Reconstruction in Louisiana After 1868
by Ella Lonn

Address:
HardPress
8345 NW 66TH ST #2561
MIAMI FL 33166-2626
USA
Email: info@hardpress.net

RECONSTRUCTION IN LOUISIANA

AFTER 1868

BY

ELLA LONN, Ph.D.

Assistant Professor in Grinnell College

G. P. PUTNAM'S SONS
NEW YORK AND LONDON
The Knickerbocker Press
1918

The Knickerbocker Press, New York

PREFACE

THE attempt to disentangle the complicated story of Reconstruction in Louisiana needs no justification. Rather is it a matter of surprise that it has been left for a northerner to do. From the point of view of the writer it has seemed an advantage to do the work long enough after the events herein related for party passions to have cooled, and yet not too late to gain the calm judgment of some of the actors, while the accident of northern birth has left freedom in drawing conclusions without fear of the charge of southern bias.

The great extent and well-nigh inextricable confusion of the period doubtless explains why writers have veered away from a subject, otherwise dramatic and absorbing. Probably the truth can never be unveiled with regard to some of the details, particularly those in connection with the election of 1876, so that conclusions must always remain more or less a matter of opinion. For that reason I have not attempted to treat that event with the fullness which the wealth—nay, excess of source material would admit of, but have preferred to state incontrovertible facts and the conclusions to which a careful study of the available sources has led me. Neither side could then conclusively prove its contention, nor does that feat seem to-day possible.

Acknowledgment is due Dean H. V. Ames of the

University of Pennsylvania, who first awakened my interest in this subject, to General Behan, Judge Breaux, Miss Marion Brown, and many others in New Orleans who kindly contributed information. But for any errors of judgment the writer alone assumes responsibility.

I also wish to express appreciation for the uniform courtesy with which materials have been made accessible at the Congressional Library and at the various depositories in New Orleans.

E. L.

GRINNELL COLLEGE,
  January, 1917.

CONTENTS

Contents

MAPS

RECONSTRUCTION IN LOUISIANA

Reconstruction in Louisiana

CHAPTER I

A Brief Resumé of Reconstruction in Louisiana before 1869

BY January 1, 1869, Louisiana had suffered the throes of reconstruction for seven weary years, but the hostile fates had decreed for her more than another seven before she should be able to wrench herself free from the grasp of her colored and carpet-bag despots. The first uncertain attempts at reconstruction were made at the close of 1862 by Governor Shepley with the consent of Lincoln. The President's policy was based upon the belief that there existed in every Southern State a loyal element which might be made to prove the germ of a civil government owning allegiance to Washington. In the course of that year, as the North gained a foothold, he had appointed General Shepley military governor, whose duty it was to resurrect the loyal element among the people. Thanks to the vigorous grip over New Orleans of Generals Butler and Banks, a considerable body, stronger in numbers than social prestige, became firmly wedded to the Union cause. The old Douglas men sprang into evidence at Butler's arrival on the scene; members of the Irish Unionists came out strongly; while still others were won by the favors distributed with an eye to political gain.   General Shepley ordered an election on December 3 for two Congressmen.   The successful candidates proved to be B. F. Flanders and Michael Hahn, both of whom were allowed to take their seats in the National legislature.

There appeared a certain group of men eager to push on the work of reorganization, either for the plums of office, or, on the part of the old slave-holders, for the sake of saving a portion of their slaves, or for the sake of casting off martial law.   This group, the Free State Party, working through the Union Clubs, urged on in 1863 a registration and convention to frame a new constitution.   But it made such slow progress that Lincoln developed his famous "Ten Per Cent" plan by his proclamation of December 8, 1863, which offered pardon and the restoration of property to all who would take a prescribed oath; and declared that the President would recognize as the true government of any of the seceded States, except Virginia, the organizations set up by loyal citizens, provided that they constituted one-tenth of the voting population of 1860.[1]

General Banks, in accordance with this plan, ordered an election of State officers for February 22, 1864.   Hahn, the successful administration candidate, was inaugurated on March 4.   About ten days later he was invested with the "powers exercised before by the military governor."   It is of importance to note that as early as this campaign the issue in the radical party was the treatment of the negroes after emancipation.   Delegates to a constitutional convention were subsequently chosen and April 6, ninety-four[2] of the men elected met in New Orleans, a fair set of men, but already showing a tendency

[1] Richardson, *Messages and Papers of the Presidents*, VI., 214.
[2] Ficklen's *History of Reconstruction in Louisiana*, states that the highest number on the roll at any time was ninety-eight, 68.

toward that extravagance which was later to be such a blot upon reconstruction. The convention abolished slavery,[1] but restricted suffrage to white males, although it empowered the legislature to confer it on "such persons, citizens of the United States, as by military service, by taxation to support the government, or by intellectual fitness may be deemed entitled thereto."[2]   A constitution was adopted and submitted to the people, but only 8402 votes were cast in ratification as compared with 11,411[3] in the election of Hahn. . The new legislature provided for met October 3, elected two Senators, and adopted the Thirteenth Amendment unanimously. Although this government was duly recognized by the President and its ratification of the Amendment gladly counted to help embody it in the organic law, its authority was restricted to a very narrow limit—that actually within the Union military lines[4]—and neither branch of Congress admitted the members chosen by the new government, while the Presidential vote of 1865 was rejected.

The legislature of 1865, fully representative of the State, and just as fully Democratic, met in extra session to elect two new Senators in case the two elected previously be rejected as not truly representative.   With these two Senators, Henry Clay Warmoth presented himself at Washington as territorial delegate of the radical Republicans of the State,[5] his expenses defrayed by his negro

[1] By a vote of 72:13.   Ficklen, 70.
[2] Lincoln's plan.   See letter of March 13, 1864, to Hahn, Nicolay-Hay, VIII., 434.
[3] Rhodes and Ficklen differ slightly in their numbers.   Rhodes depends upon Sen. Exe. Doc., 38 Cong., 2 Sess., No. 91, 4.
[4] Within the Union lines was about one-third the area of the State, according to the census of 1860, and two-thirds of the population.
[5] Already Thaddeus Stevens had devised and won followers for his territorial scheme of reconstruction.   For a full statement see Rhodes, United States, V., 551.

constituents, who joyfully deposited their half-dollars
with their first ballots to pay the expenses of their impe-
cunious delegate. [1]

Some thirty or more of the members of the convention
of 1864 were so angered at seeing the offices of the State
passing to the ex-rebels that, with the consent of the
governor and a judge of the Supreme Court, they began
to meet and plan how they could evict them. Before
adjourning, the convention of 1864 had decreed that it
might be reconvoked at the call of the President "for
any cause, or in case the constitution should not be
ratified, for the purpose of taking such measures
as may be necessary for the formation of a civil
government for the State of Louisiana." This resolution, however, had not been incorporated in the constitution and had never been passed upon by the
people. [2]

The opponents of negro suffrage denied the right of
the convention to resume its functions and the controversy over the matter became very fierce. July 30, 1866,
the delegates who favored reassembling proceeded to do
so, according to call in New Orleans. A street procession of negroes, on their way to the hall, became involved
in a serious fight with the police and crowds of white
spectators. The number killed and injured amounted
to about two hundred and the fact stood out conspicuously that of this number only about a dozen were
policemen or their white allies. The North and, more
especially, Congress was forced by this episode, together

[1] Ficklen regards this story as well-substantiated (113), though Warmoth
himself stated that he received the money to defray his expenses from the
Executive Committee. House Misc. Doc., 42 Cong., 2 Sess., No. 211,
350. The writer has not regarded this as within her investigation.
[2] Debates of the Convention, 1864, 623. Illegal also was the effort of
the mayor to suppress the convention. See Cox, *Three Decades*, 430-2.

with the rejection of the Fourteenth Amendment[1] and the
passage throughout the South of the "Black Codes,"
to the conclusion that the colored people were not safe
in the hands of their former masters.

Hence, the Congressional plan of reconstruction, long
brewing,[2] was forced on the South in the Acts of March
2, 1867, which reëstablished military rule and provided
an entire new organization of government through a
convention, elected by negro as well as white vote, and
a new constitution, which should be acceptable to Congress[3]; in the Supplementary Act of March 23 which
placed the initiative in the hands of the military instead
of the State[4]; and the additional Act of July 19 which
substituted for the liberal interpretation of the earlier
acts by civil officials the most rigorous possible and
stripped the Executive of the power of determining removals by explicitly conferring certain powers of appointment and removal on the general of the army.[5]   Louisiana
and Texas constituted one military department, placed
first under the direction of General Sheridan, and in
August under General Hancock.   Under these two com-
manders registration was pushed on so as to record as
many·blacks and as few whites as possible.   In September
a convention of ninety-eight members was elected, consisting by previous agreement of blacks and whites in

---

· [1] Blaine regarded this as the "original mistake" of the South.   Suffrage
would have then followed as a necessity and boon to the South.   Blaine,
Twenty Years, II., 474–5.

[2] The Congressional Committee reported the plan as early as April 30,
1866.   *Globe*, 39 Cong., 1 Sess., 2286.

[3] Statutes at Large, XIV., 428.   The essential sections, 3 and 4, were
later held unconstitutional.   Cases of U. S. *vs.* Reese, 92 U. S., 214, and
U. S. *vs.* Cruikshank, 92 U. S., 554.

[4] United States Statutes at Large, XV., 2.

[5] *Ibid.*, 14.   This act was drafted by Stanton.   Gorham, *Stanton*,
II., 373.

equal numbers, all but two, Republicans. The body sat in daily session from November 23 to March 9, ostensibly to frame the new constitution, but, because of the lack of a revenue, constituting itself also a legislative body. The constitution framed by it was the most severe in its disfranchising clauses of any in the South.

It was quietly ratified April 16 and 17, 1868, and State officers chosen. H. C. Warmoth was elected governor and the mulatto, O. J. Dunn, lieutenant-governor. The military governor was removed and the governor-elect placed in power at once although his formal inauguration did not occur until July 13, 1868. The first legislature of the new régime, in which a sweeping radical victory against the unorganized, disheartened conservatives had seated a strong Republican majority, was in session from June 29 to October 20. The ratification of the Fourteenth Amendment by this body opened the door of readmission to the Union so that by the act of June 25, 1868, Louisiana was once more empowered to send W. P. Kellogg and J. B. Harris to occupy the seats in the Senate vacated defiantly seven years before by John Slidell and J. P. Benjamin. By July 18, five Representatives had been seated in the House, including the first colored person to present himself for admission to Congress; and reconstruction would seem to be a matter of history.[1]

But the military was not withdrawn, for Louisiana and Arkansas were created into the Department of Louisiana under General Rousseau. Troops were so stationed at different points throughout these States that they could be called upon to coöperate with the State authorities to preserve the peace and to sustain the new governments.

[1] *Globe,* 40 Cong., 2 Sess., 4216.

The Presidential election of the fall of that year once more centered attention on the State by an undesired and wholly unexpected victory for Seymour and Blair, and still more by the disorders and outrages on the negroes.[1] Congress was not allowed to forget that it had a right to a directing influence in the matter through committees of investigation and decisions on disputed elections to its own body.[2]

At the beginning of the year 1869 carpet-bag government was in full swing and the picture of the situation in the State is not a bright one.

The political condition might well have caused an aristocratic Louisianian to withdraw himself from the contamination of politics with a shudder of despair: a carpet-bagger the recipient of the first honor in the gift of the State, and a negro house-painter of the second. Warmoth, young, handsome, and magnetic,[3] was a native of Illinois, who had entered the army from Missouri. He had had trouble with General Grant after the battle

---

[1] For a full account of the early period of reconstruction in this State see Ficklen, *History of Reconstruction in Louisiana.* As evidence that election disorders were not wholly a result of reconstruction, it might not be amiss to call attention to the governor's valedictory message of 1856. Society in Louisiana before the war, while polite and even more—brilliant, had been far from law-abiding with its frequent encounters under the duelling oaks, the Plaquemines frauds of 1844, and the riot of 1855. See Gayarré, IV., 679.

[2] For an account of the conflicting testimony on these outrages see House Misc., Doc., 41 Cong., 1 Sess., No. 13.

[3] Based on House Repts., 42 Cong., 2 Sess., No. 92, 24–5. See also *National Cyclopedia of American Biography.* Carpenter's sketch of him to the Senate may be quoted: "There is in Louisiana a very remarkable young man, dignified in mien, of elegant presence, and agreeable conversation; a man full of resources, political and social,—gallant, daring, and with a genius for politics; such a man as would rise to power in any great civil disturbance, embodying in himself the elements of revolution, and delighting in the exercise of his natural gifts in the midst of political excitement." *Globe,* 42 Cong., 3 Sess., Appendix, 200.

of Vicksburg; was charged with circulating exaggerated reports of the Union losses while on parole North, was dismissed from the service by Grant, but restored to his command by Lincoln, evidence having shown his dismissal to be unjust. He retired from the army in 1865, went to Texas, where he was indicted for embezzlement and for appropriating government cotton. But when the case was called, no prosecutor appeared and the prosecution was abandoned. He returned to Louisiana and before reconstruction was sent as a delegate to Congress as narrated above. He was at this time only twenty-six years old, apparently at the height of his powers, social and political, for even his foes admitted the dignity of his appearance and the charm of his manners and conversation.

The balance of parties in 1868 stood twenty Republicans to sixteen Democrats in the Senate, fifty-six to forty-five in the House.[1] White members had been almost entirely supervisors of registration. Warmoth had selected for this office in the parishes a large number of men left in New Orleans as flotsam after the war. They had so impressed the negroes that they were returned to the legislature or were mysteriously counted in by the returning-board.[2] Almost one-half of the House were negroes, while there were at least seven sable-hued Senators.[3] The lower State and parish offices were given over largely

[1] *Annual Cyclopedia*, 1868, 434.

[2] Nordhoff tells of the rise of a young New Yorker who returned from acting as supervisor in an up-country parish to present returns which proved him the unanimous choice of that parish. Though not the nominee, two years later, his name appeared, strangely enough, on the tickets and, although not elected, the returning board seated him. Nordhoff, *The Cotton States*, 48.

[3] The writer has been unable to get exact figures. The *Commercial Bulletin* of Feb. 22, 1869, enumerates seven Senators; while a negro in debate stated that there were forty-two of his brethren in the House. House Deb., 1870, 281.

to negroes and scalawags, not always chosen by the governor with wisdom.[1]

The comment of one of the New Orleans papers is suggestive of the sentiment of the people toward their legislature. Speaking of the revenue bill of 1869 it said:

It was the work of the lowest and most corrupt body of men ever assembled in the South. It was the work of ignorant negroes[2] coöperating with a gang of white adventurers, strangers to our interests and our sentiments. It was originated by carpet-baggers and was carried through by such arguments as are printed on green-backed paper. It was one of the long catalogs of schemes of corruption which makes up the whole history of that iniquitous Radical Conclave.[3]

Or note the *Crescent:* "The troupe which is now playing a sixty-day engagement at the corner of Royal and Conti streets,[4] which appears daily in the farce of 'How to be a Legislature,' a day or two since introduced among themselves a bill ∴ .."[5] And that paper printed later daily the following unique "ad," "Go at once to the St. Louis Rotunda to see the astounding curiosity &."

No less important to the State than its own political condition was the attitude of the National government. The defeat of the Republican party in the South in the fall election was like a dash of cold water. To an indiffer-

---

[1] A negro Justice of the Peace issued a warrant which is a rare curiosity for bad spelling and grammar: "This is to cite, fy that i. the underseind, Justis. of. the. Peace O Pint. and in Pour. John. A. Stars. to. A-rest the Body. of Henre Evens and Bring. Hit, be four, me John Fields." Copied from *St. Mary's Banner*, a parish paper.

[2] It was not uncommon for a legislator to sign his name with a mark. —*Crescent*, Jan. 13, 1869.

[3] New Orleans, *Commercial Bulletin*, Nov. 17, 1869.

[4] At this time the legislature was convening in the Banque de la Louisiane.

[5] Jan. 13, 1869.

ence or even a desire to be rid of the whole subject of reconstruction, which had characterized Congress in the fall of 1868, succeeded a resolute purpose to take advantage of every opportunity to gain an effective and permanent control for the Republican party. Even the law passed during the session of 1868–9, which provided that equal eligibility to office should inhere in those who had had their disabilities removed by Congress and had taken the oath to support the constitution in the act of July 11, 1868, was only a party measure to win more firmly the scalawags,[1] as the list of pardons reveals the fact that most had become Republicans.[2] Grant's attitude was of importance to a degree that Johnson's was not, for he came into office early in 1869, a popular and trusted executive, who would be free, to a large extent, to direct the policy of the government in the South. But, unfortunately for Louisiana, a brother-in-law, J. F. Casey, was soon put in charge of the port there and so completely won Grant's ear that the latter approached Louisiana problems with a bias. Friction between the State and National authorities was bound to come, for already at the opening of 1869 the radicals had lost the respect of the army, and recrimination was passing back and forth between the military commander and the executive of the State.[3]

[1] The scalawag was the war-time Unionist or reconstructed rebel who had ceased opposing Congress. A negro preacher defines the difference between a carpet-bagger and scalawag as follows: "A carpet-bagger came down here from some place and stole enough to fill his carpet-bag, but the scalawag was a man who knew the woods and swamps better than the carpet-bagger did, and he stole the carpet-bagger's carpet-bag and ran off with it." House Misc. Doc., 42 Congress, 2 Sess., No. 211, 478.

[2] The writer did not find this especially true of Louisiana, but of the South generally.

[3] "Apparently the Radical authorities have lost the confidence and respect of the army. We do not think that writing to Washington letters of complaint is exactly the way to regain it."—New Orleans, *Commercial Bulletin*, Jan. 21, 1869.

Socially, the problem was largely a race question, though the bitterness of feeling toward her conquerors and contempt of carpet-bagger and scalawag enter to complicate the matter. The intensity of her bitterness toward the North found expression in such paragraphs as the following:

The black and bloody chapter of American subjugation reads so much like the scenes of the Netherlands and the Palatinate that it cannot claim even the vile merit of distinguished infamy. Let it be blotted out and closed. Let the American government publish and execute this amnesty in good faith. Let them seek new fields of glory and cease to promote men merely because they have distinguished themselves by the slaughter of Americans or by laying waste the regions that Americans have planted.[1]

In moments of calmness appeals to the better sentiment of the North are heard, coupled with promises that a spirit of conciliation would be seconded by the masses of the South, which were prepared to accept all necessary and reasonable conditions imposed by the result of the war.[2]

Their particular spleen was vented now vindictively, now humorously, on the carpet-baggers: "Only call off the carpet-baggers and you are welcome to substitute an army of hand-organists in their stead. No sounds can punish our nerves, our patience, and our tympanums so much as the 'base bawl' of carpet-baggers."[3] The host

[1] New Orleans *Commercial Bulletin*, Jan. 6, 1869. For a similar expression of feeling, *Times*, May 9, 1875.

[2] New Orleans *Commercial Bulletin*, Jan. 14, 1869. "Wise liberality on the part of the northern people and of the government that ought to represent them would certainly be followed by strict and willing acquiescence. . . . We ought to prove by our demeanor toward those who come among us to buy our vacant lands . . . that they are welcome and that liberal legislation will not be wasted upon us."

[3] *Ibid.*, Sept. 25, 1869.

of traders, capitalists, and adventurers, who had come down during and just after the war to seek a new field for investment in the conquered country, were, naturally, regarded more or less as harpies. The number was formidable, for already by the fall of 1866, between five and ten thousand Union soldiers had settled in the State.[1] The exasperating feature was that they immediately undertook to run the government for the natives, securing office through negro votes.[2] Capital, energy, and talents were desired, but not men to tend to their politics.[3]

Two great facts are to be remembered in the negro question in Louisiana. In the first place the negroes were in a slight majority. After the war the Southerner saw his former slaves avoiding him, careless, insolent, acquiring habits of vagrancy, manifesting little fear in indulging their propensity for theft, believing that under the guidance of disinterested councillors, they would soon become landed proprietors without labor, scholars without study, and the social equals of their former masters. For so many years the fear of a servile insurrection had hung over him that he instinctively tried to erect a defense against it. The officials of the Freedmen's Bureau had also helped to complicate the situation. For the most part, indiscreet army officers, often bent on their

---

[1] Ficklen gives this number, *History of Reconstruction in Louisiana*, 176.
[2] It might be noted that the following officers who figure conspicuously in the pages of this account were carpet-baggers: Warmoth, Kellogg, Lynch, McMillan, Dewees, Jacques, who will figure in the frauds of '72, Speaker Carr, Campbell, Packard, Dibble; 3–5000 settled in New Orleans, proportionally less in the parishes.
[3] See *Times*, May 9, 1875. From the evidence I have met, I do not believe the feeling against them was so hostile as it became a little later when the South was determined to drive them out. Blaine makes a real point when he says, "Northern men recalled in an offensive manner the power that had overcome and, as they thought, humiliated them,—recalled it before time had made them familiar with the new order of things." Blaine, II., 472.

own fortunes, the directors managed the work in such an
inefficient manner that the planters found it an intolerable nuisance.   In the general demoralization of labor,
the Southerner turned in despair to the legislature for
relief and its impolitic response was the so-called "Black
Codes," which subjected the negro to oppressive restrictions not imposed upon the whites and smacked strongly
of the slave codes.   But it is to be remembered that the
extremely rigorous code of this State was passed before
the dreaded holidays of 1865–6 when the negroes were
confidently expecting Uncle Sam's gift of "forty acres
and a mule."[1]   In the second place, the Gulf States had
an element of especially vicious negroes, due to the fact
that before the war criminals for offenses less than murder
were traditionally sold "South."   There were also more
free colored persons in Louisiana than in all the other
Southern States, negroes who were likely to have developed
some leadership and initiative,[2] but were on the average
less intelligent than in most of the former slave States.[3]

Every effort was made by the radicals to encourage the
negro to claim full equality with the whites, political and
social, until by 1868 they were demanding not only the
franchise, but mixed schools, a share in public affairs and
even social rights.   The Southerner, as has been said
so many times, did not hate the negro, but he did not
believe that he could rise in the scale of civilization.   He

[1] Nordhoff tells of a negro in St. Mary's parish who still in 1875 was
retaining a mule halter he had purchased in anticipation of Uncle Sam's
gift, 49.

[2] It does not seem to me that Vice-President Wilson's argument that
the experiment of negro self-government would therefore have the greatest
chance of success (*Times*, Aug. 21, 1876) here is necessarily true.   It would
rather turn upon whether the leadership they would assert were vicious
or not.

[3] Due partly to the fact that they came from the large plantations where
the civilizing contact with the white race was reduced to a minimum.

felt that most of the negroes had not sufficient intelligence to desire the franchise, and hence that it was superimposed upon him.   Nordhoff declares that "without whites to organize the colored vote—which means to mass it, to excite it, to gather the voters at barbacues, to carry them up with a hurra to the polls, to make 'bolting' terrible, to appeal to the fears of the ignorant and the cupidity of the shrewd; without all this the negro will not vote."   And it was a well-known fact that the "organizers"[1] were Federal officers with little else to do. And, in addition, the campaigns did interfere with the work rendered.   The following passage from Nordhoff, the words of the bitterest Democrat he met in the State, shows how direct this was: "And they work just about as well (as in slavery), except when some accursed politician comes up from New Orleans with a brass band, and sends word, as was done last fall, that General Butler had ordered them all to turn out to a political meeting."[2]

Nowhere, perhaps, is this sentiment more accurately reflected than in a speech of Senator Ogden's in the State Assembly: "Do you not know as well as I that all the disgust, all the anger and bitterness that arose between these different political factions was engendered by the ill voices of certain politicians, who haranguing the ignorant and superstitious, in private and in public, poured into their ears voices as poisonous as nightshade."[3]

Negro suffrage was the burning question, and they were not reconciled, even after it had become a fact, even

---

[1] A person sent into country parishes some months before election to gather up the colored vote; to hold meetings, to instruct the local leaders, mostly preachers and teachers, and to organize the party.   Nordhoff, 67.   As late as Dec., 1874, a leading negro replied to the query concerning his vote, that "they had not got the word yet."   House Rpts., 43 Cong., 2 Sess., No. 101, 89.   Pinchback understood such organization and that gave him his strength.   *Ibid.*, 67.

[2] Nordhoff, 56.   [3] Sen. Deb., 1870, 218.

when they consented, as they did in the fall of 1868, to use the negro vote. But valiantly did the Democratic party in that election turn to win them; helped them to form clubs, promised protection, and offered to give Democratic negroes the preference in employment, enlisted negro orators; and often had them speak from the same platform as white Democrats. Yet all this was but for the purpose of securing white ascendency, for it was in this very year that the Knights of the White Camelia became perfected into a Federal organization, pledged to secure white supremacy, and to prevent political power from passing to the negro. The negro franchise might be a fact, but, if organized effort could prevent it, negro office-holding should not.[1] The Southerner felt that the last scourge of defeat, Congressional reconstruction, was founded on falsehood and malice. He declared that the reports concerning outrages on negroes had been distorted and exaggerated. The only purpose he could see in the zeal to put the ballot in the hands of men too ignorant to use it without direction was to prolong party power.

This hostility to the negro vote led to ingenious modes of reasoning to evade the results of the polls. On the eve of the assembling of the legislature of 1869 one of the city papers suggested that a certain negro Senator had been rendered ineligible by the adoption of a new registry law. As his ballot had been the casting vote which

[1] Note the frank reply of a lawyer to a negro politician: "I stand ready, as far as in me lies, to protect them in their rights as citizens. Here my friendship stops; I am not their friend when it comes to official life. The colored man has just been redeemed from slavery, and in his new character he is unfit for office. It is an insult and outrage to place him over the white people as an office-holder." Granting that slavery was wrong, that did not prove "that you should be put into office to run the government before your people have learned anything about the laws." Sen. Rpts., 44 Cong., 2 Sess., No. 701, xxxv.

seated another negro, the latter held his seat illegally, and the article closes with the pertinent query whether laws made by such legislators would have any validity.[1]

Another factor in the social problem, unique to the South, was not absent from Louisiana—the numerous "poor whites" in the northern part of the State. Living close to the subsistence line on the thin soil of the pine hills back of the bottom lands, without schools, with but few churches, given to rude sports and crude methods of farming, their ignorance and prejudice bred in them after the emancipation of the negro a dread of sinking to the social level of the blacks. The dread, in turn, bred hatred, and it was from this class, instigated very probably by the class above them, that the Colfax and Coushatta murders[2] took their unfortunate rise.

And still one other element, mischievous in the extreme, must be added to the social complex—men who pursued no occupation, but preyed on black and white alike, as gamblers and tenth-rate politicians, drinking and swaggering at the bar, always armed with knife and revolver, shooting negroes now and then for excitement. This class was recruited, largely, from the descendants of the old overseer and negro-trader of ante-bellum days. With just enough education to enable them to dazzle the negro by a political harangue, they were both disliked and feared by the decent white people. According to the testimony of a Northern observer,[3] the first duty of the Republican leaders in Louisiana was "to hang them by the dozen." And it was just because they were not crushed out, except so far as the respectable conservative could combat them, that Louisiana had to endure such a drawn-out purgatory before she was reconstructed.

[1] *Commercial Bulletin*, Jan. 4, 1869.
[2] See, this volume, Chapters XI. and XII.
[3] Nordhoff, 18.

Economically the State presented no better view. Louisiana had suffered particularly from the war, as a part of her soil had been held by Federal troops through a great part of the conflict, and the plantations had been drained, in consequence, of a large part of their labor. Taxable property had been reduced almost two-thirds. The returning rebel found his plantation in the worst possible state of repair, or his title subject to dispute under the confiscation laws, while much had been seized by treasury agents or dishonest speculators. He turned, in the absence of capital, labor, currency, to the one thing he knew—the raising of cotton. Even here he had to adjust himself to a complete change of system from fixed, forced labor to payments at set times or planting on shares where he was at the mercy of his planter. It cannot be charged, on the whole, that the planter drove unjust bargains.[1] If the negro suffered, it was at the hands of the poor, small farmers, as ignorant as the negro himself. But a blighted crop in 1866 was followed the next year by an almost complete failure, while the Mississippi exacted the penalty of neglected, broken levees by a devastating flood. Only in 1868 did the planters obtain an average crop in the great staples. Grinding necessity, as well as the remorseless political ostracism, drove the better class into indifference to public concerns and engrossment in their private affairs. Moreover, ignorant, unprincipled legislation bred a certain temporary apathy even to their own interests.

Already the finances of the State were in a sad condition.

---

[1] It was Nordhoff's opinion in 1875 that few laborers as ignorant as the average plantation hand could do as well anywhere else in the world, 21. Nordhoff was a young German immigrant who visited Louisiana as reporter for the New York *Herald*, and published his impressions after an investigation which bears every mark of care and fairness. One can scarcely accuse him of Southern bias when one reads: "I have been opposed to slavery ever since I sat on my father's knee and was taught by him that slavery was the greatest possible wrong," 49.

2

Back taxes were in arrears, possibly, as was charged, because the property owners were organized in opposition to the existing government,[1] but more probably because they were unable to pay. It did not help the situation that few filling State positions were tax-payers.[2] By January 19, 1869, only about one-tenth of the amount of the city taxes for the preceding year had been collected.[3]

Inability to get in the taxes, resulted, naturally, in inability on the part of the State to meet its obligations. It had been found necessary in September, 1868, to levy a special one per cent tax to provide for the payment of the past due coupons on the bonds of the State, outstanding warrants, certificates of indebtedness, and convention warrants.[4] It was not even able to pay the interest on current debts and so it was necessary for the legislature early in 1869 to empower the governor and treasurer to negotiate a loan to meet such approaching obligations.[5] Of course, credit had suffered in consequence until by October, 1868, bonds were selling in the market at forty-seven cents on the dollar. Certain levee bonds had sunk so low at one time as to be sold for thirty and even twenty-five cents.[6] A motion offered in the House in the session of 1869 that not less than fifty cents be accepted is sufficiently illuminating.[7] Many State officials were paid by warrants and suffered, except where the Assembly favored the recipient, as in the case of the executive and its own members, the loss of the difference between their face value and the market value.

Loans were negotiated only with the greatest difficulty and on exceedingly hard terms. On November 1, 1868,

[1] Such a charge was made by a member in the House.
[2] Herbert says that ten paid taxes, *Why the Solid South*, 401.
[3] *Commercial Bulletin*, Jan. 19, 1869.
[4] Laws of Louisiana, 1868, No. 114.   [5] *Ibid.*, 1869, No. 48.
[6] House Deb., 1869, 393.   [7] *Ibid.*, 287.

the interest on $2,000,000 of levee bonds was to fall due
without means to meet it. Hence, a new loan of $100,000
was necessary, but it was secured only for the short period
of ninety days at seven per cent with the privilege of
the purchase of one hundred of these bonds at sixty cents
by the loaner. At about the same time a commission
was sent to New York to sell 1300 State bonds. They
found a general distrust of all Southern securities, but
especially of those of Louisiana. Its bonds were not
quoted on the stock exchange, and the only offer on the
street was of a lot at fifty-two cents which found no
buyers. The commission at last had to accept fifty-one
and one quarter cents and, as a preliminary condition, had
to agree that provision should be made for the payment
of interest on all bonds due in January and February of
1869.[1] Naturally, such loans were secured only at great
additional expense. The ninety-day loan cost over
$3700, while the sale of the 3100 bonds mounted up to
$2213, $1000 of which went to pay the cost of the trip of
the three commissioners.[2] The necessity of paying by
warrant involved a loss to the State not only directly,[3]
but in the depression of State credit.

An attitude of extravagance and corruption was already becoming apparent in the State administration.
The Senate at the close of its session in 1868 authorized
twelve committees to sit between sessions. Practically
every Senator sat on some committee and each member
drew pay for twenty-six days, amounting to $34,620.40

[1] House Deb., 1869, 43–4. The lack of faith in Southern bonds was
partly due to the unsettled condition, but also to the fact that just before
the war many Southern States had repudiated their debts—an action later
to be repeated.

[2] Ibid.

[3] One member asserted that $75,000 was thrown away in 1869 by
the sale of the warrants on the streets to pay members. Ibid., 1870, 15.

besides $15,000 for clerks.[1]   One committee alone drew
between $16,000 and $17,000.   Money was doubly squandered by one committee, which drew pay for its time
and pay for witnesses who were never examined.[2]   And
one clerk is quoted as having had time to serve on three
committees and drawing warrants for four.[3]   But this
corruption did not come to light until the Assembly had
entered upon its labors of 1869.

[1] Sen. Journal, 1870, 12.

[2] Lowell testifies: "I can show that the greatest fraud ever perpetrated
was the action of the Senate Committee on Election, whose clerk went out
on the streets and coaxed men to come into the committee-room to act as
witnesses in order that he might get half the fees.   I state further that
witness after witness has been paid by the Senate Election Committee who
never gave one hour's testimony."   House Deb., 1869, 12–13.

[3] *Ibid.*, 50.

CHAPTER II

A Carpet-bag Legislature in Session

THE general character of the work done in the Louisiana Assembly during the sessions of 1869 and 1870 was distinctly inferior; the tone of the debate low; and the conduct paralleled only in the worst of the reconstruction legislatures. The ignorance of the members does not appear glaringly in the records of 1869, for the more illiterate did not engage in the debate, certainly did not venture upon lengthy addresses. It is only occasionally that we are appalled by the dense ignorance revealed, as when the colored legislator Burrel broke out into a mass of incoherent repetitions in defense of the St. Charles pavement bill.[1]

The debate was distinctly partisan. The following outburst, provoked by the debate on the militia bill, is sufficiently suggestive:

Is it possible that men in broad daylight will say that we should not call on the Republican party to give security to the people? That we receive this amendment that men should

[1] "The city of New Orleans will be what we intend to make it, and we intend to make this city bloom as the rose, and we intend to enhance and increase this city of New Orleans, and we intend to open every by-road, and this very bill is going to make the city bigger, and we are going to pass this act. We intend not only to legislate for the city of New Orleans, but to stamp our record upon the door of this House of Representatives, so it will remain a century of years," etc. House Debates, 1869, 359-60; also, 415.

be organized into a militia, that will call every disturbance of the peace a "nigger insurrection"? Men should prove that they are loyal before they can be trusted to go into the militia. This amendment ought to be dammed by this House. What, this democracy to be organized into a militia to execute Andrew Johnson's policy! This amendment is full of deviltry.[1]

On another occasion even the speaker stated as a good reason why a certain bill should pass that the board to be affected by it were all good Republicans. The bill promptly passed.[2] January 19 a cool resolution was offered that the persons voted for in the parishes where a fair election had been held, the twenty-six parishes where the Democrats had had a majority being calmly ignored, should meet to vote for President and Vice-President.[3] It is significant, however, that sharply drawn as was the party line, the sectional feeling manifested was distinctly pro-Southern. When a measure was offered for a contribution to a Lincoln Monument, few spoke for it, while most felt it frankly impossible that the South could be expected to contribute.[4] On the other hand, when the appeal to help bury the Confederate dead at Fredericksburg came up the following session, even such a hotheaded Unionist as Mr. McMillan spoke reverently in advocacy of the appropriation.[5]

But worse than partisanship was the lack of dignity, even frivolity, which characterized the proceedings. So serious did this become that the speaker was frequently forced to call the members to order for their senseless

---

[1] House Debates, 1869, 110.
[2] Ibid., 354.
[3] New Orleans Commercial Bulletin, Jan. 22, 1869.
[4] House Debates, 1869, 389.
[5] Ibid., 1870, 287. See also Campbell's speech, Sen. Deb., 679.

motions and tone of levity.[1]   Amendments were repeatedly refused by the chair as absurd[2] and even improper.
It was proposed to add to the oath required by the school
bill, "shall take whiskey straight without regard to race,
color, or previous condition."[3]   Some, when ordered read
to satisfy the curiosity of the House, proved even indecent.[4]
The greatest discourtesy on the part of one member to
another prevailed, while even the president of the Senate
was guilty of recognizing a Senator in the following undignified way: "Well, just pitch in."   One member cried:
"I don't know what he is going to talk about.   I don't
wish to hear him talk at all, and I therefore call for the
previous question."[5]   Because one member read his
speech, another called out rudely, "There's that document
again."   Or again, "I move the gentleman be allowed to
speak all night.   He occupies the floor more than any
other member of this House."[6]   Freedom of speech both
as to time and language and wordy altercations made
confusion and tumult almost the rule in both houses

---

[1] "The gentleman from Lafourche has spoken of bribery.   Now, there
is another absurdity, for a member gave him a cigar for a bribe, but he
did not offer me one."   House Debates, 1869, 126.   And "I rise to a point
of order—this bill is a swindle" 264.   Again, a member proposed in all
seriousness that the House adjourn in respect to the recent marriage of
one of its members.   When the speaker objected to such levity, he retorted: "It is a very serious event for the gentleman from St. Charles."
Ibid., 135.   Another member rose to make the point of order that "the
committee had no dignity," 264.

[2] On the immigration bill the following irrelevant amendments   were
offered:

> That 2000 shall be Chinese and 1000 Arabs.
> That a thousand thugs of India be included.
> "I move to include 500 monkeys."
> That the company bring over half the population of Europe.

Ibid., 1870, 281.
[3] Ibid., 1869, 242.
[4] Ibid., 1869, 112; Sen. Deb., 1870, 771, 749.
[5] Ibid., 1870, 178.   [6] Ibid., 149.

until such a remark as the following was possible: "I hope the Sergeant-at-arms will call to his assistance a sufficient number of the Metropolitan Police to keep order and to see whether we cannot have silence, and quiet, and stillness to hear what is going on," while the president weakly added, "It is really a shame that we cannot have better order."[1] It frequently became necessary for the chair to order the sergeant to seat obstreperous members and to threaten public censure.[2] In at least one instance the threat was executed.[3] Carter even boldly said of the speaker, "I must say that the man who knows the facts of this case, as he said he did, and is acquainted with the law, and then says that I am a defaulter, is either a fool or unadulterated liar." Then less vehemently, "I will be square and honest and polite to you all, but I will be hanged if I am to be bullyragged, and I'll be switched if I am to be ridden over by the Speaker or anybody else."[4]

Reprobate and scoundrel that he proved to be, Speaker Carr[5] had a certain power of command, which made it possible for him to control the House. Whenever he called anyone else to the chair, the House broke into disorder like a set of unruly schoolboys, leaving him problems to disentangle on his return. Legislators indulged in pranks such as withdrawing a member's chair while he was speaking in order that his fall should convulse the House.[6] So notorious was the disorder that one

[1] House Deb., 1869, 139; 1870, 191, 231.   Sen. Deb., 1870, 705.

[2] Sen. Deb., 1870, 639–40.   House Deb., 1871, 87, where the gentleman from Orleans declared that he would not come to order, and did not heed the sergeant.

[3] House Deb., 1869, 294.   [4] Ibid., 1871, 90.

[5] Carr had come from Maryland in 1865, was now twenty-six or twenty-seven years old, shrewd and wily in the extreme.   House Misc. Docs., 42 Cong., 2 Sess., No. 211, 217.

[6] Crescent, Jan. 26, 1869.

member acknowledged as a well-known fact that gentlemen came from the North to see what kind of a House
they had.   The speaker found it difficult to hear the
motions, while over and over again the reporter inserted
in the debates "confusion" and a statement to the effect
that, owing to the disorder, he had lost part of the speech.
The pages, who made as much noise "as a lot of young
colts, dodging about the floor, standing up, talking and
laughing all the time," according to the speaker, added
to the disturbance.[1]   It would be difficult to read the
pages that record the proceedings on the 30th of January,
1869, without feeling convinced that the open bar, which
it was charged was to be found at the capitol, had had its
due effect.[2]   The last evening closed fittingly with a mock
session, when, as the debates assure us, "the members
had a good time, and the reign of fun prevailed for a few
minutes."[3]

Low as was the tone during the second session of the
Assembly, it degenerated even lower by the time the
Assembly gathered for the third time.   Debate descended
more often to vulgarity[4] and bad grammar and rhetoric
came to the surface more often.[5]

Mr. President, I have not expressed on none of these bills
termed political bills, but, as the gentleman who preceded
me from Orleans has not entirely represented me, I claim on
this floor the privilege.   In the first place, he says we have

[1] House Deb., 1871, 135–6.
[2] *Ibid.*, 1869, 111–12.   The following statement of the speaker estab-
lishes the fact for 1871 clearly: "I will not allow while I am speaker of
the House, to have spirituous liquors brought into the House.   I must
maintain the dignity of this House, if the House will not maintain its own
dignity.   I do not desire such a thing shall be done again."   *Ibid.*, 1871,
114.
[3] *Ibid.*, 1869, 524.
[4] Senate Deb., 1870, 222–3.
[5] See speech on the constabulary bill, *ibid.*, 223–4.

elected a demagogue,—or some such word. . . .   I say on
the other hand, if the way that he holds to that he has done
what he proposes that he should have done, it is because the
Democratic members on this floor, when some bills were
introduced in this House, opposed them bills, and they did
not become laws . . . I do not know what done it, except it
was their own classes—except it was someone that stood in
the ranks in the days of old.[1]

It was of a legislature which assembled only a year
later that Eustis told his famous story: "There was a
member of Parliament brought me a letter of introduction,
and he asked me if I had any great curiosity to show him.
I told him I had—such a curiosity as he would never see
in any other civilized country, and I took him to the
legislature."[2]

In methods of procedure gross irregularities occurred
as a result of carelessness or deliberate manipulation until
the procedure occasionally became a mere travesty of the
forms of government.   Wiltz in the House charged that
he was never notified to attend a single meeting of the
Committee on the City Charter of which he was a
member.[3]   A bill was declared on third reading when
the House had refused to engross it and had ordered it
placed on the calendar.   An interested member detected
the irregularity.[4]   A member of the Ways and Means
Committee charged that the revenue bill had been returned when only two members had been present to act
on it.[5]   One striking offense was the extraordinary om-
nibus motion put and carried amid boisterous laughter
late on the evening of February 23: "I move that the

---

[1] Sen. Deb., 1870, 222–3.
[2] House Misc. Doc., 42 Cong., 2 Sess., No. 211, 534.   Note also the
opinion of Nordhoff, prejudiced for negro rights.   He was "unpleasantly
startled," not because they were black, but because they were so trans-
parently ignorant and unfit, 49.
[3] House Deb., 1870, 236.   [4] *Ibid.*, 1870, 345.   [5] *Ibid.*, 326.

reading of the bill be dispensed with, the bill be put upon its first reading, the constitutional rule be suspended, the bill be put upon its second and third readings and final passage, the title adopted, and that the bill be sent to the Senate for concurrence."[1]   One member remonstrated at what he properly termed an "extraordinary proceeding."   "The Governor has sent in a veto of some bills, and in his message has given very grave reasons for so doing.   Now, sir, I want to see the bills.   I don't know them at all.   They were ordered to be printed this morning, and now the House desires to take up those bills, involving millions of dollars, without ever giving the members an opportunity to make themselves acquainted with their provisions."[2]   Another member was excused from voting on a bill, which he insisted on hearing read, only after the following declaration of independence: "I will throw myself back upon my reserved rights, and I will not vote, and the House may take, with all respect, the course they may think proper."[3]

Even the speaker acted on one occasion without knowing what the forms were carrying through, for, on the query of a member as to the nature of the bill under debate, he replied: "Something about taxes.   The gentleman from Orleans moves it be referred to the Committee on Ways and Means."   It was so referred.[4]

The powerful majority did not even manifest the ordinary courtesies of debate to the minority, but replied coldly to the very reasonable plea of the opposition for more time on an important bill: "It seems to be the disposition of the committee to work further."[5]   By dis-

---

[1] House Deb., 1869, 331.   [2] Ibid., 1871, 7–8.
[3] Ibid., 200.   [4] Ibid., 1869, 204.
[5] Ibid., 1870, 78.   Mr. McMillan characterized this spirit as follows: "That the House will pass it, I am convinced, for there is always something peculiar in the air which tells me when a bill of this character is sure of being put through, and I feel the breath of that air distinctly at this moment, 268.

pensing with the reading of the bill and various other devices to gain time, bills were often crowded through to adoption at a single sitting.[1]   Under the operation of the previous question, debate was peremptorily cut off until one member indignantly cried out: "It is impossible to sit here and see the funds of the State voted away without an opportunity to remonstrate against it."[2]

Charges of corruption were brought against members of the Assembly not only by the press[3] and by the leading citizens of the State, but charges were openly brought on the floor of the House.   In the debate on the Ship Island Canal bill the remark was dropped that some people thought there were millions of dollars in that bill, and similar charges were made in regard to many other bills.[4]   One member even boldly challenged another: "I want to know how much the gentleman gets to support this bill."[5]   That unnecessary clerks were employed seems incontrovertible when the House decided that the auditor might employ six clerks to do the work which had always been performed by two or three.   So notorious became the corruption in many directions that the House felt it obligatory to appoint committees of investigation, even though one member contemned the charges as beneath their dignity.   The wording of one resolution

[1] House Deb., 1869, 330.   [2] *Ibid.*, 264.

[3] "Such influence we all know has been exerted for personal aggrandizement and to such an extent that in point of fact the General Assembly was actually turned into a machine for the advancement of the individual interests of its leaders." *Bee*, Jan. 24, 1869. See also *Commercial Bulletin*, Feb. 6, 22.

[4] Charges of bribery were brought in connection with the penitentiary bill, the slaughter house bill, and Chattanooga Railroad bill.   The boldest charge came out on the paving bill: "I know who are lobbying this bill, and know the men they are using, and state upon the floor of this committee that this is simply for the benefit of that very man, and for the benefit of the lobbyists." *Ibid.*, 357–8.

[5] House Deb., 1869, 72.

offered in the House early in January of 1869 reveals a whole tale: "Resolved, that the President of the Board of Metropolitan Police be directed to furnish this House with the names of any members who have been employed as special officers, and under what assumed names they drew their salaries for such services."[1]   The debates bring out the fact that two or, possibly, four members were laboring under such charge.[2]   Likewise, the House became exercised over a complaint that members serving on different House committees were also employed in the custom-house and drawing a salary from each source.[3] The Assembly was not slow to put on foot investigations of other bodies, for corruption seems already to have vitiated most departments of the government and the institutions connected with it.[4]

Although the finances of the State were calling for the most skillful handling, the legislative body acted without even the most ordinary business prudence. While the time limit for the payment of the city taxes and for the collection of the special one per cent tax levied in September, 1868, had to be extended[5]; while the credit was so weak that it was found necessary to enforce under penalties the acceptance of the State warrants for licenses and taxes by the parishes of Orleans, Jefferson, and Bernard; while the State was in such straits that an annual tax became necessary to pay the interest on bonds[6]; and legislators were being put to the embarrassment of being

---

[1] House Jour., 1870, 21.

[2] House Deb., 1870, 10.   [3] House Jour., 1870, 46.

[4] Committees were appointed to investigate if bribery had been used in the appointment of officers of the Insane Asylum, the sale of levee bonds, the school-money, the defalcation of the Land Registrar, the councilmen of Jefferson City, the Metropolitan Police Commissioners, and Board of Public Works.

[5] Session Laws of Louisiana, 1869, Nos. 10, 88.

[6] Ibid., 1869, No. 66.

told that the Waterworks Company had suspended the water until they should pay their bill,[1] they were voting themselves their pay with a generous hand and squandering State funds in sheer extravagance. They early[2] manifested anxiety for their pay, appropriating $250,000 in 1869, $500,000 in 1870, for the mileage and per diem of members and clerks.[3] Their selfishness took the form in 1869 of instructing the warrant clerks to sell the warrants at their market value in order to pay the members in currency,[4] and in 1870, of giving their warrants the preference. Their attitude toward themselves is perhaps illuminating in explaining their actions. One member had insisted that they ought to accept their money in warrants, "in which form the government pays the community," when another angrily retorted, "I desire to assure him of the very important fact that what we, as the Legislature, give to the community . . . is without money and without price. They are so valuable that the price cannot be fixed—there is no standard."[5] And another member naïvely wants to know if he does not consider the General Assembly the State. Even more telling is the following exhortation of a member to the House: "I would like to know if there is a great thing and a good thing, in the name of God, why not let the Representatives of the State of Louisiana have a hand in it."[6]

[1] Sen. Deb., 1870, 771.
[2] In 1869, the appropriation bill passed the House Jan. 7, the Senate Jan. 12; in 1870, it passed the House Jan. 10, the Senate Jan. 12.
[3] Session Laws, 1869, No. 15; 1870, Nos. 2, 49.
[4] *Ibid.*, No. 52. The governor, unwilling to veto this bill, allowed it to become law by expiration of the time limit. Herbert says the over-issue of vouchers forced these warrants down to two and one half cents in 1871, 403.
[5] House Deb., 1870, 22.
[6] *Ibid.*, 1869, 122. The speaker of 1871 considered that he had used his patronage very sparingly when he gave "three or four indigent friends places as messengers and clerks." *Ibid.*, 1871, 136.

—

Small extravagances helped to swell the total cost of this Assembly to $264,278.06.[1]   There were certain items in the general appropriation bill which look unnecessarily large.   When a mere clerk of a district court received a salary of $6000, and the rental of a building for a state house cost $13,000 for nine months; when the always elastic clause for contingent expenses was stretched to $16,000; when printing and advertising mounted up to $183,000, the people might well begin to question and murmur.   A bit of sarcasm was unconsciously incorporated in the printing appropriation of 1870 when a motion to substitute $200,000 for the original $140,000, asking some of these liberal-hearted gentlemen to open their hearts a little wider and take in every official journal of the State, was adopted.[2]   The interest alone on bonds issued to railroads is probably accurate enough, but had reached the terrifying sum of $461,014.14.   The only spasm of economy which the House suffered during the entire session of 1869 was really a pick at the police, when a few minor officials were struck off or reduced in salary.[3]

The law which was to provide the income seemed to bear no relation to the expenditures.   Unwisely wasting their time on a bill to enforce collection of taxes already paid to the Confederacy,[4] they rushed the revenue bill through with a haste which explains its inadequacy. Urged by the Committee on Ways and Means to accept its work as complete, even the reading was dispensed with, and the act, which was referred to in a later session as a disgrace,[5] adopted by the House without discussion on the evening of March 3.[6]   A clause which provoked the

---

[1] House Jour., 1870, 62; Sen. Jour., 19–20.   It was proposed to allow the chairman of each standing committee in the House $5 extra per day.
[2] Sen. Deb., 1870, 845.   [3] House Deb., 1869, 225.
[4] *Ibid.*, 17.   [5] *Ibid.*, 1870, 83.   [6] *Ibid.*, 484.

greatest criticism was one licensing gambling-houses, which appeared in the published bill and came up for a perfect storm of debate in the session of 1870. The chairman of the committee stated that it had not been in the original law, and that he believed it had been surreptitiously introduced after it had been acted upon by the House.[1] Moreover, a bill which made no provision for the interest on the debt, which made an appropriation for an institution which did not exist,[2] and which failed to meet the liabilities of the State by $500,000,[3] indicated business financiering which sooner or later must bring the State to bankruptcy.

And just when the finances called for a policy of retrenchment was the time when the legislature saw fit to embark on a system of extensive internal improvements. As has been remarked by many reconstruction writers, there was a conscious purpose to introduce in the South the energy and methods of the North and West in the hope of similar economic results. It was recognized by the conservatives that introduction of new railroads was necessary for economic rehabilitation. But it must not be forgotten that the sable statesmen who were called upon to ponder problems of high finance were ex-slaves who had had the experience of a porter's tips or the extra half-dollars of a plantation-hand. Of the numerous bills of that nature introduced, a considerable number passed, lending State aid with a liberal hand.

The enterprises were chiefly of three kinds: canals, railroads, and the ever-pressing levees. The Mississippi and Mexican Gulf Ship Canal Company profited by this spirit to the extent of $600,000, issued in the form of State bonds under a first mortgage, running the generous

[1] Session Laws, 1869, No. 114, Sec. 3,* 30; House Deb., 1870, 9.
[2] Sen. Deb., 1870, 848.
[3] House Deb., 1870, 313.

period of thirty years[1]; the New Orleans and Ship Island Canal Company to the extent of $2,000,000 and a large bonus in lands.[2] The House did not find it necessary to debate at any great length the measure which legislated away the former sum,[3] but far otherwise was the history of the latter act. Introduced into the session of 1868, it had been thoroughly discussed in the Senate and passed by that body and came up in the House in 1869 as unfinished business. Its objectionable features had not been so clear while passing the Senate, but by the next session it had been thoroughly aired by the press.[4] It declared the system of the Drainage Commissioners of the Metropolitan District "erroneous in principle and unsuccessful from experience," and so gave over into the possession of the new Canal Company all the funds and assets of the commissioners to the amount of nearly $2,000,000 and public lands in installments to the extent

[1] Session Laws, 1869, No. 116. The company drew $36,000 in bonds and was then merged with another company for a different purpose; and fell into the hands of a man who in 1875 was doing drainage at a cost 100% higher than responsible citizens were ready to accept.

[2] *Ibid.*, No. 51.

[3] House Deb., 1869, 266.

[4] "But why dwell further on a scheme the whole aim and purpose of which is to speculate, for individual or associate profit, at the expense of the people? What more need be said to demonstrate its impracticability—its utter disregard of the interests, the welfare, the health, and happiness of this community, and the unscrupulous motives and purpose of its designers and advocates." *Picayune*, Jan. 7, 1869. Jan. 22, it advocated government aid to railroads and denounced the ship canal as an iniquitous project—wild and visionary.

"It is susceptible of proof that certificates of stock in this wildcat speculation have been freely distributed among members of the legislature and others, for the purpose of influencing their votes in favor of this impudent proposition. Not only this but the principal individual whose name heads the list of corporators has boasted of the cheap rate at which our new legislature hold themselves." *Bee*, Jan. 27, 1869. See also the *Picayune* of Jan. 7 and Feb. 10, the *Commercial Bulletin* of Jan. 11, 25, Feb. 12, New Orleans *Times*, Jan. 23.

3

of 400,000 acres, on the ground that this canal would
accomplish the drainage of the entire district.   As this
fund had been raised by assessment for the special purpose
of drainage, the opposition held that it could not thus be
diverted.   But, nevertheless, this bill was pressed through
the House January 29,[1] under heated personal debate,
extending through several days, and after having suffered
much amendment.   Although vetoed by the governor,
it passed both houses with the requisite majority March
2.[2]   Smaller sums were donated to minor enterprises,
as $50,000 for the improvement of Loggy Bayou; $20,000
for improving Bayou Vermilion[3]; and $80,000 worth of
credit loaned to the Bœuf and Crocodile Navigation
Company.[4]

Aid to railroads was equally liberal.   In its zeal the
House on February 23, without the reading of the bill,
pushed through all its stages the incorporation of the
Louisiana and Arkansas Railroad Company, granted
it exemption from taxation for ten years, a right of way
three hundred feet in width, and the privilege of all the
timber for one mile on each side of the road through
the public lands.[5]   But of all the railroad bills, by far the
most conspicuous was that which extended a helping
hand to the New Orleans, Mobile, and Chattanooga

[1] House Deb., 1869, 106.

[2] The Assembly of 1870 granted further aid against great opposition in
the form of drainage taxes, amounting to about $2,000,000 per year.
Session Laws, 1870, No. 4.   Extra Session.   This law was passed despite
the complaint that in two years not a spadeful of earth had been dug, nothing done but the purchase for cash or credit of a dredge-boat.   Sen. Deb.,
1870, 751.

[3] Session Laws, 1869, No. 147.   It is interesting that even this early
the wiser of the legislators were turning to the Federal government for
help on their problem of bayous and levees.

[4] Ibid., No. 146.

[5] Ibid., No. 140.   Its achievement was the removal of twenty stumps,
people complained.

Road. It came up in the House February 4 and was pressed to a final vote that very afternoon and its amendments concurred in by the Senate February 14.[1] The bill provided for the guarantee of the company's bonds by the State under the security of a second mortgage to the amount of $12,500 for each mile within the State west of New Orleans.[2] Parishes along the route of the Vicksburg Railroad were encouraged to aid that road by the purchase of stock or the issue of bonds, in addition to the State guarantee of its second mortgage bonds to the usual amount of $12,500 per mile.[3] Still other roads had found it worth while to besiege the legislature.

The great problem of improvement most urgently pressing was not adequately met—the construction of a satisfactory series of levees for the Mississippi River. A State loan of $4,000,000 had been provided for in 1867 for that purpose but the bonds had not been readily disposed of.[4] The Board of Levee Commissioners had made contracts for a large amount of work but the legislature of 1869 found no work accomplished—only the bonds of the State pledged for work authorized to be done—and so was placed under the necessity of authorizing the sale of the bonds.[5] The House made a valiant effort to meet the problem in the passage of a bill to issue bonds to the sum of $5,000,000 to provide means for the construction, repairs, and maintenance of the levees and other works of improvement, but the effort died there.[6]

[1] It must have been this date because it vanishes from the record after the 12th and the record of this one day is missing in the files of the paper. For the record of the Senate for 1869 we are dependent on the report in the *Commercial Bulletin*, no journal nor Senate debates being extant.

[2] Laws of Louisiana, 1869, No. 26.

[3] Session Laws, 1869, Nos. 143, 145.

[4] *Ibid.*, 1867, No. 115.   [5] *Ibid.*, No. 123.

[6] House Deb., 1869, 446. It was eloquently and lengthily debated on March 1. *Ibid.*, 399–429.

A lack of discrimination characterized the action of the Assembly on this subject. To aid all projects just because they savored of prosperity would seem to express the attitude of some thoughtless legislators. "I am glad that I have one more chance for internal improvement," generously declared one member.[1] Again, a project for the northern part of the State was advocated that no charge of partiality to the Southern part should be brought.[2] Nor is it fair to lay all the burden of debt arising from these grants of aid at the door of the radicals. It was rather a response to a universal desire for an extension of railroads and improvement of the waterways of the State, voiced by the moderate conservative press as well as the radical. "It is noteworthy as a sign fraught with good promise," says the *Commercial Bulletin*, "that the railroad spirit is alive in the Northern parishes of this State, and that those whom it inspires are evidently bent on the early accomplishment of substantial results."[3] In like strain the *Crescent* concerning the work of the Chattanooga Railroad: "It is certainly to be hoped that we shall soon have direct railroad communications with Mobile, and that all efforts to prevent the consummation of so desirable an object will fail."[4] But the *Picayune*, while on the whole encouraging the measures, was more conservative and urged that promises of aid be few, "unless they are of certain and undoubted practicability

[1] House Deb., 380.

[2] "We have passed a bill to-day for Claiborne Parish, and where is the consistency of refusing to aid improvements in the parish of Lafourche?" House Deb., 1869, 381. Senator Ray declared it one of the "fundamental principles of my political theory that the State of Louisiana ought to aid all the works of internal improvement that appear to be beneficial." Sen. Deb., 1870, 627.

[3] *Commercial Bulletin*, Sept. 21, 1869. See also the same paper, same date, for agitation of opening of the southwest pass.

[4] Jan. 3. See also issues of Jan. 26, 29, 30. This paper failed in September of that year.

and profitableness, and are secure beyond all peril of loss."[1]   Such measures were supported by members of both parties, often introduced by Democrats, in every case supported by a large majority of Democrats in both houses.[2]   The leaving movers, outside of the legislature, of these bills were men of both parties; and the lobbyists who advanced the corrupt measures were of both faiths.[3] This fact was admitted by the Democratic press.[4]

The legislature of 1869, with which the *Commercial Bulletin* sourly assured its readers the people wanted as little as possible to do, convened January 4 and sat until March 4. The governor's annual message to it, a plea for freedom from prejudice, struck a tone of optimism which subsequent events did not justify: " The issues of the past eight years have been settled, we hope, forever. Slavery has been swept away, and along with it all the train of evils growing out of its wickedness, and has left us—master and slave, white and black—with the same rights under the law, the same chance to succeed in life, and with equally unrestricted aspirations and hopes."

[1] Jan. 23.

[2] Warmoth adduces proof of these statements.   House Misc. Doc., 42 Cong., 2 Sess., No. 211, 285.

[3] In the State bond bill were implicated some of the most respectable distinguished Democratic leaders of the State.   House Misc. Doc., 42 Cong., 2 Sess., 333.   See Scott's testimony which shows a written contract between the bankers of New Orleans and certain lobby brokers, by which several millions of dollars were to be paid for getting a measure through which failed.   *Ibid.*

[4] "That there were 'rings' formed in both houses of the legislature for the sole and express purpose of blackmailing the people and plundering the treasury of the State, is perhaps a lamentable and humiliating fact. That there are men of both parties engaged in this disgraceful proceeding —men who would sell out their birthright for a mess of pottage, may also be true."   Quoted from the *Crescent* in a Congressional document.

The *Bee* says, Feb. 17, 1869, being reproached with accusing Democrats of joining in the corruption: "It was only yesterday that one of their own number, in our hearing, confessed the truth of the charge."

He professed faith in a "wise, economical, moderate, and firm administration of the nation and the State as curing animosities and bringing prosperity to the people." That portion of his message which alluded to the violence of 1868 and to his measures to allay the excitement was severely challenged by the Democratic press.[1]

The Assembly during the two months of its existence passed 152 laws, many of which were local, many personal relief bills.[2] There was beginning to be apparent that tendency to vest autocratic power in the hands of the governor, which reached, as we shall see, such a culmination in the next session. In some instances, it is true, the propositions could not muster sufficient strength to pass the Assembly, but it is significant that such propositions could be offered as Ray's amendment to the charter bill for New Orleans, which suggested vesting in the Governor power to appoint the first mayor and council until the election in 1872, and the amendment to the

---

[1] *Annual Cyclopedia*, 1869, 394. The *Bee* dismissed it with the following terse comment: "Nous n'assomerons pas nos lecteurs de cette prose peu intéressante. Une analyse succincte suffira pour leur faire connattre ce que dit M. Warmoth. . . . Après avoir distillé son venin, le gouverneur aborde les affaires sérieuses." Jan. 5. The *Abeille* or *Bee* had English pages at this time, a fact which accounts for both English and French excerpts.

The *Crescent* was no more kindly: "This portion of the message is strictly and narrowly partisan, a tissue of bold, unqualified assertions and of self-evident exaggerations which would be indecent even in a campaign document; a weak but spiteful jumble of accusatory phrases in which there is but a single pretense to an argument, and that so puerile and idiotic in its fallacy as to be simply ridiculous." Jan. 5.

"The Governor applies harsh terms to our people. He attributes to them all the violence which may have existed in the State. Does he really think that he himself and his associates have had nothing to do with this excitement? Have the publications made by Republican papers, speakers, and writers contributed nothing to these troubles?" New Orleans *Commercial Bulletin*, Jan. 7, 1869.

[2] Session Laws, 1869, Nos. 23, 27, 31, 33, 34, 41, 64, etc.

volunteer militia bill, which left to him large discretionary powers.[1]   The act which prohibited the mayor of New Orleans from exercising any police duty or authority is equivalent to an enlargement of the governor's powers, for the body with such control, the metropolitan police, was virtually his servant through his appointive power.[2] Quite as important was the negative action of the Assembly in refusing to force the governor to order elections in certain cases where for political reasons he was leaving vacancies.[3]

One group of laws attempted to deal with the race and labor questions.   A vagrancy law, which finally overcame the hostile majority in the Senate, while not so severe as those of the ''Black Code,'' did still define rather narrowly and imposed heavy penalties.[4]   This stringency arose, at least largely, from the need of labor and devotion to the crops to which economic conditions forced the planters.[5]   A measure to organize a Bureau of Immigration was passed, appropriating $20,000 to secure a share in the foreign labor which they saw flooding the North.   Unfortunately, this did not solve the labor problem, and dis-

[1] House Deb., 1869, 196.
[2] Session Laws, 1869, No. 60.
[3] Case of Minden, House Deb., 29.
[4] Session Laws, 1868, No. 87.
[5] An excerpt from *St. Mary's Banner* of Sept. 15 corroborates the statement which is often made of the planter's indifference to politics. ''Never did planters of this country show such devotion to business, such singleness of purpose to make money, and such utter want of interest in all things save crops, as at the present time.''

It is to be regretted that few of the regular parish papers were available, but we are fortunate enough to catch many reflections through the editorial bickering in the columns of the city papers, which give us fairly accurately the position and spirit and consequent influence in molding public thought of each. Members of Congress accommodatingly brought in many excerpts in the course of debate.   We scarcely need the files of the Shreveport *Times*, thanks to the assiduity of Morton and the Radicals in quoting it.

satisfaction with the Bureau,[1] and especially with its carpet-bagger chief, J. O. Noyes, was loudly voiced in the session of 1870. Efforts to secure new workers by legislation continued throughout the next session. A bill to accord negroes equal civil rights had been up in the session of 1868 but had not been signed by the governor, who was forced to explain to a body of their race assembled en masse, February 4, 1869, his reasons for not doing so.[2] And Pinchback's civil rights bill, which forbade common carriers and places of public resort to discriminate on account of race, color, or previous condition of servitude,[3] came up as unfinished business from the preceding session. As was to be expected, feeling ran high and lengthy discussion resulted, usually of a serious character. Twenty-six Senators were reported as desirous of speaking on the bill. Pinchback in debate made use of the expression "refused a drink of common whiskey in a common grog-shop," which was seized on by the conservative press as a convenient whip. The cry of the Conservatives was that the colored people had too much sense to force themselves where they were not wanted, and this view was borne out by the negroes themselves. "I consider myself just as far above coming into company that does not want me, as they are above my coming into an elevation with them. . . . I do not believe that any sensible colored man upon this floor would wish to be in a private part of a public place without the consent of the owners of it. It is false; it is

---

[1] "Every Southern State, save only Louisiana, is receiving accessions to her population from the tide of European immigration that daily strikes our shores. . . . The Bureau gives no sign. Then let it be abolished or let us have a change of personnel . . . that which individual enterprise has accomplished for other States, this State-maintained institution has lamentably failed to do for us." *Pic.*, Dec. 19, 1870.

[2] *Commercial Bulletin*, Feb. 8.

[3] Session Laws, 1869, No. 38.

wholesale falsehood to say that we wish to force ourselves upon white people." But he did insist that they receive equal accommodation.[1] The former set down the agitation to a political move to renew the strife.[2]

When the bill had passed both houses, the press took a more aggressive attitude in an effort to frighten the negroes from any attempt to claim their rights. "Will any negro, or gang of negroes, attempt to exercise the privilege it confers?" belligerently asked the *Commercial Bulletin*. "If they do, it will be at their peril. . . . He may be able to obtain a ticket of admission, but no New Orleans audience will ever permit him to take his seat except in the places allotted for colored persons."[3] The *Bee* declared that if the governor dared to sign that bill after vetoing the former, "legal means would not be lacking to set aside this arbitrary law, this outrage to the law of propriety, and to individual liberty."[4]

The civil rights bill was backed up by a measure intended to prevent the intimidation of negroes by punishing the bribery of witnesses or preventing a witness by force, threat, or intimidation from testifying in a criminal proceeding.[5] It is striking that a Ku-Klux bill—a bill "to prevent people from agoing abroad disguised"—was quickly referred and evidently died in committee.[6] An-

[1] House Deb., 1869, 258–9.
[2] "Apparently this state of calm does not suit the Radical leaders. Their continual control over the State must depend on the jealousy of the black towards the white people. They feel that the colored race have more confidence in the old citizens of Louisiana than in any newcomers. Hence the effort to revive a strife which would readily quiet itself without such stimulus." *Comm. Bulletin*, Feb. 19, 1869.
[3] *Ibid.*, Feb. 22. As a form of revenge, it published the vote with the names.
[4] Feb. 23. See also issue of Feb. 25.
[5] Another social equality bill, passed by both houses in the extra session of 1870, was returned by the governor on the first day of the next session. Sen. Jour., 1870, 290; House Jour., 327; and Sen. Jour., 4.
[6] House Deb., 1869, 195.

other effort in the next session to prevent the carrying of concealed weapons met no better fate.[1]

A measure allied to the above legislation, but of vastly greater importance because of its National character, was the ratification of the Fifteenth Amendment, which was accepted perfunctorily by a vote of 18 to 3 in the Senate; 59[2] to 9 in the House, 36 Republicans refusing to vote.

Particularly confusing were the various measures which finally evolved into the slaughter house bill.   Vigorous opposition and much ridicule manifested themselves at its first appearance in the House, but all amendments against the monopolistic features were voted down, debate choked off abruptly, all attempts at filibustering defeated, and the bill adopted by a large majority under the operation of the previous question.[3]   Scanty indeed is the record of its history in the Senate.   "After a short fight the bill was concurred in as a whole and the motion to reconsider tabled by a vote of 23 to 9."[4]   By it the slaughter of animals, except by the Crescent City Live Stock Landing and Slaughter House Company was prohibited within the city of New Orleans or the parishes of Orleans, Jefferson, and St. Bernard after June 1, 1869.   All animals destined for sale or slaughter must be landed at the live stock landings and yards of the company, occupying the levee from Common to Poydras streets, which naturally exacted a fee for each steamship and craft landing at its wharves.[5]   The excessive haste with which the bill was rushed through was pretty generally believed to be due

[1] Sen. Deb., 1870, 29.

[2] *Ann. Cyclop.*, 1869, 396, gives 55 but I think it in error as the Debates give 59.

[3] House Deb., 1869, 191.

[4] In the absence of the Senate journal or debates for 1869, I have had to rely upon the brief legislative report of the *Commercial Bulletin*, Feb. 17.

[5] Session Laws, 1869, No. 118.   See the act in full.

to the fact that legislators had bought stock with the privilege of paying at convenience.[1] A perfect hue and cry against monopoly and violation of private rights went up at the passage of this bill. Hear the *Bee:* "So the bill has passed, just as it came from the House, and with provisions so monstrously unjust that if it be not arrested by veto, and be subjected to an ordeal by the two Houses, in review, which it is believed it cannot survive, it will at least become a byword of reproach to all concerned in it."[2] Or the *Picayune:* "Nay, monopolies have themselves such elements of corruption and are so odious in the land that they can and will be set aside. It may take time and a reformation of the polluted courts of justice to bring this about, but it will be done when the people awake to the necessity of driving the money-changers and the false Scribes and Pharisees from the temple."[3]

As there were about one thousand persons employed in the business in the parishes concerned, the effect was broad-spread. The butchers held a meeting immediately to consult on the best plan to defeat the bill[4] and organized an association on July 21. Some hundreds of suits were brought in the various district courts on the one side or the other, sometimes in combinations, sometimes by individuals. The ground of this opposition was that the act created a monopoly and was a violation of the Thirteenth and Fourteenth Amendments and of the Louisiana Bill of Rights. The Sixth District Court held the law unconstitutional, while in the Fifth, in which the new company had instituted suit against the association, the verdict was in favor of the company. Appeals from these several decisions came before the State Supreme Court by what is there known as "suspensive appeals,"

[1] New Orleans *Commercial Bulletin*, Mar. 17, 1869.
[2] February 23, 1869.   [3] Mar. 14.   [4] *Comm. Bull.*, Mar. 17.

but the decision was not rendered until April 11, 1870, when the rights of the new company were upheld. In course of time,[1] the cases came before the Supreme Court of the United States when the decision of the State court was sustained on the ground of police regulation, "a power incapable of any very exact definition or limitation."[2]

[1] April 14, 1873.   [2] 10 Wallace, 36, 298.

CHAPTER III

The Climax of Warmothism

THE question of the governor's power of appointment[1] involved two serious conflicts with municipalities during 1869, from one of which, at least, Warmoth emerged victoriously. A law of 1868 provided for the filling of all vacancies of State or parish offices by appointment for the remainder of the term by the governor with the consent of the Senate, but by the Governor alone, if the Senate were not in session, the appointment to expire the third Monday after the next session of the Assembly.[2] Governor Warmoth chose to interpret this as giving him the appointment even when the vacancy occurred by the expiration of the term of office. In 1868 the legislature had amended the charter of Jefferson City, requiring an election on the first Monday of January, 1869, and every two years thereafter for mayor, treasurer, comptroller, and aldermen.[3] Section 4 also provided that the governor should remove the existing aldermen and officers and appoint others until new incumbents should be elected. Warmoth did not execute this portion of the law but allowed matters to remain as they were until January, 1869, when an election should have been held. But none was ordered, instead of which the

---

[1] Under this apparently harmless clause of the constitution he controlled even the lowest local offices in the remotest parts—constable, justice of the peace, etc.

[2] Session Laws, 1868, No. 27.   [3] *Ibid.*, No. 75.

45

governor proceeded the following May to appoint, as in case of a vacancy. The original mayor, Kreider, refused to yield office, and so the appointee applied to the district judge for a mandamus to require the delivery of the books, which was granted. The new board was installed May 19, by aid of the metropolitan police. This action called out some violent demonstrations on the part of the citizens but no serious disturbance resulted and it was decided to leave the matter to the courts. Kreider carried an appeal to the Supreme Court, which held that the term of the occupants in office had not expired, for the failure to hold an election did not vacate the office. [1]

The case of New Orleans was analogous. The term of office of one half of the Council had expired; and a special election was held May 19 to fill the vacancies. But the governor under his unique interpretation of the law made appointments to fill them. The old board claimed that there were no vacancies, as, according to law, they were to hold their offices until their successors were duly elected and qualified; namely, until the next regular election. In this form it went to the courts on July 19. A three-cornered comedy of injunctions took place; one, granted by Judge Collins, admitted the newly elected members to their seats; a second, by Judge Leaumont, placed the governor's appointees in office and a Democratic howl went up; a third, from Judge Cooley, restored the elected members, and a Republican howl went up, [2] but this latter injunction was dissolved December 25. Appeal was taken from the decision of Judge Leaumont to the Supreme Court by the city of New Orleans, but was dismissed November 19, because of a technicality. [3]

[1] 21 Louisiana Ann., 483–485.
[2] New Orleans *Commercial Bulletin*, July 19, 1869.
[3] No pecuniary interest was at stake for the city, because the positions of aldermen had no salaries attached.   21 La. Ann., 744.

At the close of the year, the Governor decided to use the "mailed fist." December 28 the sheriff of the Fifth District Court read an order before the council to exclude certain members and install the appointees of Warmoth. The approaches to the council-room were crowded. The board decided to obey under protest and the governor's *protégés* were seated and proceeded to organize. One old member stayed in his seat, but as he made himself somewhat troublesome, he was ejected and another with a commission seated. In the other chamber of the city council that same evening one of the appointees appeared within the bar. President Wiltz ordered him put out. After adjournment the sheriff entered the chamber and read the above-mentioned order of Judge Leaumont.[1] On December 30 the sheriff of the Sixth District Court called the names of the appointees and served a paper upon each from the elected members. But the attorney advised obedience to the orders of the Fifth District Court and with this action the governor remained triumphant.

The wrangle between the governor and Wickliffe, the auditor of public accounts, which extended during most of 1869 and up until March of the new year, resulted in a victory for the former. He accused Wickliffe of extortion and corruption and had him arrested on several specific charges. Fourteen indictments for malfeasance to the amount of $1800 were found by the grand jury. While awaiting the trial, the governor suspended Wickliffe and appointed L. T. Delassize, a wealthy negro, auditor *ad interim*, installing him by the aid of the metropolitan police. But Wickliffe, nothing daunted, gave notice through the papers that he had opened his office at No. 53 Conti Street, "opposite where the Auditor's office formerly was," and warned the public not to pay taxes or transact any business with the bureau until the

[1] New Orleans *Commercial Bulletin*, Dec. 29, 1869.

auditor could retake possession of his office.[1] A war
of injunctions followed: a writ from the Seventh District
Court prohibited Delassize from performing his duties
on the ground that the governor had no power to make
the appointment; a counter injunction from the Fifth
District Court, March 29, restrained Wickliffe from acting. This conflict in jurisdiction went before the Supreme
Court,[2] but before a decision could be rendered, two of
the criminal cases came up for trial, in both of which
Wickliffe was acquitted, but in the one case the judge
considered it necessary to dismiss the jury with a repri-
mand.[3] The remainder of the charges were dismissed
by the attorney-general on the ground that the auditor
could not be tried until after impeachment. Party
feeling ran high in the press concerning the controversy,
some Democratic papers coming out emphatically for
Wickliffe, due possibly to mere opposition to the governor.[4] The governor withdrew his opposition and allowed
Wickliffe to resume office. In December the auditor decided to move his archives at night into the building used
as a state house, but the governor on the 30th had his
effects removed from Mechanics Institute to the sidewalk.[5]

[1] New Orleans, *Comm. Bull.*, *Bee*, Mar. 27, 1869.

[2] The Supreme Court subsequently affirmed the judgment of the Seventh
District Court, which sustained Delassize. 21 La. Ann., 710–12.

[3] *Ann. Cyclop.*, 1869, 398.

[4] "We do not propose to inquire into the legality of the action of the
Governor in ejecting Mr. Wickliffe from his office and appointing a person
to supply his place, because we consider it too clear for dispute that Mr.
Warmoth has no such power, and that his proceeding is a naked trespass.
. . . The white population of Louisiana are entirely callous to the result,
and don't care whether 'Mossup whip Barry' or 'Barry whip Mossup.'
They are in the situation of the onlookers at the fight of the Kilkenny
cats, and would have no cause to weep if the combatants scratched each
other's eyes out." *Bee*, Mar. 27, 1869.

The *Bulletin* and the *Picayune* took the same side more conservatively.
See *Bulletin*, Mar. 27.

[5] Sen. Jour., 1870, 138 (rear of book).

But this fact created no excitement in the city, as the affair seems still to have been regarded as a petty, personal squabble.

In this shape the matter came before the General Assembly in 1870. Rumors of impeachment had been rife, [1] and even before the governor's message was sent in, a resolution had been adopted by the House for a joint committee to examine into the affairs of the auditor's office and the action of the governor in suspending the auditor. [2] In the special message promised by the governor in his annual address, he charged that the auditor's offenses had seriously embarrassed the government and rendered it difficult to pay the interest on the State bonds. He specifically accused him of extortion against individuals and the charitable institutions of the State, and of fraud against the Commonwealth and collusion with evil-minded persons. [3] The special committee of the House, to which the message was referred, offered on January 31 a resolution of impeachment which was debated at some length and adopted on the evening of February 1 with but five dissenting votes. [4] The seriousness of the question sobered the Assembly so that the proceedings were marked throughout the trial by a dignity and decorum sadly wanting in their other discussions. Articles of impeachment were ordered prepared and the act suspending him from office became effective by the prompt concurrence of the Senate on February 4. [5]

February 3, Wickliffe brought thirty-four distinct counter charges against Warmoth of violations of the

---

[1] Sen. Deb., 1870, 51.   [2] House Jour., 1870, 7.

[3] "He has extorted sums of money from the creditors of the state as a condition precedent to the issuance to them of the certificates of indebtedness or warrants to which they were entitled by law." *Ibid.*, 1870, 11–12.

[4] *Ibid.*, 1870, 141.

[5] *Ibid.*, 1870, 141, Sen. Jour., 130.

4

constitution and laws, of frauds upon the treasury,
charges of corruption in levying blackmail upon citizens,
of bribery of witnesses, and numerous other acts of malfeasance. "In short," the accusation concludes, "his
conduct in this respect is so notorious that it can be
proved that he never signed a bill of pecuniary benefit to
anyone that he did not demand and receive money or
other consideration for his signature."[1] He summed
up the frauds to the State to the grand total of
$800,000 and "untold millions from forgery." But the
only effect this venting of his spleen had upon Warmoth's
loyal vassals was to cause an investigation to be made
which enabled Warmoth to go before the people exonerated by an official inquiry.[2]

The House preferred twenty-eight articles of impeachment against Wickliffe, most of them for exacting bribes
to issue his warrants for money appropriated for printing and charitable institutions, and for exceeding the
appropriations.[3] The trial began February 14, and continued almost daily until the close of the session, when
on the evening of March 3, the Senate found him guilty
upon the fourth article by unanimous vote.[4] A resolution removing him permanently from office followed
immediately. At the last moment he tried to escape
sentence by resigning,[5] and by fleeing from the State,[6]
but the Senate proceeded calmly to ignore such cowardice

[1] House Jour., 1870, 152–5.
[2] "After a lengthy and thorough examination of all the witnesses whose
attendance your committee has been able to procure, they have been
able to find from the testimony elicited no foundation whatever, for any
one of the charges preferred by George Wickliffe against his Excellency."
Ibid., 1870, 310.
[3] See Sen. Jour., 1870, 2–7 (rear) for articles in full.
[4] Ibid., 1870, rear, 191. For full account of the trial see Impeachment
Proceedings in rear of Ibid., 1870.
[5] Ibid., 1870, rear, 176, March 3.
[6] On the authority of Herbert, Why the Solid South, 410.

and to vote him out of office. Whatever may be the fact as to Wickliffe's dishonesty, he was clearly guilty of gross irregularity and carelessness in the keeping of his records.[1] And the governor had demonstrated to the State that his hold on the legislature was sufficiently firm to enable him to crush a presumptuous subordinate.

The legislation of 1870 marks high tide in Warmoth's power. The rudder he held firmly in his hands for almost two years longer; but against an ever-increasing wave of opposition, it became constantly more difficult to steer in the direction he would. Because of friction within his own ranks, legislation did not again, after 1870, become the mouthpiece for promulgating his decrees.

There were, in reality, two sessions, but the extra session followed so closely on the heels of the first, and so much of the work was but the completion of the unfinished business of the first session, that for purposes of convenience the legislation will be treated as emanating from one body. The Assembly convened for the first session at noon, January 3. After a slight struggle over the speakership in the House, Mr. Carr of Orleans was elected and the House reported itself ready for the governor's message. Its congratulatory tone sounds a bit forced when he felicitates his people upon "the good feeling that exists among the people of both races"; and the cheerfulness with which they are accepting the new order of things, and the earnestness with which "our people are addressing themselves to further protect the great interests committed to their hands."[2] But it is taken up, for the most part, with a businesslike discussion of

---

[1] "I found that the books were not written up to date, or those that were written up, the columns were not footed up; addition had not been made. A great many appropriations had been overdrawn." Sen. Jour., 1870, 66.
[2] House Jour., 9.

the various measures which, in his estimation, called
for action: encouragement of immigration, the finances,
levees, public improvements, emendation of the school-
law of 1869, charities, and gambling houses. [1]

For the first time we hear the note of caution in regard
to the financial condition. The governor warned the
Assembly that it was not satisfactory and was such as to
embarrass his administration. He admitted that the
credit of the State had not always been used for practicable
purposes, but insisted that under proper checks it might
be safely used to a still greater extent. [2] The usual
expedients were again resorted to: loans were negotiated
to meet the interest due; and the floating debt was provided for by the issue or exchange of fresh bonds. But
the same extravagance and folly which characterized
their actions in 1869 continued undiminished. [3]

By the session of 1870 an old feature of parliamentary
tactics was introduced: the opposition, though unavailing
as to the final vote, had become thoroughly organized for
filibustering purposes and threats of recourse to its use
were held over the heads of the radicals as a whip. [4] Mr.
Lowell proposed once to make a bargain with his party,
to which he was opposed on a particular bill, by exchang-

[1] For the full text of the message, see House Jour., 1870, 9 ff.
[2] House Journal, 1870, 9.
[3] They were very generous with the fees for postage, lavish to their
officers and employees, made a specialty of special committees, passed a
most liberal and loose pension act for the veterans of 1814–15, and took
active steps for the erection of a new state house. They had learned
nothing from the deficiency in the revenue of the preceding year but proceeded to quibble about levying a tax of four or five mills though Federal
investigation would show that agricultural property could easily bear a
heavier tax.   Sen. Jour., 1870, 41, 57; House Deb., 1870, 238; Sen. Repts.,
42 Cong., 2 Sess., No. 41, Pt. i., 203.
[4] "But I say, take up the city charter bill, and if you do not, I assure
you that you will not make much progress on the school bill." Sen.
Deb., 1870, 783.   Also House Deb., 200.

ing his filibustering advantage for a grant of time.[1]   By debates on rules of order, appeals from the chair to the House, demands for the roll-call on every little insignificant vote, they were able to waste time and wear out their opponents until practically no business was done at certain sessions.[2]

Four of the five measures which were destined to become the most important of the session—indeed of the reconstruction period in Louisiana—and the storm center about which the opposition to the governor gathered, were, together with the appropriation and revenue bills, introduced into the Senate as early as the third day, thus gaining for that active body the questionable distinction of initiative.[3]   Nor did that body lose its zeal in pushing legislation, for toward the close of the session bills went through with a haste amazing even after the facility displayed on occasion in 1869.   At a single evening session twenty bills were acted on,[4] and yet, despite regular night sessions for about two weeks, the session approached its close without concluding much important legislation,[5] and without making provision for the revenues or expenses of the government.   And so, in accordance with the general expectation,[6] the governor on March 3 notified the two houses of the necessity to reassemble March 7 for ten days.   In this extra session the Assembly took up and passed the tremendous number of ninety-eight

[1] "I now make a fair, honest proposition to the friends of the bill. If they will give me time—say till to-morrow, to read this bill, to examine it—I promise then, upon my word and sacred honor, that I will not oppose its passage by resorting to those parliamentary tactics commonly known as filibustering."   House Deb., 1870, 74.

[2] Jan. 21, *ibid.*, 48–57; Jan. 24.

[3] Sen. Jour., 1870, 12, 13.   [4] *Ibid.*, 216–22.

[5] The militia, registration, and New Orleans charter bills had run the gauntlet of the Senate but were still pending in the House.

[6] The House had already consulted the attorney-general about the constitutionality of prolonging the session.   House Jour., 1870, 97.

bills, as compared with one hundred and seven in the first session.

An effort to tackle the problem of the government of New Orleans had suffered indefinite postponement at the end of the session of 1869. Both houses introduced bills early in 1870, but it was only late in the extra session, after lengthy, heated debate, numerous amendments, and the creation of committees of conference, that the two houses could agree upon a measure which consolidated Jefferson City with New Orleans, forced through by the country members, it was vehemently declared, against the vigorous opposition of the city members. The smaller city did not want to be saddled with the debt and taxes of the larger. A representative of Jefferson said: "I say, sir, here in my place, that the people—the masses—do not want to be forced to pay an additional 2½ per cent tax. . . . There are not 150 people in Jefferson who would vote for consolidation."[1] An amendment to submit it to popular vote was undemocratically voted down. The enlarged city was to be governed by a mayor and seven administrators, presiding over as many departments, who were to constitute the city council. Vacancies in these offices were to be filled by appointment by the governor prior to January 1, 1871, and subsequently by popular election.[2]

New Orleans was one of the few Southern cities which had had a system of public schools before the war. Even in 1865 there were 141 schools for freedmen and 19,000 pupils, the result of a free system for twenty-five years.[3] A school law, providing in great detail for the public education of all persons between six and twenty-one years of age "without distinction of race or color" had

[1] House Deb., 1870, 295.
[2] Laws of Louisiana, Extra Session, 1870, No. 70.
[3] Sen. Reports, 42 Cong., 2 Sess., No. 41, 279.

been passed in 1869. But it had been a failure,[1] proving in the governor's words, "cumbrous and expensive."[2] The governor, therefore, suggested that the plan be simplified, the districts enlarged, and the powers and discretion of the State board increased.[3] Shortly after the opening of the session a bill was reported in the House and received, despite attempts to choke it, full, heated discussion and amendment, section by section, passing only on February 10.[4] In the Senate it came up for a lengthy debate on the last evening, when it was crowded out by the pressure of business so that it had to go over to March 9 and 10 in the extra days of grace when, somewhat amended, it passed by a very large majority, the dissenting votes coming from the city members.[5] The House concurred in the Senate amendments the next day.

For the purposes of this bill the State was divided into six divisions, of which New Orleans formed one. The State superintendent was required to nominate to the governor, and the governor to the Senate, a superintendent for each division to hold office three years. The division superintendents with the State superintendent as president constituted a board, having the general

[1] McMillan charged ineffectiveness of the law. "There is not in my whole parish, as far as I know, a single schoolhouse, no sirs, not even a shed devoted to educational purposes. There has not been a cent of the taxes raised for educational purposes expended in Carroll Parish since the war. We have a statute providing for a system of common school education, and under that superintendents have been appointed. The salary set apart for such officers has been punctually drawn." House Deb., 1870, 115–16.

[2] "Under the law of 1869 we find that the sum of $262,000 would be required for the salaries of officers, leaving nothing with which to pay teachers, or build or rent schoolhouses." New Orleans *Republican*, Jan. 25, 1870.

[3] Governor's Annual Message, House Jour., 1870, 10.

[4] House Deb., 1870, 188. House Jour., 220. On this question and the social status the negro could wax eloquent.

[5] Sen. Jour., 1870, 267.

supervision and control of the public schools throughout
the State, while the division superintendents were to
have full control in their respective divisions. The
system of New Orleans was connected with that of the
State by the selection of a city board of directors by
the State board, thus repealing all laws granting control to
the municipal authorities of that city. The State board
was also to appoint a board for every town, city, and parish
in the State with full corporate powers to sue and be sued.
The general school tax was fixed at two mills on the
dollar in addition to a tax of two mills to be collected in
each parish. It continued, however, the provision for
the admission of all children between the ages of six
and twenty-one to the schools. [1]

A special civil court, the Eighth District Court, created
at the special session, proved of transcendent importance,
when supported by the criminal court,—created several
sessions earlier. The two had jurisdiction over all public
matters, while the power of appointing the judges was
vested in the governor, thus circumventing the constitution. All cases of a public character, contests for office,
writs of quo warranto, injunctions, mandamus had to
be submitted to the former court, to which all cases then
pending before other district courts must immediately
be transferred. [2]

Numerous petitions to the legislature of 1870 showed
that the idea of improvements had now seized upon a
large number of the constituents as well as legislators. [3]
Not only did members now propose to raise the State to
economic glory through the ordinary avenue of new rail-

[1] Session Laws, Extra Session, 1870, No. 6.
[2] *Ibid.*, No. 2.
[3] The writer noted twenty-six such bills reaching various stages of progress, besides the fourteen bills which succeeded in becoming law. There
were doubtless many more which were never reported from committee.

roads and navigable bayous, but in their enthusiasm they were willing to legislate parks[1] and factories into existence and to develop the mineral resources of the State by the same agency. Bayou Bartholomew was now to be improved; the New Orleans and Chattanooga Railroad boosted by State bonds[2]; and a large sum of stock subscribed in the Mississippi Valley Navigation Company.[3]

A number of amendments to the constitution were offered this session,[4] but only four mustered sufficient strength to pass both houses. The most noted were the one which removed the governor's ineligibility for a second term[5] and the amendment to Article 99, which removed the last restriction on the ex-rebels. It had been offered in the Assembly, both in 1868 and 1869, and the governor had urged it in his annual message in the latter year.[6] It stands out in pleasing relief to most of the partisan legislation of that period, inasmuch as it was introduced, we are told in debate, by one of the most bitter opponents of the Democrats,[7] aroused very little debate, and passed almost unanimously in both houses

[1] Session Laws, Extra Session, 1870, No. 59.

[2] *Ibid.*, No. 31.

[3] *Ibid.*, No. 84. This bill became law without the governor's signature by lapse of the time limit.

[4] The writer counted seven.

[5] It appears almost incredible that this most personal measure of all passed both houses with almost no opposition. The explanation may lie in the bribery later charged. House Misc. Doc., 42 Cong., 2 Sess., No. 211, 272–73.

[6] "In this spirit (of forgiveness) I recommend the abrogation of the 99th Article of our Constitution, and believe, if an amendment should be submitted to the people at the next general election, it would receive their almost unanimous approval. I regretted its insertion in the constitution, favored the proposition to abrogate it at the last session, and now officially recommend it." *Cyclopedia*, 1869, 394.

[7] Senate Deb., 1870, 61.

at a single sitting.[1]   Several speeches, all in favor, were
made by negroes to give, as one of them innocently said,
"a little coloring to the matter."[2]

A third amendment was intended to secure the safety
of the public funds,[3] and the fourth was a most important
restriction on the public debt, namely, that prior to
January 1, 1890, it could not be increased beyond
$25,000,000.[4]

But certain bills were of such transcendent importance that they all but effaced the consciousness of
other legislation, at least in the mind of the public.
These were the four great bills, the election, registration, constabulary, and militia bills, which, together with the constitutional amendment which
removed ineligibility for a second gubernatorial term,
made it possible for Governor Warmoth to determine
the personnel of all offices practically at will, and,
but for the stumbling-block of the nominating convention, to continue himself indefinitely at the head
of affairs.

Whatever may have been the distrust of the governor
in the State at large—and complaints were not wanting
from the first in Democratic circles—confidence in their
young leader was unshaken in the men who constituted
this Assembly.   Even when opposing individual bills,
members were careful to express confidence in War-

---

[1] Sen. Jour., 1871, 37; House Jour., 146–47.
    The House Committee reported it as a "partial proscriptive measure in
direct conflict with the spirit of the age and unnecessary."   House Jour.,
1870, 146.
    [2] House Deb., 1871, 42.   Only one voice was raised in opposition.
    [3] No person who had been a collector or had been otherwise intrusted
with public money was eligible to any office of trust until he had obtained
a discharge for the amount with which he had been intrusted.   Session
Laws, 1870, No. 21, Regular Session.
    [4] Session Laws, 1870, Extra Session, No. 12.

moth[1] in some such terms as follows: "Not that I have anything against the governor himself, but I think it improper to give such extraordinary power to any man, were he an apostle."[2]

These measures were introduced together, as has been stated, on the third day, and action on them extended during the entire period up to the very close of the extra session. The greatest effort of the opposition was expended on the election bill. This was not a new conception of 1870, for a strenuous effort to press through such a bill under cover of the excitement of the closing days of the session of 1869 had failed. The note of alarm was sounded almost as soon as this bill was reported to the Senate by the Judiciary Committee.[3] "Now, sir, here is a bill giving the governor more than imperial power —behind it is concealed an armed Grecian horse, with which he may ride over the rights of the people. . . ."[4] Debate raged every day from January 18 to 24. The party aspect of the bill was so evident that it was assailed at once as a device to perpetuate the Republican party in power.   .

"I believe," declared one member, "the only persons belonging to this State who desire this enactment are those in office, and who are afraid that unless such a bill as this is passed, they will not retain the positions they now occupy, and this fear, Mr. President, is not based on any fraud or violence that might occur at the next election in

[1] "Although I would have the greatest confidence in whatever he reported." Senate Deb., 1870, 118.
"I do not say the present governor would abuse these powers," says even a Democrat, 744.
[2] Ibid., 120.
[3] Two minority reports came in, in one of which Packard urged that a new apportionment must precede any election law. Ibid., 143.
[4] Ibid., 147.

which they might become candidates, but in the simple fact that a revolution has taken place in public opinion."[1] Even a Republican felt obliged to break from his party because of its objectionable features.[2]

Feeling reached a perfect climax of frenzy and sank to depths of despondency for which it was difficult to find language sufficiently vehement.

"Therefore, I hope you will believe me when I tell you that this is the snake in the grass—the form that the devil himself assumed when he seduced our mother Eve. I tell you that this is a devil, covered and concealed perhaps, under perfumed flowers, but nevertheless, the devil—his tail and horn comes out, and not only his tail, but his horns and hoof. I tell you that this bill is a devil of a bill—the concocters are devilish fellows, and the only way we can destroy their sulphuric power is to give them hell."[3] Another outburst was clothed in more funereal garb:

I believe really that if ever there has come a day to the State of Louisiana when the whole edifice of her political government ought to be draped in mourning, that day has come now. I believe if ever there has come a day when all the pomp and glory of the past had forsaken her—widowed as she is in affection, destitute of all those glorious sympathies that used to awaken a nobler people—we have arrived, unfortunately for us, at that miserable period.[4]

In his excitement one member cried: "By God! I do not vote when they are passing bills here to take away the lifeblood of the people."[5]

The Republicans rested their defense on the necessity of an election law which would secure to every citizen

---

[1] Senate Deb., 1870, 155–56.
[2] "I believe the object of the bill, as it stands, is to perpetuate the power of a certain political party—the Republican party." Ibid., 149.
[3] Ibid., 1870, 168.   [4] Ibid., 164–65.   [5] Ibid., 180.

entitled to vote a free exercise of his rights.[1] They
turned the debate on the Democrats by declaring that
if they could not carry an election without violence and
were unwilling to pass a law to insure a fair election, they
did not want an honest vote.[2] Radicals who were not
satisfied with the bill declared that the opposition by their
refusal to discuss it fairly and by filibustering had prevented any modification. The attitude of the mulatto
leader, Pinchback, was that it was the lesser of two evils.[3]
It reëmerged from a special committee, to which it had
been committed, January 24,[4] and which again submitted
a majority and minority report, for a second period of
debate from January 27 to 31, on which latter date,
much amended and fought to the bitter end, it was
adopted by a vote of 20 to 12.[5]

It came before the House on February 4, where it was
argued at length from February 11 to 16, in keen,
searching debate. Members did not scruple to speak
plainly: "This bill, as I believe it, and as I know it, makes
the Republican party dominant; it makes the Governor,
—not clearly, but tactily—all power; it makes the many
parishes of this State but fiefs of the Executive. It adds
one more power to those he is already endowed with."[6]
Note the succinct condemnation of it as a party measure
in the following query: "Why is the whole State outlawed
in consequence of the misbehavior of portions of it?
Outlawed, I say, for it provides for the outlawry of those
who refuse to vote a Republican ticket."[7] Party feeling
ran as high as in the other House, and members found

---

[1] Sen. Deb., 150.   [2] Ibid., 187.
[3] "If any gentleman can show me where we can repose the execution
of this law outside of the Executive of the State, I would be glad to hear it;
but we must have some protection, sir."   Ibid., 172.
[4] Ibid., 190.   [5] Ibid., 347, Sen. Jour., 110.
[6] House Deb., 1870, 213.   [7] Ibid., 207.

threatening documents on their desks, placed there, Republicans declared, by the Ku-Klux.[1] Finally, suffering much amendment here too, it was passed February 18 immediately after prayer, with a burst of party effort: with the reading of only thirteen sections,[2] the passage of the bill as a whole was moved and carried, the reading of more than fifty sections being thus suppressed, notwithstanding the protest of the Democrats at the unconstitutional manner in which it was passed.[3] February 19 the Senate concurred in the House amendments.[4]

The other measures seem almost to have turned on the fate of the election law, for the opposition evidently exhausted its great effort on that bill. There was little heat over the other measures; little filibustering, few long speeches. Such few members as spoke seemed to do so to discharge a moral duty.[5] The registration bill passed the Senate, February 9[6] without amendment and the House entirely without debate on the last evening of the regular session.

The history of the militia bill in the House was truly remarkable. It was introduced March 9 from the Senate, where the interest was so slight that only seven Senators

[1] House Deb., 217.

[2] These thirteen sections had been read February 15 and on February 18, immediately after prayer, a motion was made to suspend the rules in order to put it upon its third reading and final passage at that time. No vote was taken, but the speaker asked if there were any objection to the suspension of the rules, and immediately announced that there was none, notwithstanding the fact that Dr. Wren and many other members did object, but they were unheeded by the chair. According to the protest of the Democrats. House Jour., 254.

[3] *Ibid.*, 236, 254. Vote was 247 to 26.

[4] Sen. Jour., 1870, 188.

[5] On the final suspension of the rules on the registration bill, a Senator remarked briefly: "I object to the suspension of the rules because I wish to give the senate as much time as possible to repent." Sen. Deb., 470.

[6] Sen. Jour., 150.

were present to register their vote against the fourteen votes which carried it [1]; the necessity of considering it in Committee of the Whole was dispensed with, and it was hurried to its third reading. The story of its passage on the evening of March 14 is told in the following brief passage from the debates:

"Chief Clerk Vigers read the bill.

"I move its final passage, and on that call the previous question.

"The Speaker put the question on the final passage *viva voce*, and it was declared carried." [2]

This action caused the greatest confusion, surprise, and protest.

The registration bill threw into the control of the governor the power to declare who should vote, as the election bill allowed him to declare for whom the votes were cast. With the consent of the Senate he was to appoint a State registrar, and one supervisor in each parish—except Orleans, where the State registrar was to serve—whose duty it should be to cause every qualified voter to be registered and make out lists of the registered voters for the commissioners of election at each polling-place. [3] The decision of any supervisor was final. Courts were prohibited from interfering in any way with him or his assistants. The supervisors, in turn, appointed three commissioners of election at each poll.

The election bill vested in the governor power to take all necessary steps to secure a fair, free, and peaceable election; and gave him on election day paramount charge and control of the peace and order of the State, over all peace and police officers, and over all sheriffs and constables.

[1] Sen. Jour., 245.

[2] House Deb., 1870, 343. McMillan was refused permission to record his protest. House Jour., 360.

[3] Laws of Louisiana, 1870, No. 99.

Parish and district judges were forbidden to issue writs of mandamus or injunction or other order to compel a commissioner of election to do his duty, as the latter was to be responsible only to the supervisor and he to the governor. On election day citizens at large were expressly forbidden to carry arms except under orders of the executive or his appointees. In all parishes except Orleans, the duty and function of sheriffs were superseded by men appointed by the governor. The governor and his officers were to be able to withhold certificates of election to the General Assembly whenever in their discretion they might see fit, in all cases where fraud, violence, bribery, or other irregularity might be reported. The capstone of the structure, as it has been aptly called, was the returning-board, consisting of the governor, lieutenant-governor, secretary of State, and two Senators indicated by name—John Lynch and T. C. Anderson,—in whom was vested the entire revisory power. They were empowered to fill vacancies within their own number by a majority vote.[1]

In order fully to comprehend the opportunity for fraud in elections, it must also be noted that the State constitution gave the right to vote in any parish or in any part of a parish after a residence of ten days, so that a man, armed with his registration papers, could vote at as many polls as he could visit in one day.

The purport of the third bulwark of Warmothism, the constabulary law, was to vest in the governor special power to keep the peace. With the consent of the Senate he might appoint one chief constable in each parish, whose duty it should be to preserve the peace, quell disturbances and riots, and upon warrant of any competent court,

---

[1] Laws of Louisiana, 1870, No. 100. The power to reject votes for fraud or violence was capable of abuse and yet was held by Republicans inadequate as a remedy, as it did not add the Republican ballots which would have been polled.

summarily arrest all persons charged with murder, assaults, robberies, arson, and riots, subject to the power of the governor. The chief constable of the parish was to assign to each precinct a deputy constable to perform his duties. Offices of all existing constables were declared vacant and the governor empowered to bring in a set of his loyal followers at once.[1]

The militia bill provided the necessary military power to enforce the execution of the preceding laws. Under its provisions the governor was constituted Commander-in-Chief of all the militia and could organize, arm, equip, and uniform as many of the able-bodied male citizens between the ages of eighteen and forty-five as he deemed necessary and call the same into active service. Full lists were to be submitted from each parish to the governor from which he might assign a sufficient number of persons to make up five regiments. He was to appoint officers for terms of two years to carry out details under his direction. And the sum of $100,000 was appropriated to carry out the act.[2]

Several minor bills helped to build up this autocratic power of the executive. Against stormy debate and attacks on its constitutionality, a bill was passed which authorized the governor to issue a warrant for the arrest of any person committing a crime punishable by death or penitentiary imprisonment upon failure of the regularly constituted officials to seize him, to be tried in a parish or district court. Although the accused was assured of the service of attorney, the bill violated State feeling by obliterating parish lines, and by allowing high fees to the sheriff, levied on the parish where the offense occurred.[3] Likewise, the bill which rendered the Metropolitan

---

[1] **Laws of Louisiana**, 1870, No. 74.
[2] *Ibid.*, Extra Session, No. 75.
[3] *Ibid.*, No. 40.

5

Police Board no longer responsible to the recognized legal tribunals, [1] and which did not require a bond in case suit was brought against it, was only freeing his hands the more. Nor should the reader fail to notice in this connection, as the last link in the chain, that the governor could, under the new city charter, absolutely control the city politics until after the election, a period of seven months of grace for manipulating his wires.

Legislation so vital and revolutionary as the measures just outlined and those appropriating State aid, naturally, aroused hostility, not only within the legislature, but also outside, where it raged even more violently, if possible. The Democratic press was thoroughly alarmed; it attacked the various bills continually and held the most dire threats over the heads of the Senators who dared to support them. [2]   Fiery language was intended to stir the people to action. [3]   Feeling rose to its greatest intensity over the four most important bills. [4]   Significant calls for secret meetings, signed K. W. C. and I. C. U., [5] appeared in the papers, and mass meetings began to be held both for and against the bills.   The Republican party met in mass meeting on January 27 in the hall of the Representatives to urge the Assembly to pass these bills without

[1] Session Laws, 1870, No. 55.

[2] My authority for this is the statement of a Senator in debate. Senate Deb., 1870, 618.   But names were printed in the papers on important bills so that it is probably true.

[3] "Let us have a united meeting and prompt action to bring our lawmakers to their just responsibility to an outraged community." *Bee* of Jan. 30.

[4] "We then protest against this bill on constitutional grounds," declared the *True Republican*, "for by this bill Warmoth actually fills three offices. Now, we know that this is a moderate demand for him, who wants to be the political Brigham Young of this State.   We, Gentiles, are naturally satisfied with one office, but this political Mormon wants them all." Quoted Sen. Deb., 1870, 537.

The writer has come across no clue to the meaning of these letters. The first are, doubtless, Knights of the White Camelia.

delay. This action was probably to forestall and nullify the effect of a vast mass meeting of the opponents of the legislation, which was arranged to take place, January 31 in Lafayette Square. The call was issued to all citizens "opposed to the financial schemes now pending before the legislature, calculated to increase the burdens of the people, depreciate the bonds, and ruin the credit of the people, and cripple commerce."[1] The enthusiasm of the crowd here almost outstripped that of the leaders. Said one speaker: "It is designed not to defend, but to plunder the country, and take away the liberties of the people. What is to be done?"

"Kill them," came the prompt response from the crowd.

"Ah, no, not yet. But put your foot down and say that this thing shall not be. There is power in the fixed determination of the people, and if the bills are then passed, do as Boston did to the minions of George III. What is to be done with a Legislature that does these things?"

"Lynch them," was the verdict of his hearers.[2]

A series of resolutions was passed protesting against the proposed bills as destructive of the freedom of elections and as creating an absolute despot of the executive, and denouncing their advocates as public enemies. Men gave the world notice that they intended to use all the means in their power to prevent the payment of any bonds or other obligations of the State which were not indispensably necessary to the proper administration of the government, and threatened openly to vote for no man who would not refuse to vote any appropriations for such obligations.[3] Committees in every parish sought to obtain

---

[1] The movement for concerted action against bad legislation had begun in 1869 when the Taxpayers' Organization had been created in a mass-meeting, Oct. 23. *Commercial Bulletin*, Oct. 25, 1869.

[2] *Pic.*, Feb. 1.

[3] For the resolves in full see House Jour., 148–9.

the signatures of the citizens of the State to the above resolutions, and a delegation of one hundred citizens was chosen to present them to the governor and the Assembly.

The governor's reception of the committee was cordial, but his response contained some remarkable charges; he laid the blame for the excesses on lobbyists who knew how to manipulate the negroes, and laid the corruption at the door of individuals and corporations who represented the very best people; nor did he scruple to withhold names.

"The bill (the five million bond bill) went to the Senate. I walked into the Senate chamber and saw nearly every prominent broker of the city engaged in lobbying that bill through the Senate, and it was only by exposing the fact that one of their emissaries had come into this very chamber and laid upon the desk of my secretary an order for $50,000 that I was able to defeat it. Mr. Conway, the mayor of your city, came here and offered me any consideration to induce me to sign this bill."[1]

The visit of the delegates to the Senate on February 2 degenerated into pure farce. A long and amusing debate as to whether they should receive them or not took place before the delegates, as by some misunderstanding they had crowded into the chamber before the Senators had settled this momentous question. And Pinchback explained in great detail that he had been obliged to admit them at once or they "would go off with an additional excuse that we would not listen to the representatives of the people."[2] After the reading of the resolutions the dele-

---

[1] *Cyclopedia*, 1870, 455. One of his charges was against the leading brokers, who subsequently denied the charge against them; and other persons indicated by the governor, while admitting their attempts to bribe him, alleged that he was interested against them, or that he was not satisfied with the prices offered. Sen. Repts., 42 Cong., 2 Sess., No. 41, 202.

[2] Senate Deb., 360–1.

gates were virtually asked to leave[1] and the indignation of the Senators found wordy expression.[2] Though the suggestion to return the resolutions as "disrespectful and insulting" was not adopted, the latter were promptly tabled.

The attempt with the House on the same day met with no more success, though preliminary arrangement for a ten-minute recess prevented any such undignified parley as had occurred in the other body. But the House took much the same attitude of offense toward the resolutions and buried them in a special committee.[3]

Nominating conventions for the selection of candidates for State officers were held in the month of September by both the Republican and Democratic parties. A feature of both conventions was the appearance of a large number of colored delegates. Inquiries were sent to the Democratic State Central Committee as to the admission of colored delegates and so the committee in the regular address to the people took occasion to voice the party sentiment in the following language:

" The interests of both white and black men are identical in this struggle. Whatever rights and privileges either enjoy under the constitution are sacred, and it is the duty of every citizen to see that they are maintained. The Democratic party has always upheld and defended the constitution of the country and will now, as ever in the past, protect and defend every citizen in the full and free exercise of all rights guaranteed by that instrument." [4]

---

[1] A very pointed hint is given: "But all the Senate can do in self-respect is to intimate to this body of citizens the rules of the Senate, and their own sense of propriety should dictate to them what to do." Senate Deb., 358.

[2] "I looked upon that as an act of the grossest incivility and abuse; and sir, as a matter of self-respect and vindication of the privileges of the House, I deem it right that a rebuke be administered."

[3] House Jour., 184.

[4] *Annual Cyclopedia*, 1870, 457.

It declared its platform to be retrenchment and reform, reduction of the debt and taxation, rebuilt levees, restored confidence, and a desire to develop the agricultural resources of the State.

The election was remarkable for its peaceful character.[1] But later investigation established the fact that there was much fraud both in connection with the appointment of registrars and in the count of the election ballots. The law required the appointment of registrars six months before election. Yet in August but two had been appointed. It was charged that the governor purposely delayed appointment in order to influence the August convention.[2] He had appointed in at least sixteen parishes Democratic supervisors of registration on the score that it was hard to find competent Republicans willing to undertake it and that it was good policy.[3] The same investigation concluded that "there is no doubt that most scandalous frauds were committed by and with the connivance of some of these registrars,[4] sometimes in the interest of Republicans and sometimes in the interest of Democratic candidates."[5] An old negro, who had been nominated, was astonished at the result of the count and cried: "Is it

[1] The Governor called it "the most quiet, peaceable, and orderly election the State has witnessed for many years." Sen. Jour., 1871, 23.

[2] House Misc. Doc., 42 Cong., 2 Sess., No. 211, 121.

[3] House Reports, 42 Cong., 2 Sess., No. 92, 4.
The attempt to control the negro vote made by the Democrats in 1868 seems to have been abandoned. See Nordhoff's story of how a prominent citizen dismissed a personal servant for voting against him and then restored him with the resolution never again to try to control a black man's vote.

[4] Packard states that the registrar in West Feliciana made a contract with the Democrats whereby he agreed to give a certain vote to the Democratic parish officers in return for Democratic help in electing a Republican Senator. House Misc. Doc., No. 211, 143.

[5] Ibid., 18, 438, 439. A part of Caddo Parish where eight hundred voters lived was cut off by water and so no registrar went to that section at all, 50.

possible I have no vote come out of the box? 'Fore God, I know I vote for myself."[1]

A considerable number of registrars, clerks, and friends of registrars were returned elected to the legislature.[2] Carr, who was returned from De Soto Parish without a nomination, was not even a resident of that parish,[3] nor was his the only case of that kind. It was conspicuous that fraudulently returned members were friends of the governor,[4] and he was charged with direct complicity in two cases. Some rioting, notably at Donaldsonville and Baton Rouge, was reported.[5] This naturally gave rise to many contested elections which hung on to furnish the opponents of the governor their opportunity in 1872.

It was a clear Republican victory. Graham and Dubuclet, the Republican candidates for auditor and treasurer, came in with majorities of about twenty-five thousand each, and that party secured majorities in both branches of the Assembly. The four constitutional amendments were submitted to popular vote and adopted. The amendment to Article 99 was indorsed unanimously.[6]

An interesting fact is to be noted here. In the spring of 1868, while the Democracy was wholly unorganized and the negroes aggressive under the protection of the military government, the State went Republican, but was carried by a reinvigorated Democratic party in the

[1] Senate Reports, 42 Cong., 2 Sess., No. 457, 718.

[2] According to Bovee fifteen or twenty registrars were returned. House Misc. Doc., No. 211, 245.

[3] He was put on the ticket by the Parish Committee as the man named by the convention said he could not leave. Part of the tickets bore his name, part the name of the former nominee, so that the friends of the latter who could not read were tricked into voting for Carr. *Ibid.*, 224–25.

[4] Bovee stated: "I think there was a regular system of fraud entered into with a view of electing certain men. . . . As far as I can learn, all were perpetrated in the governor's interest." *Ibid.*, 243.

[5] Sen. Jour., 1871, 32.   [6] *Ibid.*, 1871, 24.

Presidential election of November of the same year; but in 1870 it swung back to the party in power.[1]   But there are two perfectly intelligible explanations which do not necessarily invalidate the vote for Seymour in 1868: the new election law and the Enforcement Act of May 31, 1870,[2] which imposed heavy penalties for infringement upon the right to vote.

[1] See the table which illustrates this shifting in Sen. Repts., 42 Cong., 2 Sess., No. 41, 250.

[2] United States Statutes at Large, XVI., 140–6.

CHAPTER IV

The Beginning of Warmoth's Downfall

THE first hints of dissension within what may be accurately called Warmoth's party came as early as January, 1870. The element which was to become so notorious as the "Custom-House" faction had already made its appearance in Louisiana politics. A resolution introduced into the House in the early days of the session recognized the existence of separate organizations contending for recognition as the Central Republican Club, and designated the men of the New Orleans custom-house as "erring" members.[1] A certain tension seems to have been present in the attitude of the House toward all questions respecting the custom-house. When the House sought information concerning its own members who were in the employ of the custom-house, Collector Casey refused it, as he was not a State officer.[2]

The cause of the personal opposition to Warmoth is to be traced, no doubt, to the movement for the removal of his ineligibility for a second term, which caused alarm

[1] Jan. 15, 1870. "Whereas different persons and separate organizations are contending for recognition as the Central Republican Club of the State of Louisiana. . . . Resolved That the organization thus attempted be permitted to take a back seat in the gatherings of the great Republican party of this state, and that the door of the Republican Temple shall hereafter, like gospel gates, stand open night and day, until all political sinners, including even the erring ones from the New Orleans Customhouse, shall have time and opportunity to return decently and in order to their father's house." La. House Jour., 55.

[2] See above p. 29. House Journ., 1870, 252.

to the other Republican aspirants for that honor.[1] Organizations were soon covertly started to defeat the amendment at the polls, according to Warmoth's statement.[2] Opposition, however, first became open at the Republican State Convention which assembled at New Orleans, August 9, 1870, for the nomination of a ticket and the appointment of a State Central Committee. It was felt that the governor was taking extraordinary pains to control that convention, especially as he had been elected a delegate by a club which the committee did not recognize.[3] Both he and the lieutenant-governor, who was also present as a delegate, were nominated to preside, but here the former met his first check: he was defeated by his negro subordinate. As the civil rights bill of the preceding session still lay unsigned in the hands of the governor, a resolution of censure was urged by the custom-house officials on the score that he had sold out his radical principles to the Democrats; but after a heated discussion, in which Warmoth defended his action, the matter was dropped and his conduct virtually indorsed.[4] The convention denounced special legislation and pledged its best endeavors to check it.

The State Central Committee consisted regularly of fifteen members, ten appointed by the convention, five by the chair. As organized, the five appointees of the chair

[1] Warmoth himself thought that "if it had not been for that amendment there would have been no division." House Misc. Doc., 42 Cong., 2 Sess., No. 211, 380. Dibble, however, thought that opposition began when he refused to sign the civil rights bill of 1868. *Ibid.*, 298.

[2] *Ibid.*, 298. He alleged that the custom-house party printed 500,000 tickets in opposition to the amendment and distributed them through the State. It is also significant that almost all the Republican votes against the amendment were cast in the third ward where Dunn and Lowell lived. *Ibid.*, 382.

[3] *Ibid.*, 128.

[4] House Repts., 42 Cong., 2 Sess., No. 92, 9, and House Misc. Doc., 42 Cong., 2 Sess., No. 211, 299.

were opposed to the re-eligibility amendment and won over a majority of the whole committee. Hence, the governor refused to contribute to the regular campaign funds or to encourage his friends to do so, but levied forced contributions upon all his appointees on pain of dismissal,[1] organized an auxiliary committee, and began a canvass of his own, in many instances in favor of candidates not regularly nominated by the party.[2] He had tickets printed in favor of the amendment,[3] and, as we have seen, scored a victory at the polls. To Dunn's complaint that the Warmoth faction had violated custom in organizing an auxiliary committee, he retorted that the regular committee was trying to prevent a fair expression of opinion on the amendment.

Before the legislature met on January 2, 1871, the friends of the governor entered, with his knowledge, into a coalition[4] with the Democrats of the Senate, whereby they robbed the lieutenant-governor of his patronage by taking the appointment of committees into their own hands,[5] and made Democrats chairmen and majority members of several of the committees,[6] thus insuring their seats[7]

[1] It would seem that both sides used their patronage. Warmoth accused the custom-house of using its appointment of 400–500 Federal employees for the purpose of influencing the legislature in the fight. House Misc. Doc., 42 Cong., 2 Sess., No. 211, 356.

[2] *Ibid.*, 155.

[3] House Repts., 42 Cong., 2 Sess., No. 92, 3.

[4] House Misc. Doc., 42, Cong., 2 Sess., No. 211, 384.

[5] The vote is indicative of the relative strength, 24 to 11. Sen. Jour., 1871, 11.

[6] Another bit of testimony would indicate that the bestowal on the Democrats of the patronage in their respective localities was a part of this bargain. House Misc. Doc., 42 Cong., 2 Sess., No. 211, 126.

[7] The finessing for coalition appears strongly here. A proposition had been made in writing by Dunn and Packard to the Democrats, whereby the former agreed to prevent any further legislation for mixed schools or social equality and to aid in the repeal of the obnoxious legislation, if the Democrats would help to defeat Warmoth. The offer was rejected by the Democrats. *Ibid.*, 306–7.

to certain members who had been fraudulently elected.

By the same coalition Carr was re-elected speaker on the first day, receiving every Democratic vote.[1] The committees of both houses were thus so constituted that anti-Warmoth men were powerless to rid the legislature of ineligible members. Dissatisfaction with Carr's rulings, however, was so loudly expressed that about the middle of the session he was compelled by a union of Democrats with the custom-house faction to resign, and Colonel Carter of Cameron, old and rather deaf,[2] was elected in his place.[3] Opportunity was now afforded for a reconstruction of the Committee on Elections, which, although unable to complete its investigation before the recess, by an adverse report on four members at the next session, ultimately helped to complicate an already intricate situation.

The choice of a United States Senator on January 10 to succeed J. S. Harris served still further to antagonize the custom-house faction against Warmoth. James F. Casey, collector of the port, who had, up to this time, acted in harmony with the administration party, desired this honor for himself,[4] but the governor threw his influence in favor of General J. R. West, who, supported by the Democrats under fear of the election of the negro Pinchback,[5] was elected on the first ballot in both houses.[6]

[1] La. House Jour., 1871, 1.
[2] *Ibid.*, 79. House Debates, 1871, 115. Jan. 31.
[3] On one occasion he apologized for so frequently vacating the chair, on the ground that he was sick and feeble, and broke down, "standing up and talking loud enough to keep the members in order." House Deb., 1871, 200.
[4] Packard denied that Casey wanted the office, but the burden of proof is against him. He had acted with Warmoth prior to this time and a custom-house brother approached Warmoth on the question. Warmoth's refusal to support him could hardly do otherwise than alienate him. House Misc. Docs., 42 Cong., 2 Sess., No. 211, 328–9.
[5] *Ibid.*, 327.
[6] La. Sen. Jour., 1871, 20. House Jour., 21. It is interesting to note

Casey was soon found among the governor's most violent enemies.

In view of the peaceful election of the preceding autumn and the general quiet of the State, the hopeful words of the governor's message do not sound as absurd as events destined to occur within little more than a year were to prove them:

I cannot pass from this subject to other details, in justice, without calling your attention to the general and peaceable acquiescence of our people in the results of the reconstruction policy of the general government. Their acceptance of it as a finality has been much more satisfactory in Louisiana than in any other state in the South.[1]

While urging the encouragement of public improvements, he warned the Assembly against certain schemes of plunder "which are already organizing and will continue to be organized and presented to you for votes," and insisted that the commonwealth's state of bonded indebtedness must preclude any further appropriations as subsidy. Adequate penalty for bribery,[2] which had, he acknowledged, become a "crying evil," amendments to the public land laws, the police jury system, the restoration of the old capitol at Baton Rouge, and a larger measure of home rule for New Orleans are subjects which appear in his message for the first time.[3] Although defending the legislation of the previous session, he recommended with studied vagueness of expression the modification of the election and registration laws:

Pinchback's appearance as a candidate thus early. He was a strong second though not in the race as yet. The vote stood 68 to 24, House Deb., 1871, 9.

[1] Sen. Jour., 1871, 23.
[2] There was no law against bribery in Louisiana.
[3] La. Sen. Jour., 1871, 27–9.

The violent rancor of that period (1868) having now given place to a more liberal and just acknowledgment of the true relations of all our citizens, I commend to your consideration the modification of the registration and election laws to an extent, that, while securing the inalienable rights of all, will make the usage under them less irksome and exacting to the few.[1]

Together with his message he returned without his approval ten bills to the Senate,[2] and three to the House. The veto power was very freely used by Governor Warmoth. Up to January 1, 1871, he had vetoed thirty-nine bills[3] and suffered others to become law without his approval by lapse of the constitutional time limit, because they were passed by such a majority as to have made "his veto a useless bit of friction."[4] His courage in boldly vetoing some measures very close to the hearts of his legislators should not pass unnoted, nor the strength of his influence, for only five, up to this time, were able to muster the requisite two-thirds majority in the face of his opposition.

The legislature took to heart the governor's statement that the questions most urgent were such measures as would most speedily "bring railroads, open natural water-courses, and facilitate ocean commerce," without heeding his warning of the need for rigid economy. The orgy of voting away paper money to aid paper railroads and

[1] La. Sen. Jour., 1871, 29.
[2] He later withdrew one of these vetoes. *Ibid.*, 63. Only one of these ten bills passed over his veto. He should have credit for preventing the squandering of a million and a half dollars by his veto of the Nicholson pavement bill in 1870.
[3] This statement is based upon the table submitted by the governor himself in 1872 to a Congressional committee. House Misc. Doc., 42 Cong., 2 Sess., No. 211, 286-94.
[4] By 1872 he had vetoed 70 bills and refused to sign 40. *Ibid.*, 285.

canals went on with even greater frenzy than before. It was unfortunate that the governor did not carry the courage of his convictions further and instead of vetoing but six bills, do his part to quash the thirteen laws[1] which appropriated over $800,000 in actual subsidies; which granted away valuable timber along with the right of way to a new railroad; and which granted exemption from taxation to another canal company. The loose extension of $40,000, which had been appropriated the preceding session for the removal of obstructions in Bayou Bartholomew, to "what more might be necessary"[2] is indicative of the business care applied to the State pocket-book. The governor's signature to the bill for the purchase of a site and erection of a State capitol[3] may be regarded as raising the State indebtedness by one and one-half million dollars. He suffered an act guaranteeing the second mortgage bonds of another railroad to become law without his signature,[4] but the measure which guaranteed the principal and interest of a warehouse company to the amount of over a million dollars was obliged to pass over his veto.[5] The total amount added to the State debt by this Assembly amounted to about four million dollars. Nineteen different appropriation bills were passed, aside from those granting subsidies.

But it was apparent by this time that much of this effort to stimulate development by State aid was barren of result. Some roads which had received State aid had nothing to show for it, and committees of investigation "to ascertain whether the said company has complied with the conditions of the act" incorporating it were

[1] See the laws of La. for 1871, Nos. 35, 40, 46, 53, 59, 70, etc.
[2] *Ibid.*, No. 45.
[3] *Ibid.*, No. 31.
[4] *Ibid.*, No. 28.   The Southeastern Railroad Company.
[5] *Ibid.*, No. 41.   The Louisiana Warehouse Company.

beginning to appear.[1] So strong was the feeling that the
governor recommended to the next legislature that unless
work be begun actively within six months, certain railroads should lose their charters.[2]

The vexatious levee problem seemed to have found a
solution.   When the serious crevasses which threatened
New Orleans with inundation appeared in the spring,
the governor assumed control and closed the breaks with
the aid of State engineers.   The Louisiana Levee Company
was then formed and its interests made identical with
those of the State.   The company contracted to construct, maintain, and control levees on both banks of the
Mississippi and its tributaries according to the requirements of a competent commission of three able engineers;
to construct at least three million cubic yards each year
until the levee was completed to the required standard.
To get the company started the State subscribed a considerable sum and levied a special tax of two-tenths per
cént for twenty-one years for a repair fund, and, in the
absence of any tax for the current year, issued bonds to
the amount of one million dollars.[3]

Although a number of additional schools had been put
in operation,[4] the superimposed Northern school law still
proved unsatisfactory for Louisiana and came up for
further amendment.   Forty thousand dollars was fleeced

[1] Sen. Jour., 1871, 67, House Jour., 35.   In all, the New Orleans, Mobile,
and Chattanooga Railroad Company received from the State $4,250,000 or
over $58,000 a mile besides a grant of the use of a part of the New Orleans
levee, valued at $1,000,000, for it completed only seventy miles.   It remains
to be added that two different companies of Northern capitalists offered to
build the Houston and New Orleans road without subsidy or aid, but the
legislature would not grant a charter.   Nordhoff, 58.

[2] *Annual Cyclopedia*, 1871, 474.

[3] La. House Jour., 125, Sen. Jour., 121.   For the full act see Session Laws,
1871, No. 4.

[4] In 1871 the total number of schools was 640, the number of teachers
1240, and the attendance 90,000.   *Annual Cyclopedia*, 1871, 474.

from the people annually for salaries of school administrators and incidental expenses, outside of the teachers' salaries and other expenses.   School directors were often unable to write their names.   A letter from the president of the school board of Carroll Parish, as printed in the *National Republican*, is so ungrammatical and misspelled that it is almost impossible to read it.[1]   Cain Sartain, who later figured as a Representative, now a school teacher, was appallingly ignorant.[2]   Naturally demands for the abolition of this costly and inefficient establishment were incessant.   The supplement passed this session tended to simplify the law, but the chief change was provision for the appointment by a State board of subordinate boards of school directors for the several parishes, towns, and cities, who should have charge of all the funds and

[1] Feb. 1, 1872.
" January the 9th 1872.
Cor J P York I visited new Welashe Peish in the critmas finnen the White People rebelling Jest as much as the dead When You Was on the ball field Dod Swan leven in bellvue says by god he Wald like See the Dam Yankes start a public School in bellvu are minden ore any Whare beteew monre and Scheveport he Shat down a Young man I sew Well my names Simon ford on Widarvne lone Plac all so Jhon head and Jhon alfard liven in bellvue cauth a young man name Anderson Smith Who Went to see a Young collard lady step him Struck Him 3000 licks With a new caw hide do for God Sake Send them Peple Petectheon.   I promised them that I Wold Send You "

[2] *National Republican*, Feb. 6, 1872.
"Mr. Spaker.   I ask the unimus consent of the house to rise to a question of privilege.   I find in one of the issures of the Times last week a burlest on one of my carstituent which was takened from a private letter adressed to my collegue who ocuppies a seat on this floor as a representative who sent the private letter up to the Chief Clerks desk to be read as a memoral.   I think that the gentlemen my collegue who occupies a seat on this floor he acted very injustice with one of his constituents which he stands here to represent, end not only don injustice to his constituents he have I consider Mr. Speaker have shone a disrespecte this heaverbal body by sending a privat letter up to the Clerk desk to be read as a memoral in order to flatter one of his constituent he have not had a chance of an education, as he have had &&& "

6

school records, all to be under the direction of the division superintendent. An additional tax of one to two mills was to be levied on the taxable property of the parish. Special individual provision was made for the board in New Orleans and for the levying of a special tax to the amount requested by the board. But a section of the revenue law which prohibited the city from collecting taxes in excess of two per cent[1] would have closed the schools, as the limit had already been exceeded, except for the aid rendered by the State superintendent and the city government.[2] Still the system awakened great dissatisfaction, even the colored people grumbling. The governor, by the appointment of Conway, a Republican and intimate friend, to the headship of the school-system, erected it into a political machine.[3]

Agreeably to the governor's recommendation, bills to modify both the election and registration[4] laws were introduced into the Senate about the middle of the session, but were not pressed through, largely, it was charged, because of the governor's secret opposition. An effort to tamper still further with the government of New Orleans,[5] and a generous appropriation for the militia[6] passed both houses but failed, apparently, to secure the governor's signature. Some attention was devoted to

[1] Laws of Louisiana, 1871, No. 42, Sec. 7.

[2] *Annual Cyclopedia*, 1871, 474.

[3] House Misc. Doc., 42 Cong., 2 Sess., No. 211, 40. According to the *National Republican*, Conway was "devoted to the fortunes of his Excellency just as ardently as he is opposed to the interests of the people of the State." Jan. 3, 1872.

[4] This bill immediately upon its appearance from the committee was made the special order for a certain date, but does not reappear in the Journal after Feb. 10. Sen. Jour., 1870, 102. Election law appeared Feb. 1, Sen. Jour., 73.

[5] Passed by the Senate Feb. 16. Sen. Jour., 131; by the House, Feb. 18, House Jour., 157.

[6] Sen. Jour., 220; House Jour., 222. Passed by both houses Mar. 2.

the labor problem and to the question of creating parishes. The latter subject, probably for political reasons, had been something of a mania with the legislature, until at this session[1] the proposition was urged with much force "to stop the legislature from creating new parishes unless authorized by the voters of the parishes to be divided."[2]

The extravagance and state of utter corruption of the legislative body in 1871–2 were only the natural result of the conditions started in 1868–9.

The amount of the State debt was disputed. The governor held that it was, in round numbers, $22,000,000, while the auditor claimed it to be $41,000,000, the difference to be accounted for by a contingent debt of $18,000,-000 dependent on the construction of railroads, the second mortgage bonds of which the State had agreed to indorse.[3]   The bonded debt was $19,188,300, the annual interest on which amounted to $1,403,820, besides which there was a miscellaneous debt of $3,187,490.[4]   A comparison of the debt with the period just preceding the Warmoth administration is suggestive, as it had increased over $8,000,000 since 1868, taking the conservative estimate,[5] growing by deficiencies at the rate of over

[1] Even during this session fourteen new parishes were proposed.

[2] House Jour., 68.

[3] The governor asserted that there was not the slightest possibility that those roads would be built, and that if every one were built, the State would be amply secured from ever having to pay the indorsement, as the road would be worth four times the amount guaranteed.   Sen. Repts., 42 Cong., 2 Sess., No. 41, Pt. i, 197.

[4] *Ibid.*, 193.   The governor's figures vary slightly in different statements, 194.

[5] The following total compiled by Secretary Bragdon for the governor is suggestive:

Public debt for 1860	$10,099,074.32
1868	14,347,051.02
1870	23,427,952.29
1871	22,357,999.05
1872	23,045,790.00 *Ibid.*, 200.

$1,000,000 a year.   The expenditures in 1870 had exceeded
the income by over $1,000,000 although the deficit was
more than covered by the balance in the State treasury
at the beginning of the year.   The total amount of bonds
or aid granted by the State to various corporations, prior
to 1871 and for which bonds had not yet been issued, was
over twelve millions. The auditor estimated the probable
expenditures of 1872 at something over three millions,
but as a matter of fact they far exceeded that sum.

The total amount of taxable property in the State at the
close of 1871 was $250,594,417.50 from which $4,605,-
475.02 in taxes was collected.[1] With this should be
compared the valuation and taxes in 1870 to show the
decrease.   The valuation was the same—$251,296,017.02,
—but the taxes collected were $6,490,028.[2]   The unpaid
taxes amounted in 1871 to nearly five millions, exclusive
of the taxes due for 1870 and of the taxes in a number
of parishes where no rolls of assessment had been made.[3]
The aggregate tax in the State was fourteen and one-half
mills on the dollar.[4]   So great was the burden of this
taxation that in some parishes whole forty-acre tracts
of land, as rich as any in the Nile, were sold that year by
the tax-gatherer for one dollar, and in many instances
estates absolutely found no bidders.   Large owners were
willing to give half their acres to immigrant families on
the sole condition that they should settle on and improve
the land given them.   A company was being formed
in northern Louisiana to divide 50,000 acres of land in
tracts of fifty acres to a family.   Real estate declined

[1] Sen. Repts., 42 Cong., 2 Sess., No. 41, Pt. i., 205.
$3,658,879 is quoted by Scott from the *Financial Chronicle, see* Scott,
Repudiation of State Debts, 110.
[2] Sen. Repts., 42 Cong., 2 Sess., No. 41, Pt. i., 205.   *Cf.* Scott, *Repudiation
of State Debts*, 100.
[3] Sen. Jour., 1871, 27, House Jour., 87.
[4] Sen. Repts., 42 Cong., 2 Sess., No. 41, Pt. i., 358.

within the years 1870–1 not less than twenty-five per cent.[1] What was formerly considered very good security, mortgage paper for instance, had become of little value, because in a few years at that rate of taxation no one could pass the papers, for in case of foreclosure the property bore with it the burden of five, six, or seven per cent taxes which would leave no revenue.[2] The picture of the financial state drawn by a distinguished Democrat about this time is worthy of quotation.

If we were threatened with the continuance of the power which has administered this government, the conflagration of Chicago would not be more desolating than the effect of the continuance of this legislation would be upon the city of New Orleans; and the reason of it is this: when the city of Chicago was burned to the ground the people had at least the ground left, and northern and eastern capitalists have come there to rebuild it, while with us capital is flying from the state, commerce is decreasing, and everybody who can is trying to get away.[3]

The cost of collecting the tax was excessive. Ten per cent of the amount was allowed for assessment and collection in all but portions of New Orleans where five per cent was deducted. The mere cost to the State of gathering in the taxes in 1871 was close to $500,000 out of a total of $6,500,000.[4] This made the cost of collection over twelve per cent.[5] The poll-tax in the second district of New Orleans for 10,146 persons amounted to but $1911, and

---

[1] *National Republican*, Jan. 2, 1872.

[2] Testimony of Eustis, House Misc. Doc., 42 Cong., 2 Sess., No. 211, 534.

[3] Sen. Repts., 42 Cong., 2 Sess., No. 41, Pt. i., 205.   The *National Republican* reported September 22, "The regular broker shuns all dealings with it—city paper—and capitalists scorn it, it is hawked around by its unfortunate owners—clerks and laborers—and sold to the first man who offers to buy it."

[4] $493,324.   Sen. Repts., 42 Cong., 2 Sess., No. 41, Pt. i., 358.

[5] Note Herbert's table comparing the cost in 1871 with that under the Democrats before the war, 403.

of this sum, after the cost of assessment and collection was deducted, only $800.85 was left to the treasury.[1]

The legislative session of 1871 cost $958,956.50, although the Assembly appropriated only $641,400, the average cost of each Senator amounting to about $5300, of each Representative, $7300, making the average cost of a member $113.50 per day.[2] With this statement should be compared the cost before the war, when the largest amount ever appropriated for an ordinary session was $100,000.[3] The explanation of the enormous difference is to be found in the governor's comment[4]:

It was squandered in paying extra mileage and per diem of members for services never rendered[5]; for an enormous corps of useless clerks and pages,[6] for publishing the journals of each house in fifteen obscure parish newspapers, some of which never existed, while some never did the work[7]; in paying extra committees authorized to sit during the vacation and to travel throughout the State and into Texas[8]; and in an elegant stationery bill which included ham, champagne, etc.[9]

[1] Sen. Repts., 42 Cong., 2 Sess., No. 41, 360.   Tax Collector Sheridan said that he cleared about $32,000 in 1871 and $14,000 in 1872.   Ibid., 42 Cong., 3 Sess., No. 457, 707.   Warmoth defended those figures as the usual receipts for the office.   Ibid., 713–14.

[2] House Misc. Doc., 42 Cong., 2 Sess., No. 211, 396.

[3] Sen. Repts., 42 Cong., 2 Sess., No. 41, Pt. i., 359.

[4] Governor's Message, 1872. Annual Cyclop., 1871, 471.

[5] Some committees were authorized to continue during the recess, some thirty, some sixty days, some longer.

[6] The Enrollment Committee had over eighty clerks at $8 a day, when not more than ten could be required, according to the governor's statement.

[7] The printing bill for the House journals was $68,000, exclusive of New Orleans.   House Misc. Doc., 42 Cong., 2 Sess., No. 211, 38.

[8] $20,000 was spent in extra mileage above the amount allowed by law, $40,000 for mileage and per diem of special traveling committees of the House alone.   Carter stated that there were thirty-one standing committees and twenty special committees with a full complement of clerks.   House Misc. Doc., 42 Cong., 2 Sess., No. 211, 39.

[9] National Republican, Jan. 2, 1872.

The official reporter in the Senate drew the munificent salary of twenty dollars per day,[1] while each representative of a newspaper received a generous gratuity.

The enormous printing bills were, of course, a result of corruption. The public printing had cost the State in three years $1,500,000,[2] a goodly share of which Warmoth was accused of obtaining because of his fourth interest in the State paper.[3]   Under the law the three commissioners named a State printer for the journals, laws, and debates, but they were also authorized to have the printing done by certain country papers. In addition the House and Senate claimed the right to select other country papers to publish these documents officially, to be paid from the contingent funds, so that thirty-five or forty more were so selected. The sum of $180,000 was paid to papers in New Orleans in 1871, outside of the official organ.[4]   Many of the papers were sustained only by these contracts.[5]   It was generally believed that men were sent over the country to edit these papers in order to build up the interests of the governor, while Carter, on the other hand, openly admitted that he gave his patronage to papers which would support the reform movement.[6]

[1] Sen. Jour., 1871, 74.

[2] House Repts., 42 Cong., 2 Sess., No. 92, 21.   The largest sum ever spent before the war, when they were printed in both English and French, was $60,000.

[3] This paper was said to pay a dividend of 110 per cent.   But the governor denied receiving any dividend.   House Misc., Doc., 42 Cong., 2 Sess., No. 211, 368.

[4] Ibid., 38.   Sometimes papers were opposed merely because others were entitled to the same privileges.   House Deb., 4.

[5] Ibid., 42 Cong., 2 Sess., No. 211, 39.   See House Jour., 55 and 129 for a list.

[6] Ibid.   He asserted in the Press Convention that his patronage should not be used against him, and in several cases where papers asserted this independence, the contracts were revoked.   House Misc. Doc., 42 Cong., 2 Sess., No. 211, 298.

The entire lack of conscience of the men who were administering the government came to light during the close of this year and early in 1872 with appalling vividness, until one turns away simply sickened by the tale of corruption.[1] Neither party nor class lines regulated integrity,[2] for reputable men of both sides were among the persons who offered bribes. As Carter put it, "There seems to be something in the climate here that affects both parties."[3] Under oath one man declared that it was generally understood all round that any one who wanted to get a bill through had to pay for it. He thought there was a regular office opened down on Royal Street for that purpose where there was an agent for members. He had seen money paid right on the floor of the House. After the passage of the Chattanooga bill he saw a man with his hands full of money paying it out to members with little attempt at concealment.[4] Senators under false names were incorporators of many of the companies chartered

---

[1] Phelps says: "The corruption was so general and so notorious that no one connected, directly or indirectly, has escaped from the mess without taint in the eyes of the people." *Louisiana*, 369.

[2] Moncure declared that he did not know a public official who was not worthy of impeachment. *Ibid.*, 53–4.

[3] House Misc., 42 Cong., 2 Sess., No. 211, 38.

[4] *Ibid.*, 238. Another man brought conclusive evidence and stated that he had witnessed money paid to Carr, Dewees, and Pinchback. *Ibid.*, 474. Nordhoff had the original of the following interesting document: "Gentlemen of the Finance Committee of La. Levee Co.: Please pay to Hon. A. W. Faulkner the amount you may deem proper to pay on account of Levee Bill, I being absent at the time under orders of the House. But I would have voted for the bill had I been there. Mr. Faulkner is authorized to sign a receipt for me—Stamps." Nordhoff, 59. The value of quotations from Nordhoff may be proved by stating that he declared himself a Republican, never having "voted any other Federal ticket than the Republican; I have been opposed to slavery as long as I have had an opinion on any subject except sugar, candy and tops; and I am a thorough believer in the capacity of the people to rule themselves, even if they are very ignorant, better than anybody else can rule them." 10.

and got their shares of stock after the bills were passed. [1] So wide-spread was the knowledge of their dishonesty that the story was current that the members had not even time to write their promises to vote the passage of such and such a bill, but had to resort to printed blanks. [2]

One of the dishonest measures, not mentioned elsewhere, should not be passed without brief mention, at least. In 1870[3] the legislature authorized the improvement of the old city park, a piece of ground which had been held for the purpose for many years. During the following year two politicians, Southworth and Bloomer, got a written agreement from the owners of a large vacant piece of land—the only large tract near the city—to sell it to them at a fixed price, six hundred thousand dollars. The legislature of 1871 amended the park law so as to allow the commissioners to buy land for the new park and made an appropriation for it. The governor now appointed as park commissioners, Pinchback, West, and Southworth. They next acquired title to the property, but paid only sixty-five thousand dollars, the remainder being left on mortgage. August 15 they sold one-half their purchase to the city for eighty thousand dollars, receiving sixty-five thousand dollars in cash, and one hundred ninety-five thousand in bonds. It was common street talk that Antoine complained that Pinchback had cheated him out of forty thousand dollars, which he in some way expected out of the deal. [4]

[1] Most telling is the reluctant reply of the governor to the question, "Are you able to say from your knowledge, personally or officially, that all or nearly all of these bills incorporating monopolies or granting individuals private valuable franchises are passed through the legislature by corrupt means?" "I wouldn't like to say that." House Misc. Doc., 42 Cong., 2 Sess., No. 211, 400.

[2] *Ibid.*, 534.

[3] The *Picayune* had combated this measure in 1869 as an act of folly then. Sep. 24, 1869.   [4] Nordhoff, 62.

The evidence fails of proof that the governor ever received a bribe for his action on any bill, [1] but it is difficult to escape the suspicion of his complicity in corrupt transactions, if it be true, as was alleged, that no bill which the governor favored could fail and none that he opposed could pass.   He admitted his use of his patronage to remove personal enemies and appoint friends "as a custom of governors" [2] and that the government had been guilty of some abuses created by his connivance, but emphatically denied the perpetration of any frauds, [3] declaring on oath that he stood before the Congressional committee with "clean hands." [4]   But his duplicity in other ways seems clear, while the fact stands out that with a salary of eight thousand dollars a year he testified that he had made far more than one hundred thousand dollars the first

[1] The most damaging charge against him was that of a bribe of $50,000 offered him to sign the Nicholson paving bill. Walsh published a card, saying that the governor had refused it because it was too little.   The latter, naturally, denied this and tried to disprove it by the unsupported statement of another man, whereupon Walsh sent the governor a challenge. And so the matter stood—the unproved assertion of one man against the other.   House Misc. Doc., 42 Cong., 2 Sess., No. 211, 376.

But Scott on the other hand swore that it cost more to get the governor's signature than to get it through the legislature.   It is to be regretted that the defense which Mr. Warmoth still expects to write, based, the writer understands, upon the fact that he prevented still more outrageous wrongs from being perpetrated, has not yet appeared, as it may throw additional light upon this question.   The writer has applied to him repeatedly in vain for a statement of his position now after the lapse of forty years.

[2] House Misc. Doc., 42 Cong., 2 Sess., No. 211, 380. He said that he had learned from the Democrats that "to the victors belong the spoils." 369.

[3] Ibid., 358.

[4] Ibid., 351.   He declared in a series of replies to direct questions that he had never tampered with the election of members, never counseled nor advised such tampering, never held any stock that he had not paid for, nor had stock presented to him, nor been promised stock on condition of approving a bill incorporating monopolies, and never been influenced in any way in his official acts by any reward or the hope or promise of it.   But he admitted having signed bills after expiration of the constitutional time limit in order to "quiet the people."   Ibid., 351, 371-2.

year of his administration[1] and by 1872 was reported worth a million dollars. He was surely willfully deluding himself when he uttered this boast:

I believe I have since I have been governor of the State, under circumstances and embarrassments of the gravest character, and under difficulties that I am surprised myself that I have been able to overcome, administered the State government in the best interests of the people of the State, and have produced as much harmony, good feeling, and prosperity as it was possible for me or any one else to produce under the circumstances.[2]

In a series of remarkable pen pictures the governor brought charges of dishonesty against most of the custom-house reformers—against Senators Ray, Casey, Packard, Lowell,[3] Carter.[4] His attack on Carter may be considered typical :

Mr. Carter was also, and is now, the paid attorney of the New Orleans, Mobile, and Texas Railroad Company, from which he receives $833.33 per month, or $10,000 per annum, and for which he has never done one hour's service. The contract for his employment was made with him by the company after he had kept in his pocket for thirty or sixty days a bill which had passed the legislature almost unanimously, and immediately after this contract was made, by which he became the attorney of the company, the bill was signed by him.[5]

---

[1] House Repts., 42 Cong., 2 Sess., No. 92, 25.
[2] House Misc. Doc., 42 Cong., 2 Sess., No. 211, 374.
[3] Lowell was a defaulter for a large amount.
[4] House Misc. Doc., 42 Cong., 2 Sess., No. 211, 395–6.
[5] Ibid., 396. Carter was an apostatizing preacher and ex-Confederate colonel, who had turned loyal patriot and anti-Warmoth leader.—Cox, *Three Decades*, p. 561. With this statement might be compared Carter's opinion of Warmoth as voiced in a speech in February, 1872: "Louisiana is afflicted with worse laws and worse administrators thereof than can be found in ten states of the Union. Henry Clay Warmoth is the Boss Tweed in Louisi-

Several of the men attempted no reply to these charges, and Carter's explanation served only to convince the Congressional committee that the charge was substantially true.[1]   Casey was clearly proved to have been the holder of a corruption fund of $18,000, part of a $50,000 fund raised by himself and others to bribe the legislature to pass a bill for a company in which he was an interested incorporator.   When the governor vetoed the bill, Casey unlocked the safe and Herring returned $18,000.   It required just eighteen senators to pass the bill.[2]   The president of the Louisiana Lottery Company had a list of about fifty members of the House with whom he had made arrangements for the passage of the Jackson Railroad bill with the amount that had been paid and the sum still due.   The amount with a few exceptions was $600, but Campbell and Pinchback were rated worth $2000.[3] Many members held two offices, quite content to interpret the constitution in the Louisiana way that a member of the Assembly was not a State officer.[4]

---

ana, except that that amiable villain, with all his infamies, is a gentlemen and a saint compared with the unscrupulous despot who fills the executive chair of this state."—Cox, *Three Decades of Federal Legislation*, 560.

[1] House Rpts., 42 Cong., 2 Sess., No. 92, 23.   Of course the men attacked made counter charges against the governor.

[2] *Ibid.*

[3] House Misc. Doc., 42 Cong., 2 Sess., No. 211, 475; and House Repts., 42 Cong., 2 Sess., No. 92, 26.

[4] E. W. Dewees, another leader of the House, contended with Carr and Carter for eminence.   The investigating committee of Congress reported that he had been under arrest with seven sworn charges of burglary against him, and had then obtained of the chief of police a certificate that his picture was not in the rogues' gallery.—*Ibid.*, 27.

The conclusion to which the Congressional committee came is worth noting when we recall that they were Republicans: "The world has rarely known a legislative body so rank with ignorance and corruption."—*Ibid.*, 24. In May, 1875, five members of this legislature were indicted for bribery. —*Times*.

In this evolting catalog it is refreshing to find one person free from the

The governor made a genuine effort to combat the extravagance of the legislature. In April, 1871, soon after the adjournment of the Assembly, he applied to the courts for an injunction to restrain the auditor from paying warrants for the mileage, per diem, and contingent expenses of members of the lower house, because fraudulent vouchers had been issued whereby the amounts had been increased.   The injunction was granted and the auditor, together with several experts, appointed to investigate the matter.   The governor's real object was to assail Speaker Carter by the allegation that he had coerced the chief clerk to sign a fraudulent journal of the House, which authorized five committees to sit during the recess, thus defrauding the State of $200,000.   Warmoth declared that a number of resolutions, which the speaker stated as introduced and passed the last night, had been interpolated into the journal, for it was notorious that they had not been introduced up to half-past eight o'clock that evening, and that from that moment until the adjournment the House had been in a constant state of uproar, during which time it was impossible for the House to take any action.   He advanced what seems considerable evidence of his charge, while the delay of the publication of this day's journal for sixteen days after the adjournment,[1] looks, it will be confessed, suspicious.[2]

---

taint of dishonesty.   The lieutenant-governor was regarded by the Democrats as incorruptible.   "In the view of the Caucasian chiefs, the taint of honesty and of a scrupulous regard for the official proprieties, is a serious drawback and enervating reproach upon the Lieutenant Governor."—*Times*, August 4, 1871.

[1] House Misc. Doc., 42 Cong., 2 Sess., No. 211, 396.   The fraud took the form of substituting one bill for a similar one which had been tabled but purported in the journal to have been taken up that night.   It was supposed that the delay was due to the loss of the original bill alleged to have been passed.

[2] It is only fair to add, as Carr pointed out, that the testimony of the commission did not bear out these charges.—*Ibid.*, 230.

The report of the commission sustained the charges of the governor but in part. It was shown that the amount of the warrants had in some instances been fraudently increased; that warrants to the amount of $240,000 had been issued in excess of the appropriation of 1871[1]; that many warrants for extra pay to officers and clerks had been issued on the resolution of but one house, contrary to law; that $40,000 had been fraudulently issued to committees for mileage on official duty, when, according to the journals, they had not left the city; and that the signatures of the State officers had been forged in various instances. The commission condemned the loose manner of conducting business in the warrant office, but brought no specific charges. The opposition press charged the governor with holding up this report for months and publishing it at the opportune moment for him—just before the assembling of the legislature in 1872.[2]

An important decision in regard to the limitation of the State debt was rendered in May by the State Supreme Court. The matter came up on appeal from the Eighth District Court of New Orleans, where a suit had been instituted to compel the auditor to issue a warrant on an appropriation of $50,000 made in favor of a Mr. Nixon. The auditor had refused because the law authorizing it violated the recent amendment, as it increased the debt above the constitutional limit. The Supreme Court

---

[1] *Annual Cyclopedia*, 1871, 471. The over issue of the vouchers forced the value of the warrants down to 2½ cents on the dollar.—Herbert, *Why the Solid South*, 403.

[2] *National Republican*, Jan. 2, 1872.

Strangely enough the report appeared in the *Picayune*, Dec. 29, 1871.

That paper printed one of its rare expressions of approval of the governor: "The efforts of the governor to defeat so glaring an infringement of the law will meet with general approval. The court has issued the injunction asked for by the Executive, and in consequence over three thousand dollars will be saved to the State."

affirmed the decision of the lower court in favor of the auditor, contending that "the evidence in the record leaves no doubt that the debt of the State exceeded twenty-five million dollars on or before the first of March, 1871." [1]

[1] 23 La. Ann. 402–8, State of Louisiana *ex rel.* Salomon and Simpson *vs.* James Graham.

CHAPTER V

Open Rupture

OPEN, violent rupture between the two wings of the Republican party appeared in the State convention of August 9, 1871.[1] Although this convention was called merely for the purpose of electing a central committee for the next year, according to the requirements of the preceding convention, it created the greatest excitement in the party, and each wing made extraordinary efforts to secure a majority of the delegates. It was alleged that the governor sent letters to the tax collectors in the parishes to have themselves elected delegates[2] in order to insure his control. The contest for the election became so heated that it resulted in many instances in the division of the ward and parish clubs. In the Sixth Ward, for instance, a motion was made to elect the commissioner of election as a delegate; when the chairman refused to put the motion, as out of order, he was impeached and put out of office. At once a new Republican

[1] A press convention in session about the middle of July had helped to give tangible shape to the split. About thirty Republican papers and a few Democratic papers owned by Republicans were represented and the Dunn–Carter clique scored a victory in the shape of some reform resolutions.— *New Orleans Commercial Bulletin*, July 13, 1871. The *Picayune* inclined to the view that the governor's foes had concocted the affair "to injure his chances for reëlection; and to damage him generally in the estimation of Republicans throughout the State." It hinted at "ominous clicks and vivid gleams" even in this quiet convention, July 14, 1871.

[2] House Misc. Doc., 42 Cong., 2 Sess., No. 211, 127.

ward club came into existence. This was also the history of the Ninth Ward Club and many others in parish as well as city.[1] Each faction called the other bolters. It was charged against the Packard wing that they had circulated incendiary documents throughout the State, "calculated to array the colored men of our party against leading republicans of the other race."[2] Both sides used their patronage: the custom-house had about five hundred appointments which they used to influence the election; city patronage was unscrupulously used in the interest of the governor and brought to bear on the election by tendering bribes in the form of positions[3]; and gangs of turbulent roughs[4] were hired to force their way into the club meetings to control the elections.[5] Police captains, sergeants, and privates, not only knew of the existence of the outrages, but in uniform and citizens' clothes actively participated.[6] The captains were ordered to take

[1] House Misc. Doc., 42 Cong., 2 Sess., No. 211, 300.

[2] *Ibid.*, 269–70.

This receives greater color of truth from a statement in a Democratic paper that low whites were organizing the negroes of the city into a secret society, with secret signs, grips, and passwords, meeting in secret conclave in various portions of the city.—*Picayune*, July 18, 1871.

[3] City administrators with but one exception were appointees of the governor at this time.—House Misc. Doc., 42 Cong., 2 Sess., No. 211, 169.

[4] Red Bill McMickle and Lucien Adams, of notorious fame in the riot of 1866, figured prominently in this work.

[5] One captain testified that he knew some of the men to be desperate characters who had served terms in the penitentiary.—House Misc., Doc., 42 Cong., 2 Sess., No. 211, 176. He knew this packing to occur ten times. Thirteen of the fifteen ward clubs of the city complained that "gangs of city employees and other evil-minded persons have been and are being moved from ward to ward to disturb the republican wards, in denial of the rights of their members peaceably to assemble and freely to discuss the issues involved, and freely to exercise their right, on the seventh of August, to elect delegates. Threats of death and personal violence have been freely made by said unlawful combinations and in many instances actual violence has been resorted to."

[6] See also the *Picayune* for July 12, 1871.

7

their men from their beats, without regard to the protection of the city, to coerce and intimidate clubs. This manœuver became so notorious that it was the subject of constant newspaper complaint and yet the authorities paid no attention.[1]

The testimony of a captain of police is illuminating:

I was ordered by Police Commissioner William Robinson to control the part of the eighth precinct, known as Algiers, for Warmoth, or I would lose my place. This order was repeated to me by him many times. I received, on several occasions, similar instructions from Captain Badger, superintendent of police; also to send him the names of all men in my command that I believed to be "Dunn" men and they would be forced to resign, or be dismissed. Captain Badger and Commissioner William Robinson told me that the Warmoth delegates from Algiers must be elected, no matter how.[2]

In some instances the club room would be filled by a street-gang and police in citizen clothes,[3] and members of the sub-clubs kept off from the polls by threats and brandishing of clubs, or by premeditated disturbance prevented from the transaction of business, until they were forced to retire without having had a voice in the choice of delegates.[4]

The whole radical party [declared the *Times*], including every office-holder of the Federal, State, and city government, is absorbed in this combat; public business and interest are utterly ignored, and the public money ruthlessly squandered to promote the fortunes of the one or the other faction. Every

[1] House Misc. Doc., 42 Cong., 2 Sess., No. 211, 128.
[2] *Ibid.*, 176.
[3] As many as ninety police were reported present at one time in different ward meetings.
[4] House Misc. Doc., 42 Cong., 2 Sess., No. 211, 179. Many affidavits to this effect are to be found, 176–79.

species of fraud, deceit, violence, and trickery is employed to the same end.[1]

So fierce was the contest that the credentials of not more than forty of the one hundred and eighteen delegates of which the convention should consist were undisputed. From a large majority of the districts came double delegations,[2] or contestants, claiming that the regular delegates were appointed through violence or fraud. It was felt that whichever faction secured the temporary organization would also secure final control of the convention. Packard, the chairman, and a majority of the Central Committee were opposed to the governor on the ground that he had taken the management of the campaign of the preceding year out of their hands. It was also supposed that the convention might be much influenced by the place in which it was held. The place of meeting had been designated in the call by the State Committee, but was dropped in the process of printing. This point, which was dwelt upon by the Warmoth faction, Packard dismissed as unimportant, because the committee, in any case, had the power to change the place of meeting. Warmoth wanted it to be held at the state-house, as his office was located there and he could order the presence of the police. In order to force the use of that building, he hired all the available halls in the city with the intention, he declared before an investigating committee,[3] of placing them at the disposal of the committee, which

[1] Aug. 4.

[2] There were double delegates from thirty-one districts. House Misc. Doc., 42 Cong., 2 Sess., No. 211, 156, and House Repts., 42 Cong., 2 Sess., No. 92, 4.

[3] A list of four so "cornered" is given in the testimony (laid before an investigation). It was stated that the governor later had to pay $100 for violating an agreement not to use Turner Hall for political purposes. House Misc. Doc., 42 Cong., 2 Sess., No. 211, 126.

could not reject all on the plea of securing something more
suitable. [1]

The Warmoth factionists made preparations for their
conduct if their chances for success should seem to be in
jeopardy: it was agreed in a caucus the day before the
convention, that, if the convention should assemble in any
place where they did not have a fair show, Judge Dibble
should rise, read a protest, [2] and then call the convention
to order in the name of this large majority—the sixty-five
members who signed the protest. The protest charged
Packard with intending to pack the convention but disclaimed any intention on their part of using force. [3]

A short time before the opening of the convention it
became clear that the Warmoth faction had a decided
majority. And so on the afternoon of August 8, [4] the
committee announced that the convention would be held
in the United States Circuit Court room in the custom-
house, where Packard as marshal could control affairs.
The committee also announced that the credentials of all
delegates must be submitted to them and that only those
who passed their investigation would receive tickets of
admission. The "milk tickets," as Warmoth scornfully
called them, would be delivered from the private window
of the postmaster, as that official, Mr. Lowell, was a
member of the custom-house wing. At midnight the
committee reported a list of one hundred and eighty-nine [5]

[1] On Warmoth's testimony, probably an excuse. Packard admitted that
Mechanics Institute was offered him. House Misc. Doc., 42 Cong., 2 Sess.,
No. 211, 330 and 127.

[2] For the protest see *Ibid.*, 269–70.

[3] *Ibid.*, 387. Judge Dibble also testified to the above arrangement. *Ibid.*

[4] The custom-house faction said that it was only at that late date that
they were satisfied of the determination of Warmoth to rule the convention
or break it up. *Ibid.*, 132.

[5] Numbers differ. But the congressional investigation gives 189 and so
that has been adopted as more reliable than the 175 of the *Annual Cyclopædia.*

—virtually all who filed credentials, though the call stipulated the number as one hundred and eighteen—as entitled to admission.   Naturally, the Warmoth wing denounced this action loudly as without precedent or authority, though they consented to call for their tickets at the post-office.

The city was rife with reports of anticipated violence,[1] and so Packard, besides appointing about fifty deputy marshals to help keep order, demanded of General Reynolds a detachment of United States troops to protect Federal property.[2]

On the morning of the 9th, commercial business was entirely suspended.   At about nine o'clock one hundred soldiers arrived at the custom-house with two Gatling-guns,[3] stacked their muskets, and took up their position in the rotunda at the head of the stairs.   By ten o'clock a dense mass of colored and white citizens had gathered before the custom-house.   About eleven o'clock Warmoth and a large party of his supporters arrived.   They were permitted to enter the hall but were denied admittance to the court room on the score that the committee was not ready to open the door to delegates until eleven-thirty.[4]

[1] Senator Ray was reported as saying that he was apprehensive from a conversation with General West that there would be bloodshed.   The governor's caucus had created excitement, and rumors were floating about that the governor had stated in a speech that they must take the custom-house by force.   It is fairly sure that on the morning of the convention the governor did make such a statement in a speech to a group of policemen assembled for instructions.   House Misc. Doc., 42 Cong., 2 Sess., No. 211, 131.

[2] *Ibid.*, 128.   The *Picayune* condemned this presence of the military (and the conversion of a Federal building into a private hall) as likely "to produce the very acts of violence which the Central Committee feared" though it designated both as "acts of a wily political ring-master."   August 10, 1871.

[3] Whence this convention was distinguished as the Gatling-gun convention.   Sen. Repts., 42 Cong., 3 Sess., No. 457, 284.

[4] Because the governor was lame at the time, the porter would have admitted him alone, but he refused the courtesy.   House Misc. Doc., 42 Cong., 2 Sess., No. 211, 130.

There was another smaller court room beside the large one in which it was proposed to hold the convention, and the accidental opening of a door revealed to Warmoth the presence of the opposing faction already assembled there in private caucus. His mind, quick to suspect intrigue, jumped to the conclusion that the other faction would pass to the larger room through the three communicating doors and effect a preliminary organization, while his party was entering the room by a single door from the rear. He, therefore, proceeded to the rotunda occupied by the soldiers and addressed his followers[1] until stopped by a United States officer, whereupon he proposed to adjourn to Turner Hall, there to organize an independent convention.[2] The crowd left promptly, jeered at and insulted by the marshals, according to Warmoth, and even threatened by their leveled revolvers.[3]

The Turner Hall meeting, consisting of about one hundred and eight delegates,[4] only thirty-one of whom held uncontested seats, was opened, in the midst of great confusion, as an adjourned meeting by Senator Harris, who, as a member of the State Central Committee, could give the meeting color of legality. Little was accomplished at the first session beyond the usual speechmaking, except a temporary organization and the appointment of the regular committees. At the evening session resolutions were presented and referred to the proper committee and provision made for the formation of a Congressional

[1] The possibility of a bolting convention was not an inspiration of the moment, for Warmoth had expressed the opinion that two conventions would be inevitable. House Misc. Doc., 42 Cong., 2 Sess., No. 211, 388.

[2] For the text of the full address see *Ibid.*, 305.

[3] *Ibid.* See the comment of the *Nation*, August 24, 1871.

[4] Thirty-one held uncontested seats; thirty-nine held imperfect or fraudulent certificates; six had not even filed any. About sixty-six of the number held office under Warmoth. *Ibid.*, 170. *Annual Cyclopædia*, 473.

State Central Committee. The body reassembled at noon August 10, when Pinchback was made permanent president of the convention. On the last day the two committees indicated above were organized, an "Address to the People" adopted,[1] accusing the custom-house officials of illegal practices, an unlawful assembly, and attempts "to overawe and intimidate and even to assassinate the representatives whom you accredited to represent you in the convention,"[2] and resolutions adopted.[3] Governor Warmoth made a long closing address, in which he denounced the Federal officeholders,[4] and bitterly assailed Speaker Carter for his conduct in the custom-house convention, charging him with corruption, dishonesty, and licentiousness.

Lieutenant-Governor Dunn was made permanent president of the custom-house meeting, at which seventy[5] delegates were present.[6] Speeches were made by his prominent friends, laying at Warmoth's door, because of his repeated threats of violence, the responsibility for the use of the custom-house and for the employment of United States troops. Speaker Carter even went so far as to assert that the "governor received bribes, stole the public money, and was the greatest, living practical liar."[7]

An executive committee was organized and resolutions adopted, which guaranteed a place to every child in the public schools, advocated public improvements as "abso-

---

[1] See House Misc. Doc., 42 Cong., 2 Sess., No. 211, 302 ff.

[2] *Ibid.*   [3] *Ibid.*, 301–2.

[4] So high ran the feeling against the custom-house that Pinchback vowed that he would go out as the deadly opponent of Grant if the latter supported the custom-house men. Sen. Repts., 42 Cong., 3 Sess., No. 457, 285.

[5] This number is based on the personnel as given in the Congressional investigation. House Misc. Doc., 42 Cong., 2 Sess., No. 211, 418–20.

[6] *Ibid.*, 420. Thirty-six of the number were Federal officials.

[7] *Annual Cyclopædia*, 1871, 473.

lutely necessary to the development of the great material interests of the state," approved the amendment limiting the State debt, urged the State authorities to take such measures to preserve the peace of public assemblies as will avoid "any necessity for aid from the Federal government for that purpose,"[1] and indorsed the Grant administration.   One article read Warmoth out of the party in the following language:

And we, as due to our people, ourselves, and the republican party, do denounce, whether acting through his subordinates in the several parishes of the State, or as the leader of the disorganizers and bolters from the convention of today, His Excellency, H. C. Warmoth, who has forfeited our confidence, having shown clearly that he would sacrifice the republican party to advance himself, and can no longer be safely followed as a republican leader.[2]

Not content with putting out Warmoth, they must dole out the same punishment to his organ and declared it no longer entitled to "the respect and confidence of the Republican party in the State of Louisiana or elsewhere."[3] Immediately after the adjournment of this faction messages were sent to President Grant, signed by J. F. Casey and S. B. Packard, explaining the situation in Louisiana. The Warmoth side not only sent a written statement, signed by T. W. Conway, State superintendent of public education, denying wholly the charges of the other side, but a delegation of twenty men, chosen in the convention, visited Grant at Long Branch and made a verbal report. The President's non-committal reply was that the charges were very extraordinary and that he would investigate

[1] House Misc. Doc., 42 Cong., 2 Sess., No. 211, 152–3.
[2] *Ibid.*, 153, Report of the Republican Convention.
[3] House Misc. Doc., 42 Cong., 2 Sess., No. 211, 154.

them, but despite rumors to that effect,[1] no removal of Federal officers occurred.[2] However apparent the victory over Warmoth seemed, the Democratic rejoicing was, to say the least, premature.[3]

The State Committee of the Packard wing, at a meeting on November 7, adopted resolutions which, besides reiterating some of the resolutions adopted in August, urged such modification of the printing, appropriation, revenue, and other laws as would result in a large and substantial reduction of the taxes; and urged the representatives to labor for a modification of the registration and election laws, more particularly the constitution and power of the returning officers, in order to secure a free, full, and peaceable election.[4]

November 22, 1871, Lieutenant-Governor Dunn died, whereupon Governor Warmoth immediately issued a proclamation convening the Senate in extra session on December 6 to fill the vacancy by electing a president, for, under the constitution, the president of the Senate would become ex-officio lieutenant-governor. The question of a successor was a vital matter: if a Warmoth man should be chosen, not much could be gained by a temporary suspension of the governor[5]—for the question of impeach-

---

[1] House. Misc. Doc., 42 Cong., 2 Sess., No. 211, 271–2. Judge Dibble thought that the President's personal disike for Warmoth had a great deal to do with his opposition.

[2] *Nation*, Jan. 25, 1872. New York *Times*. See also *Nation*, Aug. 24, 1871.

[3] "Governor Warmoth will soon be stripped of all power and then he becomes valueless to any party. Without personal influence, character, or reputation, except for all that is bad, he would be only so much dead weight to carry without any corresponding benefit. . . . He will soon sing that doleful song 'Farewell to all my greatness.' " House Misc. Doc., 42 Cong., 2 Sess., No. 211, 200. New Orleans *Com. Bull.*, Aug. 11, 1871.

[4] *National Republican*, Jan. 2, 1872.

[5] Under the State constitution agreement by the House to articles of impeachment suspended the functions of the governor until he was acquitted. If the Assembly could not depend on a two-thirds vote of the Senate to convict, they could suspend the trial indefinitely and thus secure all the advantages of conviction.

ment was already being mooted.   But if the House could
vote impeachment before a president could be elected,
Speaker Carter, now identified with the opposition,
would become governor.[1]   And here lay the governor's
shrewdness in calling the Senate alone.[2]   To conceal his
too evident haste, the governor set forth other reasons
for convening the Senate: measures of reform, investigation of the accounts of State officers, and action on the
appointments and pardons granted by the governor during
the recess.[3]   But the opponents of the administration
declared the convocation of one branch of the Assembly to act on miscellaneous business unconstitutional,
and unsuccessful efforts to prevent the session were
made.[4]

After the resolutions of reform were adopted by the
Central Republican Committee in November, the Democratic Central Committee was called together on
November 30 for a consultation on the question of taking
advantage of the Republican split.   But it was deemed
necessary in order to maintain the integrity of their
party to shun all political alliances with either wing of
the ruling party in Louisiana.[5]   Still an agreement for

[1] Carter was quoted as boasting of being governor in thirty-six hours.
House Misc. Doc., 42 Cong., 2 Sess., No. 211, 324.
[2] The governor alleged as one of the reasons why he wished to secure a
lieutenant-governor in sympathy with himself the fact that the latter was
ex-officio on the printing committee and could help him vacate the printing
contracts which had involved the State in an annual expense of $50,000,
made by Dunn and Carter despite his opposition.
[3] See his message, Sen. Jour., 1871, Extra Session, or Annual Cyclopædia,
1871, 473.
[4] The Second Ward Club protested against it Nov. 29, as an unconstitutional squandering of the people's money and requested the Senators of the
first ward to protest.   A similar resolution was also adopted by the Sixth
Ward Club.   National Republican, Jan. 2, 1872.
[5] In an Address to the People of Louisiana issued Nov. 30, 1871.   House
Misc. Doc., 42 Cong., 2 Sess., No. 211, 358.

unity of action with the custom-house Republicans at the extra session was effected.[1]

Thirty-four Senators, the full number, except for two who had died in August and September,[2] came together for a session which lasted only two days. Senator Blackman tried to open fire by presenting a protest against the right of the governor to convene the Senate apart from the House.[3] After some discussion and balloting on various trial points to assure the governor that he could command a majority, a ballot for president revealed a tie vote for Pinchback and T. V. Coupland, deputy collector of the custom-house, who received every Democratic and custom-house vote. Senator Lewis[4] received sudden light and changed his vote at Warmoth's request so that the second ballot resulted in the election of Pinchback by a vote of eighteen to sixteen.

The governor was on the floor of the Senate during the balloting "to stiffen the members," he declared, by "his presence, cheerful conversation, pleasant manners, and so on."[5] All further action was abruptly prevented by a resolution to adjourn *sine die* immediately after the beginning of the second day in order to prevent, in the words of one of Warmoth's Senators, "any further chance of defeat on our part."[6]

Although Warmoth asserted that his persuasive words, added to those of a Dr. Southworth, who was a "very

[1] House Misc. Doc., 42 Cong., 2 Sess., No. 211, 324.

[2] The governor had not issued writs of election on the pretext that he had had no official notice of their death. Warmoth admitted that his friends in the legislature prevented official notices being brought to him. *Ibid.*, 344.

[3] House Repts., 42 Cong., 2 Sess., No. 92, 14.

[4] Carter defined him as a "peripatetic gentleman, having no very well-defined politics" and, as supposed to belong to the parish of Natchitoches. House Misc. Doc., 42 Cong., 2 Sess., No. 211, 38.

[5] *Ibid.*, 354.

[6] Senator Campbell, *Ibid.*, 112.

persuasive individual,'' were sufficient to convert Lewis,
it became revealed in a few months that a definite corrupt
bargain had been made.   Lewis agreed to ''regularly
attend the sessions of the State Senate at Mechanics
Institute, to vote to sustain Pinchback as president of
the Senate and in all political questions with the party
sustaining the State administration,''[1] in return for which
after the adjournment of the legislature he was to receive
fifteen thousand dollars in cash.   It appears that so far
as dishonesty was concerned both sides were involved,
only the governor succeeded in getting ahead of his
adversaries.   A paper came to light in Bow's handwriting
which would seem to indicate that he offered J. R. Gallup
$5000 if the latter would change his vote to Coupland for
lieutenant-governor.   ''John: The chances are that the
vote will be a tie.   I can hold $5000 ready to place in
your hands if you change your vote to our man.   Change
vote—$5000 sure.''   It may be added that this proof is pro-
duced by Warmoth.[2]   The money for Lewis, together with
about twenty thousand dollars in State bonds, was deposited in a tin box with Mr. Van Norden, president
of one of the city banks.   When Lewis applied for his
box, the demand was refused, whereupon he brought
suit, February 26, against Van Norden in the Sixth District
Court.[3]   After several refusals to surrender the box to
the sheriff, Van Norden was cited for contempt of court
and the box finally produced—empty, except for the
written agreement.   The money had been delivered to Dr.
Southworth about a month before.

Judge Cooley sentenced Van Norden to a fine of fifty
dollars and ten days in the parish prison for contempt,
but scarcely had he reached the prison before the gov-

[1] House Misc. Doc., 42 Cong., 2 Sess., No. 211, 551-2.
[2] *Ibid.*, 308.
[3] *Ibid.*, 551-2.

ernor's pardon released him. Judge Cooley had him promptly brought before the court on March 7, and in pronouncing sentence publicly rebuked the governor.[1] Again he was released by the governor, and again he was produced in court. This time the judge ordered him committed to the court-house for safe-keeping, and here the pardon of the executive failed, as the sheriff refused to honor it. Van Norden's counsel applied to the Supreme Court for a writ of habeas corpus, which was granted. On March 8, that court held unanimously that the pardon power was absolute and the prisoner must be discharged.[2]

The question of the constitutionality of the election was sufficiently doubtful to make each side anxious, the one for confirmation, the other for repudiation, when the legislature should regularly assemble. The resolution of the Republican Committee of Orleans Parish on December 19, "that the pretended action of the Senate in electing a President of the Senate to be Lieutenant Governor was illegal, and not binding on the Senate when it convenes in regular session,"[3] was prophetic of trouble in the new legislature.

[1] "Right or wrong, the decision of that court is the law, and the governor, more than anyone else, is bound to respect it, because the constitution makes him the Executive minister, and he is even bound to furnish the army and navy to carry out the judgment of the court, but in this case he has so far forgotten his duties as to make himself the principal in a deliberate attempt to violate the law.

" In this case he has so far forgotten his duty that he has openly conspired with parties to defy and violate the laws. Such conduct as that cannot be tolerated in any community." House Misc. Doc., 42 Cong., 2 Sess., No. 211, 551.

[2] State of La., *ex rel*. W. Van Norden *v*. C. S. Saurinet, 24 La. Ann. 119–23. "It is not for us to deal with this subject on the basis of inquiry into the motives of the Executive in granting the pardon to the prisoner in this case, nor to pronounce the act discreet nor otherwise."

It should be added that two of the justices were not present at the hearing of this case. [3] *National Republican*, Jan. 2, 1872.

CHAPTER VI

Rupture in the Assembly

BETWEEN the close of the extra session and the opening of the regular assembly opportunity was afforded for the definite formulation of plans for a change in the speakership,[1] a step which was intended to lead up to impeachment of the governor. A Democrat declared that proceedings were intended only if the governor made himself an obstacle to reform,[2] but the probability is that they had little expectation of his acquiescence. It was understood that the seven Democratic Senators who had voted for Coupland would act with the eleven reform Republicans in the assembly of 1872. The governor's tremendous power was objected to by every faction: by the custom-house ring, now that it was wielded against them; even by the negroes, whom he was alienating by 1872[3]; and most of all by the Democrats, whose patience with the Warmoth administration was at breaking point. Packard brought numerous charges of corruption and illegality against the governor,[4]

[1] The *Picayune* came out December 31 with the following: "A reorganization of the House at the present juncture will effect infinite good, if only the Conservative members will vote for one of their own members or a man whose fidelity to the reform movement is unquestionable."

[2] Moncure's testimony. House Misc. Doc., 42 Cong., 2 Sess., No. 211, 51.

[3] Joubert regarded the carpet-baggers as the worst enemies of the South and of the negro and their expulsion from the State the best possible blessing. *Ibid.*, 454.

[4] See his thirteen charges before the Congressional Committee. *Ibid.*, 123-4.

and claimed that nine out of ten Republicans without official position were in antagonism to him. Attacks by the custom-house organ were ceaseless.

Nominal reformation is a mockery [it exhorted the assembled legislature], and no man who loves his country can consent to the continued existence of the present personal dynastic government of Louisiana, and in the public estimate, any partisan who would in the presence of the record of the past three years of maladministration of good and the oppressive enforcement of questionable laws, continue power and patronage in the hands of the present irresponsible Executive of the State, is fitted either for the madhouse or the State Prison.[1]

Even the governor himself admitted that he had too much patronage and that provincial vacancies ought to be filled by the parochial authorities instead of by the governor.[2]

The onslaughts on Carter by the governor's wing were just as violent. There had been a good many movements to remove him even during his month of chairmanship in 1871, though none were successful. The members engaged in them remained in New Orleans nearly all summer, and were formed into a secret society, called the Figures—from the practice of designating the initial names of members in alphabetical order by numbers—pledged to remove him at the beginning of 1872.[3] The question of his removal was openly discussed in the papers and accusations of bribes brought.[4] Ward clubs were issuing

[1] *National Republican.*

[2] House Misc. Doc., 42 Cong., 2 Sess., No. 211, 394.

[3] *Ibid.*, 5. The Carter faction had no oath-bound organization, but formed a club about a week before the session commenced to see how many supporters he had. *Ibid.*, 22.

[4] "It is currently reported in the streets that the partisans of Warmoth are using $200,000 to be expended in the purchase of legislative votes to secure the election of a new speaker." *National Republican*, Jan. 2, 1872.

instructions to their representatives. The First Ward Club, for instance, wanted its members to support the speaker who acted in accord with the State convention of August 9, 1871, and called upon one Representative to resign for not supporting reform measures.[1]

The balance of parties in the legislature had changed considerably from the body elected in 1868 by the time its members gathered on January 1, 1872. There were twenty-eight Democrats in the House; only six or seven, however, in the Senate.[2] When the roll of the Senate was called, but sixteen men responded to their names.[3] On the second day of the session the sergeant-at-arms, after a prolonged search, reported that there were no Senators to be found. A member stated that he had heard that the revenue-cutter had left the city with the absent Senators aboard. And this proved to be the case. In order to prevent a quorum until the arrival of certain Senators, whom they expected to act with them, in constituting a majority for reform, in order to elect an anti-Warmoth man as lieutenant-governor, three Democrats and eleven reform Republicans had taken refuge on the first day of the session in the friendly shelter of an upper room of the custom-house, until about midnight, when the captain of the United States cutter *Wilderness* received them aboard his vessel with orders to move about the river in order to

---

Again on Jan. 3 this paper printed: "We dare him to deny that he did not yesterday afternoon solicit through several of his Lieutenants the assistance of the Democrats, offering to give them a Democratic Speaker, and whatever else they might exact! And what was their answer, Mr. Warmoth." Under the caption, "A Silly Rumor," he denied it on Jan. 4 in his organ.

See also *Picayune*, Dec. 20, 1871.

[1] *National Republican*, Jan. 3, 1872.

[2] House Misc. Doc., 42 Cong., 2 Sess., No. 211, 358.

[3] Throughout these exciting sessions the numbers given in the different sources vary. I have accepted the Senate journal in this instance.

prevent their arrest. It is probable that they expected,
as they claimed, to return the next day, but circumstances
combined to keep them prisoners aboard the vessel for
almost a week. They kept below most of the time to
avoid being seen. During this time Marshal Packard
kept in constant communication with them so that in
case other Senators arrived and were seized by the sergeants they might immediately come in. He went aboard
several times to encourage such "great sacrifice for the
good of the State," manifesting his appreciation by the
gift of champagne and cigars.[1] Among this group of
men, living and eating together on board the vessel and
at an hotel in Mississippi, whither they fled on January
6 after the Secretary of the Treasury peremptorily ordered
the landing of the cutter,[2] were two colored Senators, so
that one of the negro Representatives boasted that the
coalition established one thing: the Democrats would
swallow the negroes if they could get their votes.[3]

Meanwhile the course of events in the House was
creating the greatest excitement. That body adjourned
on the first day out of respect to Lieutenant-Governor
Dunn. On the second day, after no little excitement
caused by filibustering motions, a resolution of confidence[4]
in Carter, pledging him support for the rest of the session, passed by a vote of forty-nine to forty-five.[5] This
vote revealed to the governor his weakness, and manœuvr-
ing to turn his minority into a majority began. He called
a caucus of his members of the legislature with a view to

[1] House Misc. Doc., 42 Cong., 2 Sess., No. 211, 148.
[2] It was said that public opinion forced Grant to order the *Wilderness* to
unload. Cox, *Three Decades of Federal Legislation*, 556.
[3] House Misc. Doc., 42 Cong., 2 Sess., No. 211, 375.
[4] The exact form which this resolution took was approval of the journal,
with which Carter had, it will be recalled, been accused of tampering.
[5] The numbers differ again. The above is the one accepted by the Congressional committee, based on Burch's testimony.

8

getting a sufficient vote to change the speakership.[1]   An emissary was sent to the Democratic caucus to ask a committee of conference and to buy their support by the proffer of the speakership, but it was refused.[2]

Preparation seems to have been made in anticipation of an exciting session on January 3.   Under the police law the governor could swear in any number of special appointees, and, although Carter had forbidden the metropolitan police within the hall of the House,[3] several hundred policemen[4] had appeared on the second day in citizen clothes, their badges concealed inside their coats—some upstairs, others on the banquettes, and some on the street.   On the third day a still larger number was present, so that the passage to the House was blocked. Excitement was at fever heat in the streets, a part of Warmoth's scheme to have an excuse for calling out the militia, it was said.

The skirmishing opened with a test vote to postpone the reading and approval of the journal, which showed a change of five votes overnight and a reversal of strength.[5] After some difficulty and excitement about securing the privilege, the speaker made a personal explanation of the charge of corruption and extravagance in connection with the journal of the last session which had been brought against him.   He had scarcely resumed his seat when a motion to declare the chair vacant was offered.   He ruled the motion out of order on the ground that another member had the floor on[6] the question of the appointment

[1] According to his own admission.   House Misc. Doc., 42 Cong., 2 Sess., No. 211, 389.   [2] *Ibid.*, 53.
[3] This was not a new device of the governor's.   See House Jour., 1870, 142-3, concerning the sending of police into the hall.
[4] The *National Republican* of Jan. 3, 1872, gives the number as 250.
[5] The vote stood 49 to 46.
[6] It seems only fair to accept Carter's own words here, although the opposition held that he ruled it out of order on the ground that the House had

of a committee to consider charges against certain members, notably Carr and Dewees. It was presented amid confusion so great that though it was read by the clerk a half-dozen times, probably not more than a dozen members could hear it. Twenty members were on their feet gesticulating and addressing the chair at once, hallooing and raising questions of order, which the speaker refused to entertain. Carter ordered the lobby, which was densely crowded, cleared, and assistant sergeants were appointed until order was at least partially restored. Carr was one of the disorderly members during this time who had to be seated by a sergeant. The clerk then read the charges and Carter put the motion for the previous question. Just as the clerk began to call the roll, or immediately after,[1] Carr moved that the speaker's seat be declared vacant and a member by the name of Waters be elected. He put the motion himself, because he held that the speaker refused tyrannically to recognize any but members of his own side. It is clear that there was no recognition by the speaker and no appeal to the House. Without putting the negative[2] he called on the members to place Waters in the chair, advancing amid a shout of "yeas" toward the speaker's platform with a following of about thirty men. At the decisive moment it had been

---

already voted confidence. House Misc. Doc., 42 Cong., 2 Sess., No. 211, 22.

[1] Carr stated that he had the chief clerk's word that he had not begun to call the roll. It is almost impossible to get the exact sequence of events in the many conflicting accounts of this day's session. I have used the official accounts as modified by the testimony of eye-witnesses given in *Ibid.* and the newspaper statements, *Times, Bee, Picayune,* and *National Republican.*

The comment of the *Picayune* hits the mark: "The disgraceful scenes in the House of Representatives yesterday naturally excite the reprobation of every citizen. Such an open, undisguised scramble for office and power is without a parallel in our history."

[2] Carr stands alone in saying he put the negative. *Ibid.*, 213.

expected that the sergeant would whistle and the police in plain clothes in the lobby would assist in putting Carter out of the chair, an arrangement which was not carried out, possibly because of Waters's reluctance. But Carter denounced the movement as revolutionary[1] and by his firm stand stopped the crowd advancing down the aisle toward him. His faction raised the cry "Arrest Carr!" About eight or ten men rushed out from the speaker's ante-room,[2] reporters and extra sergeants who had been sworn in several days before, so that order was restored in a few minutes.

The motion on the charge against Carr and Dewees was then put and lost by the suspension of the rule which would have prevented the members concerned from voting. Dewees himself then secured the appointment of a committee of investigation, known to be favorable to himself and Carr.

That evening some of the opposition leaders in order to suppress the "revolution" agreed in a caucus at the custom-house[3] to arrest the governor and a large body of his followers.[4] At the request of the custom-house coalition General Emory sent troops into the city at daybreak on the morning of the 4th, to protect the Carter sergeants against collision with the police.[5] As two hundred police

---

[1] Carter is quoted as saying: "I dare any one to attempt to take this chair." House Misc. Doc., 42 Cong., 2 Sess., No. 211, 6.

[2] The number is variously given from 8 to 30. It was charged that Carter had secured notorious men there in anticipation of this event, but the writer is forced to believe from the testimony that there had been no concerted plan.

[3] Carter, Lowell, and Vorhies were among the number, but the warrants were issued in the name of four partisan members of the House, two Republicans, two Democrats. Packard said he did not investigate, merely executed the arrest. *Ibid.*, No. 211, 355 and 118.

[4] *Ibid.*, 24.

[5] The governor afterward captured General Emory so that the latter

were also marched to the state-house under the governor's orders, the street in front of Mechanics Institute was filled by noon with National soldiers, police, and armed, excited citizens. Places of business were closed and life and property seemed unsafe.[1] By about eleven o'clock, the building itself was completely filled with police, who had been ordered from their beats the night before in order to report at the Institute. Members passed between double lines of police, extending from the top of the stairs to the door of the hall, twenty or thirty feet distant, admitted if the latter knew them, stopped if they were not so fortunate as to be recognized.[2] At about a quarter of twelve a United States marshal appeared in the governor's office to arrest him, together with the lieutenant-governor, eighteen members of the House, and four Senators on a charge of violation of the Enforcement Act of April 20, 1871.[3] Acting under the governor's advice, they went voluntarily before United States Commissioner Woolfley[4]

---

really acted so as to give his moral support against the custom-house. House Repts., 42 Cong., 2 Sess., No. 92, 20.

[1] *Ibid.*

[2] Carter found the private door leading to the speaker's room locked, and the chief of police standing at his door. A latch had been placed outside the door during the night so that no one could enter except through the governor's office. His ante-room and desk had been broken into. House Misc. Doc., 42 Cong., 2 Sess., No. 211, 24.

[3] United States Statutes at Large, XVII, 13, Section 3, which declared that where insurrection, violence, unlawful combinations, or violence should deprive any class of any right, privilege, or immunity, named in the Constitution, such fact should be deemed a denial by the State of the equal protection of the laws, and the violator might be tried by the marshal.

[4] The *Bee* had "no regrets to express for the degradation which Governor Warmoth has subjected himself to in being forced to submit to arrest by the deputy marshall yesterday. . . . It is fitting that the 'poisoned chalice' should be presented to the lips of those who prepared it for us, and that the tortures they devised for an unoffending population should return to plague the inventor." Jan. 5. But the *Picayune* felt that the sovereign dignity of the commonwealth is violated "whenever a legislator is falsely

and were released on bail, but the affair detained them until nearly one o'clock.[1]

The small Warmoth faction present meanwhile in the House tried to break the quorum by leaving. After a large number had passed the gate, someone raised the cry: "Our side come out,"[2] whereupon Carter forbade the gate-keeper to let any more out, but the number present had already been reduced to about forty-nine or fifty.[3] The Committee on Elections, which had been sitting through the summer, reported unfavorably on several of Carr's friends, who were thereupon unseated,[4] and six of the seven replaced by Carterites.[5]

But Warmoth's tactics of that afternoon outflanked his opponents. About half-past one or two o'clock,

---

arrested while going to, attending upon, or returning from the legislative chamber." Jan. 5. .

[1] Packard insisted that the officers had been instructed to take no member from his seat. But in view of the advantage to his partisans and the promptness with which they availed themselves of it, it is difficult to credit his statement that "it was no political move." House Misc. Doc., 42 Cong., 2 Sess., No. 211, 118. It is not regarded as necessary to go into the matter of the second arrest attempted Jan. 5.

[2] Carr admitted that he told two or three to come down, but alleged the reason to be to avoid arrest. *Ibid.*, 214.

[3] The number is of the utmost importance and yet it cannot be determined definitely. The full roll of the House was 106, but 4 had died and one seat was vacant, so that, as the governor had not ordered a new election, the number was 101. A quorum would be held to be 51 but the chief clerk later held 52. At each roll call at this session he replied "Fifty-one and a quorum." *Ibid.*, 24-5.

[4] Carter later admitted that three of the seven were illegally removed. *Ibid.*

[5] As reported by the *National Republican*, Jan. 4. What purports to be the official journal is highly amusing and suggestive in its omissions. Frequently the number is not given—merely the statement that the clerk announced a quorum. One member, after having been allowed on a plea of illness to retire to the speaker's room, was hauled out, protesting and resisting, to cast the vote which his innate honesty forced him to cast in opposition to the majority. He probably had tried to escape with his Democratic confrères.

after the House had adjourned, he issued a proclamation calling the Assembly together in extra session at four-thirty that afternoon, because of the action of that body in unseating members while it was without a quorum. The governor notified the clerk of the House and the sergeant, who sent messengers throughout the city to summon members to appear.[1] The Warmoth faction was, by the governor's advice, assembled in a club-house across the street,[2] where it was naturally easy to receive notice, while most of the opposition, scattered throughout the city, saw the proclamation for the first time in the papers the next morning.[3] Undoubtedly no great effort was made to notify more than a few of the other wing— this much in order to give the call the semblance of fairness.[4]

At four-thirty the House convened with fifty-three members present,[5] including those unseated by Carter, seven of which entire number were Democrats. They voted to expunge all the record subsequent to the arrest of the members, expelled Carter for his conduct, and elected Brewster speaker. After passing a vote of confidence in Warmoth and urging the governor to arrange for the protection of the Institute, the body adjourned.[6]

[1] House Misc. Doc., 42 Cong., 2 Sess., No. 211, 344.
[2] The governor admitted that he advised his crowd "to go over there and await his proclamation." *Ibid.*, 355.
[3] Testimony of Carr. Even he had no personal notice. He just understood that such a thing "was going to be done."
[4] *Ibid.*, 325. The governor cited only two Carter men who had been notified.
[5] Again the numbers differ. One source gives 56. *Ann. Cyclopedia*, 471.
[6] *Annual Cyclopedia*, 1872, 472; *National Republican*, Jan. 5.
The *Bee* has an interesting prophecy in its issue of Jan. 4: "The conduct of these men yesterday warrants a belief that the attempt will be renewed to get possession of the Chair by fraud or by violence, and it is not improbable that they will make the attempt by occupying the building, which

On the morning of the 5th, Carter and his supporters found the capitol guarded by the entire available police force of the city,[1] under the admitted instructions of the governor.[2] Carter was, of course, denied admission. The leaders met in a caucus at the Cosmopolitan Club[3] and sent a committee to General Emory for advice. In accordance with his counsel forty-five or forty-eight[4] members gathered as the "legal" legislature, in the hall over the Gem Saloon,[5] on Royal Street. Loyal members dodged around and made the entire circuit of the city in order to reach the building. An immense throng of citizens which was addressed by the mayor and Representative Vorhies[6] gathered in front of the Gem shortly after they had assembled, filling Royal Street from Canal to beyond Custom-house Street. As it was deemed best for the body to continue in session all night,[7] a multitude of the "best citizens," according to the *National Republican*, cheered them on in their resolution by again congregating outside at about half-past nine and calling so loudly for Carter that he was obliged to appear and make a short address.

Meanwhile the Warmoth body had been in session

---

they can do, with the assistance of the Governor, before the regular hour of meeting, and organizing the House in their own fashion."

[1] The opposition press was, of course, loud in its denunciations of such a spectacle. "No such badges of servitude were ever before imposed upon a peaceful people on this continent," declared the *Times*, Jan. 6, 1872.

[2] He denied that they had been present by his instructions on the 4th.

[3] House Misc. Doc., 42 Cong., 2 Sess., No. 211, 26.

[4] Before they had been in session many hours they succeeded by arrests and accusations in getting 50 members, but not a quorum. Twenty-five were negroes. Carter himself admitted that he never had a quorum after he left Mechanics Institute. *Ibid.*, 30.

[5] Described as a coffee-house. *Ibid.*, 10.

[6] *National Republican*, Jan. 6, 1872. A very orderly but resolute crowd according to the *Bee*, Jan. 6, 1872.

[7] It stayed in session until 11.30 the next day.

most of the day, both houses meeting in extra session from ten to eleven-thirty, adjourning only to reassemble almost immediately again at twelve o'clock. The members who had caused the arrest of the governor were temporarily excluded and the adherents expelled by the Carter faction reseated. Although the journal fails to show a quorum,[1] a committee was appointed to inform the governor that the House was now again organized. The Senate, notwithstanding the lack of a quorum, transacted business by a resolution to request the Secretary of the Treasury to direct the *Wilderness* to land at New Orleans that the Senate might enforce attendance. The governor issued a proclamation before the day closed, declaring the Gem body "revolutionary, unconstitutional, and illegal," and commanding all good citizens to refuse to support it. He invited all legal representatives to return to their seats, commanded the other faction to cease its illegal arrest of members, and gave notice that unless it desisted from its usurpations of authority he would suppress it and arrest the members as rioters.[2]

By January 7, the excitement was at fever heat. Several calls had gone out from the governor to General Emory for United States troops, which had, accordingly, been moved twice to the vicinity of the state-house. The city presented the appearance of war. The governor was protected in the state-house by a large force of police and militia, Carter in the Gem by a large number of deputies and citizens. Bloodshed was unboubtedly prevented only, as Emory declared, by the free display of the United States forces at hand, and the acquiescence which each of the contending factions and the citizens generally yielded to the United States authorities.[3] The official

[1] It records only forty-nine present.
[2] House Misc. Doc., 42 Cong., 2 Sess., No. 211, 11.
[3] *Ibid.*, 62 and 89.

organ published a statement on January 6, that several regiments of militia were to assemble at their armories, and then followed a significant hint: "Persons who may be disposed to be disorderly will take notice."[1]   As if in reply, a Carter mob armed itself by the seizure of guns from the United States armory at Jackson Square on the 7th.   Detestation of the metropolitan police, "unknown émigrés and worthless grog-shop spouters, directed by unscrupulous time-servers and officered by incapable but willing tools,"[2] was loudly expressed in the press, while the ward clubs sent out the most inflammatory notices.

Republicans of the First Ward to the Front [they exhorted], Public Thieves and Corruptionists must resign their offices. Robbing the People is done away with.   Assemble in our Hall, corner of White and Melpomene, on Monday night, Jan. 8, and demand that Warmoth and his horde leave the State.   Speak in VOICES of THUNDER.[3]

The opposition papers vied with one another in their efforts to break what they termed the lethargy of the citizens.

Let us cast off our lethargy and arise to the importance of the occasion.   Let us tear away the mask which covers these whitened sepulchres and look fearlessly at the decaying and hideous faces which the mask concealed.   If we do not move in the matter at once, we shall become the victims of disease, and disappear from the face of the earth.[4]

The *Bee* threw its challenge directly at the legislators:

It is evident, in short, that we no longer have any government—and are in a state of complete anarchy—We repeat,

[1] *Republican*, Jan. 6, 1872.
[2] *National Republican*, Jan. 3, 1872.
[3] *Ibid.*, Jan. 7, 1872.   [4] *Ibid.*, Jan., 1872.

therefore, that the Senators and Representatives who do not
wish to indorse the responsibility of the usurpation committed
by Warmoth, must take measures to constitute themselves
legally, and, in a legal form, put an end to the dictatorship.[1]

The *National Republican* did not scruple to foment
rebellion within the police force and openly proclaimed:
"The ranks are open for all good and honest men. Fall
in!"[2] Reflections from the parish press indicate a great
distrust of the governor and a vital interest in the political situation.[3] Many of the sub-clubs indorsed the action
of Carter and pledged him their allegiance.[4] The Fourth
Ward Democratic Club brought coercion to bear by publishing the names of recreant members and called upon
the people to "remember these faithless representatives."
But Warmoth was not entirely without support. Delegations came from Feliciana and Attakapas to instruct their
Senators to support Warmoth; and some men of wealth
and standing cast their influence for him.[5]

Notice of a mass meeting of all citizens opposed to
corruption, to be held in Lafayette Square on the evening
of January 8, was published in the Sunday papers by the
Democratic Parish Committee. The crowd was largely

[1] *Bee*, Jan. 6, 1872. *Picayune* counseled citizens to keep out of the disreputable affair altogether, Jan. 6, 1872.

"No terms can be too strong," declared the *Times*, "to express the
popular denunciation and disgust for this exhibition in the very center of
our peaceful city of the Hall of Representatives, and of our state Capital,
environed by lines of armed hirelings with bristling bayonet and cannon and
Gatling guns posted to sweep the streets in threatening array."

[2] *National Republican*, Jan. 9, 1872.

[3] See Monroe *Telegraph*, *Republican Pioneer*, Baton Rouge *Gazette*, *Banner*
and *Courier* (New Iberia), Ascension *Leader*, Thibodaux *Reformer*, Tangipahoa *Advocate*, *Planters' Banner*. All quoted by city papers.

[4] Tenth Ward Club, Jan. 7; Third Ward Club, Jan. 13; West Feliciana
Executive Committee, Jan. 13; First and Second Ward Clubs, Baton
Rouge, Jan. 13.

[5] *National Republican*, Jan. 13.

composed of Democrats, but was addressed not only by Democrats, but also by custom-house factionists, and even by two colored Republicans.   There were fifteen thousand people in the square and environs.   Many inflammatory denunciations of Warmoth were cordially responded to by cries of "hang him."

Let us go in with zeal and vigor [the crowd was urged], let us wipe out from existence all of these corrupt officials.   Let us inaugurate such measures of reform that will relieve this city and State from the bonds that hold it.[1]

Resolutions were adopted denouncing the conduct of Governor Warmoth as revolutionary, and demanding his immediate resignation.   A committee was appointed to send Grant a true statement of affairs.   Warmoth's sheet got out several extras on that day to reiterate his purpose of reform.   His satellites were also accused of being busy through the crowd, pretending that it was merely a faction quarrel.[2]   But despite the intensity of feeling the troops ordered to Rampart Street proved unnecessary.

To recover three members who had been arrested by the Gem body, writs of habeas corpus were issued from the Eighth District Court by Judge Dibble.   Since the summons was treated with contempt, the governor, about four o'clock on the afternoon of January 7, sent a detachment of about eighty metropolitan police to protect the sheriff while he served the writs.   The news spread like wild-fire and immense crowds gathered opposite the Gem, the merchants near-by closing their shops in true Parisian fashion.   The police and militia marched through the rain, the sheriff served his writs, and then the columns

[1] *National Republican*, Jan. 9, 1872. See also the account in the *Picayune*, Jan. 9, and in the *Times*, Jan. 9.   [2] *Ibid.*

marched past the Gem, the militia manifesting by cheers their sympathy with the crowd.[1]

Each faction sent sergeants-at-arms to coerce the attendance of its opponents.[2] The Warmoth body stayed in perpetual session and members were cautioned not to go beyond the lines, as Carter sergeants were out.[3] Some arrests were made and one death occurred as a result of such action. A Warmoth man was taken from his bed at three o'clock in the morning; another house was searched at a late hour of the night; and one house surrounded for an entire day and night. When Mr. Wheyland, a contestant for a seat, was killed on the 9th[4] in an effort to arrest him, the Warmoth House made much of the event, attending the funeral in a body on the 10th. Carter and three of his supporters were charged with the murder, but to prevent his arrest before a hostile court, Judge Abell of the First District Court issued a bench warrant without affidavit at the instigation of the Democratic Central Committee.[5]

It was in connection with this accusation that the governor dispersed the Gem body. A sergeant came to execute the warrant on Carter at three in the morning, but as he failed of admission, a force of metropolitans went at five on the morning of January 10, three hundred

[1] This is the account of a sheet favorable to the Gem wing.

[2] A story is told of how one negro member of the Gem faction re-emerged from beneath his seat after due assurance that the Warmoth sergeant had not been able to effect an entrance. Such a display of bravery was by no means new. In the debates of 1871 occurs the following statement: "Mr. Speaker, I hear members talk about knocking people's teeth down their throats. I am afraid. I do not like to be where there are people of that kind." House Deb., 84.

[3] Carter commissioned a great number of sergeants—several thousand altogether.

[4] Some reports say the 7th. House Misc. Doc., 42 Cong., 2 Sess., No. 211, 312. *National Republican, Picayune, Times,* Jan. 9.

[5] House Misc. Doc., 42 Cong., 2 Sess., No. 211, 323.

strong, and took forcible possession. It prevented a
session at the Gem that day, though about twenty met
every day afterwards until January 24, first at the custom-
house, and then in a room on Canal Street. Carter appealed to Emory to aid him in recovering his hall, but the
general refused to lend him the troops. In consequence
of this move by the governor the excitement was greater
on January 11, than at any previous time. Knots of
men, many of them having large interests, assembled
on the streets near the custom-house, where it was errone-
ously reported that the House of Representatives was
holding its session. But one subject was discussed—
the legislative fight. From Old Levee to Royal Street
there was almost a solid line of men who intercepted every
acquaintance with eager inquiries for news. Many wild
rumors were circulating about the city.[1]

When Carter appeared before the First District Court
on January 12, the judge held that the governor's act was
a clear case of conspiracy, and that the evidence clearly
established that Wheyland had been shot by a policeman.
His release was greeted with hearty demonstrations by the
immense throng of his partisans assembled in the court-
room.[2]

In still another relation, the governor had recourse,
somewhat later, to the courts. He asked for an injunction to restrain the Carter faction from holding an assembly elsewhere than at the capitol and to restrain the
auditor and treasurer from paying any claim issued by that
body. Judge Dibble decided that the injunction ought
not to issue to forbid the body meeting, but that the one
against the auditor and the treasurer might issue and that
Carter should be restrained from appointing sergeants-at-
arms to arrest members of the legislature.[3]

[1] *National Republican*, January 12, 1872.
[2] *Ibid.*, Jan. 13, 1872.   [3] *Ibid.*, Jan. 25, 1872.

Meanwhile the Warmoth House was trying to bring
pressure of its own on the other body. On January 8,
members resolved that if the absentees had not returned
by one o'clock on January 10, they would expel them.[1]
On the tenth one member from the Carter branch took
his seat, but the threat was put into effect against the
four members who caused the arrest of January fourth.
On the eleventh the enforcement was postponed, but on
the nineteenth those refusing to attend were expelled by a
vote of forty-seven to eight.[2] The measure was reconsidered on January 20, to admit one applicant and on
January 22, to seat two. Changes in the personnel
occurred in both bodies from the vacillation of certain
members. On January 17, a Warmothite appeared at
the Gem, and that faction gained two accessions on the
eighteenth of men who declared they had attended
the other session but were "heart and soul here."[3] On
the other hand, on the nineteenth two declared their
faith in the Warmoth House as the legal body and
asserted that they had affiliated with the other faction
only to gain it over.[4] Cain Sartain tried to stand in with
both by declaring himself an adherent of neither faction,[5] while another member passed back and forth
several times.[6] One of the men admitted by Carter
went over to the other House, and one, claiming to be
disgusted with the whole business, went home, although
it was pointed out suggestively that he was rewarded by
Warmoth with the lucrative post of tax-collector.[7] Two
others withdrew from the contest for their seats and

[1] House Jour., 1872.   [2] Ibid.
[3] Proceedings as published in *National Republican*, Jan. 19, 1872.
[4] *Ibid.*, Jan. 20, 1872.
[5] The statement was made on Jan. 18, in the Carter House. Issue of
Jan. 19, *National Republican*.
[6] House Misc. Doc., 42 Cong., 2 Sess., No. 211, 27.
[7] *Ibid.*, 25.

went home when they were reimbursed for their mileage and expenses.[1]

Three distinct attempts to gain possession of the state-house were made by Carter on January 13, 14, and 22. On the first date the Carter faction assembled in Canal Street with six thousand citizens *en masse*. A scene of unprecedented excitement followed. A committee of three demanded that the police be removed from the state-house so as to admit citizens and members. The demand was verbally refused by the governor. Then the committee waited on Speaker Brewster to demand of the House the reinstallment and organization of January 4; but the latter refused to receive the committee. This body then decided to adjourn until Monday but legally to preserve its integrity. The speech announcing to the crowd the action of the committee was received with intense enthusiasm, which vented itself by going to army headquarters and crying vociferously, "Turn out Warmoth."[2]

Carter next proposed to General Emory to appoint with his consent enough sergeants to oust the police and seat his members. But Emory evidently felt that Carter was trying to take advantage of the presence of his troops, and so on January 14 he announced that he deemed it his duty not to bring the troops to the city again "in the present imbroglio without further orders from the government."[3] But when Colonel Carter published his letter and one of his adherents circulated an inflammatory article broadcast, calling the crowd together to attack the governor, Emory reversed his decision, recalling the troops to the city to suppress any riot which might arise from the article.[4]

Naturally, all this time efforts were made to draw the

[1] House Misc. Doc., 42 Cong., 2 Sess., No. 211, 25.
[2] *National Republican*, Jan. 14.
[3] House Misc. Doc., 42 Cong., 2 Sess., No. 211, 91.   [4] *Ibid.*, 92.

government at Washington and, more particularly, President Grant, into the affair. Telegrams passed to Grant and Secretary Boutwell from both legislative bodies, and just before Carter's attempt to seat his members forcibly, the Warmoth branch passed a concurrent resolution asking the President for troops to put down domestic violence. But Grant wished to avoid recognition of either body.

Of course [he said to Secretary Belknap] if there is danger of bloodshed and riot, I should like to prevent it; but I prefer the testimony of others interested in peace and quiet, rather than those interested in establishing the claims of either of the two factions to be the legitimate legislature of the State before taking action.[1]

Governor Warmoth was all excitement again on the morning of January 15, and requested Emory to send troops to prevent violence, which he feared was very seriously threatened. Accordingly, the General telegraphed that the excitement in the city was increasing hourly and if the wish of the President were not decisively signified, Warmoth's opponents would become so overwhelming that the United States troops would be powerless to subdue the riot.[2]

Under this condition of affairs the question of martial law was mooted: January 9, Emory suggested it, although he withdrew his proposition the next day; the Committee of Fifty-One, constituted at a mass meeting held a few weeks before to note the condition of affairs and representing the property and substance of the city, after vain efforts to reconcile the contending factions,[3] on January 11, handed to General Emory resolutions re-

[1] House Exe. Doc., 42 Cong., 2 Sess., No. 209, 15.
[2] Ibid., 12.
[3] A group of citizens requested the governor that a committee be appointed by the state-house to meet a committee of Carter's people to adjust matters, but the governor disapproved.

9

questing martial law[1]; the State Central Democratic Committee on January 10 asked the President to declare it; a large number of members of the bar presented a petition urging it[2]; the press approved it[3]; the absconding Senators telegraphed to the President to like effect[4]; and the mayor of New Orleans applied for it.   But the President replied to the request of the mayor that it would not be proclaimed in New Orleans "under existing circumstances."[5]

A few attempts of the two bodies to get together—a request from the Carter body for a committee of conference and a renewed invitation from the Warmoth House to the bolters to return—came to nothing so that Carter made his great attempt on January 22, which proved decisive. On the Saturday preceding, he circulated through the entire city handbills of the most inflammatory character:

TO ARMS! TO ARMS! TO ARMS!
COLORED MEN TO THE FRONT!

Warmoth's SLAVES at the Mechanics Institute pretended to-day to expel Antoine, Adolph, Burch, Wilson, Kearson,

[1] They had been passed at a very exciting meeting of the Committee on Jan. 11, House Misc. Doc., 42 Cong., 2 Sess., No. 211, 148.

[2] *National Republican*, Jan. 12, 1872.

[3] "We congratulate the Committee upon their act. The temporary disadvantage of martial law to our citizens will be fully compensated by the overthrow of an unscrupulous and venal governor and his horde of associate corruptionists." *Ibid.*   And this: "It is hard to have arrived at a point to wish for the establishment of martial law, but if the crisis does not end in the triumph of the legislative honor, we see no other solution, and perhaps it would not be the worst in order to arrive at the reform of all the abuses which have bankrupted our city and State." *Bee*, Jan. 6.   The *Picayune*, however, "heard it with regret" and felt that it must warn citizens against "the greater evil which they invoke as an antidote, believing it to be more virulent than the poison, and more lasting in its damaging effects," Jan. 10.   And the *Times* asked that "the issue between the two parties be tried like other political and civil contests, without a resort to brute agencies of force and arms." Jan. 8.   See also the *Bee*, Jan. 12.

[4] House Misc. Doc., 42 Cong., 2 Sess., No. 211, 148.   [5] *Ibid.*, 94.

Williams, Tureaud, Geddis, Johnson, Laurent, Kenner, Harper, Harry Lott, J. B. Lott, and other colored members of the house of representatives. Warmoth will next attempt to remove Ingraham and Antoine from the senate.

Rally, on SATURDAY at one o'clock at the corner of Rampart and Canal Streets, and let those who have dared to trample on your rights as freemen and citizens tremble until the marrow of their bones shakes. Let the cry be

DOWN WITH WARMOTH AND HIS THIEVING CREW.
RALLY! RALLY! RALLY!
LIBERTY OR DEATH. [1]

Sunday he published an address to the people in the morning papers, saying that he should the next morning at eleven-thirty, through the sergeant-at-arms of the House over which he presided, proceed to remove the police from the entrances and hall of the House of Representatives and place said House, with its organization intact as on January 4, in its hall at Mechanics Institute. He concluded by inviting the people to meet him at Rampart Street near Canal at ten o'clock Monday morning for the necessary orders. He also advised all persons in the neighborhood to close their doors and keep out of the streets. [2] It was reported that he had sworn in nine hundred sergeants-at-arms. But his party was evidently divided as to the advisability of fighting; the leading Democrats discountenanced it, while the organization of "76" [3] openly advised against it. [4]

[1] House Misc. Doc., 42 Cong., 2 Sess., No. 211, 318–19.

[2] *Ibid.*, 317–18. See also the *National Republican*, Jan. 21, 1872.

[3] This was a secret Democratic organization concerning which the writer has been unable to gain much information. I came across a call for a meeting issued in the papers Jan. 5, after the extra session, in which these numerals occurred.

[4] Emory reported Jan. 20: "The leading Democrats having determined to discountenance riots, I do not at present apprehend any." House Exe. Doc., 42 Cong., 2 Sess., No. 209, 17.

The faction began preparations by robbing an armory at Algiers of its rifles on Sunday night. By seven o'clock on Monday morning four hundred thousand men were enrolled, while Mechanics Institute, on the other hand, was guarded by a thousand men. Carter made a last demand on Warmoth and the speaker of the House, which was unheeded by the governor and returned by Brewster. But just at that critical moment the following telegram, addressed to Emory, was handed to Carter: "The President directs that you hold your troops in readiness to suppress a conflict of armed bodies of men, should such occur; and to guard public property from pillage or destruction."[1] Instantly he changed his tactics, read the message to the people, and urged that there be no violence. Thereupon the crowd dispersed. Emory later represented that the repeal of the offensive laws, of which note will be made directly, had taken from the Carter faction the power to raise a force sufficiently strong to dislodge the governor, and so disastrous defeat would probably have been the result of the attempt.[2]

Meanwhile the Senate, in the absence of a quorum, had been adjourning from day to day. On January 8, Anderson appeared, whereupon that body, under the encouragement of having one-half its number present, passed resolutions condemnatory of the action of the absentees and in favor of the "most thorough and efficient Legislative reform in all existing laws which experience has proven to work injury to the rights and property of the people of this State."[3]

The absent Senators were first heard from January 9 by a card which they sent to Carter, urging him to remain firm and promising, if necessary, to remain absent "the entire session rather than submit to the revolutionary

[1] House Misc. Doc., 42 Cong., 2 Sess., No. 211, 322.   [2] *Ibid.*
[3] *National Republican*, Jan. 9.

government at the State house.''¹ After the arrival of Senator Anderson but one more was necessary for a quorum. Warmoth's resources were equal to the emergency. He sent a letter to Senator Thomas, a Democrat, who was remaining at his home one hundred and eighty-eight miles distant, promising exemption from arrest if he would come to the city. At his interview with the governor at the state-house, bills repealing the obnoxious legislation were drafted then and there and the Senators present assured him of their passage before his consent to return to his seat was won.²

And so January 15 saw a change in the situation. Counting Pinchback, there were eighteen and a quorum so that the Senate chamber hummed with the unwonted stir of business. The governor and House were notified of the organization of the Senate; the governor's annual message was received; by a suspension of the rules, the election and registration laws were repealed by a vote of sixteen to two³; the constabulary law was repealed by eleven to seven; and the printing bill was repealed.⁴ A joint select committee to consider new laws on these subjects was then created. The House promptly passed the repeal bills⁵ of the Senate on the same day. In a speech to the House after adjournment, the governor promised to sign the bills that evening. "Extras" issued by the city papers stated that he had done so, though the

¹ House Misc. Doc., 42 Cong., 2 Sess., No. 211, 48.
² Ibid., 359.
³ Pinchback voted in the negative.
⁴ Senator Barber believed that the foundations of the Republican party were being voted away while Campbell voted repeal to avoid riot, hoping proper legislation could be had afterwards. House Misc. Doc., 42 Cong., 2 Sess., No. 211, 110.
⁵ The *National Republican* printed on Jan. 17, that one member was opposed to repeal, when Warmoth was heard to say: "Never mind, Charley, we'll pass new ones and worse."

approval of the press was distinctly tempered. "To the reform he reviled, he has abjectly succumbed, and with an anxiety that confessed the war which his crimes had challenged was irresistible. If his acquiescence were cordial, why was it so tardy? Too late, you Charlatan!"[1] But the measures never reached the governor. This failure to keep faith with Senator Thomas was explained later on the ground that the returning Senators raised the objection that eighteen was not a legal quorum.[2]

Thomas's return forced the hand of the absentees. On the sixteenth they had returned to the city but not to Mechanics Institute. Instead, they sent a statement that they could not return to their duty while the statehouse was guarded by armed militia and police, nor did they recognize Pinchback as legal president of the Senate. "When these armed forces are removed, and not until then, will we voluntarily consent to take our seats in your body and participate in its proceedings."[3] On January 20, they appeared in the Senate, expecting a majority to dispossess Pinchback, but at the last moment a Senator went over to the other side and so the negro leader was assured of the chair.[4] Even then the vote was so close that it stood a tie except for Pinchback's own casting vote. A resolution, declaring the extra session of December 6, 1871, constitutional, passed as a matter of course by the same vote.[5]

[1] *National Republican*, Jan. 16, 1872.
"We are not inclined," says the *Bee* , "to give Governor Warmoth credit and his adherents for their reformatory action of yesterday and shall reserve further comments thereupon until we see some evidences of their sincerity." *Bee*, Jan. 16.
[2] House Misc. Doc., 42 Cong., 2 Sess., No. 211, 359.
[3] *National Republican*, Jan. 17, 1872.
[4] House Exe. Doc., 42 Cong., 2 Sess., No. 209, 17. Emory rightly said: "The result of that effort will be decisive." The exact form it took was a refusal to elect a president.
[5] *National Republican*, Jan. 21.

The Gem faction of the House was now left powerless. One or two of the members had sneaked back to the Institute; then they came in by two's and three's, but a nucleus stayed out. They had waited for the Senate to organize, thinking it would recognize them, but by a strictly party vote, it had recognized the governor's House. The Senators then advised the Carter group that the struggle was ended. And so on January 24, at eleven fifty-five, the rump went over in a body and demanded their seats. But Rule 32, which forbade any but members on the floor, was enforced against them and they were obliged to retire to the lobby while they were acted on separately. All were restored except two white Republicans and one negro.[1]

The session was almost half over before the legislature was finally organized,[2] so that the work accomplished in the remaining thirty odd days was meagre.[3] Without dwelling upon the matter, it is sufficient to say that the House was a turbulent, noisy, useless, frivolous body, which the governor was irritated into rebuking, as the most disgraceful body he had ever seen.[4] He urged the modification of the registration, election, constabulary, revenue, and printing laws, the repeal of the metropolitan police law, and action on the State railroads. He made a brave show of personal sincerity.

[1] House Misc. Doc., 42 Cong., 2 Sess., No. 211, 12. Burch says four were excluded, but I think this an error. Even as late as February 20, the organization of the House was a matter of friction. At an evening session on that date, as the opposition found the House adjourned, it proposed to elect another speaker. Much excitement ensued but the body adjourned without having transacted any business.

[2] Standing committees were not appointed until Jan. 26, in the Senate; Jan. 28, in the House.

[3] The *National Republican* charges as an additional reason that the champagne paid for by the advocates of a certain bill flowed too freely, Feb. 23.

[4] Record in *National Republican*, Feb. 25.

The delay by your honorable bodies in responding to these recommendations and adopting measures of reform has given rise to suspicion and doubt as to the sincerity and good faith of the professions of your members, especially those who are supposed to be coöperating with me in the administration of the State government.   It is to set at rest all doubt, if there could be any, as to my own position in these matters, that I address you on this occasion.[1]

The message occasioned much ridicule.   Campbell proposed a reference to a mythical "Committee on Sermons and Exhortations."[2]

A new election law was passed late in February, retaining the obnoxious returning-board, which was now made elective by the Senate, so that there was little substantial change, though the bill was to have great importance later.[3]   A registration bill was also passed, which preserved the appointment of registrars by the governor, but with the consent of the Senate.[4]   The House managed to repeal the constabulary law, and the Senate passed new police and printing laws, and at the close, in the boisterous, hurried session of February 29,[5] both were able to consummate the passage of these half-measures.   But

---

[1] *National Republican*, Feb. 6, 1872.

[2] All the credit he received from the opposition press for this action was the following: "Warmoth attempted again to throw sand in the eyes of the people last night.   Immediately after the adjournment of the House he was called on—by preconcerted arrangement—to make a speech.   He told his creatures in the Legislature that they were naughty boys for not passing any reform measures, and for squandering valuable time.   The people, however, know that the wise legislators are only following out the program laid out for them by their lord and master, the gubernatorial imposter; and, hence, speeches—empty words—will not whitewash the corrupt Executive."   *Ibid.*, Feb. 25.

[3] Session Laws, 1872, No. 98.   See this book, Chapter IX.

[4] Passed the Senate Feb. 8, the House Feb. 10, amendments concurred in by the Senate Feb. 22.

[5] A handicuff scene occurred at this session, cheered by the lobby.

as these bills do not appear in the statute books, except the election law, they evidently suffered defeat at the hands of the governor.

By February 25, it was the settled conviction of the community that the legislature would pass no laws for the relief of the people, and that its action in seeming to pass them was only a ruse to avert, for the time, an impending riot.[1] The *National Republican* charged that "No adequate reform financially has been accomplished, except in the law regulating the expenses of the General Assembly,[2] and to a very limited extent in the Revenue Bill by reducing the rates of assessment and collecting of taxes." And so it justly stigmatized the reforms as nominal and superficial, not real and substantial as the grossness of the abuses proposed to be corrected demanded.[3] The business community sighed with relief at the final adjournment. "No hoar frost ever gladdened the sight of a fever-stricken people with more sincere joy, than the lowered flag which told that the epidemic of legalized fraud was at an end."[4]

[1] House Exe. Doc., 42 Cong., 2 Sess., No. 209, 25. This was the opinion of General Emory.

[2] Session Laws, 1872, No. 12.

[3] March 1.   [4] *Picayune*, March 1, 1872.

CHAPTER VII

Conventions and Entangling Alliances

THE preliminaries of the election of 1872 opened unwontedly early. Indeed, all factions seemed hardly able to restrain themselves until it should be time to begin the campaign fight. In the breaking up and shifting of parties but one fact seemed fairly clear: Governor Warmoth would probably not be his own successor. Violent as had been the onslaughts on him before, they seemed to double in ferocity with the approach of the election period. By 1872 language did not exist sufficiently vehement to convey the depth of detestation with which he was regarded by certain factions. He was variously termed a human vulture,[1] a Dives, uncrowned king of this dominion, our Caesar, a political leper,[2] the personification of brazen falsehood,[3] and that pest in our Executive chair.[4] His honesty had been impugned until there was absolutely no confidence reposed in his word. That he had come to the State in such utter poverty that he was invited by one landlady to move because he converted his room into an office and was sued by another for his board and lodging[5] and yet was extremely wealthy in 1872; that he had received vast sums from the State as part

[1] *Picayune*, 1872.
[2] *National Republican*, April 5, 1872.
[3] *Ibid.*, Feb. 9, 1872.   [4] *Ibid.*, Jan. 27.
[5] New Orleans *Commercial Bulletin*, Aug. 24, 1871.

138

owner of the official paper[1] were matters of common notoriety, whether true or not.   He had, as we have seen, been read out of the Republican party by the custom-house wing in August of the preceding year, and that faction was unremitting in its attacks through the platform and press.   On January 7 its organ, the *National Republican*, came out in bold-faced type: "He is a Traitor to the State and to the United States, and his Factious Cabal, self-dubbed a House, and the Metropolitan Thugs of New Orleans are his Right and Left hands to ply his Treason."[2] More controlled, the Democratic mouthpiece was just as emphatic: "If we were to sum up in one accusation the crimes of which Governor Warmoth has been guilty, we would say that it consists in his having stabbed public virtue to the heart and trampled it under his feet."[3] Even his faithful negro henchmen seemed to be deserting him.   Their organ, *The Times*, wrote as early as 1870:

He is giddy with the authority he already holds.   He gained his chair by no spontaneous summons of the people, but simply by that stealth which highwaymen employ in plying their vocation.   He is not the growth of honest sunlight, but of a ring's shadows.   By sinister means he attained a place which his wildest dreams had never promised him, and for which he has the fitness of neither moral courage nor culture, nor that nice discrimination which experience imparts.[4]

And January 27 several hundred colored men joined in a large meeting at the Louisiana Hotel to protest against his despotism.   All the best element of the State was arrayed against him; one wing of his own party; and at least a part of the negro population.   In addition the economic condition was crying out against him.

[1] His share of the profits was said to be $676,000 in two years.   *National Republican*, Jan. 25, 1872.   [2] *Ibid.*, Jan. 7, 1872.
[3] *Bee*, Jan. 7, 1872.   [4] Nov. 14, 1870.

The first move toward a nominating convention for 1872 came from the so-called Reform Party as early as February. A Committee of Fifty-One citizens had been appointed at a public meeting in New Orleans on the first of December, 1871, to secure reform in the administration of affairs in the city.[1] They had found that the troubles in the municipal government were due in large measure to "State interference and the manipulation of municipal affairs by the State authorities," and felt that reform in the city must be preceded by reform in the State. As the leaders in the movement saw that the reform measures desired were not being passed by the Assembly of 1872, they called a reform meeting for February 17 in front of the city hall. Ten thousand people responded. The report of the Committee of Fifty-One, setting forth its futile effort to present certain reform bills to the legislature was read. "Disheartened by the unblushing deceit of the executive and legislative branches of your State government, and convinced that no relief is possible while that government, as now constituted, remains in existence," the Committee recommended "the rapid organization of the people of this city and all over the State of Louisiana, not into secret, oath-bound associations, but into one grand party of reform."[2] It invited the parishes to send delegates to a convention to be held April 23 to adopt a platform of principles for the Reform party and nominate candidates for State offices whom all honest men could support.[3] Mass meetings for the reform cause were held at various points through the State,[4] and ward clubs were organized through the city against the opposition of the Republicans. A provisional State

[1] See above, 129.　　　　　[2] *Annual Cyclopedia*, 1872, 474.
[3] *National Republican*, Feb. 18, 1872.
[4] Those at Covington, Amite City, Franklinton, are noted by the *National Republican*, Feb. 2, 1872.

Central Committee met and organized March 8, which a few days later postponed the proposed State convention to June 4. In its address of postponement it attributed the frightful spoliation and robbery, of which the State was the victim, to a lack of sympathy and coöperation between the two great races inhabiting the territory. The city wards were requested to elect delegates June first and to keep constantly in mind the great principle of equality in representation that, "as nearly as possible, the convention might be composed in equal proportions from the two races."[1]

The Democratic State Central Committee was equally prompt, for February 16 found it in session, adopting resolutions, fixing the date of the convention for April 18, apportioning the representation, and issuing an address to the Democratic and Reform voters of the State. Members held that the tremendous obstacle they had to overcome in the registration and election laws necessitated an early and complete organization. In the light of subsequent events one clause in the address is interesting:

The alternative was presented to engage in a flagrant conspiracy with the Governor to fraudulently defeat the popular will and imposing upon ourselves the debasing humiliation of electing him governor or to endeavor by honorable means to obtain the desired relief to our people.[2]

It justified the union of Democratic and anti-Warmoth Republicans, and upon one question of vital importance took a determined stand:

Every candidate, Democratic or Republican, white or colored, is entitled to the office to which he has been elected by the people. Any section of the election law which leaves

[1] *Annual Cyclopedia*, 1872, 474.
[2] *National Republican*, Feb. 25, 1872.

to the discretion of a board of individuals the power to change
that result is revolutionary in its *design*, its *operations*, and its
purpose, and must be treated by the people as not upon the
statute-book.[1]

Before the Democratic convention could assemble,
however, the Liberal party had made its appearance in
Louisiana politics under the protection of the versatile
governor. Opposed to Grant for some time,[2] he was too
astute to come out in open hostility until he saw possi-
bilities for success with another party.[3] But by March
he thought he saw his opportunity in an alliance with the
Greeleyites and left, accordingly, on the sixth of the month,
for New York. On April 11 the Liberals held a mass meeting to consider measures to insure harmony and unity in
their party. At best, however, it was but a small gathering
with about seventy-five adherents on the platform and a
small crowd in front, so that even the *Republican* was forced
to admit that it was a "failure to a considerable extent,"
because the people are not ready to enter the political
turmoil so far in advance of the end of the decisive campaign."[4] Its purpose did not seem clear even to the
participants, for, while some assailed Grant, others offered

[1] *National Republican*, Feb. 25, 1872.
[2] As early as 1871 Burch said that he had hoisted the name of Grant
for President and it had given offense to Warmoth. House Misc. Doc.,
42 Cong., 2 Sess., No. 211, 19.
[3] Warmoth had declared for Grant at the August convention of 1871
only on condition that the Federal officials in Louisiana be removed. But
even in Feb., 1872, before the Congressional Committee he was most cautious: "I have made no statement, nor said anything, nor done anything,
to give them reason to believe that I would not support the President
in his re-election." *Ibid.*, 395. But his message of Jan. 5, '72, to Grant
was couched in disrespectful terms.
[4] April 18, 1872. The *Times* is not so scathing in its condemnation of
the Liberals as the *National Republican*. The former spoke of the meeting as a "respectable gathering, considering the absence of all excitement
to attract the masses of the party." April 18.

resolutions of indorsement of Grant as well as Warmoth. Shortly afterwards a document appeared signed by about five hundred citizens, urging that delegates be sent to the National convention at Cincinnati.

Inasmuch as the New York State Democratic Central Committee had decided on April 11 to coöperate with the Cincinnati malcontents, "should they assume the democratic basis," the Democracy of Louisiana became greatly exercised for fear that Warmoth might control their convention.   While the *Times* urged the convention to await the action at Cincinnati,[1] the *Bee* notified Governor Warmoth and his friends "who call themselves Democrats, that they cannot and shall not control the convention.   Indeed, they have no right to show their faces there, and we think the very first duty of the convention will be to refuse to recognize the credentials of those delegates who have notoriously involved themselves with Governor Warmoth, either as an attorney-at-law or in some other capacity."[2]

Still Warmoth influence was present in the convention in the decision which permitted a majority of those present to vote for the absent.   The attitude of many of the Democrats seemed to be voiced in the significant words of a country delegate: "We have been oppressed through bad laws, and are entitled to deliverance by these questionable means."[3]   Even thus early, however, the party was not a unit on the Warmoth question: union with him was openly debated, but a resolution declaring Warmoth "unworthy of the respect and confidence of the people and that any

[1] *Times*, see the issue of April 18.
"Meantime the Democrats will act wisely by deferring action as a distinct party, and by adjourning their convention to a day sufficiently remote from the transactions at Cincinnati, to enable them to adjust their relations and programme to the new conditions and circumstances which will then surround them."
[2] *Bee*, April 16, 1872.   [3] *National Republican*, April 24, 1872.

political connection with him would be dishonorable and injurious to the best interests of Louisiana" secured reference and was incorporated in the final resolutions. Nominations for the State ticket were postponed probably to see what action would be taken at Cincinnati,[1] and the convention adjourned to June 3 with the agreement that the people might choose other delegates to represent them if they wished. On the last evening the Committee on Resolutions reported an address so vituperative and bitter against Warmoth that a sharp fight ensued. The resolution passed amid much confusion by a vote of 20 to 2 or 3, the majority not voting.[2] It declared that the present struggle of the people was for their homes and liberties, that their courts were but a mockery, and their

Executive a tyrant, who exercises an open and boasted control over the Legislature. It is time, fellow-citizens, [it urged] to assert your manhood and dignity—to cleanse the Augean stables—to reestablish the rule of law and justice, of economy and constitutional liberty. It is time to put the brand of infamy upon the brows of those who have dishonored and plundered Louisiana; to expel them from their high places, and to make them give way to honest and capable men—the only fit representatives of a free and truly Republican people.

It declared the union of all honest citizens necessary to defeat the unprincipled party in power and earnestly invited the good people of the State to support the candidates who might be presented for the work of reform.[3]

Moved by the trend of events, the Republican State Central Committeemen bestirred themselves, bidding fc Warmoth's followers in its address of March 12, fc

[1] Blair telegraphed to urge delay. *National Republican*, April 21, 1872.
[2] *Picayune*, April 21, 1872.   [3] *Annual Cyclopedia*, 1872, 475.

it declared that his refusal to abide by the National Republican nomination will "relieve the Republicans who have been acting with him from any further obligation, and will clearly show them the objects he has had in view—either to rule the party for his own advancement, or break it by joining his opponents."[1]   Members, therefore, pleaded with all Republicans to stand by the regular organization, waving valiantly, as an inducement, the banner of reform.[2]

Before the regular Republican convention met, it was felt wise to hold a preliminary mass meeting in Lafayette Square where from eight to ten thousand men assembled and adopted resolutions which reaffirmed their faith in the National Republican Party under the leadership of Grant; which, while arraigning Warmoth bitterly, denounced the entire Labor Reform and Liberal movements, and refused even to recognize a split in the party.[3] The speakers ridiculed the Warmoth organization as unworthy of consideration or even notice.   Warmoth hirelings were accused by the friendly press of trying in vain to break up the meeting by shouts and cries.[4]

This device of using the metropolitan police and rough characters to break up Republican meetings, if we can trust Republican charges, was a favorite device of the governor's throughout the spring and summer.   Republican clubs were very active, but the opposition element was just as active in taking possession of city and parish meetings and in reversing elections and resolutions.[5]

[1] *National Republican*, March 14, 1872.
[2] "The ultimate carrying out those measures of Reform is a leading object of the Republican party, and we recommend that no candidate of that party shall be supported for any office at the next election who does not fully and unequivocally pledge himself to carrying out, in their true spirit and intention, those reform measures, both political and financial." *Ibid.*
[3] *Ibid.*, April 16, 1872.   [4] *Ibid.*   [5] *Ibid.*, June 6.

The Republican State Convention convened at the National Theatre in New Orleans on April 30 to elect delegates to the National convention.   The body of about one hundred and ninety-six delegates,[1] in which every parish was represented, was called to order by Packard.   After some confusion as to the order of business, a permanent chairman was chosen in the person of the negro Antoine, and delegates to Philadelphia elected. Lengthy debate occurred on the proper efforts to secure harmony in the party.   But opinion was unanimous against Warmoth: his name was greeted with hisses, and, on the other hand, a resolution repudiating him received with cheers.   As a measure to promote harmony, Pinchback, who, although heading a party of his own, had been elected an alternate, was invited to come before the convention on the evening of the second day to express his views on union.   He appeared and urged the colored people to stand by the Republican party.

A long series of resolutions, constituting the platform, was unanimously and enthusiastically adopted on the second day.   They heartily indorsed Grant personally as "a wise and just ruler," his management of domestic and foreign affairs, and approved the National legislation; they arraigned Warmoth and deemed his expulsion a matter of congratulation, reiterated the pledges of reform given in the address of the State committee, invited the coöperation of all honest men, even though it required the concession of their personal considerations, and urged on Congress the extension of the Enforcement Act of February 28, 1871, to all parishes in order to thwart Warmoth's control.   The question of harmony was disposed of by instructing the State committee to exert all its power and influence to bring back any bolters "if

[1] Some papers state one hundred and fifty-two.

it can be done on a just basis." The body adjourned *sine die* without nominating State officers.[1]

Still a fifth faction remains to be noted—the Pinchback wing of the Republican party. The split between Warmoth and his lieutenant-governor dates back to 1870, notwithstanding the fact that it was through the machinations of the former that the latter was elected president of the Senate in the extra session of 1871. As early as January, 1870, Pinchback said in the Senate: "It is well known, as far as I am concerned, that I have no partiality for the Governor of the State; I have not stood at his back as one of the supporters or admirers of that distinguished gentleman. I am not a lover or worshiper of his."[2] Pinchback would seem to have been undecided about Grant during the latter half of 1871 because of an hostility to the custom-house faction. Clearly, it would seem that the paths of the governor and lieutenant-governor must diverge after Pinchback, on March 1, declared for Grant, contingent on what would be done for the colored people,[3] and after the former had indorsed Grant at the Colored Men's Convention at New Orleans on April 15; yet Warmoth tried to claim his former ally as president of the Liberal State Central Committee.[4]

But by March 20 the Pinchback Committee issued a call to elect delegates to a convention on May 28 which should choose "true republican" delegates to the Republican Convention at Philadelphia and nominate a State ticket. The address of the "Parish Executive Committee" was an appeal to the colored Republicans to forsake Warmoth:

---

[1] The above account is based on the official proceedings as published in the *National Republican*, May 1 and 2, 1872.

[2] Senate Debates, 1870, 172.

[3] The *Times*, March 11, 1872.

[4] *National Republican*, March 19, 1872.

You must be aware of the political record of Governor Warmoth during the last few weeks, which unquestionably places him without the pale of the Republican party. . . . And with this record we regret to say that there are men, calling themselves Republicans, who will sell to H. C. Warmoth their rights and ours.[1]

This group, too, declared themselves in favor of reform and to that end cordially invited all men without regard to party, who desired to see honest men in office, and a faithful execution of the laws, to join themselves to it.[2]

The convention, which met according to call, professed to acknowledge the Philadelphia convention, but had one faction in favor of Grant, one hostile, while even some Liberals were present as delegates, among whom was the governor himself. The majority of the delegates were office holders under Warmoth. Pinchback opened the session with an address, in which he set forth as one of the purposes of the party the determination to declare anew their unswerving attachment to equal rights, justice, and liberty, and harped, as always, on the race question. So much dispute arose over credentials that the body failed to effect a permanent organization until the second day. The convention passed resolutions of almost fulsome praise of Warmoth[3] and Pinchback,[4] approving

---

[1] *National Republican*, April 7, 1872.   [2] *Ibid.*

[3] "Resolved, That we recognize in Governor Warmoth an officer who has combined with an efficient discharge of public duties an unimpeachable fidelity to the principles and the policy of the party by which he was elevated to his high position; that to him the Republican party largely owes whatever of credit may be its due for the fulfillment of those obligations which it assumed toward the people of the State in carrying out the principles of justice and equality which are the basis of its organization, &c." *Ibid.*, May 30, 1872.

[4] "Resolved, That in our honored fellow-citizen, Lieutenant-governor Pinchback, we have a bold, able, and manly leader in the Republican party, one who can be trusted in the future with its interests as he has been in the past, and that we indorse him to be our first choice for Lieutenant Governor." *Ibid.* See same issue for the whole platform.

them as its first choice for governor and lieutenant-governor.   It also indorsed the Chicago platform of 1868, insisted on equal educational, civil, and political rights, declared its earnest desire for union in the party, and condemned the recent action of Federal officials in interfering with the right of the people to assemble.   The race tone is dominant throughout the resolutions, which alleged that abundant evidence was to be found in the tone of the press and the speeches that the sole object of the Democrats and Reformers was the political overthrow of the negro, and that to this end they were subordinating the Presidential as well as all other questions.

In a speech to the convention on the second day Pinchback indulged in a display of conceit which is, perhaps, without parallel.   Against the desire and expressed wishes of a number of his people, he told the convention, he had withdrawn his name as a nominee for governor, to which high position he had great confidence of being elected had he allowed his name to remain.   He knew too well the condition of the State to fear failure; the colored people were strong and would vote for him to a man.   There was not then in Louisiana any man who had one-tenth as good a chance as himself who would have held back so long. [1]

Governor Warmoth made a short speech in which he stated that he did not desire the convention to accept his preference for President.   He thought it better to eschew National politics altogether and unite all Republicans on a State ticket, which object could best be accomplished by adjourning to Baton Rouge, to the time when the Republican convention was scheduled to meet, when both conventions

[1] *National Republican*, May 30, 1872.   To the investigating committee he replied frankly to the query whether the governor acknowledged his strength: "Oh, yes; he always acknowledged he couldn't get along without me.   I have to tell you the truth."   Sen. Repts, 42 Cong., 3 Sess., No. 457, 721.   He estimated his strength at about twenty-five thousand votes.

could come together on delegates and nominees. ' The convention acted on this suggestion and adjourned without further action to meet at Baton Rouge, June 19. No concerted plan appears to have governed the action of the convention.

June 13, Warmoth wrote to decline the proffered governorship at the hands of the Pinchback faction, since it appeared to be the

intention of the majority of the members of the convention on the reassembling at Baton Rouge to attempt an alliance with the custom-house party for the purpose of reuniting with those whom I consider the most dangerous enemies of the country and the State, with the arrogant, dictatorial, and corrupt administration of General Grant.

He preferred to place his trust in the rescue of the country from "Grantism and its attendant tyranny and corruption" in a thorough union of the "parties and portions of parties which had that object in view."[1]

The series of State conventions began a new round with the reassembling of the Democrats at the French Opera House in New Orleans on June 3. Four parishes were wholly unrepresented while considerable debate arose on the question of the number to be allowed to each because of the new parishes created since 1867. New delegates appeared and some of those present were also in the city in the capacity of members to the Reform convention which was scheduled to reconvene the next day.

The president opened the convention with an impartial statement of the complexities and entangling alliances before it:

Perhaps the question may arise whether or not the Cincinnati Liberal Republican platform should be endorsed, or the

[1] Published in the *Republican*, June 14, 1872. See *Times* also.

Democratic party of the State should steer clear of Federal politics in the present attitude of national parties, and look alone to the redemption of our own down-trodden and tax-ridden State from her present and impending ruin[1]—

and then followed a statement of the probability of propositions of conference from the Reform and Liberal parties.

Coalition was, however, undoubtedly, one of the objects of the convention, for a committee of eleven delegates was created for the purpose of conferring with any committee of the Reform party, "looking to a union with the Democratic Party," and no action was taken until the third day, when the chairman of the committee presented its report, declaring that there was no possibility of effecting a union of parties,[2] but asking for a new committee to select a State ticket to be supported by both parties. The old committee was continued, and again business in the convention stood still, awaiting the result.

The expected advance from the Liberals came. The Democratic body was not united after the first day when a speech suggesting coalition with Warmoth was hissed. On the third day the remark was dropped that the Democrats could not accomplish anything without a coalition and the speaker preferred Governor Warmoth's faction. It was greeted with both cheers and hisses and created great excitement. It is impossible to state whether the Republican charges that the galleries were crowded with disguised metropolitan police and that money changed hands are true or not, or how far these facts may have had to do with the slightly changed temper of the house. In any case, a third speaker was emboldened to say that "when

[1] *Nat. Rep.*, June 4, 1872.
[2] The hostile press attributed the failure to Warmoth's machinations, as union would spoil his plans.

an alliance with infamy is effected for the good, prosperity, and welfare of a people, it is noble, it is grand."[1]   But when the communication from the Liberals came, asking a committee of conference in the interest of an ultimate coalition of all the political strength of the State in a fusion ticket "that will restore honesty and intelligence in the administration of State affairs and a return to the constitutional government bequeathed by its founders," it was not at first entertained.   On the next day, however, a substitute, authorizing the conference committee jointly with the Reform committee to confer with any political organization in the State, was adopted by a large vote. The election of some delegates to the Baltimore convention concluded the work of the fourth day.

The nominations submitted by the conference committee on the fifth day were received with loud cheers, but a minority report which favored ascertaining from the convention its wishes in reference to further conference with the Liberals before nominating, and submitting the nominations to the conventions caused so much debate and confusion that the reports were not acted on until the sixth day, when the report of the minority was adopted by a close vote.   The convention, however, nominated a straight Democratic ticket.   The suggestion of McEnery for governor was not satisfactory to all and created such excitement as to prevent the reading of the resolutions so that the convention adjourned *sine die* without a platform.[2]

Meanwhile the Reform convention had been meeting in adjourned session from June 4 to 8 in the same city with a very fair attendance.[3]   A committee of conference had

---

[1] *National Republican*, June 6, 1872.
[2] Accounts of the daily proceedings are found in the issues of the *National Republican*, June 4 to 8.
[3] One hundred and forty-nine were present on the fourth day.   *Ibid.*, June 8, 1872.

been negotiating with the Democratic convention as
already detailed. A communication from the Liberals
was referred to the committee for similar treatment to
that accorded the Democratic offer. But on the fourth
day, when the Liberals appeared with a proposition for
coalition on the condition that Warmoth be made governor,
it was rejected without a dissenting vote.

The platform of the party, unanimously adopted, favored exclusive attention to State affairs with no active
participation in the Federal contest and a cordial reconciliation of the two races, accepting the political and
civil status of the negro as fixed, and declaring it

to be the policy of the party to receive assistance from any
source looking to the deliverance of our people from this
dreadful oppression under which they labor, while at the
same time it is distinctly understood that we will reject any
unworthy proposition or corrupt coalition, and that the
administration of our affairs for the future must be confided
to men of known integrity and capacity.[1]

On the fourth day the nominations for the chief offices
reported by the conference committee were unanimously
adopted, subject to the ratification of the Democrats,
although the ticket bore the names of but two of the
Reformers; but when the report came from the Democratic convention late on the afternoon of the next day

---

[1] *National Republican*, June 7, 1872, also McPherson's, *Handbook of
Politics*, 1872, 162.

The cardinal object of the party was declared in an address to the people
of July 8 to be " the complete overthrow of the present putrid government
of our State—the judicial condemnation by our whole population, sitting
as a court on the first of next November, of every individual connected with
the frauds and villainies systematically perpetrated upon us in the past few
years by every department of our State government."

And yet the *National Republican* pointed out Oct. 9, 1872, that the
very man who wrote the above words was then canvassing with Warmoth
and commending him to the confidence of the people.

that they had rejected the conference ticket, the men adjourned subject to the call of their Central Committee without ratifying the Democratic candidates or selecting a ticket of their own.

The fusion of the Democrats and Reformers was evidently effected about July 8[1] through the central committees, when the latter adopted the Democratic ticket, and agreed to a common platform of eight planks. Acknowledgment of the civil and political rights of all citizens was made; the rejection of all fraudulently contracted debt advocated, together with rigid economy; the restoration of "home rule" to cities and parishes, abolition of the extraordinary powers vested in the executive, and the enactment of severe law against bribery and speculation in State securities urged.[2] A vast assemblage of respectable people held a jubilee for the fusion on July 12, which became also a ratification of the nomination of Greeley and Brown.[3]

Next in chronological order came the adjourned conventions of the two wings of the Republican party at Baton Rouge, set for the same day, June 19, undoubtedly, with the hope of coalition. The custom-house wing experienced much loss of time over the credentials and difficulty in effecting an organization. Even there the governor seemed to be seeking some sort of an alliance with the Republicans, for he sent a telegram urging the convention

[1] On account of the liberal attitude of McEnery, the *Republican* declared that the "Last Ditchers should wear a weed." July 20. The denunciations of the Conservative nominee by Warmoth's organ were severe in the extreme. See issue of July 19.

[2] The platform is given in the issue of the *National Republican* for July 9.

[3] The Liberal Republicans had already ratified them on July 10. It truly seemed, as one of the papers said, a meeting convened more for the purpose of denouncing that cold-blooded tyrant, Warmoth, than for the ratification of either Greeley or McEnery, for his name was received with curses, groans, hisses, and shouts of execration. Cries of "Kill Warmoth" and "Drive the robber out" were heard. *Ibid.*, July 13, 1872.

to indorse Greeley and adjourn to the first Monday in August, evidently hoping that when the Liberal convention met, coalition might result; but the convention declared by hisses that it would have none of him.

Union with the Pinchback wing, however, was regarded in an altogether different light, for on the third day a committee of eleven was appointed to confer with a similar committee from the other body,[1] negotiations to be conditioned upon indorsement of Grant and repudiation of Greeley and Warmoth by the latter body.

Meantime in the Pinchback body, a resolution that the convention was not favorable to Greeley and Brown had caused the greatest excitement, and had been carried only by a very close vote. Hence, the condition of the Packard convention was read in deathly silence, followed by shouts of "never" and denunciatory speeches. A curt refusal was sent back, coupled with resolutions for the other body to act upon. When they were rejected and returned at the evening session, intense excitement prevailed and the evidence of Greeley and Grant factions became more conspicuous than before. The body suddenly decided to adjourn to New Orleans with the result that the next day a steamer brought about half the original number to Mechanics Institute, where they vented their spleen in resolutions condemnatory of the custom-house factionists for having betrayed the Republican party, and refused to be bound by their acts, or to support their candidates. Without making any nominations, they adjourned to August 9, unless sooner convened by the Central Committee.

Meanwhile the custom-house faction at Baton Rouge proceeded to make its nominations: W. P. Kellogg for governor and C. C. Antoine, a negro, for lieutenant-governor. A long series of resolutions was adopted, indorsing

[1] President Campbell had opened the convention with a speech for harmony between the two wings.

the platform and nominations of the National convention, approving the resolutions of the executive committee of November, 1871, and lauding the party as a whole.[1]

The Liberals were left in April when their five hundred adherents constituted scarcely the germ of a party. It had been kept alive only by the most strenuous exertions. A small body of perhaps thirty met in the governor's office on April 23, to consider what action might be taken with regard to the Cincinnati convention. Even the German Liberals, a somewhat more vigorous group, under the leadership of the editor of the *Gazette*, were hardly a help to Warmoth, because they refused to coalesce, and decided at their meeting on April 26, when about a hundred men were present, to send eight delegates of their own to Cincinnati.[2] Yet one hundred and twenty-five men, one-fifth of whom were negroes, made their way North to the convention under the lead of Warmoth. By May 14, the party had created a State central committee, but efforts to claim prominent men as adherents by placing them on the committee met only in most cases with refusal. May 15, the *National Republican* asserted that there were but fifty Liberals in the State. June 12, the *Republican*, their organ, published an address to the people, asking them to elect delegates to a nominating convention to meet in August. Their paper represented fourteen thousand votes as cast in New Orleans for delegates,[3] but the *Picayune* cited three thousand as nearer the truth.[4]

[1] Even here some were sufficiently disgruntled with the choice of Kellogg to create a new faction—negroes under the lead of Carter—which held a mass meeting in Lafayette Square, June 29, and strove to link hands with Warmoth.

They declared that Kellogg's nomination had been brought about by fraud. Sen. Repts., 42 Cong., 3 Sess., No. 457, 284.

[2] *National Republican*, April 27, 1872.

[3] *Republican*, July 23, 1872.

[4] July 23. It claimed that not one-fifth of the white people voted.

Numbers of the Germans, however, undoubtedly followed the Liberal movement and the German *Gazette* finally supported Warmoth, though professedly independent, until it was dubbed by the Republican press "the German edition of Warmoth's Republican." The party had also a rather strong parish press.[1]

August 3, a rally to drum up interest seems to have been a complete failure. Only about two thousand men, the roughest class of the city, appeared in the parade; the leaders were not allowed to speak but were hissed from the stand and obliged to retire in their pomp to the St. Charles Hotel. The crowd cheered for McEnery and flung out disparaging jeers until the Liberals had to abandon the fight. Some speeches were made in the rotunda of the hotel at eleven o'clock.[2]

The convention opened August 5, in New Orleans, many parishes wholly unrepresented, some by aliens, it was charged, and only a few by respectable men. A committee of thirteen was appointed to confer with the Pinchback, Reform, and Democratic committees, but the convention dragged to the fifth day, many meanwhile

[1] The following parish sheets were known as Liberal papers: Shreveport *Times*, St. Mary *Register*, Houme *Patriot*, Baton Rouge *Journal*, the Donaldson *Chief*, Thibodaux *Sentinel*, Baton Rouge *Advocate*, Alexandria *Democrat*, Baton Rouge *Gazette-Comet*, and Clinton Parish *Democrat*; and the following subsidized by parish printing: Opelousas *Journal*, St. James *Louisianian*, Mansfield *Reporter*, Claiborne *Advocate*, Bossier *Banner*, Franklin *Sun*, St. Tammany *Observer*, Iberia *Banner*, St. John *Meschacebe*, Assumption *Pioneer*, Natchitoches *Times*, Minden *Democrat*, Morehouse *Conservative*, and *Union Record*. The *Republican* held that there were fifty Liberal clubs with a membership of fourteen thousand in all.

[2] The transparencies are indicative of the humor of the time. One represented a disconsolate individual struggling in the waters of the last ditch; another was a green frog's head, peeping out of the ditch; Grant's scepter—a bayonet, dripping with blood; a large frog with staring eyes represented the Last Ditchers before and after the convention; a fish's head, Grant's minister of state; a jug of whiskey and a box of cigars— "Grant's Councillors." *Republican*, August 4.

leaving in disgust before the conference committee reported its failure. Finally, on the sixth day, tired of
waiting for a union which refused to materialize, D. B.
Penn was put forward by the body as its choice for governor,[1] Young for lieutenant-governor, and resolutions
indorsing Warmoth[2] as the next United States Senator
were unanimously adopted.   There can be no doubt but
that the sole object of the convention was to effect an
alliance with one or other of the parties, but the object
was not attained until some time after the convention
had adjourned.   For months Warmoth had been reaching
out in every direction, deterred by no scruples or resent-
ments, rebuffed by no snubs or insults, conscious that his
power over the election machinery could be made effective
only in alliance with one or other of the large parties
of the State,[3] for even his organ admitted that the "Penn
ticket had not been received with that favor which the
authors of the movement expected."   And his power of
control was not to be estimated lightly, for politicians
later bore testimony to a Congressional committee that it
was worth twenty thousand votes.[4]

Through his organ he said in the early spring that he
would support Grant if the latter would pledge himself to
abandon the policy previously pursued by him in Louisi-

[1] *National Republican*, August 4.

[2] There is little doubt but that as late as August 1, Warmoth still had a
hankering for his office, as his paper on that date lauded him as the unanimous choice of the Liberals for governor.

[3] A clever cartoon entitled "Political Yeller Dorg, seeking a New Bone,"
appeared about March 17.   A dog, with Warmoth's name on the collar,
Warmoth's head on his shoulders, and his tail tucked between his legs, had
run his snout abruptly against the pitchfork of "public opinion" held firmly
by the Goddess of Liberty.   From the Democratic window came the words:
"The treacherous cur cannot find a bone here."   In one corner Schurz
asked anxiously of Sumner, "Shall we take him in?"   "If we do, he will
keep up a constant howl, and steal every bone," was Sumner's reply.

[4] Sen. Repts., 42 Cong., 3 Sess., No. 457, xliv.

ana[1]; he assured the Republican party in the State that their quarrel could be readily arranged because there was really no principle upon which they were not united.[2] His enemies alleged that even late in March he made propositions to the President for a compromise but was snubbed by Grant[3]; but by April 10, he committed himself definitely to the Liberals by urging the election of delegates to Cincinnati and by attacking the National administration without reserve.[4] But even as late as July 26, his organ threatened that unless the union ticket of the Democratic and Reform parties was abandoned to rally to his support, he would go over to the Republican camp.

Although Warmoth was spurned by the Democrats at first, the current of interest which forced them to him is easily traced. The words of the *Bee* may be taken as indicative of the original feeling of the more sincere of that party.

The words bargain and coalition and compromise are thoroughly revolting to us. We pray for success, and hope for it, and our State most sadly needs it; but we cannot turn aside from the old broad beaten path. We have all faith in principle—we have no faith at all in finessing, in cunning bargains, in astute games of policy or in specious expediency.[5]

But as early as March the question of coalition with him was openly discussed in Democratic papers.[6] The

[1] *Republican*, April 6. [2] *Ibid.*, April 7, 1872.
[3] *National Republican*, March 23, 1872.
[4] *Ibid.*, April 11, 1872.
[5] The *Picayune* of June 4 urged the party to avoid all entangling alliances that might interfere with this vitally needed deliverance. The *Bee* felt, without reference to the moral aspect, that an alliance with Warmoth would "do more harm than good." June 2. As late as July 18, the *Picayune* opposed Warmoth, though to the Liberals, who were such from anti-Grantism, it bade "God-speed in their Federal contest."
[6] The *Picayune*. "We hear it stated that certain politicians who were

Times hailed Warmoth's circular of April 10 with joy, as it would create an irreconcilable breach among the Republicans of which that paper felt that the Democrats should take advantage.[1]   So patent was the trend after a union ratification meeting of the Cincinnati ticket on May 25,[2] that the Republican papers made constant assaults on the Democrats of corrupt bargain whereby the Democrats bartered the Senatorship to Warmoth for his control of the election machinery.[3]   We have seen the growing tolerance of the idea of union manifesting itself in the conventions.   Every art that Warmoth possessed, direct as well as indirect, was plied on the two conventions June 3 and 4, but without immediate success. McEnery himself was accused of expressing "proclivities in and out of the convention to coalesce with the State Liberal Republican movement."[4]   And at a meeting at Shreveport a Democrat dared to voice what became a typical opinion: "One of the newspapers has called the concessions of Reformers and Democrats to Warmoth an infamous alliance.   Well, I am ready for the infamous alliance."[5]

leading men in this State a quarter of a century ago are still working to induce the people to believe that the nomination of Governor Warmoth by the white men of this State for re-election is a political necessity." *Picayune*, March 9. As early as January, 1871, suggestions had come from the Democrats that Warmoth would be available as Democratic candidate for governor in 1872, pursuant to the terms of the bargain which sent West to the Senate, and which would finally dispatch Warmoth to the goal of his ambition.   [1] *Times*, April 10, 1872.

[2] *National Republican*, May 26, 1872.

[3] The *Picayune* also makes this charge, June 6.

[4] On the testimony of a Democrat, *National Republican*, July 4.

[5] The *Times* on August 20 printed the following: "Governor Warmoth's earnest and sincere labors in behalf of the Liberal cause, involving as it did, the abandonment of the Radical party, which up to the latest hours tempted him with its highest honors; his self-abnegation in withdrawing his candidacy upon finding himself likely to impair the harmony necessary to a Liberal success, should be a sufficient guarantee to the fair-minded of

But though rumors of a fusion came out frequently in the Republican press,[1] the Liberal convention came and passed and several weeks elapsed before it became a reality as a result of the negotiations between the several central committees. A meeting of conference committees consisting of seven members from each of the several fusion bodies was held August 27. The final result of their deliberations was compromise based upon the acceptance of a "fusion" ticket, headed by McEnery, which was, with one or two slight modifications, the ticket already accepted by the Democrats and Reformers. The fusion ticket read: For Governor, J. McEnery; Lieutenant-Governor, D. B. Penn ▬▬▬▬▬ (Warmoth party); Attorney-General, H. N. Ogden; Auditor, James Graham; Secretary of State, Samuel Armstead (colored)[2]; and for

---

sincerity in his present objects and motives." See also its issues of August 23 and 27. But the *Bee* consistently objected. On June 2 it called Warmoth a "trickster who will betray them as he has betrayed his own party, or by arguments based upon erroneous and false promises though presented by citizens who, though honorable, err in believing that virtue may triumph by an alliance with vice and that reform may come from a compromise with fraud." As late as August 16 it printed, "Le pouvoir imaginaire que l'on s'est plu a prêter au gouverneur Warmoth avait induit en erreur un grand nombre de citoyens respectables qui croyaient honnêtement que le parti conservateur de la Louisiane ne pouvait réussir sans l'intervention du gouverneur." And even August 25 it held, "Si les libéraux s'en tiennent aux prétentions qu'ils ont déjà formulées, il n'y a aucun espoir de fusion."

[1] *National Republican*, August 24.

[2] The appalling ignorance of this preacher-candidate for one of the highest offices of State is revealed in a Congressional inquiry:

Q. Do you know of any commissions having gone out of your office? (for election). A. No, sir, I do not.

Q. Would you know it if they had gone out?

A. I don't know. . . .

Q. Have you ever read your commission?

A. No, sir, I don't think I have.

Q. You can read.

A. Oh! yes, sir. Sen. Repts., 42 Cong., 3 Sess., No. 457, 499 and 501.

11

Superintendent of Public Education, R. M. Lusher.[1]
The principal concession to the Liberals was the acceptance of an electoral ticket in favor of Greeley and Brown.

The Republican press rained abuse upon the Democrats
for their alliance. The editorial of the *National Republican* is particularly striking:

> Warmoth may not be a fiend incarnate, but the Democrats
> have made him nothing less in the eyes of their children and
> the world, and as they now swallow him, their protestations
> that he has become an angel without changing will be of no
> avail. They stand stultified before mankind. He has not
> risen to them, but they have sunk to his level—aye, to his very
> feet! They have become not merely so bad as he is, but as
> bad as they represented him to be.[2]

Last of all, in point of time, came the fusion of the two
wings of the Republican party. Ever since early May
negotiations had been going on between the two factions
without success.[3] The Pinchback body, it will be remembered, had adjourned on June 22, at Mechanics
Institute without naming a ticket. For the third time
the convention assembled on August 9, almost a colored-
men's convention. Almost at once a committee was
appointed to confer with the Republican Executive
Committee. After negotiations, prolonged through two
days beause the Packard wing virtually asked that
its ticket he indorsed without any concessions on its
part, the committee recommended the nomination of a
straight ticket of their own. There was no hope of union
with the Warmoth party, for a substitute motion to adopt
the Liberal platform was greeted with hisses, cries, and

[1] *Annual Cyclopedia*, 1872, 480.
[2] Sept. 26, 1872. See also its issues of Oct. 13, 24, etc., and German
Gazette, Sept. 10, for mild sarcasm.
[3] For details of the negotiations see the *National Republican*, May 30.

groans in a perfect fever of excitement.[1]   But Chairman Campbell voiced the spirit of a strong faction when he said:

I tell you the only thing you can do is to make a trade, and it must be either with the custom-house party or the Liberals— I tell you a straight ticket is a fizzle, a humbug and nobody believes in it. . . .   If you join the Liberal party your action will do more toward the exercise of your civil rights than all the civil rights bills that can be enacted.[2]

Pinchback declared for Grant and the Republican ticket but spoke kindly of Warmoth.   He showed more political perspicacity than some of his Northern friends when he declared:

If I thought we could secure a Republican government in Louisiana by supporting Mr. Greeley, I would support him, but after a careful observation, I tell you, fellow citizens, if you wish a Republican government and the success of the Republican party, you can only secure that under the Grant and Wilson ticket.   Everybody knows how bitter I am against the Custom-house and its party; but I tell you, my friends, if it is necessary to secure the success of the Republican party I will swallow it—

and amid tremendous applause he moved the indorsement of the Kellogg ticket.
    With great enthusiasm the convention on the fourth and last day indorsed the Philadelphia platform, and pledged itself loyally to support Grant and Wilson.   It then

[1] *National Republican*, Aug. 13.
[2] Campbell left the hall followed by all the office holders amid hisses and jeers.   The bolters organized in the Senate chamber, twenty-seven parishes and eleven wards of the city being represented, for a two days' session. Whether the split was justly laid at Warmoth's door (*National Republican*, August 13 and 14, 1872) or not, he reaped the benefit, for the faction was added to the Liberals.

proceeded to the nomination of a full State ticket and put
Pinchback, amid wild acclamations, at the head, with A.
B. Harris in the second place.   The resolutions reaffirmed
those adopted at Turner Hall, August 9, 1871, supporting
the National Republican party.   The State committee
was also authorized to continue the negotiations with the
Packard Central Committee with power to make such
changes in the ticket as were necessary to gain the object
sought.   The Packard wing offered the Pinchback wing
three places on the ticket but the difficulty lay in which
three until Pinchback, on August 27, to reconcile the
differences, withdrew, when Lewis on the other side,
withdrew from his candidacy as Congressman in favor of
the former.   At a meeting of the conference committee
that day members agreed on a ticket, keeping Kellogg and
Antoine at the head and agreed on a new State Central
Executive Committee to be formed by the consolidation
of the two committees.   The action was approved by
both central executive committees, which consolidated
September 10 by the election of Packard as president and
Pinchback as first vice-president.[1]   The fusion Republican ticket then stood: For Governor, W. P. Kellogg
(Custom-house); Lieutenant-Governor, C. C. Antoine
(Custom-house, colored); Secretary, P. G. Deslondes
(Pinchback); Auditor, Charles Clinton (Custom-house);
Attorney-General, A. P. Field (Custom-house); Superintendent of Education, Brown (colored, Pinchback); and
for Congressman at Large, Pinchback (colored).   The
large number of Federal officeholders on this ticket should
not escape notice: Kellogg was sitting in the National
Senate, the auditor was a sub-treasurer at New Orleans,
while five candidates for the Assembly held Federal

[1] *National Republican*, Sep. 12, 1872.
The organs of the two respective factions, the *Louisianian* and *National
Republican*, flapped their wings lustily Aug. 22.

positions.[1]   Thus had the political sky cleared until there were but two tickets in the field, headed respectively by Kellogg and McEnery.[2]

[1] Sen. Repts., 42 Cong., 3 Sess., No. 457, 1082.
[2] A. P. U., American Protective Union, a white man's party to repress negro pretensions to political recognition, spread until by October it counted seven thousand members. It appointed its men to run as delegates in the wards for primaries and was so well-disciplined as to elect a majority in the conventions.   Hence, the Fusion ticket was in the main A. P. U. members.

CHAPTER VIII

The Campaign and Election of 1872

THE campaign was accompanied by very few disorders compared with the election of 1868. Sporadic instances, of course, are to be found; a White League was organized in St. Mary Parish on July 13, for the protection, as its name suggests, "of our own race against the daily increasing encroachments of the negro and we are determined to use our best endeavors to purge our legislative, judicial, and ministerial offices from such a horde of miscreants as now assume to lord it over us."[1] The country press resorted to bold threats and warnings to the colored people. The Natchitoches *Vindicator* printed the following on July 18:

On the other hand, should you imagine that the teaching of your former rulers is correct and you elect to attempt, for it will only be an attempt, to continue their rule—then you must take the consequences. For we tell you now, and let it be distinctly remembered that you have fair warning, that we intend to carry the State of Louisiana in November next or she will be a military territory.[2]

A highly inflammatory letter signed by two hundred and twenty Republicans came in from Caddo to the governor

[1] *Republican*, August 13, 1872. This was now a Liberal paper under Warmoth, but it consolidated after the election with the *National Republican*, which had started in the summer as a Grant organ.
[2] Quoted in a government document.

in August[1]; a Democratic rally in New Orleans late the same month provoked a few shots[2]; and the report of a Ku-Klux outrage in Carroll Parish on October 8 furnished capital for Republican papers, but turned out to be merely the destruction of a Republican printing-press.[3] Hence, the temper of the State is seen to have been uneasy, ready to break out upon the least provocation. But, fortunately, the provocation does not seem to have arisen, and complaints took, for the most part, a different turn.

The registration was to begin September 2, to continue until October 26, but almost immediately complaints began to be heard that the registrars were, almost without exception, Warmoth tools, and that the appointment of registrars was being unduly delayed.[4] Disputes between United States inspectors and State registrars arose, which led to a definition by Supervisor Blanchard of the powers of Federal commissioners, in which he guarded State rights as far as possible.[5]

A few days before the election Blanchard issued private instructions to the effect that commissioners of election should receive no votes or affidavits supplied by

[1] "Great God! what sort of a government is this? Shall we live in peace, or shall we go to war? If the latter alternative is forced upon us, we have nothing to defend ourselves with. . . . Great God! Governor, is it not possible to have something done that will put a stop to the monstrous acts of the men who have determined to inaugurate a reign of terror in order to accomplish their political ends?" New Orleans *Republican*, August 9.

[2] *National Republican*, August 27.

[3] *Ibid.*, Oct. 15.

[4] Pointe Coupee complained September 23 that they were still without a registrar in that parish. *Ibid.*, Sept. 29.

[5] A test case came before United States Commissioner Weller, September 12. For the definition of their duties see the *National Republican*, Sept. 13: The Federal commissioner might arrest for offenses committed in his immediate presence; he had a right to inspect the books during the hours fixed by law; but he had no authority to copy, make lists, or claim the inspection of certificates of registration.

the Radical party unless the person offering to vote was known to have been wrongfully refused; and what was more important, that after the election they should count first the votes cast for Presidential electors and members of Congress on separate tally lists, completing the statement of voters of each poll; they should then close the box and reseal it until the National count was completed; then count the State and parish votes, bearing in mind the fact that United States supervisors of election and deputy marshals "have no right whatever to scrutinize, inspect, or be present at the counting of the State and parish votes."[1]   Packard, in behalf of his party, requested the appointment of one Republican commissioner of election at each poll, but the request was refused.   But he was himself equally partisan in his appointments.   He placed one to four special deputy marshals at the polls in every parish and over six hundred in New Orleans, but confined himself exclusively to his own party.   Furthermore, in issuing instructions concerning the supervision of the vote for State and local officers, he gave directions only to the United States supervisor of his party.[2]

The election occurred November 4, one day before the time set in other States.   All parties were urged by their respective leaders to preserve peace on election day. "Let no word or act of ours give pretext for violence" seemed to be the motto of each party.   Until the Republicans began to fear defeat, it was admitted by all parties and by all the newspapers that the largest vote ever cast was polled on that date, and that it was as peaceable and fair as any ever held in the State.[3]   Even the *National*

[1] House Exe. Doc., 42 Cong., 3 Sess., No. 91, 12.
[2] Sen. Repts., 42 Cong., 3 Sess., No. 457, lxiv.
[3] *National Republican*, Nov. 5, 1872, and *Republican*, Nov. 19.   The *Republican* assured the President that no people were ever more orderly or obedient to law than the people of New Orleans and Louisiana in the

Republican pronounced it a "remarkably quiet and orderly election."

The size of the vote was not in itself indicative of fraud. The total vote for governor, exclusive of three parishes from which only irregular and informal returns were received, summed up to 128,402; while the total vote in 1870 was only 106,542.[1] But several facts contributed to bring out a larger number of voters than before: the disfranchising clause of the constitution, although abrogated at the election of 1870, became operative for the first time at this election and might reasonably account for a great part of the increase; the census of 1870, taken by men, none too intelligent, was gathered in the summer when many of the white citizens were absent[2]; and there is some evidence that the white people took a more general interest in this canvass than before since reconstruction,[3] due to the fact that they now thought they saw some hope of success. Then, too, the Radical party was losing its small element of respectable Southern whites through a natural divergence of feeling over the negro, while some of the better carpet-baggers were returning North. On the other hand, it was by no means a safe method of procedure to count the negroes solidly for the Republican ticket—or substantially so. It is impossible to say how many colored people supported the Fusion ticket, but considerable numbers were to be found, especially in the northwestern part of the

---

State and Federal election recently held, and that the relations between the races were kindly. Admitted by leading Republican papers as late as Dec. 9 and even Jan. 24, 1873. Even Packard regarded it in a majority of the parishes "as fair as you usually have it in any State election." Sen. Repts., 42 Cong., 3 Sess., No. 457, 913.

[1] House Exe. Doc., 42 Cong., 3 Sess., No. 91, 82.
[2] Sen. Repts., No. 457, 282.
[3] Evidence of McMillan. *Ibid.*, 282–3.

State[1]; cases arose like that of Tangipahoa Parish, where the negroes were apathetic because of the personal un-popularity of the Republican candidate[2]; and many voters, so densely ignorant as were the negroes, could easily be carried over to support, to some degree at least, the Liberal cause. [3]

But by November 7 the Republican papers began to be full of charges of trickery, fraud, and intimidation in many of the country parishes. [4] Although charges of violence during registration and election were brought against the Democrats in some ten parishes, [5] and although the Democrats, in turn, charged two instances of negro rioting just after election, these cases were exceptional rather than general, [6] and were based upon affidavits, some of which, at least, were open to question. It is noticeable that most of these parishes lie in the northern part of the State. A large body of voters of Bossier Parish swore that a body of Ku-Klux, commissioned as constables, practised wholesale intimidation throughout the parish under threats of reviving the massacre of four years before[7]; St. Landry lay readily open to the same charge, because of her previous record; in Grant two hundred and fifty

[1] Sen. Repts., 42 Cong., 3 Sess., No. 457, 702.
[2] Testimony of a Republican Federal commissioner. *Ibid.*, 570–1.
[3] Even Armstead, Secretary of State, did not know how McEnery came to supplant Penn on the Liberal ticket, nor why he himself was changed from candidate for Congress to Secretary of State. *Ibid.*, 496 *ff.*
[4] See *National Republican*, Nov. 12, Lafourche *Times*, Nov. 9, Providence *Republican*, Nov. 9.
[5] Caddo, East Baton Rouge, Jackson, Bossier, St. Landry, Livingston, Grant, St. Tammany, Webster, and St. Helena. House Exe. Doc., 42 Cong., 2 Sess., No. 91, 124, 128; Sen. Repts., No. 457, 314. The writer found evidence for ten. See Map II.
[6] Terrebonne and Iberville. These the writer believes are trustworthy but not characteristic. House Exe. Doc., No. 91, 128.
[7] *Ibid.*, 126–7. I should question the reliability of most testimony from Bossier, as investigation shows the evidence from there vitiated by fraud.

negroes were represented as deprived of their votes, while others were compelled against their wills to vote for Greeley.[1] It is very likely that a number in Webster and Union Parishes were coerced by threats of employers. Credible also are the allegations in St. Helena,[2] St. Tammany, and Jackson Parishes,[3] where Democrats were placed under heavy bonds for participation in Ku-Klux activities.

Some violence was undoubtedly practised toward United States supervisors by State registrars, who drove them from the polls under threats, made serious in one or two instances.[4] Especially were the National supervisors excluded from the count after the ballots for electors had been examined.[5] A negro supervisor of Caddo related how the State supervisor refused to recognize the former's authority and forcibly ejected him outside the polling-room. When he took his station by a window, the commissioner cried, "This d— nigger has got his book and is taking down the names and numbers of the voters." When he still held his ground, though the Democrats strove to drive him off, he was abusively ordered away, quiet being restored only by the arrival of a Federal soldier. At the close of the election he was not allowed to see the box closed,[6] but he persisted in following the State official when he started off with the box, though persecuted for three miles by the threats and curses of a crowd of men who rode around him.[7] But isolated cases certainly do not establish the fact of general disorder.[8]

---

[1] House Exe. Doc., 42 Cong., 3 Sess. No. 91, 128.   [2] *Ibid.*, 128–9.   [3] *Ibid.*
[4] Two supervisors were wounded in Jackson Parish, House Exe. Doc., 42 Cong., 3 Sess., No. 91, 128.
[5] Affidavits to that effect were filed from Caddo, *ibid.*, 124; from St. Mary, 126; Pointe Coupee, 127; Madison, 127; and Webster, 128. Complaints to that effect are too general to be disregarded: 112, 113, 127, and 128.   [6] *Ibid.*, 112–3.   [7] *Ibid.*, 113.
[8] See Maps I and II. A comparison of the disorder of 1872 with that of 1868 shows a certain parallelism in location, but much narrower extent.

But the great feature which virtually vitiated the election in parts of the State was fraud, fraud on the Democratic side offset by false affidavits on the Republican, until it is almost impossible to determine the truth.   It took many forms.   In the first place, polls were too few, were placed at remote and inconvenient points, were improperly distributed, and not properly announced. In Caddo Parish, for instance, two boxes were provided for a remote, thinly-settled white section, where less than two hundred votes were polled, while only four were allotted for the remaining three thousand votes of the parish; in Shreveport only two boxes instead of the usual five were provided; in Plaquemines Parish the six polls were all distributed in the lower part of the parish where were settled the whites, while there was not a single poll for the negroes in the upper part where were congested more than one-half the voters; and in Bossier, the most conspicuous example, the four polls, at which it would have been impossible to cast the full registered vote of two thousand three hundred and eight-two votes in a single day, lay in the northern half of the parish where not more than one hundred and ninety voters lived.[1] The result of such distribution was that many men had to go from thirty to fifty miles, usually on foot, to cast their ballots.[2]   The inconvenience of the polls could only be the result of labored study.   Besides being too few, they were deliberately placed at points remote and well-nigh inaccessible.   Some were on islands in lakes and bayous,

[1] Sen. Repts., 42 Cong., 3 Sess., No. 457, 315.   See Map III.   In Natchitoches, a parish of eighteen hundred square miles, where there never had been less than eleven polls, four were opened for this election.
[2] In St. Bernard each voter had to go an average of fourteen miles, 171.
In Bossier the river front from the poll at Benton to the most southern portion of the parish was more than a hundred miles, most of which included the most populous part of the valley.   Note Map III.

some in log-cabins, some in the pine hills,[1] and one in a fodder-house, three miles from the place announced.   In Natchitoches, where the last named case occurred, notice had been given that a poll would be opened at Beulah Church, but the Federal supervisor finally found the box at noon on election day in a fodder-house, three miles from the church.   The Democrats gathered about the church all day to inform their friends in whispers, as they arrived, to take a certain unknown road.   The supervisor finally followed some Democrats and found the box.[2]   The announcement of the location of the polls was often delayed or concealed.   The official publication for New Orleans did not appear until November 3, in many parishes not until the morning of the election, when Federal supervisors were sometimes denied information and misled.   The supervisors in Bossier and Caddo Parishes refused to give notice where the polls would be opened, despite repeated demands upon them.[3]

A second group of frauds took the form of illegal hours and places of registration and election.   One supervisor was accused of closing his office at three o'clock while fifty men were still waiting for their certificates[4]; another of not keeping his official hours strictly; from one poll came complaints of not opening until seven-thirty[5]; from another, of votes cast by candlelight before the

[1] In Natchitoches, House Exe. Doc., 42 Cong., 3 Sess., No. 91, 4.
[2] *Ibid.*, 112.
[3] A supervisor in Bossier called on the State official on the morning before election to ask the location of the two new polls which that official was supposed to open.   The reply came that that was a secret.   Upon imperious demand for a reply, he was told that only the original four would be opened.   In haste he sent word to the extreme southern part that there would be no poll in that section.   By daybreak many Republicans passed the nearest polls to give their more tardy friends a chance.   Sen. Repts., 42 Cong., 3 Sess., No. 457, 316.   In St. Mary no announcement was made.
[4] House Exe. Doc., 42 Cong., 3 Sess., No. 91, 111.   East Baton Rouge.
[5] *Ibid.*, 115.

hour for opening[1]; from two parishes came charges of serious delay—as much as seven and nineteen days respectively—in beginning registration.[2]   A supervisor in Rapides Parish systematically obstructed the registration of colored men, dodging them and refusing to appear at the time and places advertised.[3]

A third source of complaints was wilful delay and refusals to accept registrations or votes.   Complaints of unfairness were admitted as "well-founded" by a Last-Ditch Democrat, while the letter of a Fusionist admits that it was not the fault of Republicans that they could not comply with requirements.[4]   Much delay was achieved by the peremptory refusal of supervisors to permit clerks to make entries[5]; again, the supervisor deliberately frittered time[6]; in Bossier almost every voter was challenged[7]; at one point every negro was sworn as to the correctness of his papers so that a large number did not have time to vote; indeed, the process of delay became such a fine art at one point in Bossier that only four hundred and fifteen votes were received in twelve hours and more than three hundred Republicans deprived of the opportunity to vote.   But the complainant tersely adds, he had heard of only two Democrats at any poll in the parish who did not vote.[8] Refusals of ballots were made under various pretexts: a number of men were disfranchised in New Orleans as they were unable to read the notice which charged them with

[1] House Exe. Doc., 42 Cong., 3 Sess., No. 91, 112.
[2] Ibid., 128–9.   [3] Ibid., 125.
[4] National Republican, Nov. 16.
[5] House Repts., 43 Cong., 2 Sess., No. 101, Part ii., 34.
[6] House Exe. Doc., No. 91, 126.
[7] Another scheme to deprive negroes of their vote, which I have seen nowhere in print, was told me by several old residents of the State.   Negroes in the country were kept moving from poll to poll by the statement, "You don't belong in this ward; you must go to Gold-dust," etc., until the poor negro had walked away his chance to vote.
[8] Sen. Repts., 42 Cong., 3 Sess., No. 457, 317.

fraud[1]; for failure to register[2]; for informalities in registration papers[3]; because they did not "appear" of age, though Democrats under age and unnaturalized citizens were accepted[4]; or for registration in another ward, though no poll had been opened in the voter's own ward.[5] Registration was frequently refused on the pretext of having exhausted the blanks, though they promptly materialized for whites.[6]

Dishonesty in the vote and count constituted another source of fraud. The negroes were duped by counterfeit Democratic tickets, palmed off on their ignorance for Republican ballots.[7] The preparation made by the Democrats for such deception seems conclusive of their intention.[8] Fraudulent registration papers were voted by minors and foreigners; ballot-stuffing occurred not only in the ordinary way of inserting one hundred tissue paper ballots as a single ballot, but in some cases boxes had been prepared beforehand[9]; double and triple voting occurred—indeed, one name in New Orleans was said

[1] House Exe. Doc., 42 Cong., 3 Sess., No. 91, 129.

[2] In contrast with this rigid adherence to rules stands the case of a man whose vote for the Fusion ticket was accepted on a registration paper on which the ink was scarcely dry. Sen. Repts., No. 457, 179.

[3] House Exe. Doc., No. 91, 125, 112.

[4] *Ibid.*, 125, 128.

[5] At Ward No. 2 in Natchitoches.

[6] House Exe. Doc., No. 91, 112. We are told that often as many as one hundred negroes were waiting at once.

[7] In Union Parish the Democrats boasted that they had deceived two hundred colored voters. *Ibid.*, 129. The registration also does not seem to have been fair. One hundred voters were registered from a single house in New Orleans.

[8] Packard stated that he had proof of one establishment engaged in printing tickets during the count. It was like the regular Republican ticket, except that there was a private mark on the back, and a small hole in the corner of the blue shield which left a white spot on the printed blank. Sen. Repts., No. 457, 905–6.

[9] House Exe. Doc., No. 91, 64 and 128.

to have been voted seventeen times—and the same
registration papers served for one hundred ballots at
different precincts in Terrebonne.[1] Boxes came in
improperly sealed, or indeed wholly unsealed[2]; the
contents of one box were emptied into another supposed
to be stuffed[3]; and Democratic names were read from
Republican tickets or a Republican ballot slipped under
a Democratic ticket.[4] When the ballots were counted
behind bolted doors as in St. Mary,[5] or in a private room
at an hotel, as at Rapides,[6] or when the boxes did not
arrive at their destination until many days after election,[7]
the presumption is that the alteration of ballots had something to do with the delay. The evidence of tampering
with the ballots is overwhelming. To cite but one case of
many, the experience of the Federal supervisor of East
Baton Rouge may be related. After some dispute with
the State commissioner about where the box should be
taken, they drove together about eight miles from Port
Hudson, when they were stopped by a shot and the State
officer called by name. He declared his intention of
spending the night there, and started off with the box.
Although parties tried to prevent the Federal officer
from following, he did make his way through a lane to a
shanty about sixty yards from the road. But in about
fifteen minutes the commissioner returned, stating that
he would, after all, go to town. Followed by several

[1] Sen. Repts., No. 457, 415.
[2] House Exe. Doc., No. 91, 119.
[3] *Ibid.*, 128.
[4] *Ibid.*, 112.
[5] *Ibid.*, 126.
[6] The supervisor followed the State officer to the hotel and learned that
he was locked in one of the rooms. On demand the former was admitted
but told that no interference would be tolerated. *Ibid.*, 114.
[7] *Ibid.*, 118. One arrived as late as Nov. 29. Sen. Repts., No. 457,
1042.

men on horseback, they reached the court-house only half after midnight. [1]

Irregularity and tardiness in signing the returns arouse, to say the least, suspicion. In Carroll they were signed fifteen days later than Warmoth swore he had opened them; in Lafourche, one hundred miles from New Orleans, they were signed the same day they were opened; in Grant, three hundred miles distant, on the 13th, one day before they were opened. Finally, the returns from Madison, Grant, Pointe Coupee, and East Baton Rouge would appear to be forgeries, as all the signatures seem to be by the same pen. [2]

The last device was, according to the allegation of the Republicans, frauds committed purposely by the Demo-

---

[1] House Exe. Doc., No. 91, 65. I have selected this case as probably trustworthy since the actual personal testimony of the supervisor is on record. The following charges speak for themselves: The candidate in St. Mary for the Senate was returned with only 100 Republican majority, when the Republican candidate for Congress, whose vote was counted in the presence of the Federal inspector, received 500 votes. One supervisor of Union Parish knew that 783 colored and 80 white men intended to vote the Republican ticket but only 489 ballots were so counted. Another supervisor saw 460 Republican votes cast as against 63 Democratic, but during the night the 460 votes "melted to 20"; the National supervisors in Jefferson Parish swore that 500 Republican ballots of a peculiar device were put into the box, yet, when opened, it contained 555 straight Liberal tickets so that even the State supervisor cried, "Here is a palpable fraud." And a Republican candidate for justice of the peace in Pointe Coupee had his tickets written in pencil, yet at the count they came out written in ink with another name. In Grant Parish the box was alleged to have been wrested from the United States supervisor, kept in a private residence all night, and showed next day unmistakable signs of having been broken open and blunderingly repaired. A hole was left through which to stick additional bogus ballots, if necessary. House Exe. Doc., No. 91, 26, 129, 127, 128, 113, and 128.

I have ventured to cite these cases as they seem from the evidence on record to be fairly reliable and because nearly all the Federal supervisors complained similarly.

[2] Partisan testimony, it must be pointed out. *Globe*, 42 Cong., 3 Sess., 1869.

12

crats in Republican sections in order to cast out the whole poll.[1] The entire vote of Iberia, St. Martin, and St. James was thrown out on these grounds. And in Terrebonne the fact remains that the supervisor, after counting eight boxes, which turned out heavy Republican majorities, resigned and left in the night, thus creating a pretext for throwing out the entire vote on the ground of a technical irregularity.[2]

Against the charges of fraud and dishonesty laid against the Democrats must be arrayed the evidence of a resort to trickery on the part of the Republicans in their affidavits. Previous to the election, one man asserted, it was common talk in the marshal's office that it made no difference how the State went, that they would get up affidavits after the election to gain the victory.[3] One of their tools took 25,000 affidavits, printed before the election,[4] to Bossier Parish and brought back 1900,[5] while a certain Jacques took 2000, which had been signed in blank by an obliging judge, to the Red River district. Jacques's methods in Plaquemines are illuminating. He read the affidavit form to about three hundred men who had not voted, because of indifference or because it was too far to the polls, and excited their anger by telling them that they had been cheated out of their vote. He then took their names and signed the forms at his leisure, on the ground "that they regarded that as voting." As this method did not yield large enough returns, he got a thousand more names from the poll-book of 1870, under the orders of General Sypher, who, as a Congressional

---

[1] The colored registered majority in Iberville was thus annihilated. House Exe. Doc., No. 91, 127.

[2] *Ibid.*, 128–9.

[3] Testimony of Jacques. Sen. Repts., 42 Cong., 3 Sess., No. 457, 530.

[4] Admitted to be true by Packard. *Ibid.*, 903, *i. e.*, that such affidavits were prepared.   [5] *Ibid.*, 535.

candidate, had some interest in the election.[1]   Whether
the men were dead or had moved away made little difference.   So notorious was the dishonesty on these affidavits
that it is said Bovee, on receiving the affidavits in the
presence of the Lynch returning-board, expressed his
appreciation by the words, "Jacques you are a hell of a
fellow," while Lynch was in the habit, when he met him,
of asking laughingly if Plaquemines had yet quit voting.[2]
A United States commissioner found everything "fair"
in Tangipahoa Parish, but the Republican representative
declared that that would not do.   "That will defeat us;
we have got to get testimony."   And so the two started
out and procured a list of names which the commissioner
used later as sworn affidavits until he had sufficient to
overcome the adverse majority against him.[3]   This
witness, when brought before the Congressional committee, admitted frankly that his report was "mythical."[4]

Jacques's testimony is a commentary on Louisiana
politics.   He affirmed that forgery was so common that
it was done without persons thinking anything about it
and drew a fine distinction as to the purpose involved.
"If a man signs another man's name for the sake of
money or anything of that kind, then we look upon that
as forgery, but it is not so in political matters."[5]   He
admitted that his conduct was criminal but never thought
anything of it as it was being done by every registrar in
the State, and he regarded "political tricks as all fair and

---

[1] He testified: "General Sypher wanted me to extend it to 3500 if the
registration books would allow it.   There were 4000 names on the books.
'Can't you make 3500 on that?' was Sypher's query.   'The books ought
to bear it.' "   Sen. Repts., 42 Cong., 3 Sess., No. 457, 529.
[2] Testimony of Jacques.   *Ibid.*, 528.
[3] *Ibid.*, 563–71.   Testimony of Barkdull.
[4] *Ibid.*, 515, 565.
[5] *Ibid.*, 541–2.

square.''[1]   A part of the colloquy with the Federal in-
vestigators is interesting:

> Were you aware that it was forgery in every instance?
> I am aware that it is probably.
> Were you aware at that time that you were committing
> the crime of forgery in the case of every one of these sig-
> natures?
> No.
> Are you aware of it now?
> I don't think I am.[2]

In the face of the conflicting testimony and the differing
opinions of the Congressional committee, it is extremely
difficult to decide upon the truth.   The following facts
can, however, I believe, be safely regarded as established:
There was but little accusation of unfairness brought
against the city election; but notorious frauds were
charged in twenty-four country parishes, and established, probably, in the parishes indicated by Packard,
who had unusual sources of information through his
position as chairman of the State Executive Committee
and through his thousands of subordinates scattered
through the State and who was, moreover, reasonable in
his accusations.[3]

---

[1] Sen. Repts., 42 Cong., 3 Sess., No. 457, 553. Jacques probably
betrayed Sypher because the former was not rewarded with the custom-
house position promised, but there is an absolute openness about his
evidence which sounds true and the committee, which had the advantage
of his personal presence, did not question the truth of his revelations.

[2] *Ibid.*, 523.

[3] The parishes concerning which Packard had no doubts were generally
those against which others brought charges: Pointe Coupee, Iberville,
Grant, Jefferson, St. Tammany, Catahoula, Lafourche, Claiborne, St.
Martin, Iberia, St. James, St. Mary, Terrebonne, and De Soto. See Map
No. II.

CHAPTER IX

A Louisiana Canvass

THE decision on the question of the frauds was a matter for the returning-board. By the law of 1870, under which the election was held, the board was composed, as has already been explained, of the governor, lieutenant-governor, secretary of state, and two Senators—Anderson and Lynch. All the members except Anderson gathered in the governor's office on November 12,[1] two weeks after the election. Business was transacted only so far as to elect the governor president and Lynch secretary of the board. Then a motion was made to declare Pinchback and Anderson ineligible, as they were candidates for office. The governor held this action discourteous in the absence of Anderson, and, with some difficulty, secured a postponement. It is probably true that Warmoth had become satisfied that the board as constituted would not do his bidding and sought time to perfect his schemes for reconstructing it.

On November 13 the same four met again with Chief Justice Ludeling present to administer the oath. Pinchback left after the justice had expressed an opinion adverse to his eligibility. To the utter astonishment of Secretary Herron, Jack Wharton[2] appeared with a brand-

[1] The secondary authorities say November 13, but this is incorrect as the minutes prove. See Sen. Repts., 42 Cong., 3 Sess., No. 457, 779.
[2] He had already taken his oath of office to Judge Cooley at eleven o'clock that morning. *Ibid.*, 725.

new commission as secretary of state, and claimed a seat
on the returning-board.   Herron made an effort to move
that General Longstreet and Judge Hawkins be elected
to fill the vacant places, but the governor stopped him by
declaring that he no longer had any right to act, proposing
instead the names of Hatch and Du Ponte.[1]   The Lynch
minutes record that Lynch and Herron voted aye, and,
constituting a majority of the board, had thus elected
their candidates.   But the governor put his motion and
declared it carried by the votes of Wharton and himself.
Although Mr. Lynch, who was reading the order of Herron's suspension, did not vote at all,[2] Herron declared
that he had voted in the negative.   Hatch and Du Ponte
were immediately summoned and sworn in by Judge
Cooley.   Just as the governor began to open the returns,[3]
Lynch retired from the field without protest, taking with
him the still-dazed Herron and the minutes of the previous
day[4] as evidence that he and his colleague constituted
the legal board.   They proceeded to the office of the chief
justice to be sworn in.[5]   The governor's victory called
forth the following outburst from the hostile press:

In his fevered delirium he spits upon all decrees of law, and
spurns every acknowledged rule of social quietude and well-
being.   He strides this little State of ours like a new Colossus,
and his dicta and the acts of his hirelings must be accepted,
he tells us, perforce, as law and gospel.[6]

[1] It is impossible to determine the exact time at which these motions
were put.   House Exe. Doc., 42 Cong., 3 Sess., No. 91, 151.
[2] Some of the witnesses testify that he did not vote at all, which conduct
would be natural because of his preoccupation in reading the order.
[3] The testimony is conflicting, naturally, as to whether the returns were
opened before Lynch and Herron succeeded in leaving the room or not.
The point involved is obvious.
[4] Sen. Repts., 42 Cong., 3 Sess., No. 457, 590.
[5] For the minutes of the returning boards—see *ibid.*, 650 ff.
[6] *National Republican*, Nov. 14, 1872.

In order to understand the tangle of law suits which now ensued, it is necessary to return to the days which immediately followed the closing of the legislative session of 1871. The Assembly had passed, against the protest of the city government and of the citizens, the Crescent City water-works bill which intrusted the city water supply to a private corporation. This bill, with some others, was sent to the governor's home at eleven-thirty Saturday night, where his landlady receipted for them. Warmoth refused to receive them and on Monday suggested to one of the interested members that they be sent for, as he did not receive bills at his residence.[1] The point in question was important: if the bills were considered as delivered before midnight Saturday, he must either sign or veto them before Thursday or they would become law without his signature. The clerk of the House accordingly sent for them and delivered them to the governor's secretary. The legislature adjourned the following Thursday before the five days allowed for executive veto had expired, according to the governor's count.

After obtaining the opinion of the attorney-general that the bill had become law by lapse,[2] Bovee procured from the speaker and lieutenant-governor an imperfect copy of the bill, even though the governor had told him that he intended to veto it at the next legislative session, and promulgated it in the *German Gazette* of August 29.[3]

The governor demanded an explanation of the secretary, whose failure to produce one to the satisfaction of his

[1] His home was considered a sort of office, but his housekeeper had not receipted before. House Misc. Doc., 42 Cong., 2 Sess., No. 211, 241.

[2] Bovee had represented the hour of delivery as 9 P.M., Saturday. Upon hearing the governor's version, the attorney-general decided that Bovee had no right to his action. Sen. Repts., 42 Cong., 3 Sess., No. 457, 1083.

[3] It had already been published at Carrollton, in the *State Register*. House Misc. Doc., 42 Cong., 2 Sess., No. 211, 240.

chief resulted in an executive order of suspension under the "law of necessity to protect the government from the acts of dishonest and corrupt officers." That afternoon,[1] when Bovee went to his office as usual at three o'clock, he found Mr. F. J. Herron there under the protection of four policemen, who refused his demand for possession of the office. A struggle for possession of the seal ensued, with the result that Bovee presently found himself in the police station on a charge of assault and battery. He lost the suit which he brought in the Eighth District Court, October 20, under the intrusion act, on the ground that the executive had power to suspend until the legislature could act by impeachment,[2] while the appeal carried to the Supreme Court was dismissed on a technicality.[3] As we have seen, the session of 1872 did no work for about thirty days, and, when action was had, the governor's message, charging Bovee with this and other offenses, was referred to a special committee. This body, at the close of the session, at the request of Bovee, asked that the investigation be continued until the next session, on condition that the status remain unchanged.

Immediately after adjournment, Bovee revealed his hand by instituting another suit, alleging that, although his removal be legal, Herron's term had expired, as he had been appointed only until the legislature should meet and act. In the absence of impeachment, he argued, he was entitled to his office. His view was sustained by the lower court and confirmed by the Supreme Court, December 2, 1872.[4]

But before this decision was handed down, Herron found that his head was to fall as suddenly as his pre-

[1] *I. e.*, August 29.
[2] 23 La. Ann., 807. 1871. Among the list of cases not reported.
[3] *Ibid.* Because it had not been taken within the prescribed ten days.
[4] 24 La. Ann., 594-5.

decessor's in this political tragedy. Although the Democrats held that the governor's action was prompted by his discovery of a plot between Herron and Lynch to falsify the returns, based on the fact that Herron had ordered a duplicate of the State seal,[1] it was due, no doubt, to the simple fact that Warmoth had learned that Herron would follow his own counsel. But the specific charge on which the governor issued his order of removal November 13 and appointed Wharton was that Herron had failed to adjust his defalcation of some one thousand dollars as tax collector for 1871, which was supposed to have been settled before he was appointed.[2] As matters now stood the fight would come between Bovee and Wharton.

Judge Elmore of the Eighth District Court threw obstacles on December 4 in the way to prevent Bovee's taking his office by refusing to order the execution of the judgment until the six judicial days allowed by law for appeal by the defeated party had expired, although Bovee and Herron had mutually agreed to waive that privilege. The day of the decision Bovee went into the secretary's office to take possession. The police, at Warmoth's request, forcibly put him out, as the latter did not recognize the decree of the Supreme Court. Before the six days had expired, the Federal troops took possession of the state-house, excluded Wharton, and inducted Bovee into office. Yet he had acted on the Lynch Board from the day of the decision.[3] Elmore's act of contempt

---

[1] House Exe. Doc., 42 Cong., 3 Sess., No. 91, 76. The governor charged that the secretary had been out of the city three months, had been at his office but once or twice until the meeting of the returning-board when he promptly materialized.

[2] Statute 21, 1870, made it unlawful for the governor to issue a commission to any person who might appear to be a defaulter unless he pay the amount in ninety days of the date of election or appointment. The governor had given him fourteen hundred dollars to pay the defalcation and thought he had done so.

[3] Bovee was ineligible to serve on the board in any case as he was a

brought upon his head on December 9 judgment from the Supreme Court in the form of a fifty-dollar fine and ten days' imprisonment. But that very afternoon he was released by the governor's pardon.[1]

There were meanwhile two returning-boards in existence. To maintain the appearance of legality, the governor was notified of the first meeting of the Lynch Board. When he failed to appear, Lynch was made president and a resolution was adopted on November 14, instructing the attorney-general to institute suit in the Eighth District Court against the Warmoth Board to enjoin the said parties from pretending to act as the returning-board or in any way hindering the other board.[2] This injunction was served on the morning of November 15, whereupon the board dutifully refrained from making any returns, although tabulation by clerks went on.[3]

The Warmoth Board, in turn, brought suit the following day, November 16, in the same court and under the same judge, to restrain the Lynch Board from counting or promulgating any returns and to force it to pay one thousand dollars in damages. Judge Dibble granted the injunction in both cases.[4] It should be noted that Dibble was only holding over as an appointee and was, therefore, directly interested in restraining any canvass of votes, as he would continue in office as long as the injunctions prevented a legal canvass, for it was admitted by all

candidate at the election, but as Carpenter said, "he was not going to be stopped by a little difficulty of that kind." *Record*, 43 Cong., 1 Sess., 1042. He had acted as assistant secretary of the board up until the time he was restored.   [1] 24 La. Ann., 619–24.

[2] House Exe. Doc., 42 Cong., 3 Sess., No. 91, 70.

[3] Sen. Repts., 42 Cong., 3 Sess., No. 457, 142.

[4] Injunctions were such a common event at this time that Bovee said: "I never looked at them much. I merely put them away." *Ibid.*, 441.

parties[1] that his opponent, Elmore, had been elected by a vote of two to one. On November 19, Judge Dibble tried both cases before a large and curious crowd, ordered the injunctions in favor of the Lynch Board to issue,[2] and pronounced an oral opinion which contained a famous passage:

But much has been said at bar in regard to the acts of the Executive in his efforts to defeat the will of the majority of the returning-board, as constituted on the 14th of November, and his acts have been so frequently designated as a brilliant *coup d'état*, that I feel called upon to say that the *coup d'état* is not an American institution; it belongs to another country, where they have barricades, and where they meet to organize governments at midnight. Our Anglo-Saxon liberty proceeds under processes of law, and an individual has no power to change the government of the people.[3]

He held, therefore, "that Herron is still Secretary of State; that his vote of the 13th of November determined the election of Longstreet and Hawkins to the board; and that he was Secretary of State *de facto*."[4] And, as a necessary corollary, Warmoth's plea for an injunction was refused. This whole controversy in relation to the returning-board was appealed to the State Supreme Court and came up January 13, 1873, as will be detailed later.

November 21 a motion for a rehearing in these two suits was made, set for November 25 before Judge Dibble, but subsequently postponed to December 3. This was part of a scheme concocted by the governor,[5] for he had

---

[1] Sen. Repts., 42 Cong., 3 Sess., No. 457, 862.

[2] The governor stated that Dibble had confessed that if he had not rendered the above decision, he would have been arrested by the United States marshals. *Ibid.*, 863.

[3] For the full decision, see House Exe. Doc., 42 Cong., 3 Sess., No. 91, 150–2.   [4] *Ibid.*

[5] The writer ascribes this move to Warmoth because his counsel made the motion for a rehearing, though the Congressional Committee assume

devised a way to secure a favorable decision from this troublesome court. November 21 he issued a commission to W. A. Elmore, Fusion candidate, and to W. P. Harper, as judge and sheriff respectively of that court and to other judges of New Orleans, thus virtually defying the order of the Federal Circuit Court. At that time no returns had been made, but Warmoth swore before a Congressional Committee that he commissioned them "upon general notoriety of their elections," and because he was convinced that "if the suits went on, the returns would be tied up six to twelve months perhaps." In accordance, therefore, with his duty, he had examined the returns and commissioned these men, as he believed he had a right to do in such an emergency.[1]

On the same day[2] Elmore proceeded with an adequate armed force to seize the Eighth District Court before the hour to which the court had adjourned. At eleven o'clock Judge Dibble's arrival and order to his sheriff to open the court caused something of a commotion. He left, however, without forcible ejection, though he claimed the right to his office[3] and appealed to the Supreme Court for relief.

Although to achieve his ends Warmoth wished the support of the courts, the versatile governor was not dependent upon them. On November 20 he drew from his pocket, where it had been reposing ever since March, the election bill of the preceding session,[4] to which allusion has been made, and signed it. The second section pro-

---

that he appointed Elmore after the motion had been made in order to save himself.

[1] Sen. Repts., 42 Cong., 3 Sess., No. 457, 862.

[2] The Congressional record, which says Nov. 22, is incorrect, for the papers report it on that date as among the preceding day's events.

[3] See his letter to Elmore, House Exe. Doc., 42 Cong., 3 Sess., No. 91, 154.

[4] See above this volume, p. 136.

vided for a returning-board of five persons to be elected by the Senate. Warmoth claimed that the effect of this act was to abolish all previously existing boards, and that, inasmuch as the act took effect during the vacation of the legislature, he was authorized to appoint the members under his constitutional power of appointment during the vacation.[1] He chose to disregard the irrationality of the canvass of an election compiled under a law signed sixteen days after the election had occurred. Both the law under which the election was held and amendment ordered that compilation should begin ten days after the election. But he appointed on the evening of December 3 P. S. Wiltz, Thomas Isabelle, J. A. Taylor, De Feriet, and J. E. Austin to constitute the board. And amid all this excitement he issued on the same day a proclamation convening the legislature in special session on December 9.[2]

The importance of having a favorable judge on the bench appeared December 3 when Elmore granted a motion for a new trial in both cases. Upon the ground that this new act abolished all former boards, he dissolved the injunction granted against the Warmoth Board and dismissed both suits.[3] Warmoth knew that the Eighth District Court had exclusive jurisdiction of such cases in Orleans Parish and shrewdly reasoned that appeal could not lie to the Supreme Court as no salary was attached to the positions on the board and hence that the sum of five hundred dollars, required by law, was not in controversy. And so the governor soon commenced a new suit himself in this court, obtained an injunction restraining the Lynch Board on the ground that the new election law abolished that board. Lynch applied to the Federal court to remove this suit on a certiorari which the State

---

[1] Sen. Repts., 42 Cong., 3 Sess., No. 457, ix.
[2] This proclamation appeared in the *Times* and *Picayune* on the evening of November 21.　　　　　　　　　　　　　[3] 25 La. Ann., 5.

court treated with contempt.   No proceedings were taken in the Federal court.[1]

However, on December 17, A. P. Field, attorney-general elect, according to the Lynch returns, presented his petition to the superior district court for intervention and appeal in the case of the State *versus* Jack Wharton on the ground that his salary placed more than the requisite amount at stake.[2]   His prayer was granted.   The decision handed down January 23 declared that Field was entitled to an appeal, but did not declare that he was entitled to his office, reversing the judgment below merely on the ground that it was erroneous as to the Lynch Board, which had not appealed.   It held that that body might have appealed as, although it did not involve a pecuniary interest, it was very important to the people. And it declared the board composed of Warmoth, Herron, Lynch, Longstreet, and Hawkins to be the legal board.[3]

While the Lynch and Warmoth suits and counter-suits were being fought out in the State courts, a contest over the same question was being waged in the Circuit Court of the United States.   Kellogg, the Republican candidate for governor, filed a chancery bill, November 16, against the Wharton Board, against McEnery, and against the publishers of the official journal of the State on the allegation that ten thousand negroes had been excluded from the polls on account of their color.   They were,

[1] Sen. Repts., 42 Cong., 3 Sess., No. 457, xv.   Also *National Republican*, December 3.

[2] House Exe. Doc., 42 Cong., 3 Sess., No. 91, 152.   At the same time he presented his commission to the First District Court and to the Supreme Court, in both of which it was recognized.

It should also be noted that on November 24, Ogden, to whom Warmoth had issued a commission as attorney-general, presented his credentials to the Supreme Court with a request for recognition.   The court merely replied that the matter would be taken under advisement.   But the application was never passed upon.   *Ibid.*, 152–3.

[3] 25 La. Ann., 14.   Sen. Repts., 42 Cong., 3 Sess., No. 457, 30.

accordingly, restrained from canvassing any returns
except before the Lynch Board; the governor was ordered
to refrain from permitting any but the Lynch Board to
have access to the returns; and he was further ordered in
the discharge of his duty to submit them to that board;
McEnery was forbidden to set up any claim to the governorship; and the journal was forbidden to publish the
evidence they might furnish.[1] The bill professed to be
for the preservation and perpetuation of the evidence of
the election and to have reference to the support of a
suit which Kellogg might have to bring to recover the
office.[2] He also tried to bring a rule for contempt as
Warmoth continued to do what he was restrained from
doing. Warmoth pleaded as excuse that his clerks were
going on with the work of tabulation, as he had not
believed that the restraining order was intended to direct
him to interfere with mere clerical labor. If he had erred
in this respect, it was ignorantly and with no intention of
violating the order of the court.[3] And the other members
swore that they had done nothing as returning members
since the injunction was served.[4] This matter was
progressing slowly when the governor, to escape trial
before the Federal court, on November 20, approved
the revised election law of the last session, as we have
seen, which legislated both boards out of existence.
Although he thus took the whole subject away from the
National court, the case was continued, was argued at

[1] See Court record quoted in full, House Exe. Doc., 42 Cong., 3 Sess.,
No. 91, 157–217 and 239–253. The restraining order is given on 98–9.

[2] The opinion of the Congressional Committee on the jurisdiction of the
court is interesting: "The only legitimate purpose of this bill was to preserve testimony, and the subsequent attempt of the court, on a bill for
equity, to determine the title of Warmoth, Wharton, and others to act as
State canvassers, was a matter wholly beyond the jurisdiction of Federal
courts." Sen. Repts., 42 Cong., 3 Sess., No. 457, xiii.

[3] House Exe. Doc., 42 Cong., 3 Sess., No. 91, 286.   [4] Ibid., 296.

great length with unequaled interest by a great array of legal talent, but did not receive formal decision until December 6.[1]

Before that date, however, certain important events had occurred to alter the entire situation. The date set for the casting of the electoral ballots, December 4, was upon them, and prompt action was necessary if the State were not to lose her vote. On December 4 the Lynch Board declared a result of the count for Presidential electors, according to .which eight Grant electors had received a majority of all the votes in the State. It was not declared in the official organ, but the results made out and the electors given the certificates of election, by Bovee on the morning of December 4. They met that day and cast their votes for Grant but were obliged to detain them some days until Secretary Bovee should obtain possession of the State seal.[2]

The De Feriet Board, which, it will be recalled, had been appointed on the evening of December 3, canvassed the returns with remarkable celerity and announced the result on December 4. There had been no canvass made of the returns for electors by the Wharton Board, but upon the request of the secretary of state, his assistant had examined them, not in the presence of the board and had made a compilation during the life of that board which gave an average majority of six thousand to the Greeley electors.[3] Returns were made in the governor's presence but without authority under the law. And so December 4 he issued a paper in which he named eight Greeley electors as chosen and placed a copy of this statement in the hands of each. These men met and cast blank

[1] For the full argument see House Exe. Doc., 42 Cong., 3 Sess., No. 91, 157–189; for reply, 189–217.
[2] Sen. Repts., 42 Cong., 3 Sess., No. 457, 144.
[3] Ibid., 580.

ballots for the President, but their solid vote for Brown for Vice-President.[1]   And so at the time the electoral vote was cast the returns had never been canvassed by any competent authority.

The governor issued his proclamation the same day, promulgating the full result of the canvass, and published the certificate of the secretary of state, giving the list of the members of the legislature.[2]

Although the victory seemed for the moment to lie with the governor, his action stirred Judge Durrell of the Circuit Court to his extraordinary "midnight order." He probably thought that he was acting in accord with the wishes of the National administration, for certain messages had passed back and forth just before his famous order was issued.   On November 27, W. P. Kellogg sent a highly inflammatory letter to the Attorney-General at Washington in which occurred the following significant sentence:

So audacious and flagrant have been the means resorted to within the last few days by Governor Warmoth . . . that I should not be surprised to see the supreme court of the State, which is known to sympathize with us, and which has incidentally passed upon the legality of our returning-board and the illegality of the action of Warmoth in issuing commissions before the result of the election is declared according to law, ejected from their seats by force, notwithstanding that the constitution provides they can only be removed by impeachment.[3]

Coupled with this was an appeal to party prejudice.

But it must not be forgotten that this is a systematic and organized attempt to destroy the republican party in this

---

[1] *Globe*, 42 Cong., 3 Sess., 1302.
[2] For the proclamation of the governor, see Sen. Repts., 42 Cong., 3 Sess., No. 457, xvi.   [3] House Exe. Doc., 42 Cong., 3 Sess., No. 91, 6.

13

State, to outrage every principle of justice, to override all
constitutional and legal restraints, and to inaugurate a condition of things that will jeopardize the peace of the community
and the security, hereafter, of the black as well as the white
republicans of the city and State.[1]

In the absence of any call for troops, there can be little
doubt that the telegram sent to Marshal Packard by the
Attorney-General, December 3, ordering him to enforce,
with the aid of troops to be furnished by General Emory,
the decrees and mandates of the Federal courts, no matter
by whom resisted, was a response to the above letter.[2]

Because Warmoth had, in violation of the restraining
order of the court, issued a proclamation of the returns,
Durrell on the night of December 5 between nine and
eleven o'clock issued from his private lodgings an order
to the marshal forthwith to take "possession of the
building known as the Mechanics Institute, and occupied
as the State house for the assembling of the legislature
therein," to hold the same subject to the further order
of this court, and meanwhile "to prevent all unlawful
assemblage therein under the guise or pretext of authority
claimed by virtue of the pretended canvass," but he was
directed to allow the ingress and egress to and from the
offices of "persons entitled to the same."[3]   A Southern
writer says that it was generally believed that the judge
was intoxicated, his signature being referred to as one of
the evidences.[4]

The marshal then called for a detachment of United

---

[1] House Exe. Doc., 42 Cong., 3 Sess., No. 91, 7.
[2] Sen. Repts., 42 Cong., 3 Sess., No. 457, liv.
[3] For the order in full see *ibid.*, xvii.
[4] Herbert, "Why the Solid South," 414.
  The *Times* says, its "besotted letters fairly reel with intoxication."
This charge was so constantly reiterated without contradiction in Congress
that there is no reasonable room to doubt it.

States troops under command of Captain Jackson to act as a *posse comitatus* and seized the state-house at two o'clock on the morning of December 6. Troops were quartered in the Senate chamber and in the hall of Representatives while officers and a deputy marshal took up quarters in the governor's ante-room.[1] Two soldiers were posted at the entrance with crossed bayonets to suffer no one to enter except by permission of Packard. These troops continued to occupy the building for more than six weeks.[2] Soon after daylight the news began to be noised about the city so that Canal and Dryades Streets were soon thronged with people. But as the morning advanced the court-house became the center of attraction, for it was well known that on that day Durrell would deliver his opinion in the Kellogg case. By eleven o'clock every available seat in the court room was occupied by a crowd in the best of humor, but one largely in favor of the custom-house.[3]

The judge granted the injunction to restrain Warmoth from canvassing the returns. He declared Warmoth's returning-board illegal and ordered the returns forthwith placed before the legal board, adding that the legislature announced by it would be protected by that court.[4] As the investigation by Congress charged, his opinion mis-

---

[1] *North American*, Dec. 7, 1872.

[2] Trumbull searchingly queries: "Can it be that the Attorney-General sent his telegram, and that Captain Jackson was ordered to New Orleans with his batteries, in anticipation of the unauthorized orders of United States District Judge Durrell to seize the State-house and prevent the legislature from organizing except with such persons as he should declare legally elected?"

[3] New York *World*, Dec. 7, 1872.

[4] Casey's comment to Grant is significant: "The decree was sweeping in its provisions, and if enforced, will save the republican majority and give Louisiana a republican legislature and State government, and check Warmoth in his usurpations." House Exe. Doc., 42 Cong., 3 Sess., No. 91, 14.

stated the allegations of the bill and ignored the fact that the governor had appointed a new returning-board.   His attitude, although admitting the validity of the new law, was that it was his duty to continue the old laws until the old boards could have a reasonable opportunity to complete all business before them.[1] Even the affidavits which the judge adduced in support of his decision contained no charge of denial of the franchise on account of race or color.

Durrell's order created a perfect furor of excitement and indignant protest,[2] which did not subside until Northern papers,[3] the Congressional committee, and even members in Congress had expressed their emphatic disapproval of the interference of this Federal official with the internal affairs of a State.   "Judge Durrell's action looks too much like a conscious prostitution of his court to the services of one side in a vile partisan squabble," said the New York *World*.[4]   The New York *Herald* held, "Disguise it as we will, cover it up in any phraseology we may please, the result is revolution—a displacement of the State authorities by Federal bayonets."[5]   The onslaughts of the New Orleans *Times* were violent in the extreme. Articles appeared with glaring captions, as "Gibbeted,"[6]

[1] For full opinion see Sen. Repts., 42 Cong., 3 Sess., No. 457, xviii–xxvi.

[2] Foulke characterizes it well: "It was practically an order of the Circuit Court organizing the legislature of Louisiana." *Life of Morton*, II., 278. See Cooley's *Commentaries*, II., 1814, note.

[3] See New York *World*, Dec. 7, 8, 9; New York *Herald*, Dec. 9, 26; *Nation*, Dec. 19, 26, Jan., 2.   Some papers are favorable, as see the *North American* of Philadelphia, Dec. 9.   As late as Mar. 6, 1873, the *Nation* insists that Durrell ought to be impeached.

[4] Dec. 11, 1872.

[5] Dec. 7, 1872.   It follows a pertinent query on Dec. 26, "Is this a Republic and is Louisiana one of the United States?" by an emphatic assertion that she is, coupled with a condemnation of the imperial policy being pursued toward her.   [6] Dec. 8.

"The Situation and Duty of Manhood," the "Crowning Infamy,"[1] and "Carthago est Delenda."[2] On the morning of December 8 it came out with an article under headlines in mourning:

"Hung be the Heavens in Black." Let us make Monday a day of mourning and of solemn protest. "Hung be the Heavens in Black." Let our enemies feel that the public finger is pointed at them, and the public conscience has recorded its anathema. Let the stores be closed. Let the hum of business for one day be checked. Let the church doors be opened, and prayer ascend to the King of Kings. Our case is one in which we are helpless without the aid of the Mighty. If a protest thus solemnly and sincerely enunciated against the encroachments of unauthorized oppression and corruption be not effective, then is American liberty a myth and republican self-government a base delusion! If liberty in this land is to be buried, let Monday's meeting be a funeral.

Nor were the other papers far behind. Thus the *Picayune:*

James II. had the festive, jovial, and remorseless Jeffries to aid him in his attempt to reestablish himself in absolute power in England and the Radical Administration at Washington has the festive and remorseless, but not jovial Durrell to aid in the work of making Louisiana a subject province.[3]

The defense of the *National Republican* was quite unavailing against the avalanche of adverse criticism.

[1] Dec. 8.   [2] Dec. 15.
[3] *Picayune,* December 7.
Note also the following Gallic outburst from the *Bee:* "En prenant la défense de notre pauvre Louisiane, si accablée et si meurtrie, nous avons laissé deborder l'amertume et l'indignation dont notre cœur était rempli. Mais tout s'use, même le ressort de l'indignation; et en voyant passer hier matin de deux mitrailleuses et marchant au bruit d'un tambour qui battait lentement le pas d'enterrement, nous nous sommes dit 'voilà la liberté qu'on enterre, la république est morte, vive l'empereur Grant I er.'" December 7, 1872.

All honor to the noble judge, whom adroit leaders could not bewray, whose eminence no partisan hand dares seize to dissuade him from the performance of duty, and who, reverently conscious that he is an accredited priest at a sanctuary of the people, affords asylum to the humblest and blackest suitor, yet, launches a mandate at the boldest and most powerful conspirator within the borders of Louisiana. All honor to him that he has dared to be right![1]

Again and again in varied phrase the Congressional committee return to the subject and in their own words, "know no language too strong to express their condemnation of such a proceeding." In their report they say:

Viewed in any light in which your committee can consider them, the orders and injunctions made and granted by Judge Durrell in this cause are most reprehensible, erroneous in point of law, and are wholly devoid for want of jurisdiction; and your committee must express their sorrow and humiliation that a judge of the United States should have proceeded in such flagrant disregard of his duty, and have so far overstepped the limits of Federal jurisdiction.[2]

And they approve the sentiment of certain Louisianians in their Address to the People of the United States, where they affirm,

without fear of contradiction, that the foregoing statement exhibits on the part of the United States court the most highhanded usurpation of jurisdiction and authority of which the annals of jurisprudence afford any example.[3]

[1] December 7, 1872.
[2] Sen. Repts., 42 Cong., 3 Sess., No. 457, xxvii.
[3] House Exe. Doc., 42 Cong., 3 Sess., No. 91, 80. It may be noted, as evidence of the impression produced at Washington, that about a year later the House of Representatives required the Judiciary Committee to report on whether Durrell should be impeached.

After delays for almost two years, in order that the government might

After the decision by Judge Durrell on December 6, Armstead, secretary of state on the Fusion ticket, filed a bill in the Eighth District Court against the members of the Lynch Board and obtained an injunction commanding them to make no canvass of the November election, except upon the returns made in pursuance of law. Again a writ of certiorari issued from the Federal court, only to be again disregarded by the State court, with the result that no proceedings were had in the Federal court and that the injunction remained in force.[1]

And still the tangle of suits became more hopeless as the critical date for the assembling of the legislature approached. Antoine, Republican candidate for lieutenant-governor, filed on December 8 against the Warmoth Board on the equity side of the United States Circuit Court the most remarkable bill of a truly remarkable series. It was directed against the Warmoth Board, the De Feriet Board, Lieutenant-Governor Penn, the clerk of the House, the secretary of the Senate, the assistant secretary of state, Armstead, Blanchard, the metropolitan police, all the men reported members of the Assembly according to the De Feriet returns—over three hundred persons in all. It appeared in the official journal of the State Sunday, December 8, under the caption, "Protection to the State Legislature. Hands off, all around. Read, ponder, observe." Although a long and tedious arraignment, it differed from the Kellogg bill only in that it included the prevention of the forcible constitution of a legislature for the purpose of declaring the plaintiff not elected, and tried to compel all the parties strictly to follow the statutes of Louisiana which required the secre-

find other grounds, he escaped this disgrace only by resigning. *Record*, 43 Cong., 2 Sess., 321-2.

[1] Sen. Repts., 42 Cong., 3 Sess., No. 457, xxvii.

tary of state to transmit lists of the members elected to the Assembly to the clerks of the House and Senate.[1] The court granted a temporary injunction and a bill returnable December 11. But the very act of Congress under which this proceeding was instituted by express words excluded members of the State legislature from the right to maintain any proceedings in a Federal court to obtain their seats,[2] so that in the words of the investigating committee, the writ was issued for "the sole purpose of accomplishing what no Federal court has the jurisdiction to do, the organization of a State legislature."[3]

Finally, on the evening of the 6th[4] the Lynch Board promulgated the returns for the legislature, according to its canvass. A second demand[5] for the returns had been made upon the governor by General Longstreet and Bovee a few minutes after Durrell's decision on December 6.[6] As the governor refused to see them, Bovee left a copy of his instructions, but without allowing time for the reply, which there was no reason to expect, the Lynch Board met that evening to complete its canvass, and promulgated the returns in the official journal on December 9[7] for the chief officers of State, Senators, Representatives, and Presidential electors. The results for Congressmen, for parish and city officers were promulgated on varying dates, extending from December 9 to 27.[8]

The reader will agree with the investigating committee that there is "nothing in all the comedy of blunders and

---

[1] House Exe., Doc., 42 Cong., 3 Sess., No. 91, 99–102 and 234–8.
[2] Act of May 31, 1870, U. S. Statutes, XVI., 146, Sec. 23, and Act of Feb. 28, 1871.   [3] Sen. Repts., 42 Cong., 3 Sess., No. 457, xliii.
[4] Published in the papers of the 7th.
[5] The first demand had been made Nov. 15.   [6] *Ibid.*, 251.
[7] December 6, 7, and 9 are given in the secondary sources, but the above is correct.
[8] See the returns of the Lynch Board, Sen. Repts., 42 Cong., 3 Sess., No. 457, 188–250.

frauds under consideration more indefensible than the pretended canvass of this board."[1] Only one of the actual returns[2] was before the members and their methods were as fraudulent as the frauds they were trying to establish. They had copies of full returns from less than half the parishes, at a generous estimate, as the United States supervisors made returns only on the vote for Presidential electors in most cases. In some cases they had reports made by Republican Federal supervisors in the parishes where those supervisors were permitted to remain for the State count; in certain parishes, what were supposed to be certified copies by one[3] of the State supervisors; in others, affidavits of individuals; in some, informal statements of the result from the State registrars, giving an abstract, not a copy; in other cases they had nothing but letters, newspaper statements, or personal testimony, in which the witnesses were not generally on oath; and, finally, as a climax of absurdity, where they had nothing whatever to act upon, they made an estimate, based upon their knowledge of the political complexion of the parish, of what they thought the vote ought to have been. They assumed authority in many cases to throw out the entire vote of particular polls and wards,[4] thus rejecting, they

[1] Sen. Repts., 42 Cong., 3 Sess., No. 457, xxvii.

[2] In one parish only, Terrebonne, was the return based directly on the ballots put in the box, as the United States supervisor sent them the original return. *Ibid.*, 415.

[3] Lynch stated that he did not remember a single case where his returns were signed by both supervisors. *Ibid.*, 404.

"We had," he says, "from quite a number the result in the different polling-places and in one or two a complete copy. . . . We had them from a large number, but not generally from State officers." The following was exceptionally good evidence: "The State supervisor from Carroll Parish submitted to myself his returns, from which I made an abstract, that was the evidence upon which we acted." *Ibid.*, 148.

[4] To accentuate the absurdity they threw out Bossier Parish entirely and then counted the affidavits of 1159 who said that they had been denied

believed, not over six thousand votes,[1] and, on the other hand, counted deliberately about ten thousand affidavits purporting to be sworn to by voters who had been wrongfully denied registration or the right to vote.[2] "Honest" John Lynch's defense is worth quoting as an instance of perverted political morals. " We had not the technical evidence before us. We were what I considered in the midst of a revolution, and in order to get at the results of the election as near as we could, as an officer acting, I availed myself of every kind of information within my reach, not only the affidavits, but my former knowledge of the political divisions of the inhabitants of the State as corroborative of the evidence placed before us."[3] In another place he added that "on the whole we were pretty correct."[4] Of course, such methods did not afford complete returns and so in a burst of generosity Lynch declared that in parishes where they had nothing to guide them, they gave the results as given by the other side, as they were generally Democratic parishes.[5] He admitted that they took the National vote as their principal guide, leaving entirely to conjecture whether the same men voted for Kellogg as cast their ballots for Grant, and in a doubtful case giving the Republicans the benefit of the doubt, for they were, in their own words, "determined to have a legislature."[6]

---

the right to vote. Sen. Repts., 42 Cong., 3 Sess., No. 457, 150–1. Natchitoches was also treated in the same way.

[1] *Ibid.*, 158.

[2] House Exe. Doc., 42 Cong., 3 Sess., No. 91, 86. The false affidavits that Jacques handed to Bovee in the presence of the board should be recalled. See above p. 179.

[3] Sen. Repts., 42 Cong., 3 Sess., No. 457, 155.

[4] *Ibid.*, 158.   [5] *Ibid.*, 149.

[6] The testimony of Bovee is worth quoting:

Q. You said you had the affidavits of the Federal supervisors upon what? What did they show?

It is significant that each member of this returning-board was immediately rewarded with a lucrative office by Pinchback: Longstreet became levee commissioner at $6,000 a year; Hawkins, judge of a newly created court[1] at $5,000; Herron a recorder of mortgages, an office worth $10,000–$20,000, created after the canvass; while the position of inspector of live stock, worth $12,000, was offered to John Lynch's son. And yet Lynch[2] testified that there was no bribery.

And still one last returning-board was destined to appear on the stage—the fourth, the so-called Forman Board. When the Warmoth legislature convened December 11, as will be set forth in the next chapter, his Senate elected another board to replace the governor's appointees, consisting of two Democrats, two Republicans, and one Reformer: Forman, Mitchell, S. M. Todd, F. Hunsaker, and S. M. Thomas. The last-named, after canvassing the vote for State officers and the Assembly, resigned and Southmayd was elected to fill his place.[3] The trunks containing the returns, which had been secreted in a room of the St. Charles Hotel, were delivered over to them by the assistant secretary of the previous board. Hunsaker and Todd acted with the board up to the time Southmayd was elected but forsook the party then so that the returns

---

A. They showed a very doubtful case. I think just as likely one was elected as another.

Q. Did they show fraud?

A. Not particularly.

Q. What did you decide about it?

A. To give that to the Republicans.

Q. You gave them the benefit of the doubt?

A. We were determined to have a legislature.—Sen. Repts., 42 Cong., 3 Sess., No. 457, 484–5.

[1] See below, p. 210.

[2] It seemed best for him to resign later.

[3] Sen. Repts., 42 Cong., 3 Sess., No. 457, 79.

were signed by but the three men.[1]   The canvass had been practically completed by the De Feriet Board and the result for the legislature and State officers already declared.   But the Forman Board reëxamined the result, working all one night and until 10 o'clock the next morning, when they promulgated, on December 12, the results for State officers, those for parish officials being published later.   But the returns for Presidential electors were not reëxamined.   From two parishes no returns were received at all[2]; the vote of three parishes was cast out for violence and fraud[3]; while from some, the returns were so meager that the board was unwilling to take the responsibility of declaring the result and so referred the returns to the Senate itself for determination.[4]

Hence, the result of the canvass of the election of 1872 was the existence of two distinct governments in the State, with two complete sets of State officers and two distinct Assemblies, in which only a few of the members were accepted by both houses.[5]   According to the Lynch returns, the House had 77 Republican, 32 Democratic members; the Senate 28 Republican, and 8 Democratic Senators,[6] out of which number 68 were negroes.   On the other hand, the Forman Board announced but 103 of the full 110 to which the House was entitled: 75 Liberals and Democrats as opposed to 35 Republicans.[7]   In the Senate,

[1] West in 1875 charged that someone forged the names of two members and that the third denied ever signing the returns.   *Record*, 43 Cong., 2 Sess., 873.   [2] St. Tammany and Terrebonne.

[3] Sen. Repts., 42 Cong., 3 Sess., No. 457, 77.

[4] *Ibid.*, 95.   Iberville and St. James.

[5] I find varying statements.   One says 45; another gives 58 in the House. (Sen. Repts., 42 Cong., 3 Sess., No. 457, 323) and 8 in the Senate (*Ibid.*, 326), another 71 in both houses.

[6] House Exe. Doc., 42 Cong., 3 Sess., No. 91, 102.   Packard's official notice, 107 by count.   I find various figures given: 73 Republicans to 33 Fusionists in the House, and 27 to 6 in the Senate.   [7] *Ibid.*, 303.

which should consist of 36 members, there were 15 holding over, to whom the Forman Board would add 19: 15
Fusionists and 4 Republicans. The division as to color
was 46 negroes in the House, 10 in the Senate. In all, 66
members were returned by both boards, concerning
whom there need be no dispute: 58 in the House, 8 in the
Senate.[1] But each party had sufficient strength to make
its claims serious when the issue should be drawn in the
extra session of December 9.

[1] Sen. Repts., 42 Cong., 3 Sess., No. 457, 320–326, also 266.

CHAPTER X

A Period of Dual Governments

GOVERNOR WARMOTH had issued his call, as stated in the preceding chapter, for the legislature elected November 4 to convene in extra session for ten days at Mechanics Institute on December 9, because the present condition of affairs presented "an extraordinary occasion." But the seizure of that building by United States troops three days before the Assembly should meet, interfered with his plans and ultimately produced a result which could have been anticipated only in Louisiana—two legislative bodies in session at the same time.

On the morning designated, between two and three thousand people crowded the street in front of the Institute. The law prescribed that the legislature should be organized by the last secretary of the Senate and clerk of the House, in accordance with the list furnished by the secretary of state. Naturally, the issue would turn upon whom Pinchback and the speaker should recognize as secretary.

The Senate and city did not need the additional wave of excitement with which the lieutenant-governor inundated them at the opening of the Senate by accusing Warmoth of an attempt to bribe him with an offer of fifty thousand dollars to allow the organization of the Senate in a "manner not prescribed by law," presumably by the old members.[1]

[1] Pinchback claimed that he held the offer in abeyance overnight in order to obtain proofs, and then proudly replied, "I have slept on the

There were present in the Senate when Pinchback dropped his gavel at noon on the 9th, fifteen left-over Senators together with fourteen of the twenty-one new members,[1] of which number the Republicans could claim twenty. The Warmoth faction had expected the old members by prompt organization to dominate the situation, but Pinchback refused to recognize any motion and insisted, even against Republican protests,[2] on swearing in the new members at once, accepting the Bovee list as conclusive evidence of membership. It was stated in investigation that several men withdrew at once, including six holding over, because of the mode of organization. Certain it is, that two names do not reappear in the records after the first session. Three new Senators, while responding to their names, refused to take the oath, while one so far declined to participate as to refuse to serve on the committee which notified the House of their organization.[3]

Only a portion of the one hundred and ten members,

---

proposition you made last night, and have determined to do my duty to my State, party, and race." He exposed it as a conspiracy in which Democrats and some Republicans were implicated. House Exe. Doc., 42 Cong., 3 Sess., No. 91, 52, *National Republican*, Dec. 10. 14,000 copies of an extra containing this rumor were exhausted on Dec. 10. I find no proof of this accusation, though Warmoth's defense sounds more like proof than a denial, "I object to Mr. Pinchback being allowed to make a statement here unless I be permitted to bring evidence to disprove the statements which he has made. . . . It will necessitate sending for witnesses from New Orleans, and I think we will show that Mr. Pinchback is not in the habit of resisting such temptations." Sen. Repts., 42 Cong., 3 Sess., No. 457, 392.

[1] Numbers differ but I am giving those recorded in the official journal, though I am well aware that there might be cause for jugglery. The extra number is accounted for by the fact that there were several vacancies which had not been filled during 1872. Pinchback claimed there were but fourteen holdovers. Sen. Repts., 42 Cong., 3 Sess., No. 457, 326.

[2] House Exe. Doc., 42 Cong., 3 Sess., No. 91, 82–3.

[3] Sen. Jour., Extra Sess., 3.

who legally constituted the House, assembled.[1] Sixty-five members, fourteen of whom were said to be Democrats, are registered present in the journal at the initial roll-call,[2] increased by four more before the evening session adjourned. Twenty-seven[3] of this number had been returned by both boards and so were subject to no question. The body organized by the election of Postmaster Lowell as speaker and then created a joint committee with the Senate to wait upon the governor. This group soon reported that the governor had not been in his office the entire day; that his secretary was too busy to see them; and that they had thus been obliged to leave with the door-keeper a written notice of organization.[4]

The custom-house cabal sated its thirst for a revenge, long-burning, upon the governor by promptly voting impeachment by the overwhelming majority of 57 to 6.[5] The vote by which the Senate resolved itself into a court of impeachment is significant—17 to 5.[6] Six Senators who had responded to the first roll-call were not now present, but two reappeared at the evening session. As Pinchback would now be obliged to perform the duties of governor during the latter's suspension, pending impeachment, the Senate elected A. B. Harris, president by a practically unanimous vote.[7] At an evening session— for they had learned the danger of adjournment by

---

[1] The Lynch Board, it will be recalled, returned only 107, and so, according to their count, 54 would constitute a quorum. 19 were necessary in the Senate for a quorum.

[2] House Jour. Extra Sess., 1872, 3. Other numbers are given in various records.

[3] 45 is also given. The writer believes 27 by actual count to be correct. Sen. Repts., 42 Cong., 3 Sess., No. 457, 323–5, 1070.

[4] House Jour., Extra Sess., 4.

[5] Ibid., 5. Certain formal regulations that provided for a hearing before a House committee were ruthlessly ridden over.

[6] Sen. Jour., Extra Session, 1872, 5.   [7] Ibid.

the experience of the preceding January—[1] twenty-one Senators[2] were organized by Chief Justice Ludeling as a court of impeachment, only to adjourn until the 16th to afford time for the preparation of the charges. Pinchback qualified and took possession of the governor's office the same night. Hope waxed high with the Republican party, for Packard reported duly to Washington: "It is believed that all the Democrats, members of the general assembly, will qualify and take seats tomorrow."[3]

Two of the three men who had refused to take the oath concluded on the second day to cast in their fortunes with the body which seemed to be in the ascendant.[4] Pinchback felt called upon, as Warmoth had declined to communicate the object which led him to convene the Assembly, to recommend such legislation, as in his opinion, the public good required.[5] He urged a speedy trial of the governor; investigation of the frauds at the election, seizing this opportunity also to deliver a sermon on the "necessity of coöperation with Congress" to secure freedom of the ballot[6]; modification or repeal of oppressive laws, for the passage of which he promised an extension of the session if necessary; and, lastly, the conduct of all business, not in the interest of any class, but in the interest of all.[7]

The interesting event of this day's session was the count of the vote for governor and lieutenant-governor. Although one Senator, whose loyalty might be open to suspicion,[8] tried to secure postponement until the regular January meeting, the Senate assented to the eagerness

[1] See above, this volume, p. 119.
[2] Although the journal states 20, it records 21 names.
[3] House Exe. Doc., 42 Cong., 3 Sess., No. 91, 14.
[4] Sen. Jour., Extra Sess., 6.   [5] Ibid., 7.   [6] Ibid.
[7] Ibid., 1872, 7.
[8] Mr. Vorhees, who joined the Warmoth faction on Dec. 11.

14

of the House.   The official returns of the Lynch Board were, of course, accepted so that the journal duly records 72,890 and 70,127 votes for Kellogg and Antoine as opposed to 55,249 and 57,568 for McEnery and Penn, respectively.[1]   The former were thereupon proclaimed chief executives for the four years beginning the second Monday of the following January.

By the third day the Warmoth faction had succeeded in making itself felt as a disturbing element, and legislators were indignantly denying statements of their presence at the Warmoth legislature, as reported in his organ,[2] while the Senate was deigning to notice acrimoniously the desertion of members to the Lyceum Hall body.[3]

Legislation was remarkably rapid, as the bill for abolishing the Eighth District Court and creating a superior district court for Orleans was pushed through all its stages in a single day by constant suspension of the rules in both houses.[4]   There was thus an interesting circle created.   Hawkins counted in spurious members of the legislature, that legislature created a governor, who made Hawkins judge, and Hawkins then decided the legislature to be legal.[5]

---

[1] Sen. Jour., Extra Sess., 1872, 8.   Four members were sworn into the House this day and three after the joint session, bringing the total up to 76.

[2] House Jour., Extra Sess., 17.   Sen. Jour., 12.   One member in his zeal published a card, denying participation with the "mass-meeting of a crowd of revolutionists at the City Hall."   *National Republican*, Dec. 12.

[3] It appointed a committee of investigation, as it appeared that certain Senators had "taken part in the illegal assemblage at Lyceum Hall, and have, in further violation of the dignity and authority of this honorable body, proceeded to recognize H. C. Warmoth as legally in the exercise of Executive functions."   Sen. Jour., 11–12.   A similar committee was appointed in the House.

[4] Sen. Jour., 10.   After several days, Warmoth wisely decided not to let litigants incur needless expense by the trial of further cases.   *National Republican*, Dec. 14.

[5] Sen. Repts., 42 Cong., 3 Sess., No. 457, lxii.

As soon as Warmoth saw that the Federal power was being turned against him, he tried to forestall his opponents by an attempt to organize informally in Lyceum Hall, two days before the date set for the extra session and by making the first plea to Grant. Fifty-two men were present at this meeting.[1] About sixty men, returned by the De Feriet Board as Representatives, met in a caucus at the city hall, December 9, assembling in regular session the next day at Lyceum Hall, where they gained four accessions.[2] In this body appeared thirty persons returned by both boards.[3] The question of a quorum is a vital matter and yet difficult to determine. Adherents of Warmoth insisted that the House had had a quorum of the one hundred and three members,[4] officially returned by their board from the first, but so strong a partisan as McMillan held that ten were questionable and, hence, that it was six or seven short of the required number.[5]

As we have seen, practically all of the Senators reported at Mechanics Institute the first day, but dissatisfaction with the arbitrary organization led eleven members of the House and eight[6] of the Senate to secede from the Pinchback House to the Lyceum body on December 11 and thus enabled that body by the evening of the third day[7] to declare a quorum in both houses and to organize in defiance of the restraining order secured by Antoine.

---

[1] On the authority of the *National Republican*, Dec. 8, which would have no object in making the number larger than it was.

[2] Sen. Repts., 42 Cong., 3 Sess., No. 457, 263.

[3] *Ibid*. See also *National Republican*, Dec. 12.

[4] As the De Feriet Board pronounced only upon this number, it was held that one-half, or 52 constituted a legal quorum.

[5] He held 56 to be a quorum, whence neither House had the legal number. *Ibid.*, 263–5.

[6] Based on the report itself of the Senate journal, 15. Among them were the three who had refused the oath on the first day. A ninth had never been at the state-house, as he came late.

[7] Warmoth only claimed 21 Senators, but his opponents gave him 24.

H. J. Campbell was chosen president of the Senate, J. Moncure speaker of the House, and a message from Warmoth read to each house.[1]   Two proclamations which he issued that same evening in an extra of the *Times* did not tend to quiet the disturbed condition of the public mind.   The first declared the Pinchback legislature a "revolutionary and fraudulent assemblage" and their leader a usurper, against whom officers and citizens were solemnly warned; while the second legislated the city hall into the status of official state-house, as the lease of Mechanics Institute had expired.[2]   As noted earlier,[3] the Forman Board was created to canvass finally the returns.   It found the clerical labor of tabulation performed, but reviewed it poll by poll, ward by ward, and tested its accuracy, finding in the whole body only one or two insignificant clerical errors.   It differed only slightly from the De Feriet promulgation.   But this was the only work accomplished.[4]   The accusation brought by the *National Republican* that the extra session was called for the sole purpose of discharging to Warmoth the debt for fusion—his election to the United States Senate—received no color of truth from any action taken by this assemblage.[5]   On December 13 this body adjourned to the first Monday in January, possibly, to avoid the humiliation of seeing edicts which it could not enforce contemned, and because it was evident that it would soon be further weakened by the loss of the militia.

Pinchback had placed General Longstreet in command of the militia.   The former had repeatedly commanded the officer in charge of the State armory, a henchman of Warmoth's, to turn over all the arms and ammunition of

---

[1] See *Philadelphia Inquirer*, Dec. 12, or *Ledger*, Dec. 17, on this message.
[2] House Jour., Extra Sess., 1872, 21–2.
[3] See above, p. 203.
[4] Sen. Repts., 42 Cong., 3 Sess., No. 457, 699.   [5] Nov. 24.

the State, but had been as often refused.   A large armed
police force was unable to take the position on December
13 and there seemed imminent danger of a conflict.[1]
But the militia offered to surrender to any Federal force.
Under orders to recognize the Pinchback government,
General Emory sent an officer to ask the evacuation of
the arsenal and the dispersal of the armed forces.   The
demand was promptly complied with and the arsenal
turned over to the Pinchback authorities on the morning
of December 14.[2]

Meanwhile, Warmoth had, with his usual passion for
the courts, appealed for what legal support he could
secure.   December 10 he had promptly sued out an
injunction in the Eighth District Court against Pinchback to restrain that individual from performing the
functions of governor, on the score that his term as
Senator had expired.   A nice judicial point is involved
here.   It was held by one party that he was only acting
lieutenant-governor by virtue of his election as president
of the Senate in November, 1871, and hence that he lost
office with the expiration of his Senatorial term, November 4, 1872.   By the other faction he was regarded as
actually becoming lieutenant-governor and entitled, therefore, to continue in office the length of time for which
Dunn had been elected; namely, until January 2, 1873.
It strengthened his cause not a little that Warmoth had
recognized him on the returning-board, November 13, and
on December 8 by his attempt to bribe him, if the charge
be true.   Pinchback made no reply,[3] but continued to

---

[1] See *National Republican*, Dec. 14 and 15, for a circumstantial account
of this attempt.
[2] House Exe. Doc., 42 Cong., 3 Sess., No. 91, 25–6.
[3] Pinchback's own opinion is of some interest: "I think, under the
constitution, it (his term as Senator) expired on the 4th of November,
when that election took place.   If in the minds of anyone, there had been

act as chief executive.   As a rule for contempt was likewise ignored, Judge Elmore sentenced him to ten days'
imprisonment and fifty dollars' fine.[1]   In this game of
contempt, it is of passing interest to note that a sergeant
was directed to arrest Elmore for contempt in issuing the
injunction against "their Governor."[2]   And when the
case came before the State Supreme Court for adjudica-
tion in March, 1873, it held the view maintained by Pinchback's friends.[3]

Both parties brought the greatest pressure to bear
upon the President to secure recognition.   The Republicans opened fire on the very first day of the session by a
concurrent resolution, calling on the President for protection against "certain evil-disposed persons," reported to
be forming combinations to disturb the public peace and to
"defy the lawful authorities."[4]   Grant guardedly assured
Pinchback that "whenever it becomes necessary in the
judgment of the President, the State will be protected
from domestic violence."[5]   December 11 and 12 the
telegrams poured in at Washington.

Parties interested in the success of the Democratic party,
particularly the New Orleans *Times*, are making desperate
efforts to carry the people against us.   Old citizens are dra-
gooned into an opposition they do not feel, and pressure is
hourly growing; our members are poor and adversaries are
rich, and offers are made that are difficult for them to withstand.   There is danger that they will break our quorum[6]

---

any doubts about my being the legal lieutenant-governor of the State,
it seems to me that when my term expired the courts or somebody in
authority should have called my attention to it."   Sen. Repts., 42 Cong.,
3 Sess., No. 457, 329–330.

[1] Sen. Repts., 42 Cong., 3 Sess., No. 457, 860.

[2] *National Republican*, Dec. 12.   But reconsidered and indefinitely
postponed.   [3] 25 Louisiana Ann. *ex rel*. Morgan *vs*. Kennard, 243–4.

[4] House Jour. Extra Sess., 1772, 5.   Sen. Jour., 4.

[5] House Exe. Doc., 42 Cong., 3 Sess., No. 91, 18.   [6] *Ibid*., 19.

urged Casey. Kellogg joined with Pinchback in the effort to secure a recognition of the Radical body, urging the danger of an immediate conflict between the two houses and hence the importance of recognizing Pinchback.[1]

On the other hand, the Fusionists turned to the same source to ward off danger. At noon on December 10, they gathered, eight hundred strong, in front of the city hall in an indignation meeting. Speeches were made by Warmoth and McEnery, which did not fail in incendiary language. A Committee of One Hundred Citizens, drawn from the best element in the city, was selected to present a petition to President Grant. The chairman of this committee and McEnery each sent a telegram, begging him only to defer action until after the arrival of the Committee.[2] Notwithstanding this reasonable plea, the President on December 12[3] recognized the Pinchback organization as the lawful government of the State, to which he would lend all necessary assistance "to prevent disorder and violence."[4] He followed this promptly by a consistent reply to McEnery to the effect that the visit of the citizens would be unavailing, as his decision was irrevocable.[5] But still the people could not be convinced that a deaf ear would be turned to their arguments, and so thousands went to the station in a drizzling rain to bid their Committee Godspeed as it departed for Washington, December 14.[6] The men arrived on the 18th and waited

---

[1] House Exe. Doc., 42 Cong., 3 Sess., No. 91, 19, 20.   [2] *Ibid.*, 21.

[3] Since the hours are not stated on the telegrams, it is impossible to know whether Grant had received the request for delay before he sent his recognition, both being received on Dec. 12.

[4] House Exe. Doc., 42 Cong., 3 Sess., No. 91, 23.   [5] *Ibid.*

[6] A fair-minded Radical felt that this group, although sincere men, could not present the facts fairly, as they were from New Orleans, where the election had been fair, and knew nothing of the country, where the frauds had been perpetrated. *Ibid.*, 26.

on Grant the following day.[1] Their memorial was naturally fraught with feeling, although it gave, in the main, a fair presentation of the facts.

It is not surprising that a widespread feeling of indignation, disgust, and distaste prevails at these extraordinary proceedings. They are without parallel in the annals of the United States. They betoken a spirit of malice and mischief, a determination to prostrate all the bulwarks of law and of social order, under the guise and cover of judiciary action, to secure ends purely selfish and personal. They manifest a contempt for the institutions of the country, the peace of society, the guaranties of life, liberty, and of property, that has created alarm and insecurity.[2]

And it concluded with three specific requests: that Justice Bradley be appointed to the Circuit Court of New Orleans, that the Federal troops be no longer employed there, and that the President and Congress refrain from recognizing either government before an investigation be made.[3] Though they were courteously received, the measures of relief applied for were refused.[4] But, meanwhile, these attempts of the Democrats did not seem to be altering the trend of affairs in the Pinchback legislature, which was quietly meeting day after day. A few shifts and additions occurred. Two of the eight deserting Senators were expelled,[5] and two saved

[1] A part of the group went on to New York to advise with some Congressmen.

[2] House Exe. Doc., 42 Cong., 3 Sess., No. 91, 22–3. One record states that they asked an investigation of three men.   [3] Ibid.

[4] Ibid., 81. Every possible pressure had been brought to bear on Grant—from absent bank presidents and other influential men who could not go, from a group of Northern business men doing business in the city, and from the attorney-general. Ibid., 28, 49, 87.

The *Nation* scored Grant severely for his interference and attitude toward this committee, Dec. 26, 1872.

[5] Campbell and McMillan, Sen. Jour., Extra Sess., 16–7.

their heads by returning to Mechanics Institute after the adjournment of the other body, evidently on the principle of being in with both sides[1]; December 13 one Senator appeared, while members were seated as late as December 27, and even on the last day of the session.[2] But it must be confessed that one regards with some suspicion the insertion in the Senate journal on December 16 which records that on the 12th instant three Senators had qualified and taken their seats.[3] It may or may not have relation to the fact that about this time the Senate began to have difficulty in mustering a quorum.[4] The House continued in daily session, legislating, making a brave show of activity without much result until the date of the regular Assembly, largely because it was afraid to adjourn for fear that Warmoth would get possession.

Some skirmishing, preliminary to the convening of the regular Assembly, occurred, for it was evident that neither side intended to lay down its arms. The first move came from the Democrats, who held another mass meeting, January 3, to express their opposition to the Pinchback faction and their determination to support the McEnery government. Since their appeal to the President and Congress had failed, they tried to shout their grievances into the public ear. A Committee of Two Hundred, selected irrespective of party from the most prominent business men and heaviest tax-payers, issued an "Address to the People of the United States" in which it adroitly

[1] Hunsaker straightened matters to the satisfaction of that body by a declaration that, "I regard this as the legal Senate of the State and I came here to take my seat and stay." Sen. Jour., Extra Session, 1872, 18.

[2] House Jour., 55.

[3] Two of the names do appear in the roll-calls of Dec. 12, but the other can be found nowhere except on Dec. 16. See Sen. Jour., 22.

[4] On December 24 they were obliged to adjourn to the 26th, on which date they were again obliged, on account of lack of a quorum, to adjourn until the next day; and on the 29th the requisite number was obtained only by ordering the sergeant to bring in absentees.

focused attention upon the Congressional attitude by declaring:

We confidently anticipate that Congress will promptly appoint a committee to investigate fairly and impartially the facts of the case, and in view of the gross and palpable wrongs which have been committed, we cannot doubt such a committee must admit and report to Congress the necessity of prompt and complete relief.[1]

They did not allow themselves to despair because the Republican party had a large majority in that body. After an arraignment of carpet-bag rule, fair if severe, they revealed the purpose of the address.

We have everywhere and at all times proclaimed our conviction that the body, styling itself a Legislature, now in session at the Mechanics' Institute, does not and never did comprise a quorum of members elected by the people; . . . and we feel justified by the language and action of the President himself in regarding that recognition as merely provisional and temporary,[2] subject to the future action of the Congress of the United States, to which tribunal the President has submitted us for relief. We are equally convinced that the body which recently assembled at Lyceum Hall in that city did comprise a quorum of lawfully-elected members of the State assembly.

And so, while advising studious abstinence from a collision, they recommended that the people of the State give their moral support to the legislature about to assemble and "such material aid as may enable them to assert and maintain by legal means the rights of the people of this state to local self-government."[3]

[1] *Annual Cyclopedia*, 1873, 444–5.
[2] This remark provoked from Grant the assurance that "the recognition is final, and will be adhered to, unless Congress otherwise provides." House Exe. Doc., 42 Cong., 3 Sess., 91, 33.
[3] *Annual Cyclopedia*, 444–5.

As an offset to that plea appeared the "Executive Address" of Governor Pinchback on the same date, a series of counter charges against the Warmoth government,[1] and an "Address to the President and People of the United States" from the Republicans. Pinchback attempted in his address to plant himself firmly against permitting the assembling of the Fusionist legislature, distinct from what he termed the "legal body.'

The governor-elect, as returned by the Legislature in session at the State House, will, on the day provided for in the Constitution, be inaugurated [he declared], and the legislature recognized by the President will meet, but no pretended governor shall be inaugurated, . . . no pretended General Assembly shall convene and disturb the public peace. Parties participating . . . are public wrongdoers, and shall be promptly dealt with as such. The whole force of the State shall be used for this purpose.[2]

But the reply from Washington was prompt and unexpected, "I think there ought to be no forcible interference with any proceedings to inaugurate McEnery, if they are not accompanied by violence, and there is no attempt to take control of the State government."[3]

The victory of one side or the other in securing possession of the minor State offices, city, and parish positions, and recognition of the one faction or the other in the certificates of election would ultimately make for strength in the struggle of the Assemblies for recognition. No objection was raised to the fact that Wiltz had been elected mayor of New Orleans; the only criticism passed was as to his mode of taking office. November 27 he and the new administrators,[4] on the strength of certificates

[1] *Annual Cyclopedia*, 444–5.   [2] *Ibid.*, 1874, 445, gives excerpts.
[3] Jan. 4.   House Exe. Doc., 42 Cong., 3 Sess., No. 91, 31, a telegram from Attorney-General Williams to Packard.
[4] All but two who refused to install themselves.

from Supervisor Blanchard, although they held no commissions, demanded their offices. Very quietly they entered upon their duties November 30 and were sustained, as usual, by the Eighth District Court.[1] All the Republican parish officers returned by the Lynch Board —and they constituted about one-half—accepted their commissions, naturally, from Governor Pinchback. As the boards agreed very closely in Orleans Parish in conceding Democrats elected, the latter were willing to accept commissions at the hands of the Radicals. This question was discussed by Warmoth and his counsel, and the advice issued to accept the commissions from Pinchback, as it was well known that if it were not done, his obedient legislators would abolish the offices and his courts expel the Democrats by force in order to install the men who did accept his commissions.[2]

The position of the Supreme Court could not but be a weighty factor, and both sides, especially the Kelloggites —for it was known that the judges were in sympathy with them[3]— strove during these days which intervened between the election and the regular assembly to secure a favorable opinion by the highest legal authority. Suits were pending between the Warmoth and Lynch Boards, through the intervention of Field as has been recounted. In addition, two other cases had arisen. Perhaps it was fortunate for the McEnery faction that these decisions were not made until the two bodies were in session and so had only the weight of a legalistic opinion on a *de facto* situation.

A contest arose between Clinton, the Republican candidate, and Graham, the Fusion nominee, for possession of

[1] *National Republican*, Dec. 1.
[2] Sen. Repts., 42 Cong., 3 Sess., No. 457, 866.
[3] Relatives of three Supreme Court judges held office at the hands of Pinchback. *Globe*, 42 Cong., 3 Sess., 1746.

the office of auditor.[1]   But this suit failed to come on to
the highest tribunal, as the injunction of the Eighth
District Court was not recognized after the Pinchback
Assembly legislated it out of existence.   But a dispute
over the position of associate justice of the Supreme Court
did obtrude itself upon that tribunal's attention.   Early
in December, Pinchback nominated P. H. Morgan to fill
a vacancy on the bench created by resignation.   The
nomination was confirmed, but J. H. Kennard, who had
been previously appointed by Warmoth, refused to surrender his seat, thus forcing Morgan to institute a proceeding, which came by appeal before the highest court.
That body but confirmed its earlier decision in the case of
Field when it held on January 31 that Pinchback was
lieutenant-governor, and by the impeachment, acting
governor; and that Morgan was entitled to his seat.
Incidentally, the court passed upon the Kellogg legislature,
as the validity of a law, passed by that body, January 14,
came before it in this case.   That act was passed to
promote the speedy trial of contests for judicial offices by
providing that such bills should be tried within twenty-
four hours without jury and by preference over all other
cases pending.[2] While the court held that judges could not
determine judicially the persons who composed the legislature, yet they could take judicial notice of the body
constituting the legal legislature and the law in question
had been passed by the legal legislature.[3]

Practically the same body of men who had been meeting
for nearly a month in Mechanics Institute reconvened
January 6, a few minutes after the final adjournment of the
extra session, with scarcely anything to indicate that they
were entering upon a new session.   Both houses con-

[1] *National Republican*, Dec. 12, 1872.
[2] Session Laws, 1873, No. 11.
[3] 25 *La. Ann.*, 243–5, and Sen. Repts., 42 Cong., 3 Sess., No. 457, lxxii.

tinued the same officers, while Pinchback did not feel called upon even to distinguish the day by an introductory message.

Fourteen Warmoth Senators and forty-seven Representatives met peaceably at Odd Fellows Hall,[1] despite the large crowd in front of the building. There was a general closing of places of business to allow the entire population to turn out, while United States troops were in readiness to preserve order. There seemed to be a general determination, if Pinchback's threat to interfere with the meeting of the Assembly were executed, for the citizens to form and defend their Representatives against any force. But the crowd soon dispersed, as the legislature was obliged to adjourn almost at once because of the lack of a quorum. On January 10, six Republican Senators,[2] including the two vacillating men who had returned to the Kellogg body after the adjournment of the Warmoth legislature, transferred back to the latter, justifying themselves on the ground of the "revolutionary organization" of the houses in swearing in persons notoriously defeated, and so for the "public good," they determined to take their seats in the body, "truly representative of the people."[3] This addition gave McEnery twenty-one members and a quorum.

January 13, the Radical houses met in joint session in Mechanics Institute to listen to the inaugural address of Kellogg and to Pinchback's farewell speech.[4] At the

---

[1] Although Warmoth had designated Lyceum Hall as the state-house, the city council had excluded the legislature from that building and so he was obliged to resort to the above-named place.

[2] 13 of the 15 holding-over Senators were Republicans. Sen. Repts., 42 Cong., 3 Sess., No. 457, 466.

The Sen. Jour. shows that the number was six by declaring certain seats vacant. See 75 and 58.

[3] *Annual Cyclopedia*, 1873, 445–6.   Sen. Repts., 42 Cong., 3 Sess., No. 457, 1094.   [4] La. Sen. Jour., 1873, 60.

same hour John McEnery was being inducted into office in Lafayette Square, which a complete cessation of business had thronged with people. The metropolitan police were under arms; the artillery was harnessed and ready for action; Federal troops were drawn up on some of the principal streets. But though grave and intense feeling was manifest, the day passed without outbreak.

The one transaction of far-reaching importance of the McEnery legislature was the election of McMillan on January 14 to the seat in the United States Senate, left vacant by the resignation of Kellogg. At about the same time, the Kellogg body was acting on the same subject. By a flattering majority, twelve as opposed to nine for all other candidates, Pinchback was elected Senator for the term beginning March 4, while John Ray was chosen to serve out the unexpired term of Kellogg.[1]

With the vacancies due to incomplete promulgation by the canvassing boards, the expulsions[2] and shifting, there was considerable change in the personnel of the houses, especially of the Senate. Two members were seated arbitrarily, as there were no returns from certain wards; others, where gentlemen did not appear to claim their seats, were seated subject to contest. After due debate, the governor was given notice of the vacancies, and orders were issued for special elections on February 1, 10, 15, and 17, with the result that seven of the vacant places were filled before the close of that month. And the House journal shows that about a week before the close of the session, some Representatives returned to the Kellogg body.[3]

[1] Sen. Jour., 1873, 62, 66.   Ray's election occurred the next day, to be exact.

[2] Sen. Jour., 59.   But the House resolution for expulsion, after numerous postponements, gave way to a spirit of conciliation.

[3] House Jour., 1874, 38.   A resolution offered in the next assembly, Jan. 14, proves this. "That the Committee on Contingent Expenses report

Although the McEnery legislators continued to assemble day after day and transacted business until the very close of the session, the work of their rivals is that which stands recorded on the statute books of the State. One of the first acts was to legalize beyond all question the work of the extra session by a retroactive measure. And, to make sure beyond all peradventure of the legality of Kellogg's title, the vote for governor was recounted and re-declared on January 7.[1]

The impeachment trial of Warmoth, instituted the first day of the special session, dragged over the first weeks of the regular assembly. It began in earnest on December 16 and went on apace. It was, naturally, hailed with delight by the custom-house press.[2] The House brought charges under seven heads, the most serious of which were the issuance of commissions of election before the legal returns had been canvassed; his attempt to bribe Pinchback[3]; an attempt by bribes and threats to induce supervisors to reject legal voters, and to alter votes; and the appointment of a tax-collector during recess after the Senate had rejected his name.[4] As was

---

to this House what payments, if any, have been made to these members of the General Assembly whose names appeared on the roll of the House, but who were absent in attendance upon a revolutionary body until within a week of the close of the last session." In this body, 68 of 140, or more than half, were negroes. Cox, *Three Decades*, 563.

[1] House Jour., 1873, 59-61.

[2] "The impeachment of Governor Warmoth yesterday by the Legislature opens a new era in the history of Louisiana, and brings gladness and hope to every loyal heart throughout the State. It is the bow of promise in our political sky, the dawn of a brighter day, and a sudden termination of lawlessness, turbulence, dishonesty, and corruption." *National Republican*, Dec. 10, 1872.

[3] This charge rested, it must be remembered, on the unproved accusation of a man who had become his enemy.

[4] Impeachment because of his removal of Bovee savors of *ex post facto* legislation, while the charge that he had assumed to act as governor on Dec.

to be expected, Warmoth did not heed the summons to appear on December 18, but when the court reconvened on December 23, counsel for the accused did appear[1] to ask until January 9 for the preparation of the defense. On that date, when the Senate sat as a court, the governor's counsel read a series of remarkable counter-charges, denying the legality of the Assembly, which caused much indignation and controversy. Warmoth's pleas were rejected and he was ordered to file an "answer" within twenty-four hours,[2] a period later extended to January 16. The question then arose as to the wisdom of continuing the prosecution when Warmoth's term had expired, but the trial dragged until January 27, when the chairman of the House prosecution found himself too busy to attend the sessions of the court, and the chief justice delivered his opinion that they could not impeach after the term had expired.[3] By a three-fourths vote the Senate then decided to discontinue the trial.[4]

The issue which would determine whether the Kellogg government could win substantial support or not was the manner in which it fulfilled its promises of reform—and that meant, primarily, of the finances.   Already the question of repudiation must have presented itself to the mind of Kellogg, for, after pointing out the heavy obligations of the State, which it would not be able to meet, he denied any idea of repudiating any portion of the "legitimate" debt.[5]   The Assembly made a brave show of sincerity in

---

11 scarcely constituted grounds at the time when impeachment was voted. For the articles in full, see House Jour., 1872, Extra Sess., 20-1.

[1] This recognition of the Pinchback legislature by Warmoth is difficult to explain unless he had begun to fear the strength of the Fusion government and meant to try for a vindication before the government which might win out.   [2] Sen. Jour. Supplement, 1872-3, 11.

[3] He also condemned it as an unwise expense—an unusual bit of economy.
[4] Sen. Jour. Supplement, 1873, 14.
[5] House Exe. Doc., 42 Cong., 3 Sess., No. 91, 30.

reform by at once creating a committee on retrenchment and reform, [1] by offering numerous bills to reduce unnecessary expenses for justice and jury fees, expenses in cancelling official bonds[2]; by turning to the light fraudulent warrants of the preceding Assembly for registration and election purposes[3]; by an inquiry into the condition of the railroads and canals; and by an act to provide for systematic collection and payment of money into the treasury. [4] But the sum total of accomplishment was small, even allowing for the immense difficulties under which they were laboring.   In a positive way, the treasurer was peremptorily prohibited from registering any warrants, [5] and the appropriation for the General Assembly was placed at $270,000 but rendered nugatory by an additional grant of $95,000 or "as much thereof as might be necessary."[6] From the attitude of the citizens on the payment of taxes, it was clear that the problem of securing any funds would be a most difficult one.   As Durrell had refused to allow an appeal from the Circuit to the Superior Federal Court, the Tax Resisting Association[7] determined to test the legality of the Pinchback government by refusing to pay their assessments.   Neither government made any effort in the early weeks of 1873 to collect the taxes, while McEnery forbade the citizens to pay them to the other government.[8]   But toward the close of the session the Kellogg government passed an act to enforce their collec-

---

[1] Sen., Jour., 1873, 78.   [2] Ibid., 204.
[3] Ibid., 177–192.   [4] House Jour., 1873, 199.
[5] Session Laws, 1873, No. 44.   [6] Ibid., Nos. 38 and 50.
    [7] This association had been organized in May, 1872, for the purpose of resisting the extortionate taxation of the Warmoth régime by testing the validity of the taxation in the Federal Supreme Court, but became now an engine against the Kellogg forces.   By January, 1873, a large number of the citizens of New Orleans were involved in suits.   Sen. Repts., 42 Cong., 3 Sess., No. 457, 457–60.
    [8] February 15.   For his order see the Globe, 42 Cong., 3 Sess., 1852.

tion under speedy and severe penalties, forbidding a delinquent the right to bring suit or be a witness in his own behalf in any court of the State,[1] and calling out the militia to aid in the collection. It did not allay popular feeling that this was followed by a relief measure, remitting all penalties to delinquents, provided they paid the taxes promptly, for the Resisting Association had already been largely recruited. Finally, Kellogg issued a proclamation against resisters, warning all against taking any part in the association, active or passive.

A great deal of tinkering was done to previous legislation without much real improvement. The metropolitan police was mustered in as part of the militia[2]; the charter of New Orleans was again modified; the independence of the city in its financial difficulties still further curtailed[3]; and an attempt to solve the perpetual problem of a school system ineffectually made.[4] It recognized the recent election disturbances by amending the election law, providing a sufficient number of polls but retaining the odious feature of the returning-board; by declaring it a crime to usurp a public office; and by providing for forfeiture of office by any person recognizing such usurper.[5] A civil rights bill at last gained the requisite majority

[1] Meetings were held in many parishes during April, Livingston leading off, to agree to recognize only the McEnery government, and to pay no taxes to the other government. In St. Helena a sportive mob shaved the mane and tail of the tax-collector's horse; Tangipahoa gathered on April 13 the largest meeting ever held there. *Picayune*, April 21. In New Orleans a standing committee of seventy was appointed to organize resistance to Kellogg, who was burned in effigy. April 20. *Ibid.*, April 22.

[2] Session Laws, No. 37.

[3] The taxes of New Orleans were defined; its indebtedness limited; and the funding of the floating debt authorized. This bill the governor vetoed, as he felt it "unwise to saddle the present State administration with the responsibility of conducting the affairs of the city of New Orleans." House Jour., 1874, 16.   [4] Session Laws, Nos. 36 and 82.

[5] *Ibid.*, Nos. 19 and 41.

this session.   It required all common carriers, inn-keepers, and managers of places of public amusements to afford equal accommodations to citizens without regard to race or color, imposing severe fines and imprisonment on those making such distinction. [1]

While relations between the two legislatures in session for two months in the same city were necessarily strained, there was no conflict until the very close, when the McEnery factionists resolved on aggressive action.   February 26 their executive called on all able-bodied men between the ages of eighteen and forty-five in Orleans Parish to appear as the State militia on March 1. [2]   In a mass meeting assembled on that date, resolutions of support for the McEnery government were passed, asking the alternative of withdrawal of Federal protection from the Kellogg government or martial law, pending a new reconstruction.   On the evening of March 5 the opponents came to blows.   The police, though armed with rifles and artillery and supported by several companies of Federal infantry, were able to frustrate an effort by an unorganized body of citizens to gain possession of the police stations only after considerable bloodshed.   This attempt was disclaimed as premature and unauthorized by the McEnery party.   But it furnished ample pretext for the action of the following day.   A body of armed police took possession of Odd Fellows Hall and marched the members of the McEnery legislature whom they found in session there between files of sharpshooters as prisoners to the guard-house. [3]   McEnery promptly inquired of

[1] Session Laws, 1873, No. 84.
[2] *Globe*, 42 Cong., 3 Sess., 1852.   This summons was issued in accordance with a resolution passed by the McEnery legislature authorizing the governor to use the civil and military power of the State to reinstate the district court judges of Orleans Parish—of the Third, Fourth, Seventh, and Eighth Courts.   [3] *Annual Cyclopedia*, 1873, 449.

Colonel Emory if the action were by his authority.   That officer, while disclaiming responsibility, assured him that if it were the authorized action of the Kellogg forces, he would prevent violent interference. [1]   McEnery could only issue another impotent address to the people of Louisiana, recounting his difficult position.

If we resist the Executive of the United States, which with arms defends this usurpation, we are rebels; if we do not resist it, we submit to and acknowledge its authority and power. . . . We appeal to our brethren in the other States for their sympathy and support of a position which they are all interested in maintaining, thus vindicating a cardinal principle in our political system. . . .   We can only assert our rights, refuse submission to usurpation, and abide the judgment of the American people in our case. [2]

[1] For reply see *Annual Cyclopedia*, 1873, 449.
[2] This account is based upon the reports in the New Orleans *Times*, *Republican*, *Picayune*, and the *Annual Cyclopedia*, 1873, 449.   Though many Northern papers condemned this action as "foolish and wicked," the *Nation* was fairly sympathetic to the malcontents, who, they felt, "had the 'good wishes of all those in all parts of the country who wish to see Custom-House and Carpet-bag rule with their attendant disorders quickly and forever ended.'"   It scored the United States Senate as responsible for the situation.   March 13, 1873.

CHAPTER XI

The National Government and the Louisiana Problem

WHILE Louisiana was sending out her frantic appeals for help, Congress, the one power which could have altered the trend of events, was standing by passive.

The House of Representatives noticed first the turmoil produced by the election dispute. "Whereas the State government of Louisiana is now administered by orders from the Federal courts, supported by Federal bayonets,"[1] it called upon the President on December 16 for information. On the very same day it passed a resolution instructing its Judiciary Committee to "inquire what legislation is necessary to guard against the dangers threatening the liberties of the people of Louisiana, Alabama, and Arkansas."[2] Evidently, the situation in Louisiana seemed to call for special action, for on the very day on which the President submitted the documents, January 13, but before they were duly presented, a Louisiana Representative moved that a joint committee be created to inquire into the election, especially as to whether there were any legal and established government there. After an animated discussion the President's documents were referred to the Judiciary Committee with orders to report what action was required by Congress.[3] But not until the closing hours of the session, March 3, did it submit a

[1] *Globe*, 42 Cong., 3 Sess., 226.   [2] *Ibid.*, 228.   [3] *Ibid.*, 550–1.

230

report, which merely recommended a continuation of the investigation, as the committee had not had time to consider the legality of Durrell's action in upholding the Lynch Board, as to which the gravest doubts existed.[1]

The Senate, on the other hand, let the matter rest until it reassembled after the holidays, when it directed the Committee on Privileges and Elections to inquire into the election in Louisiana and Arkansas and report measures to prevent similar contests in future Presidential elections.[2]   And on January 16 it was further instructed to report whether there was any existing "legal state government in Louisiana."[3]   Before it was ready to make any report, another question had been raised on January 22 by the presentation of the credentials of Ray and McMillan,[4] rival contestants for the unexpired term of Kellogg, which would terminate March 4.[5]   The two returning-boards responded to the summons of the committee and arrived in Washington on January 26 with some trunks full of the much bandied-about election returns, whereupon the committee began its investigation.

The composition of this committee requires a moment's consideration.   The chairman, Senator Morton, was a Republican of Indiana, with whom were associated, on the committee, four colleagues of the same political faith— Logan, Alcorn, Anthony, and Carpenter.   Opposed to them were but two Democrats, Trumbull of Illinois and Hill, a Georgian.   As the Presidential count was close at hand, the committee reported on February 10 on that portion only relating to the electoral returns.   This report merely stated the facts, leaving it to the Senate to go back of the governor's certificate, if it desired: One

[1] *Globe*, 42 Cong., 3 Sess., 2133; also House Repts., 42 Cong., 3 Sess., No. 96.   [2] *Ibid.*, 42 Cong., 3 Sess., 339, 368.   Jan. 7.
[3] *Ibid.*, 641.   [4] *Ibid.*, 766.
[5] Both credentials were, oddly enough, presented by Senator West of Louisiana.

board was not legally qualified to make the returns, and
the other did not.[1]   When the electoral vote was counted
on February 12, objection being immediately raised to
both sets of returns, the houses agreed, acting separately,
not to count the vote of Louisiana.[2]

Senator Carpenter on February 20 submitted a majority
report, signed only by himself and three of his Republican
colleagues, on the remainder of the questions referred to
it; namely, whether there was any existing government
in Louisiana, and on the credentials of Ray and McMillan.
After a full presentation of the facts, which denied entirely
the jurisdiction of the Circuit Court and condemned
scathingly the proceedings of Judge Durrell, it swept
away the Lynch canvass as an indefensible fraud with no
semblance of integrity; and denied jurisdiction to the
State Supreme Court in the Field case, as the Lynch Board
did not appeal and the party who tried to intervene had no
cause of action against either of the litigants.   It was
their opinion that the canvass of the De Feriet Board
would have been acquiesced in and the McEnery government quietly accepted but for the interference of Durrell
and the Federal troops, a measure which had resulted
in establishing the Kellogg government *de facto*, "so far
as there is one."   They, therefore, concluded that if the
election held November, 1872, were not absolutely void for
frauds, McEnery and his associates "ought to be recognized as the legal government of the State by Congress, or
Congress must provide for a re-election."[3]   But as a consideration of the testimony forced them to the conclusion
that the Kellogg government was defeated by fraudulent
manipulation of the election, they felt it impossible to
say that the State had any government whatever.   The

[1] Sen. Repts., 42 Cong., 3 Sess., No. 417, 4–7.
[2] *Globe*, 42 Cong., 2 Sess., 1305.
[3] Sen. Repts., 42 Cong., 3 Sess., No. 457, xliv.

McEnery government, so-called, approached more nearly a government *de jure*, and the Kellogg government a government *de facto*.[1] The question was a political one which Congress must decide. The "alternative of civil war or the maintenance by military power of a State government not elected,"[2] the committee felt exceedingly embarrassing and found the best solution to lie in a re-election under Federal authority, recommending at the same time, the passage of a bill which they had prepared.[3] As to the credentials of the contesting Senators, naturally, they felt that neither was entitled to a seat.

Together with the majority report came three dissenting opinions. Trumbull favored a recognition of the McEnery government as legal, as he felt that the frauds were not sufficient to vitiate the entire election and made out a strong case by showing that the election had been confessedly quiet and peaceful, that there were more whites than blacks in the State,[4] and that over eight thousand negroes voted for McEnery as opposed to less than half that number of whites casting their ballots for Kellogg.[5]   Morton, ultra Radical that he was, believed that the Kellogg

[1] Sen. Repts., 42 Cong., 3 Sess., No. 457, xlv.

[2] The prophecy which fell from Carpenter's pen is worth quoting in the light of the events of March 3 and September 14, 1874. "Should Congress adjourn without making provision for the case, one of two things must result: Collision and bloodshed between adherents of the two governments, or the President must continue the support of federal authority to the Kellogg government." *Ibid.*, l.

[3] *Ibid.*, li. Both Warmoth and McEnery were accused of being in the lobby of the Senate, January 30 and February 2, to engineer a new election. But the risk of a new election was more than Kellogg was willing to run.

[4] According to the census of 1870.

[5] Reports, lxv. He regarded the machinations which had put Kellogg in power as part of a political manoeuver to preserve the State for the Republican party, and he condemned in no uncertain terms the "unfeeling and despotic answers sent by order of the President to the respectful appeals of the people of Louisiana." *Ibid.*, lxi.

government, as the *de facto* and legal government, should be left in control, especially as the United States had no right to interfere.[1]   And Hill held that Congress ought not annul an entire election which was conceded to be fair, but that those members of the two houses whose election had not been disputed might convene, organize, and count the election returns in order to "seat only such members as may appear by said returns to have been elected to the particular house, and to announce the election of a governor and lieutenant-governor, who shall thereupon be inaugurated."[2]

What boots it to rebuke the illegal and tyrannical assumptions of a judge [he wrote], if his orders and decrees must have all the effect he designed to give them?   Of what consequence is it that his violations of law should be reviewed and censured, if the effect is the same as though he had not exceeded his jurisdiction and abused the authority of his office.[3]

Carpenter's bill provided machinery which would insure a fair election.   It would reinstate Warmoth and all the old officers until a new election occurred in May, 1873. Judge Woods of the Federal Circuit Court should conduct the election by appointing two registrars, citizens of the State of opposing political faith, who should appoint two supervisors of registration in each parish and in each ward in New Orleans.   Supervisors of election were also provided for, who should appoint two commissioners for each poll.   A complete new registration would thus have been effected in March.   Proper location for all polls and full publicity of the count was insured; and cause for dispute

[1] Sen. Repts., 42 Cong., 3 Sess., No. 457, lxxviii.   He was able to think that a decided majority of the people of Louisiana sympathized with the Kellogg government and desired to see it maintained.   *Ibid.*
[2] *Ibid.*, lxxx.   [3] *Ibid.*, lxxix.

avoided by vesting jurisdiction in cases of appeal in Judge Wood.[1]

Anxious for action by Congress on the Louisiana affair because the session was drawing near its close, Grant sent in a message February 25, in which he invited the attention of that body to the "grave complications" growing out of the election.[2] The message clearly reflects his opinion and constitutes a defense of his action in recognizing the Pinchback government. Although he made no specific recommendations, he earnestly urged action before Congress should adjourn, clearly defining his policy to adhere, in the absence of legislative action, "to that government heretofore recognized by me."[3]

There had been a straggling debate every time Louisiana had been mentioned, but now with the President's message and the report of the committee before it, and only a few days of the session left, the Senate settled down on February 27 in Committee of the Whole to earnest consideration of the Louisiana problem. Carpenter, as father of the bill, opened the debate with an extremely brief speech, the strength of which lay, perhaps, in his statement that substantially all parties to the controversy approved his proposed solution.[4] Hill immediately offered an amendment in the nature of the suggestion contained in his dissenting opinion for the State to settle the

[1] The details can be found in the *Globe*, 42 Cong., 3 Sess., Part iii., 1850–1.

[2] Morton had a tremendous influence with Grant and to him mainly must be attributed the President's message of February 25. Up to this time Grant had been constant in his support of Kellogg, but after interviews with Carpenter and Conkling it appeared that he was favoring a new election. Morton drove to the White House to ask that the support on which he had depended in undertaking the defense of the Kellogg government be not now withdrawn. Grant gave the desired promise. Foulke, *Life of Morton*, II., 284–5.

[3] Richardson, *Messages and Papers of the Presidents*, VII., 212–3.

[4] Carpenter had shown a draft of his bill to many persons representing all sides of the controversy.

controversy itself through the members whose title to their seats was not contested.[1] Morton opened the general debate in a strictly party speech, aggressive and denunciatory, appealing to the war and blood spirit and ringing the changes on the massacre of 1866. He felt that it was not necessary to pass a law to overturn an existing government.

I recommend masterly inactivity. I say let that government alone, and if Congress adjourns and leaves it just where it is now, all will be well. If McEnery attempts to make any trouble, Governor Kellogg is able to take care of him without any assistance from the Government of the United States; but if he requires it he will get it. The President has said he would give it.[2]

Debate became heated and lengthy, Morton, Thurman, Carpenter,[3] Schurz, and Trumbull taking the leading

[1] *Globe*, 42 Cong., 3 Sess., 1851. He made out from the returns twenty-two Senators and fifty-eight Representatives legally elected.

[2] *Ibid.*, 1872.

[3] In response to a request for fuller information Carpenter rose again to support his bill by substantial arguments, in the course of which he became involved in a personal controversy with Morton. The constitution, he said, provided that the United States should guarantee to every State a republican form of government. Louisiana had a constitution, providing that the returns of all elections should be sent to the secretary. The election law of 1870 conflicted with this in providing that these returns should be made to the governor.

Protected by the Federal troops, the Kellogg legislature had been organized. Morton had insisted that if this fraud were not sanctified, State rights would be violated. Carpenter took a little malicious pleasure in seeing the Senator from Indiana driven to a State-rights platform. After Federal interference had established a government, to say with a straight face that State rights required that it should be sustained showed a gravity which he did not possess.

The returns showed that McEnery had been elected; the testimony had satisfied the committee that the election had been a monstrous fraud; but if one of the two governments must be recognized, the McEnery government was the only one with pretense of right.

parts. The split in the Republican ranks was clearly manifest in this debate—Morton for the extreme Radicals, while Trumbull and Schurz,[1] as well as Carpenter, came out for the more conservative wing. West, sent to the Senate by the Radicals, felt that he could best display his loyalty by supporting Morton's position. Debate raged all day long on February 27, all night, and until the late morning of the 28th.[2]

At the time the committee made its report there was a considerable majority of the Senate in favor of a new election. Morton was the only member of the committee in favor of the Kellogg government. The fate of the bill was largely due to his determination that action should not be taken, and to his efforts, both on the floor of the Senate and outside in personal interviews with fellow Senators.[3]

Morton interposed: "You prefer that fraud?"

Carpenter answered that he preferred it for the obvious reason that it was the smaller fraud. Morton's admiration of greatness extended to frauds as well as virtues.

Thereupon Morton rose to the defense. It was said that Louisiana was without a government. This was not true. There was a government in complete operation, held legal by the Supreme Court of the State in at least three formal decisions. With all due respect to Carpenter the Supreme Court of Louisiana understood the question of its own jurisdiction much better than the Senator from Wisconsin. His trump card was that if Congress could interfere in this State, it could in every State of the Union.

[1] Trumbull, Schurz, and Hill made out a strong case along the line of Trumbull's report. Schurz based his arguments on the possible source of authority for Federal action and found it in the right to guarantee a republican government. None of the speeches were more trenchant than his in his queries of Morton. "Will he tell me what requisite of republican government that Kellogg government possesses? Has it been elected by the people? . . . Had the Kellogg government, I ask, any origin in the world but the usurpation of a Federal judge supported by the force of bayonets?" *Globe*, 42 Cong., 3 Sess., 1874.

[2] The House adjourned at 7.45 A. M.

[3] There was also personal feeling behind the bill. Conkling enjoyed the distinction of rivalship with Morton for leadership in the Senate. Because of Carpenter's brilliancy in debate he was pushed forward on this occasion as the champion of the anti-Morton forces in the hope of breaking the

When the measure came to a vote, Hill's amendment was voted down, as might have been anticipated; an amendment to recognize the Kellogg government as the *de facto* government was accepted; but the bill, so amended, failed by the votes of the Democrats, aided by a few conservative Republicans.[1]

The judgment of Rhodes on the attitude of Congress is eminently sound. Congress followed the worst of three possible lines of action. A new election was clearly the fairest procedure, but substantial justice would have been rendered by merely withdrawing support from Kellogg, whereupon a bloodless revolution would have permitted McEnery to come into control.[2] Failure to take action merely continued a situation which had already proved a failure.

And so Congress adjourned without action of any sort, throwing back upon the Executive, responsibility[3] and opportunity, if he could but have seen it. His attitude was, however, exactly what one should expect from a soldier, not a statesman. As a military man, he stood for action and rigid order. Nor should we forget that element in his character which had brought upon his head

---

latter's influence. But Morton, relying on the support of the Radical Senators of the South, spent his time winning over the doubtful, while Carpenter was working up his "fine speeches," with the result that the Hoosier Senator came out of the controversy the undoubted leader of the party. Foulke, II., 283-4.

[1] Oddly enough, Carpenter voted for the bill so amended, as the best practical result attainable, Morton against it. *Globe*, 42 Cong., 3 Sess., 1896. Comparatively few were present at the final vote. It stood 18 to 20, absent 35.

[2] Rhodes, VII., 111.

[3] Due weight may be allowed to Schouler's explanation of the indisposition of Congress to interfere as a conscious determination to keep the country Republican and to throw the odium on the President, trusting to his military popularity to bear the strain. *History of the People of the United States*, VII., 258-9.

the charge of nepotism.   He was probably particularly biased in Louisiana matters by his relationship to one of the leaders in the Kellogg faction.   The South had been the most constant source of anxiety and friction of all the executive problems which he was called upon to solve. A factor which could scarcely have failed to affect his feelings and judgment was the brutal attacks from the Southern press, not the least violent of which were those from New Orleans, which had battered at him continuously during the Presidential campaign of the preceding year and which he could scarcely have forgotten.   The following is but one of dozens of similar assaults by the *Times:*

Such are some of the many disgraces which have been brought on this proud republic by the great folly of elevating to its Chief Magistracy a boorish soldier, whose ignorance of the laws, usages, and policies of nations and the duties of government is only equalled by the perversity of his favoritism and the intensity of his egotism.   It was this folly which the mad Roman emperor so bitterly satirized by investing his favorite charger with the imperial purple.[1]

Could he have been impervious to such thrusts as this: "To the yielding members of his political and military family, Grant is sufficiently grateful.   While chiding any approach to independence, on their part, he has little hesitation in billeting the faithful on the public crib."[2]

[1] July 29.   See also the issues of July 12, 31, Oct. 18, 25, and 29.   That of July 31 is particularly virulent: "Never before did the Chief Magistrate of the Republic occupy a position so low as that now held by Grant.   The feeling of distrust and dissatisfaction against him is all but universal, and would be entirely so, but for the influence of interested officials and debased politicians.   Analyze the popular cry, 'Anybody to beat Grant,' and in it will be found the very superlatives of condemnation.   This condemnation is, to the popular mind, the legitimate result of that stubbornness and stupidity, which have been the prime characteristics of the Grant administration, and which, in case of a re-election, would be maintained in a still more exaggerated form for another term."   [2] Oct. 29, 1872.

Yet so desirous was Grant of shifting the responsibility that he called the Senate Committee of Privileges and Elections before him to urge on them his eagerness for Congress to take action and assume the responsibility which properly rested on the legislative department in a political question.[1]   And, as noted above, when the session was drawing perilously near March 4 without such action, he addressed a message to Congress, in which he fairly warned the members that failure on their part to act would constitute a recognition of the Kellogg government.[2]

Subsequent events in Louisiana, first of which in point of time came the Colfax massacre, served only to confirm his opinion of the lawlessness and violence of the white Conservatives.   The riot which broke out in Grant Parish in the Red River Valley about three hundred and fifty miles from New Orleans, was the direct result of the bad counsel of leaders, certainly on the side of the negroes.   In most of the Red River parishes, the colored population predominated in numbers, particularly in the low lands. And their political leaders, to maintain their ascendancy, were constantly instilling in their minds suspicion of a desire, on the part of the whites, to enslave them, thus producing a feverish and unsettled condition of society. The whites knew only too well how brutal infuriated negroes become, and so were easily alarmed.   In the words of Marshall of the Congressional Committee, they feared, "that the bloody scenes of San Domingo might be reënacted on our soil," and the whites were compelled by every motive to see that no such rising prove a success.[3] Colfax, the parish seat, was a small village of four or five homes, and two or three stores, while all around it stretched

---

[1] According to the statement of Senator Alcorn in debate.   *Globe,* 43 Cong., 2 Sess., 1343-4.
[2] Sen. Exe. Doc., 42 Cong., 3 Sess., No. 47, 2.
[3] House Repts., 43 Cong., 2 Sess., No 261, Part ii., 11.

large plantations bearing a dense negro population.   As early as 1871, Longstreet reported that arms were being issued there carelessly to a militia company, which was parading lawlessly under a desperado negro captain, who suffered arrest for the illegal way in which he was arresting men and even committing theft, murder, and arson. Though the company was discharged, the band kept their arms and continued their outrages.   Here as elsewhere, both Warmoth and Kellogg had commissioned parish officers so that loyalty was divided.   In Grant Parish two Fusion judges and a sheriff, under commissions from Warmoth, held office until March 25, 1873, when Kellogg's candidates took forcible possession.   That very night the newly-installed officials summoned armed negroes, several hundred strong, into Colfax under pretense of a sheriff's posse.   But deposing the sheriff, the band assumed a semi-military character, arming, drilling, and mounting cannon on earthworks in the court-house yard. Mounted squads scoured the country and permitted no white people to pass into the village.

The alarmed whites, in an attempt at a compromise, called a mass meeting at Colfax for April 1, to which the negroes were invited.   Though unarmed, according to instructions, delegates from Montgomery were stopped by the negroes so that the meeting came to naught.   Affairs grew more alarming after April 5: two hundred blacks fired on fifteen armed whites approaching Colfax; an outrage was perpetrated upon a judge's dead child; and an unprotected house was assailed.   Riot, murder, and robbery held sway until more than forty families left.[1]   April 7 the court, after opening, was unable to hold its session. Though this condition was reported to Kellogg, April 9,

---

[1] Nine of the men tried were twenty miles away on the day of the fight, as was conclusively proved.

16

no military force was sent[1] and the district attorney, also refused to act, as the Ku-Klux Act protected negroes only. The Democrats firmly believed that the leaders who had fomented the trouble left Colfax secretly the night of April 8. During the week prior to the conflict, Sheriff Nash, the Fusion officer, was busy summoning a posse of whites to retake the court-house and put down lawlessness. By Easter Sunday, April 13, he had gathered about one hundred and fifty men and secured a piece of artillery. Under a flag of truce he went to Smithfield, a negro quarters a half-mile to the northwest of Colfax, to order the negro commander to disperse his men. Refusal was followed by the threat of an attack in one-half hour. The negroes fled, about one hundred taking refuge in the court-house. The whites claimed that two of their number, who had been sent to the building to demand surrender, were shot, whereupon the enraged whites set fire to the structure, regardless of a shirt and the leaf of a book displayed as flags of truce, and killed a number of negroes as they rushed out from the flames. About thirty-seven, who were captured, were shot down in cold blood at dark after being told that they were to be set at liberty. The wildest stories of outrageous cruelties and barbarities by the white men were rife.[2] Fifteen or sixteen of the

---

[1] It was felt that Kellogg was indifferent purposely to have such a story for political capital.

[2] See Morton's speech in Congress over this affair. "The evidence before the grand jury . . . shows that three or four men would seize a colored man and another man put his pistol in his mouth and blow his brains out, and that they were mutilated and their abdomens ripped open after death. . . . Some thirty were captured and marched back in front of the court house after dark, and there they were put in lines and shot as Virginius prisoners were shot in Cuba. A large number were taken to the bank of the river after dark and shot, and thrown into the water. . . . The evidence further shows that when this massacre took place at night on the bank of the river, they tried experiments on them with their arms. They put them breast to back, three or four or five each, and then a man would stand at the

negroes had lifted the boards and taken refuge under the floor, but were all captured. A few of the wounded escaped by feigning death. In addition to some charred remains, fifty-nine dead bodies, which had been left unburied until the following Tuesday, were found near the court-house. [1]

The *Nation* regarded this "horrible massacre" as a not "unnatural consequence of the position in which Congress left the dispute" between the factions, and pointed out that there had been no outcry "over the disgraceful connivance at Washington at the state of things which has converted Louisiana into a South American Republic" parallel to the outcry which went up for the punishment of these "demons." [2] And it scorned Kellogg's impudence in accusing McEnery of planning and ordering the massacre as "tenth-rate politics." [3] But a large majority of the North [4] were far more inclined to agree with the verdict of the majority of the investigating committee, voiced in the following words of Hoar:

---

end of the line to see how many bodies he could send a bullet from his rifle through." He would make the number so killed over a hundred. *Record*, 43 Cong., 1 Sess., Appendix, 42.

[1] The account given here does not agree exactly with that given by Rhodes. It is based on the majority report of Hoar, Wheeler, and Frye, and on the minority report of Marshall, House Repts., 43 Cong., 2 Sess., No. 261, Part ii., iii., 847, 891, 409, 532, and also the *Annual Cyclopedia*, 1873.

[2] *Nation*, April 24, 1873.   [3] *Ibid.*, May 1.

[4] See the New York *Times* of April 18, which denounced it as a "fiendish deed, wholesale murder"; the New York *Evening Post* of April 16.

The Democratic press of Louisiana attempted to place the responsibility on Kellogg. "La responsibilité du sang qui vient de couler, remonte à celui dont l'ambition insensée a été la cause primière du conflit, à William Pitt Kellogg qui, non éligible à la place de gouverneur et non élu, a, par des moyens que toute conscience honnête ne peut s'empêcher de flétrir, usurpé l'exercise d'un pouvoir auquel il n'avait aucun droit." *Bee*, April 1. In a similar strain the *Picayune* blames the "pretender's ambition and misuse of troops." April 22.

"This deed was without palliation or justification; it was deliberate, barbarous, cold-blooded murder. It must stand, like the massacre of Glencoe or St. Bartholomew, a foul blot on the page of history."[1]   Nor did it tend to allay their sense of outraged justice that obstacles were opposed to the conviction of the persons indicted by the Federal Circuit Court for participation in the riot.   Kellogg, in his next annual message, declared that the most influential residents of New Orleans formed associations for the relief of the "Grant Parish sufferers"; that the entertainments given for their benefit were the most popular of the season; and that the massacre was still regarded as a justifiable assertion of white supremacy.

Grant's conviction, only deepened by this affair, is clearly seen in the message he sent to Congress almost two years later.

On the 13th of April [he stated], a butchery of citizens was committed at Colfax, which in blood-thirstiness and barbarity is hardly surpassed by any acts of savage warfare. . . .   It is a lamentable fact that insuperable obstacles were thrown in the way of punishing these murderers; and the so-called conservative papers of the State, not only justified the massacre, but denounced as Federal tyranny and despotism the attempt of United States officers to bring them to justice. Fierce denunciations ring through the country about office-holding and election matters in Louisiana, while every one of the Colfax miscreants goes unwhipped of justice, and no way can be found in this boasted land of civilization and Christianity to punish the perpetrators of this bloody and monstrous crime.[2]

. A few other violences, arising from conflicts over the court appointees, at about this time, contributed their

[1] House Repts., 43 Cong., 2 Sess., No. 261, 13–4.
[2] Richardson, *Messages and Papers*, VII., 308.

share in prejudicing the North, notably those in St. Mary's and St. Martin's Parishes.   In the latter, a public meeting was held, where the people bound themselves to resist the collection of taxes by Kellogg.   Citizens successfully resisted the metropolitan brigade for several weeks until in May they bowed to the mandate of a commander of United States troops.[1]

And these events explain the President's proclamation of May 22, 1873, in which he publicly recognized the Kellogg régime, since "Congress had tacitly recognized that government by refusing to take any action," and ordered the "turbulent and disorderly persons to disperse and retire peaceably to their respective abodes" within twenty days and to submit themselves to the laws and constituted authorities of said State.[2]

[1] For the full account see *Annual Cyclopedia*, 1873, 450.   And House Jour., 1874, 11.

[2] Richardson, VII, 223–4.

CHAPTER XII

Democratic Desperation

A SECOND legislative session under the Kellogg régime came and went without affording relief to the property class—indeed, it rendered the situation even worse. January 5, 1874, about the same number and the same men as had adjourned at Mechanics Institute the preceding March reassembled at the same place.[1] There were some vacancies to fill from death and resignation, some members added by the determination of contested election cases, and some of the defeated candidates seated, subject to contest, on a simple report of the Committee on Elections.[2] But a faction of the McEnery adherents, who had absented themselves all through 1873, while not convening, refused to lower their flag, even though the governor's annual address held out a bid and tried to stir their dormant consciences by warning them that if it should appear that their votes would have prevented bad legislation or have secured the passage of measures in the interest of the State, they would have incurred a grave responsibility.[3] They contented themselves with a telegram of protest to Congress, which the Senate resented because of its form.[4]

[1] There were present 25 Senators and 83 Representatives on the first day. Sen. Jour., 1874, 1, House Jour., 1.

[2] One was sworn in as late as Feb. 13. *Ibid.*, 147.

[3] Sen. Jour., 15. Jan. 12 the two members of the first ward of New Orleans were given one day's notice to appear or forfeit their seats. House Jour., 34.   [4] *Nation*, Jan. 8. 1874.

The money problem of how to enable the business of the State to keep going was the question which exclusively interested the State. It is only fair to allow Governor Kellogg to present the situation of the treasury in his own words. Hear first his excuse for not accomplishing more during his first year:

The treasury was empty. The total amount of taxes collected during the previous year was less than the amount returned delinquent. As against the various exhausted funds a mass of unpaid warrants had accumulated, aggregating nearly $2,250,000. This disgraceful result of the maladministration of the resources of the State during several years past, was left as an inheritance to be added to the other embarrassments of the present administration. The interest on the heavy bonded debt of the State had fallen in arrears to the extent of nearly $300,000. All receipts from the immense delinquent lists . . . were tied up . . . and devoted exclusively to the payment of the old outstanding warrants. . . . A system of espionage, which it seemed impossible for the treasury to shake off, had been established by the dealers in those warrants, whereby they were informed the instant a dollar was turned into the treasury. . . .[1]

The present situation, while not without its discouragements, afforded, he felt, just grounds for congratulation when compared with that of the previous year. Revenue, exceeding $4,000,000, had been collected with less loss and expense to the State than for many years. The large amount of overdue interest was paid early in the year, and since then the current interest had been paid promptly at maturity with the exception of the interest on some $6,000,000 worth of bonds held in abeyance, subject to the action of the courts, and there was money to pay that, if it were found legitimate. The board of examiners,

[1] Sen. Jour., 1874, 5.

which he had appointed, reported the State debt $53,000,-
000, from which it struck off $30,500,000 for unwarranted
guarantees.   But even then the State was bankrupt; it
could neither pay the debt nor meet the annual interest.
The board recommended repudiation to the amount of
$12,000,000.   In his annual message the governor virtually
recommended repudiation and defended it with the terse
statement: "I am not willing to advise the continuance
of a rate of taxation which is not far removed from
confiscation."[1]

His specific recommendations were to confine appropriations within the revenues; to make the revenues of each
year take care of the expenditure of that year; and, lastly,
to forbid the auditor to issue a warrant unless the funds
for it were in the treasury.   He suggested as a solution for
the debt, "a well-digested funding bill" and constitutional amendments which would convert the whole debt
into consolidated bonds at the rate of sixty cents for
each dollar of out-bonds; which would limit the rate of
taxation to fourteen and one-half mills, and reduce the
debt, as soon as possible, to fifteen million dollars.   He
condemned the fees of notaries, clerks, and sheriffs, the
fees paid for conviction of criminals, and the charges of
city coroners as excessive and urged their reduction[2];
and felt that the fees of tax collectors were still too large,
especially when as much as fifty million dollars' worth of
property passed unassessed.[3]

What executive action could effect, Kellogg endeavored

[1] Sen. Jour., 8–9.   The *Nation* regarded Kellogg's message as "in itself
no bad document for the McEnery party to use as its memorial." Jan. 8,
1874.   [2] *Ibid.*, 1874, 12–13.
  [3] The Committee on Retrenchment reported Mar. 2 that "the present
enormous and unnecessary expense of assessment and collection of taxes
by State, city, and the several parishes does not fall far short of the anticipated income of the general fund for the present year—$1,050,000." Sen.
Jour., 243.

to do. When he learned that the New Orleans, Mobile, and Chattanooga Railroad Company, to which the State had donated three million dollars in bonds, had become insolvent after completing some ninety miles of road, and had been sold in the United States Circuit Court in June, 1873, he instituted suit to annul the sale and assert the rights of the State as a creditor; and then recommended to the legislature that the State purchase and manage the road, if no one else would undertake it.[1] And he endeavored to thwart unwise legislation by vetoing nine of the unwise bills of the last session.[2]

But his corrupt[3] legislature, having tasted the joys of a liberal income, went its own happy way. It did pass a few measures of reform which did not affect its own perquisites: it reformed the collection of taxes, reducing the cost of assessment by substituting quadrennial revision—a saving of $250,000 to the city and State each four years; it reduced the number and compensation of assessors and collectors, at the same time increasing their responsibility—a change which diminished by two-thirds the clerical force in the auditor's office; and it provided for proper legal action to refuse portions of the debt as illegal. Likewise, the constitutional amendments which he had recommended passed both houses unanimously[4] in the form of five sections: One, indorsing the funding bill and consolidated bonds; the second, reducing the State debt to fifteen million dollars and limiting taxation to twelve and one-half mills; one, devoting annual revenues to the expenses of the same year[5]; another, limiting the debt of

---

[1] Sen. Jour., 1874, 9–10.   [2] House Jour., 16. Sen. Jour., 16–17.

[3] Venality was boldly charged, as before, on the floor of this Assembly.

[4] Sen. Jour., 37. House Jour., 58.

[5] Session Laws, No. 4. Ratified by a larger vote than that cast for either of the party tickets, according to the governor's annual. Sen. Jour., 1875, 6. The *Times* advocated these amendments; 12,000 Conservatives voted for them.

New Orleans; and the last, placing the State election on the same day as that of the Presidential election.[1]   The Assembly also passed a law to establish official parish journals[2]; a law incorporating a company as a Society for the Prevention of Cruelty to Animals, which was translated into a society for cattle-stealing[3]; a joint resolution indorsed Durrell's "upright and fearless" action as "emanating from the purest motives"; a Superior Criminal Court with powers of highest criminal jurisdiction, writ of habeas corpus, and mandamus was created for Orleans Parish to take cognizance of all offenses with the penalty of life imprisonment or hard labor for more than five years, for all violations of election and registration laws, for all offenses against State officers, and for conspiracy and malfeasance.   Two important laws, intended to prevent the complaints of 1872, wrestled with the registration and election questions.   A new general registration must occur under the supervision of a State registrar, a supervisor for each parish, and an assistant for each ward in New Orleans, their appointment vested by habit in the governor.[4]   A revision of the election law gave the supervisors supreme power to strike a name from the list at will or to refuse registration.   The improvement spirit was not yet dead, for this assembly authorized the incorporation of the Shreveport and Southwestern Railroad Company, at the same time encouraging the

[1] The purpose of this amendment was to reduce the expenses of election as well as for uniformity with the practice of other States.

[2] Session Laws, No. 59.

[3] The legislature gave this society exclusive charge of all the pounds in the city with authority to seize all animals in the streets, charge the owners five dollars a day for detention, and after eight days sell them.   The summary arrest of the goats in the outskirts very nearly precipitated a riot of Irishwomen.   The company once began to arrest horses left standing in the streets while their riders were transacting business.   Nordhoff, 61.

[4] Session Laws, No. 155.

city of Shreveport to donate $300,000; steamships built in the State were relieved from wharfage fees[1]; and the monopoly of certain bayous was granted for a quarter of a century.

New Orleans had not thriven very much better during the year of Democratic rule than under Radical control,[2] but there can be no doubt but that Mayor Wiltz and the administrators were hampered, as they alleged, by the Assembly. The city debt had mounted from $16,000,000 in 1868 to $20,000,000 by November of 1871,[3] a large proportion of which had been accumulated for railways, levees, and water-works,[4] while the bonds brought but about three-fourths of their par value, thus augmenting the debt by one-third. The assessed value of property had declined during the preceding year $1,434,622[5] and the amount of taxes which it was possible to collect had declined even more relatively.[6] Such contradictory statements appeared as that in the *Times* which held that the reduction in the city debt under Conservative rule approximated $800,000[7] and that in the *Republican* which charged that the certified city debt had increased from June, 1872, to June, 1874, $750,000.[8] But there was

---

[1] Session Laws, 1874, No. 145.

[2] The *Republican* states that the rulers were accused of having permitted a ring in their assessment office, and of having applied the wharf receipts to other purposes than wharf reparation.   April 4, 1875.

[3] House Repts., 42 Cong., 2 Sess., No. 41, 205.   The *National Republican* reported Sep. 22: "The regular brokers shun all dealing in it (city paper) and capitalists scorn it.   It is hawked around by its unfortunate owners— clerks and laborers—and sold to the first man who offers to buy it at 58–60 cents on the dollar.   The merchant who sells the city necessary supplies, the contractors and others in the jobbing lines, take good care to add the discount."

[4] The papers complained Aug. 8, 1872, that the city was spending $20,000 a week on "about as perceptible city improvements as a flea upon an ox's hide."   [5] House Repts., 42 Cong., 2 Sess., No. 41, 201.

[6] *Ibid.*, 207.   [7] July 17, 1874.

[8] *National Republican*.   Note the caustic comment: "These apologists

no gainsaying the fact that the city was in a very bad way indeed. The rate at which the tax had mounted was appalling: before Warmoth's administration it had been 15 mills on the dollar; in 1869 it was 23¾; in 1870, 26⅓; in 1871, 27½ mills[1]; and in 1873, 30 mills; but in 1874, it stood again at 27½ mills. The city's seven per cent gold bonds sold at forty-eight cents,[2] and then were taken up only by local charitable organizations, banks, and adventurers. The list of delinquent tax-payers to the city covered four pages of fine print in the *Republican* of August 4, and the list of properties offered for sale by tax-collectors was appalling.[3] Sales were made for pitifully small amounts. From 1871 to 1874 four hundred and ninety-one seizures had been made in the city. And, here, again, credit for effort is due the governor, for he laid before each House a series of fifteen measures intended to curtail all expenses possible of reduction, and insure the end of all waste, the ones presented to the House having been drawn up under the supervision of the city council and a committee of the Chamber of Commerce.[4] Of all these, only the amendments which prohibited the further increase of the city debt in any form and which provided that after the first of January no certificates of indebtedness should be issued by any officer, except against cash, passed.[5] But others of the legislator's own initiative passed: one, to abolish fees of jurors in coroner and criminal cases[6]; another to levy a police tax, regulate levies of

---

say that it is no fault of the Fusion Administration that they abused their trust, but of the Republican legislature and Democratic lobby that did not put it out of their power to do so." July 17.

[1] Herbert, *Why the Solid South?* 406.

[2] A little later. See the *Times*, July 9, 1874.

[3] See the New Orleans *Republican*, Dec. 18 and 23. See also the *Republican*, Jan. 1, 6, 10, and 22, 1875.

[4] Sen. Jour., 1874, 138–40, House Jour., 138–9.

[5] Session Laws, 1874, No. 22.   [6] *Ibid.*, No. 69.

taxes and tax-suits; to authorize the funding of the city floating debt[1]; to provide the time for the payment of taxes, allowing a discount for taxes paid prior to March 20[2]; and to reduce the cost of inquests and give salaries to coroners. [3]

Greater folly than ever characterized their expenditures. The governor had estimated that the legislative expenses ought not to exceed $150,000; yet the Senate cost the State for that one session almost $68,000, [4] while it added to the vouchers thirty per cent to cover the loss of selling the warrants and authorized $35,000 rental for the capitol offices[5]; and the House, as usual, authorized any number of additional fees for messengers and clerks, encouraging also contests for seats by paying the per diem and mileage for all claimants back to 1872. The governor found that the public lands were not proving the source of help which they should. Of eight million acres available for cultivation, over five million remained for sale, while the forty-seven thousand acres sold during 1873 were sacrificed at the absurd price fixed in 1871, twelve and one-half cents per acre.

It is small wonder that the Conservatives saw no hope of relief so long as negroes predominated in their councils, and that in sheer desperation they determined they must carry the fall election, a feat which could be achieved, they felt, only by a white man's party. They had made their effort, sincerely and honestly, in 1872 to win the black vote, but apparent success had not brought results. Phelps's statement of this position is lucid:

It was plain that if they could establish a legal and orderly government, the Federal troops would be withdrawn. There

[1] Session Laws, 1874, No. 128.   [2] Ibid., No. 40.   [3] Ibid., No. 157.
[4] Found in a report of the Committee on Auditing and Supervising Expenses of the Senate. Appropriation was for $228,000. Ibid., No. 2, 32.   [5] Sen. Jour., 243.

remained, consequently, but one hope and one duty—the determination to rectify the blunders of negro suffrage and annul the pernicious influence of his vote.

And so now the *Times* stood alone among Fusion papers in a sincere effort to gain black ballots.[1]

Leaders found their excuse in the insolence of the black police and in the plea of the Black Leagues, survivals of the Liberty Leagues of six years earlier.   To what degree this latter plea was founded on facts is difficult to determine, but concerning the arrogance and brutality of the colored militia there can be no question.   Many prominent citizens testified to the Congressional Committee that white ladies in every portion of the city were assaulted and indignities offered them; while the conduct of the negro police became oppressive and even bold enough to threaten without cause prominent citizens.[2]   Arrests were frequent, often for trivial causes, and without duly executed warrant.[3]   The police would violently and unnecessarily beat the person arrested.   An attorney testified that it was impossible to get a colored policeman to arrest negroes committing these offenses, or to secure conviction of a policeman.   Indeed, he cited a case where the judge complimented the police for what seems plain brutality.   It was the practice among the policemen, when they arrested a man, to strip him of all the valuables about his person.[4]   Also in the case of a colored Democrat, arrest and trial were usually so hurried that there was no opportunity for defense.[5]

In June the whites were becoming alarmed by the ship-

---

[1] See later, July 17, 18.   So far as reflections from the *Bee*, *Picayune*, and *Bulletin* can be caught, they stood emphatically for a white man's party.   But see House Repts., 43 Cong., 2 Sess., No. 101, Part ii., 222, for the position of certain leaders.

[2] *Ibid.*, 221–2.   [3] *Ibid.*, 221 and 211.   [4] *Ibid.*, 222.

[5] *Ibid.*, 217.

ping to the country of large quantities of arms to be distributed to the blacks.   Nearly every steamboat carried some in the hold.   About July 1 a story of an apprehended negro uprising was current, which the *Times* declared took its rise from the *Picayune's* publishing and spreading a canard of a negro uprising, scheduled for early July.   On July 4 the last-named paper published the constitution, signs, and pass-words of the "Republican Alliance," the official name for the Black League.   About the same time the *Bulletin* dropped an unfortunate hint about arms being shipped to the Cane River.[1]   The *Times* and *Bee* denied that the people believed it, but, on account of being copied in several parish papers, it caused excitement and tense feeling.   The writer found unmistakable evidence of negro duelling and of the collecting of arms in La Fourche[2] and New Orleans.[3]   But these were only a few isolated instances.   Perhaps the *Times* put the situation fairly when it said:

We do not believe there is an organized "league" for any purpose among the colored people; if any person has reliable evidence to that effect we shall be very glad to receive it and comment on it in proper terms.   But the clannish spirit manifested by them in many localities is patent to everybody. . . .   It is used by the worst specimens of their race and ours for purposes not at all necessary to their self-protection.[4]

Before election, however, the race line had become very clearly drawn.   The colored men of Orleans Parish held a separate convention in October and published an address in which they, as constituting nine-tenths of the Republican party, asserted their title to nine-tenths of the offices, but declared generously that they would be satis-

[1] July 4.
[2] House Repts., 43 Cong., 2 Sess., No. 101, Part ii., 31.
[3] *Ibid.*, 217, 275, 211.   [4] July 22, 1874.

fied with one-half.[1]   Nordhoff relates a story told him by
a Republican of one parish where the blacks wanted to
put in office an entire set of colored men.   As the Republicans had been honest there, they did not want the blacks
to run them into debt.[2]   Kellogg testified that the first
positive indication of negro organization appeared in
April, in the famous Todd resolutions of a village in St.
Mary Parish, whence the movement branched off to Bienville,[3] while some time before a formal White League was
heard of organizations had been formed at Opelousas.'[4]

As early as June, parish papers, with the approval of
the city papers, were urging the propriety of organizing
a new party on a strictly white basis, the first step in
which was to be the enrolling of the whites in "White
Leagues."[5]   The address of the White Men's Central
Club of Webster Parish defines the position sufficiently
well:

Their [the negroes] recent attitude toward the white people
is one of open defiance, inviting an issue of the races, by
organizing and arming their leagues throughout the state,
with the determination to gain complete supremacy in Louisiana.   Our own safety and that of our families demand that we
cease our apathy and prepare to meet this issue by a thorough
organization of the white race in every parish in the state.[6]

War was declared on carpet-bagger and scalawag and
on every white who should refuse to coöperate.   Leagues
sprang up obediently all over the State: July 2 we hear
of the Crescent City White League[7]; July 25 of a meeting

---

[1] New Orleans *Republican*, October 26.
[2] *Cotton States*, 66.   These Republicans rejoiced in September 14, as it had
terrified the negroes from carrying out the above plot.
[3] House Repts., 43 Cong., 2 Sess., No. 101, Part ii., 185.
[4] Phelps, 376.   [5] Mansfield *Reporter*, June 29, copied by the *Times*.
[6] Webster Parish *Democrat*, quoted by the *Times*.
[7] *Picayune*, July 2.   The *Bee* felt the necessity of prompt organization,

at Colfax Court House for the purpose of forming a White League[1]; July 25 of one at Iberia[2]; July 13 of one in St. Mary Parish; and July 27 of one in Natchitoches.[3] One can scarcely suppress a smile when we read in the *Sugar Bowl* that the colored Baptist Church at Petite Anse pledged its support to the White League there.[4]

The story of the inception of such a body in New Orleans is told by the chief leader, Frederick Ogden, himself.[5] An effort was made to dissociate the organization entirely from politics,[6] but it evidently broke down. However, some of the men interested went off and organized white leagues in the city, among whom was Ogden, who organized a group on July 1 for purely "defensive" purposes as the Crescent City White League.[7] Other groups followed the example until twenty-five to twenty-eight hundred men were enrolled in separate leagues.[8] It assumed a military character to the extent of appointing and obeying officers. This explains the confusion in names: in New Orleans it was an armed, defensive organization, in the parishes often a political party. So marked was this distinction that from some four or five parishes came double delegations to the convention at Baton Rouge.[9] The movement spread until by the last of August the number of armed and

---

for "La population blanche de la Nouvelle Orléans peut être dans la nécessité de se protéger elle même contre des aggressions subites, ou elle peut être appelée à envoyer des secours aux blancs des paroisses menacés par des soulèvements."   August 30.

[1] *Republican*, Aug. 2.   [3] *Sugar Bowl.*
[2] *Vindicator*, July 28.   [4] August 20.

[5] Ogden was the first president and Behan was vice-president, under whom were soon enrolled the best men of the State.

[6] The resolutions proposed are to be found, House Repts., 43 Cong., 2 Sess., No. 101, Part ii., 224.

[7] *Ibid.*, 206–7.

[8] Only three thousand were enrolled after September 14.   *Ibid.*, 219.

[9] *Ibid.*, 225.

17

organized leaguers was given as fourteen thousand.[1]   That
the White League proper had any considerable relations
outside of New Orleans, or that it was intended in any
way to interfere with the rights of the colored citizens
does not appear.   But that the White League would
coöperate to overthrow the Kellogg régime, the Congressional Committee did not doubt.   "So will substantially
all the white citizens of Louisiana,"[2] is its terse comment.
In some of the parishes, as Attakapas, it was warmly
received; in others it was treated with indifference,[3] much
as the Reform party was treated in 1872.[4]   Some of the
old staunch Democrats did not seem eager to abandon
their party name and organization for the League.[5]
While the leaders were, no doubt, conservative, the
younger element introduced features which led the papers
to denounce it as simply an offshoot of the Ku Klux Klan.[6]
The costumes and instruments were gone, but the spirit of
proscription was present, it was felt.   Thus voiced the
Shreveport *Times* the feeling which actuated the leagues:

> Their career [carpet-baggers] is ended; we are determined
> to tolerate them no longer, and if they care for their infamous
> necks, they had better stop their work right now, and look
> out for a safer field of rascality.   If a single hostile gun is
> fired between the whites and blacks, every carpet-bagger and
> scalawag that can be caught will in twelve hours be hanging
> from a limb.[7]

[1] *Bulletin*, August 25, a Radical estimate.
[2] House Repts., 43 Cong., 2 Sess., No. 101, Part ii, 9.
[3] The following parish papers opposed it: Mansfield *Reporter*, Lafayette
Advertiser, June 27, Attakapas *Register*, July 3.   Encountered through the
columns of the *Times* and *Republican*.
[4] Baltimore *American*, July 13.
[5] See New Orleans *Times*, July 7, *Bulletin*, July 14, 1874, to show the
attitude of a Democrat leader.
[6] Baltimore *American*, July 13; see also *Republican*, Aug. 13.
[7] Copied.   The organization was strong around Shreveport.

It should, however, be realized that to many White League was but another name for the old-time Democratic party.[1]

The platform of the White League in St. Mary Parish formulated its creed succinctly. It declared the purpose to be the protection of the white race, the purging of offices from "such a horde of miscreants as now assume to lord it over us"; it pledged the members to hearty support of all that the League determined upon; it condemned no white man for his political opinion, if he but joined them; and it declared it to be the duty of all members to socially proscribe all white men who united themselves with the Radical party and to employ only those in alliance with themselves.[2] The exhortation of the Natchitoches *Vindicator* of July 25 throws additional light:

Your only succor lies in your own right arms, and you must immediately be prepared to meet any and every emergency. Let each ward organize and establish a concert of action so that if the worst comes, we can have it said that we, at least, made some show of resistance. Better that we should occupy unnumbered graves than live as recreant cowards.

The leagues of New Orleans drilled and marched in cotton presses, halls, and in the streets[3] of New Orleans under many difficulties, usually at night and without arms. As complaints were made to the advisory board, the Fusion leaders directed all drilling on the streets to cease with such success that Packard admitted that "no instance occurred after that up to the time of the election."[4]

[1] After the election, Packard stated that this organization was known as the McEnery militia in some parts of the State. House Repts., 43 Cong., 2 Sess., No. 101, Part ii., 27.

[2] Sen. Exe. Doc., 43 Cong., 2 Sess., No. 13, 31. Adopted July 13.

[3] Usually in Commerce Street because of its width.

[4] House Repts., 43 Cong., 2 Sess., No. 101, Part ii., 26.

But not only did the movement meet with the condemnation of the Radical press of the State,[1] but also of other papers and organizations, Conservative as well as Radical. The Natchez *Democrat* and *Courier* of July 10 predicted the violence and Radical outcry which it actually provoked. It was condemned by the Chicago *Tribune* and New York *Journal of Commerce* and advised to be cautious by the Boston *Post.*[2] In much the same strain spoke the editor of the *Nation:*

The Leaguers may have better information than we of the decay in the North of the feeling that, as regards the negro, the South will bear to be watched. Some decay there has been; how much, nobody yet knows; but how much there was of the feeling to be removed the Leaguers can partly guess by reflecting on the equanimity with which the North has now for years regarded the condition of Louisiana herself and South Carolina.[3]

The Boston *Advertiser* is mild when it says:

The white people of Louisiana, being, it may be acknowledged, under some provocation in view of the way things have been managed in that state, have rushed madly into the worst scheme to remedy the difficulty. . . . Things have occurred in Louisiana within the past ten years that tend to discourage any confidence that the worst outrages would not be resorted to if they were thought to be expedient . . . The peaceable submission to the situation after a firm and ineffectual protest,

---

[1] The New Orleans *Republican* stripped away all non-essentials and put the case clearly, if baldly, "Their Democratic friends in the North are now endeavoring, by misrepresentation to create a public opinion that will induce the President to keep his hands off while they go in, and by killing a few hundred negroes, carry the election triumphantly for the Democratic party, by returning six Democratic members of Congress and electing a Democratic legislature for Louisiana." Aug. 4. See also issues of July 19, Aug. 1, where it speaks of the "White League Lunacy," of Aug. 4 and 6.

[2] July 22.   [3] Aug. 13, 1874. Vol. XIX, 97.

did something to restore a more favorable opinion toward the Louisiana people.   But its force will be quickly dissipated if they persist in this folly of a White League, the meaning of which is a perpetuation of the antagonism of races, out of which their woes have sprung.[1]

Thus more belligerently the Cleveland *Leader:*

If we were to name that organization of the United States which nearest approaches in malignancy and wickedness the old slave power, we would say it is the lately formed "White Leagues of Louisiana."[2]

Or hear the Washington *Republican:*

If as is threatened, the forthcoming election shall be conducted upon these principles; if a reign of murder is inaugurated, the white leaders in Louisiana mistake the temper of the North, if they suppose it will stand by with folded hands and sanction it.[3]

The Republican State Convention of Pennsylvania saw fit to incorporate in its platform a plank condemning the "frantic efforts of the Democrats to bring on a war of races in the South with the design of depriving a portion of its citizens of the rights which belong to them."[4]

The New Orleans *Republican* made an eloquent plea to the colored population for strong nominations, and for freedom from prejudice at the convention, which should meet August 5 in the state-house to name candidates for State treasurer,[5] new State Central Committee, members of Congress, and for the State Assembly.   The first two

---

[1] Copied by the New Orleans *Times*, July 13.
[2] Quoted.   [3] August 20.
[4] New Orleans *Republican*, Aug. 26, 1874.
[5] It is significant that Clinton, the auditor, declined August 13 to serve longer with "such an associate as the nominee of the Republican convention." *Republican*, August 13. Dubuclet had been renominated.

days were largely lost because of a lack of decorum, defiance of the chairman, and because of the delay in action on the credentials. It threatened to be difficult to preserve the unity of the party, as the story of dissensions and disorder was eagerly spread broadcast by the opposition. The convention completed its work on the fourth day by the adoption of the resolutions. It reiterated its faith in the Republican principles as enunciated at Philadelphia; indorsed Grant and the Kellogg government, which "in the face of unparalleled difficulties had achieved substantial reforms"; approved the Civil Rights bill, then before Congress, the funding bill, and certain of the amendments; and pledged itself to the reduction of State expenses and to a fair election, coupling with this a condemnation of the spirit of violence "manifested in certain localities by the Democratic party."[1]

The Democratic Central Committee summoned the State convention for August 24 at New Orleans, appealing to all Conservatives for support in its battle against Radicalism for constitutional principles, "principles in violation of which this usurpation has been foisted on Louisiana, and our people subjected to political and judicial persecution."[2] This party, too, had dissension to battle with in its ranks: the Democrats in the parishes objected to the place of assembly because of the thugs,[3] the editor of the Shreveport *Times* going so far as to appeal to the constituencies to appoint no delegates.[4] The Committee of Seventy, men of property, and of large landed and business interests, who had spent large sums to prevent the installation of Kellogg, urged the State Committee to

[1] This account is based on the issues of the *Republican* and *Times*, August 6–10, and the *Annual Cyclopedia*, 1874, 476–7.

[2] *Times*, July 8.

[3] Baton Rouge *Advocate*, copied by the *Times*, July 8; a meeting at Donaldsonville is recounted in the *Picayune*, August 20.

[4] Copied by the *Times*, July 26.

amend its call so as to summon "all the elements opposed to Radicalism to assemble at Baton Rouge instead of New Orleans," to which convention should be remitted the shaping of the canvass. [1]

And so the convention gathered at Baton Rouge, in concession to that request, on the day designated; made its nominations, advised against the amendments, and adopted its platform. Its preamble gives utterance to the party policy: "We, the white people of Louisiana, embracing the Democratic Party, the Conservative Party, the White Man's Party, the Liberal Party, the Reform Party, and all others opposed to the Kellogg usurpation. . . ." It denounced Kellogg as a usurper, maintaining himself in opposition to the will of the people; condemned his party for inflaming the passions of the negroes; denounced the social legislation of Congress; took its stand unequivocally for white rule as "most helpful to both races"; it denounced the election laws, termed the portion of the State debt added by the Republicans fraudulent; and urged the Democrats to vote down the amendments. [2] The Democracy of the metropolis ratified the resolutions in a mass meeting on Canal Street on September 1. But the stand on the color line was seen to be so foolish that as soon as the convention had adjourned, the very members of the convention did nominate colored men in the parishes.

The situation over the registration law was full of difficulties. Although it was said that Kellogg had pledged himself never to sign the law, he did affix his signature. On July 29 this law was the sole topic of conversation. The prevalent feeling was one of disgust, indignation, and resentment. Men were saying to each other that the game was up; that any theory based on the use of the ballot-box was simply idiotic; that the mission of the

[1] *Picayune*, July 31, 1874.   [2] *Annual Cyclopedia*, 1874, 477.

new law was evidently to guarantee their defeat beforehand, and that since the means afforded by the law were
fully adequate to the end contemplated, people might as
well discard that method of making themselves heard.
It was openly said, "Supervisors can't refuse our suffrages
on *one* basis we know of."[1]

With such a determination on the part of the Democrats
to go the very limit of desperation and a situation with
regard to parish offices provocative of friction, it was not
to be expected that the summer could pass without
violence.   Rumors of coercion and murder[2] by bands of
White Leaguers, who were forcing parish officers to resign,
came from Martinsville,[3] from Bossier, and from Natchitoches[4]; came from Lincoln Parish, where the effort
was termed a conspiracy to "overturn the authority of the
majority and place the parish in line with the insurrec-
tionary movements in other parishes in that part of the
State"[5]; from Marksville and Avoyelles, where the tax-
collector was forced to resign and was driven from the
parish[6]; from Caddo, whence the New Orleans *Republican*
drew a fine story of outrage[7]; in fact, from many parts of
northern and western Louisiana.   Of course, it is difficult to determine how much of this reported terrorism
was Radical newspaper artillery, fired off to influence
the National government.   But the *Picayune* admitted
that the people had waited on parish officials with a

---

[1] *Picayune*, July 30.   [2] *Republican*, Aug. 22.
[3] But note that the *Picayune* states that nearly all the officials requested
to resign here were white, while those invited to retain their positions were
nearly all black.   Sept. 1.   See the *Republican* of Aug. 18 for St. Martin
Parish.   See also issues of August 8 and 9.
[4] According to the Natchitoches *Vindicator* there was a Committee on
Resignations there.   Copied by the *Republican* about Aug. 18.
[5] *Republican*, Aug. 18.   [6] *Ibid.*, Aug. 25.
[7] Denied in a letter signed by two hundred and twenty Republicans of
the parish.   *Picayune*, Aug. 21.

demand for their resignations in "some half a dozen parishes."[1]

Clashes of this sort could not occur without great likelihood of a serious climax somewhere and that climax came in Coushatta, a city perhaps a hundred miles farther up the Red River than Colfax, well up in the northwestern corner of the State.   On one side it was alleged to have been a merciless war waged by the whites upon the blacks, while other reports attributed the origin of the trouble to the uprising of the blacks.   The outbreak followed several sporadic cases of conflict between the races.   A body of the White League assembled to compel the parish officers— all Republican—to resign.   The sheriff summoned a posse of sixty-five men, white as well as black, to protect the officers in their rights and duties.   This posse, overpowered by a superior force, surrendered after a number on each side had been killed, under a clear guarantee of their lives, conditioned upon the departure of the more prominent Republicans and the resignation of the six Radical officeholders.   The following day, Sunday, August 30, while these officials were being conducted in fetters to Shreveport by an armed guard of about seventeen men from the place where they had been confined over night, they were set upon by another band, presumably White Leaguers, who had been seen to leave Shreveport the night before, and "deliberately murdered in cold blood."[2]   Though the people of the Red River Parish issued an address, trying to show that they were not hostile to negroes, Kellogg immediately notified the President that "a more wanton outrage was never com-

[1] About Aug. 21.
[2] According to Kellogg. The *Annual Cyclopedia*, 1874, 478, gives two versions, Kellogg's and that of the Conservatives of the parish. I also used Sen. Exe. Doc., 43 Cong., 2 Sess., No. 17, House Repts., 43 Cong., 2 Sess., No. 261, Part ii., 9–10, 773–80, and the *Bulletin, Ibid.*, 884–8.

mitted in any civilized community." He followed this
action on September 3 with a proclamation declaring
martial law and offering five thousand dollars for the
capture of each person implicated.[1]

The report of this outrage, added to others elsewhere
in the South,[2] led the President to take measures to suppress them, whereby instructions were issued to all
Federal marshals and attorneys in the State to detect
with all possible dispatch, to expose, arrest, and punish
the perpetrators of these crimes. Federal troops were
ordered stationed at convenient points to give all necessary
aid.[3]

Although the Committee of Seventy tried to find
excuses and to avert the blame from the Democrats, and
although the better Conservative papers condemned the
act,[4] these apologies did not silence the roar of indignation

---

[1] "The effect of this (the declaration of martial law) is that all truly
honest and honorable people are filled with serene satisfaction while the
rogues and ruffians are trembling in their boots." New Orleans *Republican*,
Sept. 6.

[2] There is no doubt but that the Vicksburg murder, occurring a little
later, in September, 1875, and a negro riot in Alabama blackened matters
sadly for Louisiana. According to Morton, 500 White Leaguers from
Louisiana offered their services. *Cong. Record*, 43 Cong., 2 Sess., 373.

[3] *Annual Cyclopedia*, 1874, 479. The order to Belknap is quoted there
in full.

[4] See the excerpts from the Delhi *Chronicle* and Ascension *Leader;* but
Grant in his report of the affair declared that the Conservative press of the
State denounced all efforts at punishment and boldly justified the crime,
"and hence he concluded that the spirit of hatred and violence is stronger
than the law." *Cong. Record*, 43 Cong., 2 Sess., 415.

The *Times* charged this "atrocious deed as the direct and legitimate
outgrowth of the violent Red River White League Organizations," and
for it the able and diabolical White League organ, the Shreveport *Times*,
responsible (Sept. 2, 1874). But the *Picayune*, while disclaiming any desire
to "mitigate any of the horrors of the Coushatta tragedy," felt it well
"that all the circumstances thereof should be clearly ascertained" (Sept. 5).
This paper hardly felt the gravity of the case until it heard the click of guns
through the President's proclamation: "A few whimpering carpet-bag-

and wrath which went up again over the country.[1] The
Republican press of the State seemed never to tire of the
subject ."of Lives taken for the Crime of Northern birth
and Republican principles."[2] Day after day the New
Orleans *Republican* made some reference to Coushatta,
laying it, of course, at the door of the White League.[3]
And as late as September 10 some Louisianians telegraphed that the reign of terror continued unabated at
Coushatta with a camp of Leaguers established in the
town and murders occurring daily.[4] There was even a
loud demand in the North for a special session of
Congress to consider Southern questions.

---

gers have fled the neighborhood they despoiled; a few swaggering ruffians
have shrieked with terror at the worm their cruelty goaded into turning; half a dozen conspirators and inciters of bloodshed have met rude
sentence from their victims" (Sept. 4). And, "as for torturing it into a
war upon the negro, there is absolutely nothing in the affair, from beginning to end, to warrant such a construction" (Sept. 3). And the *Bee*
explained it as a radical plot: " Les chefs du parti radical auraient voulu,
sans doute, avoir une seconde édition du massacre de Colfax, afin de four-
nir au parti un moyen d'influencer les élections d'automne et d'avoir un
prétexte pour obtenir l'envoi de quelques troupes fédérales" (Sept. 3), and
denied it as an act of the League.

[1] See Washington *National Republican*, Sept. 2, Chicago *Times*, Sept. 5,
Cleveland *Leader*, Sept. 3, St. Louis *Republican*, Sept. 4, Philadelphia *Bul-
letin*, Aug. 31, Philadelphia *Dispatch*, Sept. 4, Cincinnati *Times*, Sept. 1,
Baltimore *American*, Sept. 1, *Inter-Ocean*, Sept. 2, Milwaukee *Sentinel*,
Sept. 1. The *Nation*, however, shows no positive condemnation
Sept. 10.

[2] The *Republican* printed its account of the Coushatta affair Sept. 1,
under the above headlines.

[3] See its issue of September 2.

[4] Sen. Exe. Doc., 43 Cong., 2 Sess., No. 13, 12.

CHAPTER XIII

The September Rebellion and the Election

THE country was given scarcely two weeks in which to recover from the Coushatta story, before New Orleans roused it to fever pitch in very truth by the action which marked the limit to which the Conservatives could be driven in their efforts to recover the reins of control and in their despair of securing a fair election under the recent law. The revolt of September fourteenth may have been suggested by the feeling that Grant was relenting, based on the fact that in the course of the summer he had withdrawn all the Federal troops except a small garrison in New Orleans. Proof of the existence of a belief that Grant meant to leave the South alone is found in a letter from Kellogg to the President on August 19, in which he decries the industrious circulation of that impression.[1] A certain restlessness in the city had been sufficiently manifest so that the militia was not sent to Coushatta until United States troops had arrived, while on September 2 patrols were massed to counteract the rumored movement of the White Leaguers.[2] The Conservatives had been especially irritated by the seizure by National officials of arms, shipped to private citizens in New Orleans, presumably for the White League.[3]

---

[1] Sen. Exe. Doc., 43 Cong., 2 Sess., No. 13, 9.
[2] *Picayune*, September 3.
[3] Phelps, 377. The *Picayune* reflects this feeling strongly when it char-

They felt that there was no security for life or property unless they enjoyed their constitutional right to bear arms.[1] They had been disarmed while passing along the street even on returning from a hunting excursion.[2] A mass meeting of the citizens had been called on September 4 to condemn the action of the police in taking private property.[3] It may be true, as Ogden claimed,[4] that the masses did not know on the morning of the fourteenth of any purpose to overthrow the Kellogg government but underneath lay, undoubtedly, the determination to do so if a favorable opportunity presented.[5]

On Saturday night, the 12th, in anticipation of a seizure from the steamer *Mississippi* on Monday morning, posters appeared about the city, calling on the citizens to assemble Monday at eleven o'clock on Canal Street. In the *Bulletin* Sunday morning, appeared an incendiary article, signed by many business firms, calling on the citizens to close their business doors, and in "tones loud enough to be heard the length and breadth of this land, declare to the janizaries and hirelings, as well as the prime instigator of all the outrages heaped upon us, that you are of right, ought to be, and mean to be free."[6]   On Monday

---

acterizes this affair "as one of the most tyrannical and high-handed outrages which has yet disgraced the memory of freedom in this century." Sept. 10.

[1] Guns, not pistols, for almost every citizen had his own pistol.

[2] House Repts., 43 Cong., 2 Sess., No. 101, Part ii., 216.

[3] *Ibid.* .   [4] *Ibid.*, 218.

[5] *Ibid.*, 216.   See also Fleming, *Documentary History of Reconstruction*, II., 144–5, where extracts from the diary of D. F. Boyd, President of the State University, show that rebellion was in prospect.   There was very bad feeling between the races and parties at the time.   Things had reached so serious a condition that men felt that they must take a chance on improving it by forcing some kind of a change—it mattered little what.   The great object, it was felt, was to make an impression on the North, and this, they held, was partially achieved when Massachusetts at her next election went Democratic.   Opinion of Judge Breaux.

[6] Even the women appealed to the men out of the depths of their humilia-

morning about three thousand[1] armed men met quietly at the Clay Statue[2] and adopted a resolution accusing Kellogg of ulterior motives in the new election law, of wrongs in the registration, and demanded, therefore, in the name of the citizens of New Orleans,"now in mass meeting assembled, and of the people of the State of Louisiana, whose franchise has been wrested from them by fraud and violence, and all of whose rights and liberties have been outraged and trampled upon, his immediate abdication." When the committee reported that he declined to receive them on the plea that he regarded their assemblage "as a menace," a loud and angry shout went up.[3] Penn, who in the absence of McEnery was acting executive,[4] "constrained from a sense of duty," in an inflammatory proclamation called on every man between the

---

tion and despair, "By all that is dear and sacred to the human heart to be true to your country, to yourselves, and to us." *Bulletin*, Sept. 13.

[1] Variously estimated from 2000 to 5000. The testimony makes it quite apparent that at least a large number had no exact knowledge of what was to occur, and yet in respect to a rumor that the whites were going to exterminate them "not a house servant that day dared to show his ashen face beyond the back gate."

[2] It might be noted that in the hundred odd years of her history, New Orleans had had ninety-two tumults.

There was a tradition in New Orleans that men met in La Fayette Square to talk, at the Clay Statue to act. This statue then stood on a high pedestal with an iron railing. Told the writer by Miss Marion Brown.

[3] The demand had to be forwarded through a member of Kellogg's staff to the custom-house.

[4] McEnery, a resident of the northern part of the State, was not in perfect sympathy with the attitude of New Orleans at this time, and so it was suggested that he might conveniently leave the State in order to allow Penn, an old Confederate soldier, to take charge. On the authority of Judge Breaux. This attitude on the part of McEnery, not in any way to seem to revive the issues or spirit of the war, was characteristic of this gentleman. Mr. McEnery's son told the writer that he had never heard his father talk of the war nor reconstruction; neither did he wish to hear others discuss the past.

ages of eighteen and forty-five to arm and assemble as the militia to drive out the usurpers.[1]

An interval of silence and waiting now came over the city. Some frightened negro officials gathered about the custom-house for protection; near the state-house were more negroes. With bolted and barred doors some thirty metropolitan policemen paced the gallery, while a few persons entered through a double file of police. At the Supreme Court Room some two hundred police under arms might have been found. But by three o'clock large numbers of armed men, marching in perfect order[2] with grave mien, began to assemble in Poydras and the neighboring streets, where in true Parisian fashion, they erected barricades of lumber and boxes, horse-cars, and paving-stones. Just about four o'clock five hundred metropolitan police, armed with artillery, appeared near the river on Canal Street, between the custom-house and the levee, where they deployed as the insurgents opened fire upon them with the old rebel yell.[3] The police, demoralized after a ten-minute fire by the fall of about forty-four men,[4] retreated to the custom-house leaving two Gatling and one twelve-pound gun in the hands of their opponents.[5] Barricading began then near the custom-

[1] The account is based largely upon the *Republican* and *Times* of Sept. 15, as modified and corrected by the *Congressional Record*, but Phelps and the *Cyclopedia* have also been used. For Penn's proclamation see *Cyclop.*, 480.

[2] Packard a day or two later ironically complimented them on their handsome, soldierly appearance and marching. He felt that many more joined the League after this affair. House Repts., 43 Cong., 2 Sess., No. 101, pt. ii., 26.

[3] Longstreet, an ex-Confederate officer, had been execrated for accepting office as head of the militia under Radicalism. When he recognized many of the "boys" who had served under his command in the war and heard the yell, he blanched. Told the writer by General Behan.

[4] Ogden reported twelve killed on his side.

[5] It was said that Federal soldiers cheered their old antagonists. Phelps, 380.

house in the midst of fiery excitement. Badger, captain of the metropolitans, fell, though not killed. The encouraged Leaguers demanded that the city administration resign. Extras came wet from the press, in one of which Penn issued a proclamation appointing Ogden general of the militia and reassuring the negroes that they need fear no harm. Pickets were posted along Canal Street, and detachments of the League bivouacked in the street all night. No cars ran after four o'clock.[1]

At eight o'clock the next morning, all the metropolitan police and colored militia stationed in the state-house surrendered. Kellogg sought his favorite haven of refuge, the custom-house, while all the State and city property was seized by the insurgents. The old officials were deposed by those who had been elected with McEnery two years before. Penn, formally inducted into office that afternoon, proceeded to install the men "legally elected" in 1872, and to reorganize the police and judiciary. At eleven o'clock Ogden ordered the barricades removed and business resumed, but the effect of such an unprecedented event could not so quickly be effaced and shops were not opened that day. After a triumphal parade through the streets at three o'clock in the afternoon, the men were dismissed. In the evening the armed men were removed from the city-hall and Wiltz resumed his old duties as mayor. The McEnery legislature was summoned to meet and impeach the judges who had sustained Kellogg. Barricades were erected for the Leaguers as they

[1] It is hard to reconcile Ogden's insistence that the overthrow of Kellogg was only incidental to the overthrow of the enemy, by which word he designated the police. For his technical account of the fight, see House Repts., 43 Cong., 2 Sess., No. 101, Part ii., 213–5. But a genuine fervor rings in his last paragraph: "To that God who gave us the victory we commit with confidence and hope the spirit of our immortal dead; and strong in the consciousness of right, record anew our holy purpose that Louisiana shall be free." *Ibid.*, 215.

came pouring in from the country.[1]   According to General Emory the revolt could only have been suppressed with troops and gunboats.   But even Casey admitted that the city was orderly.

The joy of the Democratic papers was unrestrained. In headlines the *Picayune* heralded the victory thus: "Last rites and obsequies of the Kellogg Government. Closing Scenes of the Revolution.   All quiet along the Line."   Under them came the following comment:

So ends the Kellogg régime.   Big, inflated, insolent, overbearing, it collapsed at one touch of honest indignation and gallant onslaught.   Its boasted armament dissolved before the furious rush of our citizens; its thieving, sneering, unscrupulous chieftains hid like moles, and its mercenaries fled like stampeded cattle.[2]

The *Bulletin* could not resist another over-confident fling at Grant:

For the first time since a drunken and corrupt judge, backed by the arbitrary power of the thing who disgraces the office formerly dignified by Washington, Jefferson, and Madison has succeeded in fastening on our necks the galling yoke of the knaves and plunderers who have so long tried the patient endurance of our people, an opportunity was furnished by the oppressers themselves to teach them a lesson they cannot soon forget.[3]

Congratulations poured in from all over the State, even from other States.[4]   September 15 ten thousand

[1] A Texas Senator said that a company of his State went to the station ready to help Louisiana, but were deterred by a telegram stating that they were not needed.   *Record*, 43 Cong., 2 Sess., 275.   [2] September 15.
[3] Sept. 15. See also the *Times*, the evening edition of the *Picayune*, Sept. 16.
[4] For excerpts from the press of other States, see House Repts., 43 Cong., 2 Sess., No. 261, Part iii., 835.

18

citizens of St. Louis assembled in mass meeting at the court-house to express their hearty sympathy with the citizens of Louisiana, and to offer congratulations at their success.   Likewise at Mobile a large gathering on the same date was for the purpose of felicitating New Orleans.[1] The Vicksburg *Herald* prayed fiercely, after offering New Orleans her best wishes, that the "fiercest wrath of God may light upon their oppressors."[2]   Even the clergymen raised their voices in the pulpits in exultation over the renaissance.

Resistance to tyranny is obedience to God.   He who would be free must himself strike the blow.   I feel like a new man to-day, and my inmost soul is lifted up with a confident hope of the dawn of a yet far brighter future for poor, stricken, down-trodden Louisiana.   Vengeance is mine, saith the Lord. God be praised.[3]

The example set by the metropolis was quickly followed in the northern part of the State and a bloodless revolution would seem to have effaced the events since the election of 1872.[4]

But such action did not escape the emphatic disapproval of Grant.[5]   On application from Kellogg for aid to protect Louisiana from domestic violence, he issued, on September 15, a proclamation which sharply ordered the turbulent persons to disperse within five days and to submit to the laws and constituted authorities of the State.[6]   Orders

---

[1] *Picayune*, Sept. 15 has an account.   [2] *Ibid.*
[3] House Repts., 43 Cong., 2 Sess., No. 261, Part iii., 836. He refused to believe in the failure of the revolt.
[4] In New Iberia, Baton Rouge, Amite City, Franklin, and Shreveport. A committee at the last named place declared that the "last vestige of the Kellogg government has disappeared from northern Louisiana without a word or act of violence to any person, white or black." *Republican*, Sept. 17.
[5] It was said that Casey besought the President not to interfere.
[6] Richardson, *Messages and Papers of the Presidents*, VII., 276–7.

were also given for United States troops[1] and three men-of-war to proceed to the Crescent City. General Emory was instructed under no circumstances to recognize the Penn government. In compliance with his instructions, he suppressed the insurrection on September 17 by a general war order. General Brooks demanded the surrender of the arms and State property and took command until the legal government could be reorganized. At seven o'clock that evening the buildings were formally surrendered under protest by McEnery, who had returned the preceding day, as "in response to formal demand for surrender or accept the levying of war upon our government by the military forces of the United States." The two executives issued a protest against the action of the Federal power but urged the people to be law-abiding, "painful though it be to give up our most cherished rights."

On the 19th Kellogg returned quietly to the state-house; the metropolitan police resumed their functions without disturbance; but the displaced Kelloggites were restored in the parishes more slowly. In Rapides the clerk of court held office till election; the recorder was still in office in January, 1875.[2] And once more the desperate struggle of the white citizens to throw off the yoke of their oppressors had failed because it ran counter to the wishes of the general in the White House. The fact that the most intelligent and substantial citizens were driven to such a step weighed not at all as to the "crime" in his mind.

The cry which went up from the defeated Conservatives was hardly what one would expect and the more pathetic

[1] By Sept. 22 there were 28 companies of troops in the State, all but one in New Orleans. The *Picayune* says the Federal troops were cheered by the citizens. Sept. 15.

[2] House Repts., 43 Cong., 2 Sess., No. 101, Part ii., 92.

on that account.   It seems free from rage but the more quietly determined.   The Morehouse *Clarion* and the *Sugar Bowl* of Attakapas may be cited as suggestive, if not typical.   From the former we read:

No, no, the great moment has not yet ended; the events of the 14th of September cannot be rolled back on the march of time.   It constitutes the first step in the mighty progress of revolution, which will end, as we verily believe, in the restoration of Louisiana to her proper place in the Union as a free, independent, and sovereign State; or, if not in that way, then in the overthrow of Republican governments in all the States.[1]

The latter in more pessimistic mood:

We have already been too patient; we can endure no more. Shall we not listen to the last appeal of our sunny South and wrench it from the hands that polluted it?   Yes.   Let us kneel on the grave of the "Lost Cause," and swear to Heaven to defend our rights.[2]

The Committee of Seventy published, a few days later, an Address to the People of the United States in defense and explanation of their revolutionary action.   Their chief ground of objection had been the arbitrary way in which the registration under the new law was being handled in the interests of the Republicans.   They added an explanation of the object of the White League, declaring it to be a restoration of honest and intelligent government to Louisiana.   And they laid at Kellogg's door, because of his usurpation, responsibility for all the blood

---

[1] House Repts., 43 Cong., 2 Sess., No. 261, Part iii., 765–6.

[2] *Ibid.*   Sometimes their remarks were stamped by folly, as the following from the same paper: "For the moment we are insolently thwarted, but sooner or later freedom shall be ours, and we make no thoughtless threat in saying that it is very apt to be accompanied by another and successful secession."   *Ibid.*

and excesses of the past two years.[1] The expected reply from Kellogg came in the form of an Address to the People of the Union on September 30, an effort to refute the charges of corruption and oppression made by his opponents, coupled with the counter-charge of a determination to overthrow Republicanism. He gave credit for no honest motive to justify the "misguided and disastrous revolt";[2] but attributed it solely to greed for office.

Although the Democratic governor of Ohio tendered fifty thousand men to suppress the revolt in Louisiana,[3] and the Radicals of the State called loudly for punishment,[4] the tone of the Northern papers was, in the words of one of the Republican organs, "very perplexing,"[5] for many of the most ultra-Republican papers argued that Louisiana had only exercised her divine right of revolution.[6] The *Nation* thus epitomized the feeling of a large part of the North:

We must say frankly that we know of no case of armed resistance to an established government in modern times in which the insurgents had more plainly the right on their side. We know of no mark of justifiability in a revolutionary movement, except one, which this Louisiana movement did not possess. . . . Had the same state of facts arisen in London or Paris, or New York, or Boston, there is no candid or impartial person, no lover of order or progress, at the North who would make use of any argument against a resort to force except the improbability of success.

It felt that there was just one thing the North could do: immediately withdraw Federal support from the knaves

---

[1] For the full address see *Ann. Cyclop.*, 1874, 483–4. It is dated Sept. 23.
[2] *Ibid.*, 484–5.
[3] Denied later, *Republican*, June 26, 1875.
[4] *Republican*, Sept. 16, 17, Oct. 3. On the latter date it called for vengeance.   [5] *Ibid.*, Sept. 17.
[6] Chicago *Times*, Sept. 15, St. Louis *Democrat*, Louisville *Commercial*.

in control in Louisiana.[1]   Liberals were divided in sentiment; some called it the story of the violated State, others,
among them Schurz, maintained that the President had
now no option but to support the Kellogg government,
whose original bad title had been confirmed by possession.[2]
But above all, the revolt had shown conclusively how
entirely the Kellogg government rested on Federal support.   Nobody but the governor himself seemed to think
that he could maintain himself unaided.   Not alone
Conservatives, but officers of the army, had assured Carpenter that if Federal troops were withdrawn, the Radical
government could not last a week.[3]

As soon as the excitement attendant upon the September
revolt had subsided, the State found itself in the throes
of the fall campaign.   All through the summer complaints
had been coming in from the parishes of Democratic aggres-
siveness and acts of coercion.   The spirit is similar to
that noted in 1872 but much more outspoken in its determination to use every pressure short of physical force.
Some of the pugnacious remarks of the organs were,
to say the least, unfortunate.   Such words as those of
the Shreveport *Times* could hardly conciliate a Grant:
"There has been some red-handed work done in this
parish that was necessary, but it was evidently done by
cool, determined, and just men who knew just how far to
go, and we doubt not if the same kind of work is necessary, it will be done."[4]   It warned the carpet-bagger and
scalawag that if a single hostile gun were fired between the
races, every one of their kind caught "would in twelve
hours therefrom be dangling from a limb."[5]   No wiser
was the *Vindicator:*

[1] Sept. 24. It could find no parallel except the support of Austria to the
petty princes of Italy, except that it was an insult to those rulers to compare
them to Kellogg.   [2] Merriam, Bowles, II., 234.
  [3] When he was in New Orleans in May, 1874.   [4] July 27.
  [5] House Repts., 43 Cong., 2 Sess., No. 261, Part iii., 765.

The White Man's party is determined to rescue Louisiana from the polluting embraces of such a hybrid pack of lecherous pimps as Kellogg, Packard, Durrell, Pinchback, Dibble, Casey, and their followers, who were conceived in sin, brought forth in pollution, nursed by filthy harpies, and dropped in Louisiana, to show to the world to what depths of corruption, disgrace, and infamy human nature can stoop, when the flesh is weak and the spirit willing.[1]

The Shreveport *Comet* vowed by the Eternal Spirit that rules the universe that it would "battle against negro rule to the day of our death if it cost a prison or a gallows."[2] The Shreveport *Times* thought that the public should use hemp or call upon the defeated candidates counted in.[3] Again and again, in varied phrase, men declared their intention to carry the election or remand the State to a military territory. Nowhere is this more unmistakably enunciated than in the Natchitoches *Vindicator:*

Should you imagine that the teaching of your former rulers is correct and you elect to attempt, for it will only be an attempt, to continue their rule, then you must take the consequences. For we tell you now, and let it be distinctly remembered that you have fair warning, that we intend to carry the State in November next or she will be a military territory.[4]

---

[1] House Repts., 43 Cong., 2 Sess., No. 261, Part iii., 283.

[2] Quoted *ibid.*, 754.

[3] *Ibid.*, 755. The part played by this paper in the campaign is significant. One person declared that he had never known a paper to get such an ascendancy over the public (363). A man hostile to it still declared it the ablest and fairest exponent of public opinion. The Conservatives in mass meeting indorsed it. In like strain wrote the Franklin *Enterprise* of St. Mary Parish and the Alexandria *Democrat*, all quoted in the above report.

[4] July 18. One hears the same tone in the *Southern Cross* of Marksville, and Mansfield *Reporter*, *ibid.*, 762, 765.

It is very likely that McEnery said some unwise things
during his campaign speeches, but he was also doubtless
maligned when he was reported as saying, "We shall
carry the next election if we have to ride saddle-deep in
blood to do it."[1]   One witness before the Hoar Committee
quoted from a speech, which he claimed to have taken
down from McEnery's lips, as follows: "Get public
opinion up to a white heat.   Make every carpet-bagger,
scalawag, radical, and negro vote our ticket or leave the
State.   Let us be peaceable if we can, but if necessary,
apply force in all cases."   To Judge Myers he was reported
as saying insolently before a public meeting, "Run your
hand down to the bottom of your pocket and pull out the
money you have got from the Kellogg government."[2]

By various devices they planned to carry the election:
By a general conscription from all labor of negroes who
voted for Republicans[3]; by a refusal to hold business
dealings with anyone who voted the Radical ticket[4];
by refusal to make advances to planters who employed
or rented land to Radical laborers[5]; by opening a black
list, in which all who adhered to the negro party should be
reckoned negroes[6]; by humiliating all whites who failed
to register by publishing their names[7]; and, in a few in-

---

[1] At Lebanon in Bienville Parish. .House Repts., 43 Cong., 2 Sess., No.
261, Part iii., 789.   [2] *Ibid.*, 299.

[3] It was stated that handbills in French and English were circulated,
"To save your country, do not employ the negro. Wild beasts can only be
tamed by hunger."   New Orleans *Times*, July 30, Baton Rouge *Advocat*,
Sept. 7.   But Kennard says that such a measure before the White League
of the capital had found slight support, and that the planters paid slight
attention to it.   House Repts., 43 Cong., 2 Sess., No. 261, Part iii., 219.

[4] See the merchants' compact of Shreveport, Sen. Exe. Doc., 43 Cong.,
2 Sess., No. 13, 5.   [5] Shreveport *Times*, Oct. 14.

[6] Some butchers were to lose their patronage for acting with a Radical
club. *Bulletin*.

[7] Baton Rouge *Advocat*, Sept. 6.   Adopted by the White League of that
city. "Most contemptible of all was the man who would in this crisis

stances, by forcibly breaking up Radical meetings.[1] The threats grew ever more bold. A Ku Klux notice was posted in one place addressed to all Radicals: "Your fate is sealed. Nothing but your blood will appease us."[2] The *Caucasian* tried to drive every white man to the polls by declaring him otherwise a "traitor and deserving to be ruled forever by negroes."[3] Even the *Bulletin* of New Orleans openly advocated "the rapid organization of all men who are willing to do battle for everything that is dear to an American citizen."[4] The *Bee* early urged the enrolling of a volunteer force to prevent frauds after election.[5] Furthermore a Democratic meeting declared its purpose to send bodies of men to the polls to see that every vote was counted fairly, peaceably if they could, by force if they must.[6]

On the other hand, the Conservatives were complaining of the use of the Federal soldiery in political struggles. Packard was availing himself of his position as marshal to arrest white citizens summarily. He appeared in several parishes with warrants of arrest to drag his Democratic foes to New Orleans for bail, where all possible obstacles were thrown in the way of release,[7] whence they

---

accept a nomination from the negro party. He would be banished from decent society and universally condemned by the community, for such a crime." Shreveport *Times*, copied, House Repts., 43 Cong., 2 Sess., No. 261, Part iii., 764. See also the excerpts from the Franklin *Enterprise*.

[1] I discredit most of these charges, as I found but few direct complaints.

[2] The intelligent whites disapproved of these extremists, yet submitted to their dictation. *Ibid.*, 16. [3] *Ibid.*, 528. [4] Sept. 11. [5] August 31.

[6] *Times*, July 26. Ogden said that the Crescent Club placed twenty men under an officer at each poll to watch the election and keep order but not to interfere with anyone's vote. They had had word that the Republicans would create a disturbance and put the blame on the League.

During the unsettled days of October there seems to have been an attempt made on Kellogg's life.

[7] Well substantiated. House Repts., 43 Cong., 2 Sess., No. 101, Part ii., 84. See also the absurd requirements made in Iberia Parish, *ibid.*, Part i., 6.

could return home at their own expense. Nordhoff
heard from army officers of several cases where such unwarranted arrests caused alarm and suffering to the
families of the victims; and of other cases where innocent
men lay out in the woods for days in fear of these warrants.[1]   It was reported that as late as this, negroes were
summoned from the field to political meetings by order
of General Butler.[2]   Negroes reported threats of arrest
by the Federal cavalry, unless they voted the Radical
ticket, boldly made in the very presence of their employers.[3]   It is notable that no warrants were sent out
after the election.   Packard explained the presence of
the soldiery in Natchitoches by the anarchy there, and the
necessity for arrests by the Coushatta massacre; he
expressed disbelief in arrests in Bossier Parish on election
day; and insisted that he had given instructions not to
interfere with men's rights as voters[4]; but admitted that
several men were brought to the city in default of bail.
This action awakened animosity, not only toward Packard,
but also toward the bluecoats themselves.[5]   Democrats
resented as oppressive and unjust the obstacles placed in
the way of naturalized Democrats in trying to register,
the rejection of white registration while blacks were freely
recorded,[6] and the enrolling of colored crews of transient

[1] *Cotton States*, 64–5.   [2] *Ibid.*, 13.   [3] Nordhoff, 66.
[4] House Repts., 43 Cong., 2 Sess., No. 101, Part ii., 24.   Blank warrants
were charged by Arroyo, but this Packard denied.
[5] Thus did the *Bulletin* relieve its feelings: "If soldiers choose to get
mixed up in broils with which they have no concern, they must expect to
come out with punched heads and torn uniforms.   The time has passed
when a blue-coat stuck upon a pole can make us bow in abject submission
as before a Gessler's cap."   More temperate, the *Picayune* declared,
"The propriety of letting them interfere in local and domestic concerns
which the engaging parties are perfectly competent to regulate is, and
always will be, open to very grave doubts."   August 27, 28.   *Picayune*,
August 27.
[6] The lists of 1874 showed colored registered voters proportionally more

boats. To all this was added the grievance that State courts were prohibited from interfering.

It was realized that pretexts would be sought to deprive the Conservatives of any victory they might win, and so by October 1 many of them tried to conciliate the blacks, voted down the non-employment propositions which had been advocated earlier in the campaign, and threatened all who were guilty of such coercion with arrest.[1] In some parishes a union ticket of colored and white Conservatives was put out and elected.[2] The Crescent City Club passed resolutions prohibiting interference with the returning-board. And above all it must be clearly understood that it was but a small faction which advocated extreme action.

Naturally the Radicals used the cry of coercion to its full limit, the success of which they had learned in 1872, both before and after election. The *Republican* kept up a correspondence over the State, copied belligerent remarks constantly—in a word, kept the mill supplied with grist, and turned out the product in volumes which were

---

numerous than white. Jury panels revealed the fraudulent names. Nordhoff states that it was proved that in New Orleans alone Republicans had made 5200 false registrations. Packard admitted that only 5000 officials and their relatives voted for Republicans, while that number of blacks voted for Conservatives. Nordhoff, 43. Hundreds of Northern men acted with that party in Federal politics but with the Conservatives in local. *Ibid.*, 53.

[1] House Repts., 43 Cong., 2 Sess., Part i., No. 261, 2.

[2] Terrebonne and St. Mary offered about one-half the offices to the blacks, but it was too late. Intelligent negroes voted for men they knew to be corrupt in their anger at the Conservative platform. The writer feels that she has not swung too far in her zeal to be fair to the Conservatives when she reads such a statement as follows: "No thoughtful man can see the State as I saw it without gaining a high respect for its white people. The attitude of the races there toward each other is essentially kindly, and only the continuous efforts of white demagogues keep them apart." Nordhoff, 17.

distributed as public documents.[1]   And the State Central
Committee obtruded the perpetual Louisiana question
upon Grant by a request for troops to aid them on election
day.[2]   Nor was he free from other inflammatory reports
from officers in the army and subordinate officials.[3]
But, on the whole, the actual testimony of intimidation
in this campaign is very slight, for even Packard, after
citing a case, added, "it is but just that I should add there
were very few instances of parishes like that."[4]   The
distinguishing feature was the fact that the campaign
arose from the people.   It was the Conservative boast
that there was not one politician on the State Central
Committee, that the State was not canvassed in the
ordinary sense, and that there was no engineering.[5]

Unavailing attempts were made to secure a system of
registration and canvass which should be satisfactory to
all.   By the middle of August the Democrats were besieging Kellogg for representatives of their party among
the election officials.   They asked for one of the two
supervisors and one clerk in each precinct of their party
and of their selection.   While Kellogg was willing to
concede the presence of Democrats in these places, he
was unwilling to let the selection pass from his hands.
They next asked that one of every two registration clerks
be selected from several Democratic names submitted
to him.   But the most that Kellogg would concede was
to select them from the opposition.[6]   Finally, committees

---

[1] See the sickening scrap-book of excerpts in House Repts., 43 Cong.,
2 Sess., No. 261, Appendix.

[2] Sen. Exe. Doc., 43 Cong., 2 Sess., No. 13, 15.

[3] *Ibid.*   See also Sen. Exe. Doc., No. 17, 53.

[4] House Repts., 43 Cong., 2 Sess., No. 101, Part ii., 23.   [5] *Ibid.*, 146–7.

[6] *Republican*, Aug. 15.   The distrust felt for Kellogg is evidenced in the
Nation of October 29, where it expresses the belief that the election will
turn on "how much fraud Kellogg conceives himself to be in a position to
commit."

of the two parties held a conference and agreed to an arrangement which was published September 29. The Conservatives agreed to put down all intimidation; an advisory committee of five was to be constituted—two Republicans, two Democrats, and an umpire jointly selected—to carry on the registration through the entire State. Kellogg pledged himself to act on their advice if it were constituted. And, finally, the Conservatives were virtually conceded two members on the returning-board[1] to fill the vacancies which it was expected would occur. The State Democratic Committee, after a stormy session because of the implication of party responsibility for the violence, reluctantly ratified the compromise.[2] The address in which it announced the arrangement stated that the question of the legality of the State government remained untouched and uncompromised; and no question of principle had been discussed, waived, nor concluded.[3]

This arrangement was not well received in the parishes, being regarded as an acknowledgment of guilt.[4] But the advisory board, consisting of Packard and Joubert for the Republicans, Burke and Wiltz for the Conservatives, with Bonzano, a Republican, for the fifth member, was organized October 1. Yet nearly all the supervisors and clerks in Orleans Parish—except a few selected as Conservatives, though generally at heart Republicans—were Republicans, as were supervisors in other parishes. Complaints of partisanship were brought against eight supervisors, but only one was removed. Even in the appointment of Conservatives, much delay was caused

---

[1] Even the *Republican* conceded that the board was an "exasperating circumstance with powers almost certain to be misused." Jan. 6, 1875.
[2] *Ann. Cyclop.*, 1874, 487.   [3] *Ibid.*
[4] See the opinion of the Natchitoches *Vindicator*, Oct. 12, Alexandria *Caucasian*, copied, House Repts., 43 Cong., 2 Sess., No. 261, Part iii., 761, 763.

by Republican objection; after appointments were made, Democratic clerks were not allowed to make records on the books.[1]   Although the advisory board held a number of meetings and acted on some questions, it broke down October 20 in mutual recriminations by the resignation of the chairman.[2]

In anticipation of outbreaks on election day, eleven companies of Federal troops, stationed at various points in the city and on the Red River, together with a fleet in the stream, insured the general quiet which did prevail during the voting.[3]   Shops were closed by law.   But little interest was felt by the Republicans in the municipal ticket, as they knew that the entire Democratic strength, which would certainly turn out, gave them no hope of victory there.   As in 1872, a peaceful election was reported throughout the State,[4] and, as then, the conflict turned upon the question of frauds,[5] which the Radical

[1] House Repts., 43 Cong., 2 Sess., No. 261, Part iii., 101; Part ii., 34–41. Even in New Orleans one of the few Democratic commissioners complained of lack of instructions.   *Ibid.*, 15.

[2] The Shreveport *Comet* of Oct. 8 makes charges against the good faith of the Republican members, while the *Republican* accuses the League of drilling after the compromise.   The *Bee* also had accusations of bad faith.

[3] In all the South there were but 4082 soldiers that day.   Richardson, VII., 298.

[4] See Iberville *Pioneer*, Madison *Journal*, Donalsonville *Chief*, quoted in House Repts., 43 Cong., 2 Sess., No. 101, Pt. ii., 38, 228.   Yet at some of the polls lists of negroes voting the Radical ticket were kept for later distribution in fulfillment of the threats.   But in the evidence before the sub-committee the writer did not find one case of a planter discharging a negro for his politics, the one case charged in Carrollton being disproved.   *Ibid.*, 85, Sen. Exe. Doc., 43 Cong., 2 Sess., No. 17, 55.

[5] Again the records are full of stories of fraud.   One of the most amusing is how voters were obliged to hand up ballots at the end of a pole to the second story.   House Repts., No. 101, Pt. ii., 6, 7, 35.   Equally amusing is the excuse of a negro, fifteen times a repeater on the same day, who was so alarmed when followed that he gave a false name.   See also House Repts., 44 Cong., 1 Sess., No. 442, where a House Committee unearths many frauds in Carroll and Concordia Parishes on the part of the Republican

press agitated with redoubled energy.[1] The Democrats felt that there was no question of the victory; they were only concerned as to whether they could gather its fruits.[2] And already on the evening of November 7 they held a great celebration.

At the canvass which began November 14, a committee of three from each party, counsel for each central committee, and reporters were admitted to the open sessions—all decisions being made in secret session.[3] The board consisted at that time of Wells, Cassanave, Kenner, Anderson, and Longstreet. The last named resigned at once on account of feeble health and was replaced by Arroyo, a Democrat, who was selected, it would appear, only because, as a mere clerk for thirty-one years, he was regarded as not dangerous.[4] The Democrats filed a protest against the constitutionality of the board, because the law creating it gave judicial power, and because there was a lack of fair Democratic representation upon it. In spite of previous frauds, there was a prevalent feeling that no body of men would again dare to falsify the verdict of the ballot-box. But as the proceedings went on, as the board went into secret session for ten days on December 14, feeling ran so high that on the 20th, while the president of the board was dining at one of the chief hotels of the city, two strangers attempted to assassinate him.[5] Arroyo resigned December 24[6] because the "just and

commissioners "most discouraging to contemplate," 8. This is in the contested election of Spencer vs. Morey.

[1] *Republican*, daily issues.   [2] *Picayune*, November 3.

[3] The minutes of the board are very meagre indeed—a bare record of going into executive session.

[4] House Repts., 43 Cong., 2 Sess., No. 101, Pt. ii., 16. He was evidently timid. See his reiteration about being browbeaten, 17. Probably nobody would regard Anderson as a Conservative, though he so classified himself despite the fact that he had acted with Kellogg for a year or two. *Ibid.*, 1.

[5] House Repts., 43 Cong., 2 Sess., No. 261, Part iii., 93.

[6] November 23, according to Wells.

reasonable" rules of the returning-board seemed to him a perversion of justice and because of unfair decisions with regard to candidates whom he considered unquestionably defeated.[1]

The evidence of crooked work by this board is fairly clear in the alteration of figures of compiled statements of supervisors,[2] in the disappearance of Democratic protests and evidence two or three days after they were filed, in the refusal to canvass De Soto at all, which had always shown a Democratic majority,[3] and in the acceptance of affidavits of intimidation after evidence had closed.[4] Illuminating is the attitude of Wells that he was satisfied that there was intimidation and that nothing could convince him to the contrary.[5]   The report of the Con-

[1] Petty quibbling annoyed him, when returns were rejected because a commissioner signed his initials T. B. instead of T. P.; when it was decided that evidence of informality and fraud constituted proof; that an unsigned tally sheet should be held the official record, if no fraud were charged; that affidavits should be received for each charge of intimidation; when Winn Parish was rejected because the registrar had not forwarded his oath to the secretary; when Terrebonne was thrown out because the commissioner had inclosed the returns in the boxes.   House Repts., 43 Cong., 2 Sess., No. 101, Part ii., 51–4, 47.

[2] With the aid of a magnifying-glass it was made evident that many tally sheets had been changed and signatures forged.   But when a Democrat alleged to the board that those changes had taken place since the returns came into its possession, they still refused to send for witnesses at Democratic expense.   Even a Republican supervisor proved by original returns that the sheets had been falsified since being placed with the board.   Compare with this the fact that their tender consciences threw out one poll where there was no chance for the Republicans, as they could not canvass forged returns.   House Repts., 43 Cong., 2 Sess., No. 261, Part iii., 16, 31.

One of the Democratic committee testified before the Congressional Committee that Anderson had said of the board: "We concluded to throw out the Fort Jessup poll in Sabine, which will elect the regular candidate by a majority of one," though he himself preferred another Democrat.   His proposal to fix it up so as to get in his choice was refused. *Ibid.*, 31–3.

[3] House Repts., 43 Cong., 2 Sess., No. 101, Part ii., 6–7.   [4] *Ibid.*, 7.

[5] *Ibid.*, 8.   The Congressional sub-committee had great difficulty in

gressional Committee scores very severely the action of the board as "arbitrary, and, in our opinion, unfair, and without warrant of law," concluding that this arbitrary, unjust, and illegal action alone "prevented the return by the board of a majority of conservative members of the lower house."[1]

Errors and informalities in many polls, protests and statements of intimidation, constant protests by both committees, the discovery that poll-books had been stolen, the besieging of their room by importunate candidates and their officious attorneys, the necessity of hearing testimony, and the bullying of an impatient press[2] had so harassed the board that it declared itself unable to promulgate the results until December 24. It found Dubuclet reëlected treasurer, while 53 Republicans and 53 Democrats were entitled to seats in the next House, with 5 referred to the legislature for decision. The five amendments were declared incorporated in the constitution.[3] The board reported that a large number of polls were objected to in twenty-seven parishes, all in

---

securing the attendance of Wells, who appeared reluctantly after having once pleaded his wife's illness. He admitted that he was not present at the election in Rapides, where his testimony alone was to prove intimidation. House Repts., No. 261, Part iii., 95, 99.

[1] House Repts., No. 101, Part i., 5. Rapides Parish alone changed the complexion of the lower House. The three Conservative candidates presented themselves at New Orleans January 4, ignorant of the fact that the board at one of its last sessions declared all the Republican members from that parish elected. Hoar Report of 1875.

[2] Especially the *Picayune*, according to the *Republican*. Democratic organs continued during the canvass their arrogant tone: "Therefore, we should simply give the members of that board to distinctly understand that unless they return the elections as they were returned at the polls, they and those they seek to 'count in' will pay the forfeit with their lives." Shreveport *Times*. The citizens of Caddo in mass meeting declared it their purpose "to install on January 1 all officers elected in this parish whether returned by the board or not." Quoted Sen. Exe. Doc., 43 Cong., 2 Sess., No. 17, 20, 69.   [3] See *Republican*, Dec. 25, for the full report.

some, so that if it had complied strictly with the forms of law, so many must have been thrown out that no election could have been declared, but that they had ruled out only three complete parishes. And it pronounced a long tirade against the machinations of the White League.

The day previous, the Democratic Committee, taking its cue from the Lynch Board of 1872, assumed to declare a result, from the sworn statements of commissioners, charging the board with a "revolutionary conspiracy with the present usurping governor" to overthrow the duly elected Assembly.[1] It held 4 Conservative and 2 Republican Congressmen elected, 71 Conservative and 37 Republican members of the legislature elected, and also that Moncure, Democratic candidate for treasurer, had defeated Dubuclet.[2] McEnery followed this with a denunciation of the wrong perpetrated by the board as a "more crowning infamy" than that of the Lynch Board or Durrell's midnight order.[3]

The greatest dissatisfaction with the canvass was expressed everywhere, even at the North. Even before the board was ready to proclaim results the Committee of Seventy published another of its numerous addresses to the world.[4] The Natchitoches *Vindicator* asked the sons of Louisiana if they were prepared to submit to the overthrow of their social as well as political structure.[5] The *Picayune* thus commented on a "Christmas Present from

---

[1] *Annual Cyclopedia*, 1874, 489.

[2] Moncure brought suit, which was decided by the Supreme Court adversely to him in 1876.   28 La. Ann., 704.

[3] *Ann. Cyclop.*, 493.

[4] "In this manner are we threatened with another mongrel herd of rapacious plunderers, ignorant and debauched, claiming to be Republicans, elected by Radical returning-officers, and installed in the Legislature by the potential force of the Army and Navy of the United States." *Ann. Cyclop.*, 490.

[5] Dec. 12, House Repts., 43 Cong., 2 Sess., No. 261, Part iii., 286.

the Board": "It is nothing less than the maintenance of free institutions. . . . It is time now for the American people to decide whether there shall be one rule for Louisiana and another for Massachusetts."[1] The *Bee* felt much the same about "the evil deed accomplished" and hoped that the people would not endure longer a farce unworthy of a republican country.[2]

[1] Dec. 25.

[2] "Ce que le peuple a supporté alors, il ne le supportera pas aujourd'hui. Il y a assez longtemps que les élections en Louisiane sont une force indigne d'un pays républicaine et civilisé. . . . Ils ne peuvent plus se moquer de tout un peuple en faissant et en défaisant la majorité à leur gré. Ils sont réussi élire 39 représentants; ils n'ont pas droit à un de plus et nous espérons que cela sera clairemont demontré quand la Législature se réunira." December 25.

It is striking that it was during these exciting days that Warmoth was attacked on Canal Street by the manager of the *Bulletin* with a cane, and in self-defense drew a knife, inflicting several wounds which later resulted in the death of his assailant. *Picayune*, Dec. 27.

CHAPTER XIV

The Banditti Legislature

IN fear of an impending civil war, Grant ordered Sheridan in the late fall of 1874 to make a tour through certain Southern States to ascertain the true condition of affairs, endowing him secretly with authority to assume command in the South if it became advisable.[1] And so circumstances brought it about that Sheridan was in New Orleans and played a leading part in this act of the drama which utter desperation was driving the Conservatives to place on the Louisiana stage.

Indignation at the result declared by the returning-

---

[1] Unfortunately, though the papers had published the correct facts as to Sheridan's visit, he denied the rumor that he was to take command. He was merely, he said, on his way to Havana with a party of ladies. Naturally he was before long execrated as a "liar." *Picayune*, Dec. 28, 1874, January 1, 1875. There is a curious story of why the order was secret. It was said that at a meeting of the White League at Jackson, Mississippi, it was resolved that no officer of high rank should be permitted to go to New Orleans, and that upon such attempt, the train would be wrecked. *Ibid.*, December 31.

It should not be forgotten that Sheridan had had such previous connection with this State that he was held, in the language of the *Picayune*, "more responsible for the misfortunes of Louisiana than any other man." Before the events of January 4 it printed: "We know him for the man who desolated the valley of the Shenandoah, and brought fire and the sword and famine among its people; and to whom Louisiana was a desolation to which that of fire and the sword and famine might well be regarded as preferable. Yes, we know General Phil Sheridan well enough; and because we know him for what he is, he has been sent here by the President in order to add this crowning outrage to the outrages which have already been heaped upon us." *Ibid.*, December 28, 1874.

board led to open threats of defiance. Thus the Shreveport *Times* sought to bolster any waning determination:

> The question now with the people of Louisiana is, is the work finished? We think not. The will of the people, as expressed at the ballot-box, on the second of November, and not the will of Kellogg and Company as expressed through their returning-board, must be vindicated. Every man elected to the lower house must be present in New Orleans at the opening of that house ready to take his seat. No private interest or matter of business should prevent any from being at his post of duty. If the Federal government interferes to deter the people from protecting themselves, let the State be made too hot for it. Let every man do his duty and his whole duty, be the consequences what they may.[1]

Even more pointed is the exhortation of the *Times*: "If George L. Smith is counted in over W. M. Levy, or if Twitchell is counted in over Elam, let Smith and Twitchell be killed."[2]

As the time for the convening of the new legislature drew near, the excitement grew ever more intense. Without legislative assistance they saw bankruptcy, commercial dishonor, and general impoverishment staring them in the face.[3] Furthermore, public opinion was educated

---

[1] Quoted in *Cong. Record*, 43 Cong., 2 Sess., 276.
Of like tenor was the Natchitoches *Vindicator*: "The people of Natchitoches have come at last to the wise conclusion to put a stop to being represented by these interlopers, and we will be in New Orleans in sufficient numbers to see if our will is not respected." Quoted in House Repts., 43 Cong., 2 Sess., No. 261, Part iii., 759.

[2] House Repts., 43 Cong., 2 Sess., No. 101, Part ii., 116.

[3] In his belligerent language E. A. Burke, a prominent Liberal, put into words the burning purpose which actuated the Conservatives: "I am anxious for such a government as will secure equal protection to Republicans and Democrats, black man and white man, to be conducted for the material interests of the people, and not run in the interests of ring adventurers and thieves." *Ibid.*, 37.

by this time to realize that an excited and troublous
episode was imminent.   Wild rumors of every kind were
afloat[1]: of a scheme by the Conservatives to obtain control of the Assembly by force through the calling out
of the White League, or by corruption[2]; of a plot to
kidnap Republicans; of threats of assassination to reduce
the Republican majority, said to be indorsed by the
opposition press throughout the State.   The arrest for
embezzlement of a Republican member, who was released
after the meeting of the legislature on the bond of his
abductors, was charged solely to political motives.[3]
Sheridan stated that he had repeatedly heard threats of
assassinating Governor Kellogg and expressions of regret
that he had not been killed September 14.   Because of
the danger of violence being used to influence the organization of the House, the governor placed the state-house
under the military command of the general of the State
militia and requested General Emory to station Federal
troops near the capitol.   The militia, accordingly, excluded from the building all but State officials, members
and contestants of the Assembly, and Federal officers,
including the three members of Congress who were in the
city investigating the recent election.[4]   The Radicals
met in caucus in the state-house January 3 with doors
and windows on the ground floor thoroughly barricaded.
So guarded were the Democrats in their caucus that
no one could glean any facts concerning their plan of
operations.[5]

[1] Speculation was just as rife outside the State.   St. Louis *Democrat*,
Dec. 29.   [2] New Orleans *Republican*, January 3, 1875.
[3] *Annual Cyclopedia*, 1874, 493.   New Orleans *Republican*, Jan. 3.   This
paper speaks also of another abduction.
[4] All except Potter, who was not recognized and so denied admission.
These Congressmen were invited by the Democratic caucus to attend the
opening session.   *Record*, 43 Cong., 2 Sess., 331.
[5] *Times* and *Picayune*, January 4.

By noon of the 4th the state-house was surrounded by an excited crowd of several thousand people, through which throng the members pressed their way shortly before noon.[1] The leaders of the two factions in the House appeared in characteristic mood—Hahn calm and imperturbable, Wiltz pale and uneasy, tapping his desk with his fingers. The tactics now pursued by the Conservatives remind us forcibly of those of January 3, 1872, slightly perfected as to details so that there was no slip in the machinery. Immediately after or slightly before the clerk completed the announcement of the number of members, one hundred and two,[2] fifty-two Republicans and fifty Democrats, a Conservative nominated as temporary speaker L. A. Wiltz, whom his party had agreed in caucus to support.[3] This the clerk declared out of order, as the legal motion could be only for a speaker. But Billieu hurriedly put his own motion[4] against the protest of the other party in a quick and excited manner, probably not in a very loud voice. Without waiting for the negative or an announcement of the vote, Wiltz, who had purposely taken a position near the clerk's desk, dashed upon the rostrum, pushed the clerk aside, seized the gavel, and was sworn in instantly[5] by a justice of the peace

[1] We do not lack for information on the momentous meeting of this day, as we have an account by the Congressional sub-committee, House Repts., 43 Cong., 2 Sess., No. 101; by Sheridan, Sen. Exe. Doc., 43 Cong., 2 Sess., No. 13; by the Conservatives, Sen. Misc. Doc., same session, No. 145; and by the Republicans, *ibid.*, No. 46, besides the official journal and the various newspapers.

[2] The Democrats held that one hundred and six were present, forty-five of whom were recognized by both factions. A quorum would be fifty-four.

[3] The Republicans had selected Hahn and were just as confident of seating him.

[4] In this overriding of a clerk, the memorable precedent of J. Q. Adams in 1839 was followed.

[5] The Republican account says that he drew from his pocket a book looking like a Bible and went through the form. House Jour., 1875, 15.

who had followed him upon the platform.   Wiltz, vouch-safing no attention to the opposition remonstrances, administered the oath to the members *en masse*, and upon a Democratic motion declared a clerk nominated and elected.   The latter, according to a preconcerted plan, instantly sprang forward and occupied the clerk's desk amid the wildest confusion.   In a similar hasty manner a sergeant-at-arms was elected[1]; and the chair authorized to appoint a number of assistant sergeants, all this during Republican objections.   Instantly a large number of men, who had obtained admission under various pretexts,[2] turned down lapels disclosing blue badges labeled "Assistant Sergeant-at-arms" and ejected the old officials.[3]   The House then promptly settled the five disputed cases left to it for decision and swore in as many Democrats, thus winning its majority.   Wiltz was then seated in the chair permanently by fifty-five Democratic ballots with loud cries of "yes" and "no," nearly every member upon his feet.   Many of the Republicans thereupon deemed it time to withdraw from such "illegal proceedings," but Wiltz was quick enough to save his quorum by virtually imprisoning five Republicans who were not able to make their escape with the rest.[4]   Police in the lobby pulled out Republican members as soon as they appeared, while sergeants tried to hold them back.   In the commotion which ensued some knives and pistols appeared, but fortunately no initial shot was fired to precipitate a battle.

A motion was then put to call for United States troops to preserve the peace.   A committee soon returned with General De Trobriand in civil costume, whose appearance

---

[1] The New Orleans *Republican* denies that any such motion was put. Jan. 4.

[2] Reporters, friends of members, etc.

[3] Sheridan accused these assistants of being recognized as captains of the White League.

[4] Wiltz forbade the sergeants to allow further egress or ingress.

was greeted with applause. A few words from him, after an assurance from the speaker that his assistance was necessary, to the mob in the lobby restored peace.

But business had proceeded for only about an hour,[1] during which eight additional members were seated, when the House was again interrupted by the reappearance of General De Trobriand, this time in uniform. Fifty-two Republicans had signed a petition to the governor, stating their grievances and requesting that the "legal members be put in possession of the Hall."[2] The Radicals now in their turn obtained a posse of the military, on condition that no member returned by the board be ejected. When a file of Republican members at the heels of the general endeavored to follow him into the House, they found the door closed in their faces. But the general ordered their admission and declared his intention of ejecting the five members just seated. Although Wiltz refused to point out the men, De Trobriand with Republican help identified them, whereupon the soldiers with fixed bayonets approached each one successively and thus, in the words of the journal, "expelled the five intruders."[3] The Democratic members thereupon withdrew under the leadership of their speaker, allowing the Radicals an opportunity to organize according to law in the eyes of the Radicals. The response of two Democrats before Wiltz led them out, enabled their opponents to declare fifty-four and a quorum.[4]

[1] The Republicans held that permanent organization was not effected until after the Democrats had left. [2] House Jour., 1875, 16.

[3] When the general placed his hand upon one of the men's shoulders the latter asked the speaker what to do. Said Wiltz, "I suggest to the member that he retain his seat until he is ejected by force." When the file of soldiers with fixed bayonets approached, he protested in the "name of American liberty" at this outrageous action. *Picayune*, January 7.

[4] The record of this day's proceedings in the journal is interesting in its brevity: "Immediately after the calling of the roll, disturbances and revolutionary proceedings ensued, and upon their subsidence the organization of the house was proceeded with."

The filling of the five seats left open by the board made their quorum secure.

The Democrats who had withdrawn held a caucus that afternoon, when they determined to organize a legislature independent of the one assembled in the state-house. The Senate and House, in separate buildings, were established on St. Louis Street within fifty yards of the state-house, but neither house was able to show a quorum. They continued, however, to meet twice daily. The troops remained on duty all night with cannon posted at all entrances to the capitol, De Trobriand and his staff in the office of the attorney general. On the 5th McEnery protested against the action of the Federal officer,[1] while two of the ejected Conservatives promptly brought suit against Sheridan and De Trobriand in the Federal Circuit Court.[2]

In a delicate situation which called for the most tactful, considerate handling, Sheridan bungled with the heavy hand of military discipline. His telegrams, reporting events, gave a highly-colored partisan view and went far toward aggravating the situation, already sufficiently irritated by his very presence. His first act was to assume command that very night under his secret orders. The next day he sent his famous "banditti" message:

I think that the terrorism now existing in Louisiana, Mississippi, and Arkansas could be entirely removed and confidence and fair-dealing established [he assured the President], by

[1] And yet at one o'clock of January 4 McEnery issued an appeal to the people for calmness, patience, and dignity, convinced that all would yet be well. And on January 6, when a negro was seen on the street near the capitol with a placard on an elevated standard inscribed, "Remember September Fourteenth," two Conservatives immediately took it away and destroyed it. *Picayune*, January 6.

[2] *Times*, Jan. 6. On January 11 the caucus renewed its pledge to withstand the blandishments of the Republicans.

the arrest and trial of the ringleaders of the armed White Leagues. If Congress would pass a bill declaring them banditti they could be tried by a military commission. The ringleaders of this banditti,[1] who murdered men near here on the fourteenth of last September, and also more recently at Vicksburg, Mississippi, should in justice to law and order and the peace and prosperity of this southern part of the country be punished. It is possible that if the President would issue a proclamation declaring them banditti, no further action need be taken, except that which would devolve upon me.[2]

He was further encouraged in his attitude by a message from Grant on January 6 that "the President and Cabinet[3] confide in your wisdom and rest in the belief that all acts of yours have been and will be judicious."[4]

The excitement caused throughout the country and especially in Louisiana by the expulsion of the members from the Assembly and by the designation of American citizens as banditti could not be exaggerated. Early on the evening of the 5th the rotunda of the St. Charles Hotel was thronged by men of every business and profession. The feeling was deeper than on the 4th, the

[1] It was said that Sheridan based his banditti statement on Bishop Wilmer's testimony with regard to larceny (see this volume, Chapter XVI.). Sheridan thus explained his unfortunate choice of words to a reporter of the *Times:* "I don't suppose there is a sensible man in the State who really imagines I mean that all the people were banditti, for they are not blunderers and robbers." He explained that jahhawker and banditti were technical expressions used in an opinion on the Enforcement Act, to which the White League had made itself liable. As jahhawker was not applicable, he had no choice but to use the word contained in the opinion referred to. Issue of January 11.   [2] Sen. Exe. Doc., 43 Cong., 2 Sess., No. 13, 23.

[3] This was hardly fair to Fish and Bristow, for, according to Belknap, both protested against Sheridan's atrocious proposition. J. S. Black, *Essays and Speeches*, 319, Note. It was said that Fish resigned, but Grant, prompted by Conkling, refused the resignation. Blaine publicly stated that Grant had ruined the party. Excitement at the capital was profound.

[4] Sen. Exe. Doc., 43 Cong., 2 Sess., No. 13, 25.

quiet emotion of a people "outraged as men and citizens," as the *Times* phrased it.[1]   Sheridan was simply execrated. He was the Benedict Arnold of his day.   His appearance was greeted with loud groans and hisses; abusive articles were marked and handed to him by waiters at his hotel, which he received with smiles and bows; remarks were made audibly for his benefit; threats were made on his life, because "he dared to tell the truth,"[2] but he declared they caused him no concern, and, in truth, no attempt was made to execute them.   Though constantly followed by a hostile crowd, he walked about as if utterly oblivious of its presence and ate his meals as if deaf.   Caricatures of the "extravagant telegraphist" were placed in the show windows along Canal Street.   One of the most ludicrous consisted of plaster of Paris effigies of a fierce bulldog with a very lank specimen of a banditti—the dog with a collar about his neck from which hung a card with the words, "I am not afraid."   A Sheridan partisan on February 12 shot at the window from the neutral ground[3] and covered a group of people with fragments of glass.[4] The following story has, the writer believes, not before appeared in print.   An old West Point friend was one Colonel Palfrey, of Lee's staff, a resident of New Orleans. Sheridan rushed up to him on the street one day, addressing him by his cadet nickname, "Hello, Mouse."   But "Mouse" only turned his shoulder contemptuously on the enemy of his banditti brothers.   This rebuff Sheridan betrayed that he felt.[5]

[1] January 6.

[2] Sen. Exe. Doc., 43 Cong., 2 Sess., No. 13, 25.   The *Picayune* held that these threats were the work of Radicals to discredit the Conservatives. Jan. 8.   See also the stories told by Hoar, I., 208, and the incident of Sheridan's rage when he was the guest of Barrett, told by Rhodes, VII., 125.

[3] A strip of ground running through the middle of Canal Street.

[4] *Picayune*, Feb. 12.

[5] Told the writer by the brother of Colonel Palfrey.

The jubilant defense of the *Republican*[1] and the eulogistic resolutions of a mass meeting held on the evening of January 9 to offer sincere gratitude to Sheridan "for the interest he has manifested in behalf of an oppressed and long-suffering race"[2] were entirely overwhelmed by the storm of hostile criticism. Under the headlines, "IMPENDING REVOLUTION" the *Bulletin* declared:

President Grant seems to have thrown off even the flimsy pretense of being the chief civil magistrate of the people, and grasping his sword essays to play the role of Cæsar. If the people of the United States, and if the army and navy are prepared to support him in his treasonable designs, then is the doom of the Republic sealed and liberty is dead.[3]

The *Times* hoped that

when military power is again brought to hold its proper subordinate relation toward civil authority, no raiding Sheridan will be permitted to ride roughshod over a people his equals in patriotism and his superiors in intelligence—or encouraged by the Executive head of the nation to fling upon such a people the venom of his spleen.[4]

To stop to criticize such suggestions would be an idle waste of time [declared the *Picayune*]. We presume that any attempt to influence General Sheridan by any rational argument would be as futile as the effort to make a Maori chieftain understand the binomial theorem.[5]

The *Bee*, naturally, turned to Napoleon for precedents and found one in the 18 brumaire.[6] In entirely different strain does the *Bulletin* return to the subject:

[1] "The language used by General Sheridan in the above-quoted dispatch shows that he thoroughly understands the political situation, and displays a statesmanlike grasp of thought not unworthy of the military genius of the author." January 6. See also its issues of January 9 and 10.

[2] *Ibid.*, January 12. A similar meeting was held at Baton Rouge, January 18. [3] January 7. [4] *Ibid.* [5] January 5.

[6] "En un mot, c'est un 18 brumaire que Grant vient de faire exécuter en Louisiane, en faisant expulser par les soldats les représentants du peuple." January 5.

We have heard that many a man who has been afflicted men-tally has seen, or imagined he saw, snakes, but we have never before heard of a case in which anyone so afflicted has seen banditti!!! fierce, terrible fellows who go roaming about to see if they cannot hurt somebody.[1]

An Atlanta paper was but voicing the pent-up, sur-charged emotions of Southerners outside the State when it said:

Again and again do we reiterate the hope that the citizens of New Orleans will take up the gage of battle so insolently thrown down to them.   Since blood must flow in defense of their liberties, then let the streets of the Crescent City again be the scene of the conflict of patriots against a most infamous usurpation.   We pray it—pray it, as if to God—that there may be no hesitating, no shrinking.

There is no mincing of words in this threat:

Now, let Grant declare Ogden, Marr, and the rest banditti, and then we will see who is hurt.   If any hanging or shooting is to be done, it is just possible that a braggart and dirty tool of an upstart like Sheridan may ornament a lamp-post quite as rapidly as any White League "ringleader" may grace a gallows.[2]

But it is not the fulminations of the press which impress the reader, but the surprised indignation, the dignified denials of bodies like the council of New Orleans, which noticed with "profound regret the dispatches sent by a general of the army to the Secretary of War characterizing us as 'law-defying and law-breaking'"; of a body of clergy, among whom were both the Roman Catholic archbishop and the Jewish rabbi[3]; of a group of bank presidents and

[1] January 7.
[2] Quoted in *Cong. Record*, 43 Cong., 2 Sess., 450.
[3] *Bulletin*.

cashiers[1]; of the Cotton Exchange; Merchants Exchange Association, and Chamber of Commerce; and of a group of Northern and Western men in the city on business, declaring that they had seen no spirit of defiance. Large meetings, representing various business interests, testified to the earnestness of feeling against the "libel" and slander[2]; even a body of foreigners met January 7 to deny the allegations.[3]

An excerpt from the New York *Tribune* reflects faithfully Northern sentiment without regard to party:

Now that Kellogg proposes to decide who shall belong to the Louisiana legislature and is backed by the United States army, might not President Grant better decide who shall belong to the next Congress and enforce his decisions by five or six regiments of United States troops, commanded by that truthful and just man, General Sheridan, and remove all regularly-elected members to make place for the Caseys or Dents? If he insists on fighting it out on this line, someone will play Brutus to his Cæsar without fail, which, by the way, would be a great blessing to the country.[4]

The *Nation* felt that "at this pace, we shall probably see by 1890 that the President has the right to inflict capital punishment with his own hand."[5] To the Cincinnati *Inquirer* it was the "crowning iniquity of a Federal administration not wanting in iniquities"[6]; to the New York *Herald* a spectacle which "should cause every

---

[1] *Republican*, January 8.   [2] *Times*, January 6.
[3] *Ibid.*, Jan. 8.   [4] Jan. 9.   [5] Jan. 14.
[6] Jan. 5. See also the New York *World*, *Evening Post*, Jan. 5, Cincinnati *Gazette*, Boston *Journal*, Boston *Advertiser* (both Republican), St. Louis *Democrat*, Philadelphia *Inquirer*, Jan. 6, Washington *Capitol*, Jan. 10. The following papers came out for Sheridan: Chicago *Tribune*, Jan. 6, *Inter Ocean*, Cincinnati *Times*; the following defended him mildly: Cleveland *Leader*, Milwaukee *Sentinel*, Baltimore *American*, Pittsburgh *Dispatch*, Washington *Republican*.

American to blush with shame and indignation"; while the Washington *Republican* compared it to Cromwell's purge. Vice-President Wilson deprecated it in harsh terms. Governors thrilled at the news and urged their legislatures to "protest with such emphasis and earnestness as to arrest the attention of every patriotic citizen": the governor of Indiana inveighed against the "crime"[1]; Governor Allen of Ohio urged action[2]; and the executive of Missouri urged resolutions of indignation.

The State legislatures of Ohio, Illinois, Virginia, Missouri, and Georgia considered the outrage worthy of legislative notice and severe condemnation, and as, to quote the phraseology of Ohio, "utterly defenseless in its atrocity" and calling for the severest censure and punishment on its actors, aiders, abettors.[3] The legislatures of Tennessee, Pennsylvania, and New York, the New Hampshire Democratic State Convention,[4] the Democratic State Central Committee of Missouri,[5] the Tammany Hall Committee, and boards of trade condemned the action. While the political complexion of most of these bodies was Democratic, the tone is clearly sincere and indicative of suppressed feeling. The indorsement, on the other hand, by the legislature of Kansas and the carpet-bag government of Mississippi[6] "of the President and of the valor, patriotism, and integrity of General Sheridan" were isolated instances of ultra-Radicalism.

Vast indignation mass meetings were held in many places,[7] but those in Faneuil Hall, Cooper Institute, and

---

[1] New Orleans *Times*, Jan. 9.   [2] *Ibid.*, Jan. 8.
[3] Sen. Misc. Doc., 43 Cong., 2 Sess., No. 47, 62–3.   Jan. 14, 19, 29.
[4] Jan. 5.   [5] *Times*, Jan. 8.
[6] *Record*, 43 Cong., 2 Sess., 1095, 689.
[7] There were also meetings at St. Louis; at Springfield, Illinois; at Frankfort, Kentucky; at Houston; Louisville; Baltimore; and Albany.

in Cincinnati were the most notable. The meeting in New York on January 11 was remarkable in numbers and enthusiasm. The doors were opened a half-hour before the usual time, and at a quarter after seven the hall was packed. William Cullen Bryant, octogenarian and staunch Republican though he was, had taken a prominent part in getting up the meeting and spoke with the "vehemence and fire of a man of thirty" in his denunciation of the President and military.[1] The meeting was, he declared, distinctly non-partisan, just American.

I don't exactly like the form of argument addressed to citizens of the United States—as we all are—that we must not be unconcerned nor careless about this action in Louisiana, for it may be repeated in New York. [*From the audience, cries of "Never, never."*] I don't like that form of argument to citizens. I tell you, fellow-citizens of the United States, that when it is done in one State, it is done in all. [*Applause.*] The United States, it is our boast, in its frame of government, is vital in every part, and cannot be hurt in one part without injury to all.[2]

Evarts and Curtis, also warm Republicans, spoke with strong feeling. The resolutions adopted protested emphatically against military interference, declaring that

it were better that legislative bodies shall be forbidden to meet at all, than to be forbidden to meet under their own rules and surrounded by their own officers, because nothing is more dangerous or demoralizing than arbitrary rule veiled by constitutional forms.

The body could not refrain from expressing its "heartfelt reprobation of this despatch itself, of the atrocious

[1] Godwin, *Life of Bryant*, II., 357.
[2] *Ibid.;* New York *Tribune*, Jan. 12.
20

imputation it casts on a large body of our countrymen, and of the Executive sanction which it has received."[1]

The Boston meeting was held January 15, and that in Cincinnati January 16, the latter being described as the largest held there since 1861. Pendleton addressed the gathering thus:

I am glad that it is so [that the Conservatives had exercised restraint] for it gives no alloy to the sympathy we can feel for their private wrongs, and puts no check upon the indignation and public sentiment for the unparalleled outrages upon public liberty.[2]

Dr. Wright, speaker of the Ohio House, declared that he would pray, if at all, "O God, may we not despise our rulers," and would add, "O Lord, may they not act so that we cannot help despising them."[3] Letters of sympathy with the purposes of the meeting were read from Honorable Groesbeck, Judge Hoadley, and Governor Allen, who for official reasons was unable to be present. Hoadley regarded the administration as having been engaged for three years in a conspiracy to deprive the people of Louisiana of the right to govern themselves, while Groesbeck tersely remarked that "bayonets are out of place in legislative halls."[4] Governor Allen felt that the Republican masses would not stand passively by while any man sought to assuage his thirst for power in the blood of the people.[5]

[1] New Orleans *Times*, January 12.
[2] *Record*, 43 Cong., 2 Sess., 1137. [3] *Ibid.*
[4] *Ibid.*
[5] At a banquet on January 8 he declared that a dispute which could be settled only by the legislature was settled "in the old way of despotism, by an armed body, settled by the army of the United States paid by your taxes, settled by a man who was ordered there for his lawless military despotism." *Ibid.*, 533. The marked change perceptible in the feeling of Northerners is explicable. They had believed that such intimidation

The immediate effect on New Orleans of these exciting events was to paralyze business by a lack of confidence, but by the 9th the fever had abated somewhat and the prospect of a settlement was hailed with joy.

existed in Louisiana as prevented a fair vote so that any frauds by the returning-board only afforded an equitable offset to the intimidation by Democrats. But now they were thinking for themselves and questioning the statements of their leaders.

CHAPTER XV

Louisiana Before Congress Again

WHILE the Louisiana problem was being fought before the returning-board and in the state-house at New Orleans, another battle, just as spirited, was raging in the halls of Congress at Washington. The whole matter arose in the House the very first day of the session of 1873-4 with a proposal by Butler to seat the Kellogg Representatives. But the old opposition was keenly alive to the danger of this seemingly harmless proposition. A lively debate was opened by Beck, pointing out the absurdity of Pinchback's seeking a seat in both houses, apparently on the principle that two chances were better than one. This unprecedented attitude provoked him into saying: "I know that many rights are accorded to men BECAUSE of race, color, or previous condition, but I never knew that even a negro could be both a Representative in Congress and a Senator at the same time."[1]

Two of the three Representatives were seated the second day,[2] a third the next,[3] although Kellogg had permitted irregularities in the special election of November 24, 1873, to fill a vacancy caused by death in the Louisiana Assembly. At Pinchback's own request[4]—for he was loath to be sworn into the House until every hope of the Senate was gone—the resolution to seat him was laid on the

[1] *Record*, 43 Cong., 1 Sess., 27.   [2] *Ibid.*, 28.   [3] *Ibid.*, 49.
[4] *Ibid.*, 34.

308

table, and his claims, together with those of all the War-moth contestants, were referred to the proper committee. A change was apparent on the part of certain members, who had objected to the preservation of the Kellogg rule by Federal force, to the position that such continued rule altered the expediency of making any change.

The Committee on Elections reported on only one of these contested cases and then not until the next May—that of Sheridan *vs.* Pinchback.[1]   No testimony had been taken.   They held the fact of the fraudulent canvass by the Lynch Board and the irregularities of the Warmoth Board so notorious, "that the House ought to take legislative notice of it in this contest," for the purpose of appropriate legislation.[2]   But they did not feel at liberty to report upon the evidence before them that either was entitled to the seat, and hence recommended that each have twenty days in which to produce further evidence. A minority of three would have seated Sheridan.[3]

The report came up for discussion on June 8.   The defenders of the Kellogg régime waxed belligerent in their attacks upon his opponents.

I repeat, what was met and defeated in Louisiana was in its inception a felonious conspiracy which in its progress became revolution—organized throughout a State, planned, entered upon, and nearly consummated by metropolitan police, and by confederate soldiers armed as militia; led by an unscrupulous Executive, who rallied to his support the thugs and assassins of former bloody conflicts in that turbulent State.   To defeat that organization and that revolutionary movement, avowedly and determinately bent on the overthrow of the rights and liberties of the colored race, I aver, as a proposition of law, constitutional, public, and statute, it was not only

[1] *Record,* 43 Cong., 1 Sess., 4039.
[2] House Repts., 43 Cong., 1 Sess., No. 597, 2.   [3] *Ibid.,* 40.

lawful, but supreme duty, to employ every necessary, available means, including force.[1]

Sarcasm was wielded to good effect:

Warmoth the demon, became Warmoth the angel, and the obnoxious election laws became the wisest upon the statute book.   Even the negro metropolitan police were suddenly bleached to Caucasian whiteness in the hope that they would contribute to the consummation of the diabolical plot to defraud the people and to overthrow free government in Louisiana.[2]

Or hear this cry:

Sir, the thing upon us was war—incipient, 'tis true, and not yet fully flagrant—still adjusted, impending war.   With bowed and uncovered head, here in this august presence, I thank Almighty God and bless this great nation that treason was met by that one, sole, adequate, lawful means by which it could be met—war.[3]

In his zeal one partisan was able to declare Kellogg's administration "the ablest, wisest, and purest that had existed in that State for a quarter of a century.   To assail and overthrow it by Congressional interference would be as unconstitutional and indefensible as needless and reckless."

Sheridan and Pinchback were each accorded an opportunity to be heard on the floor of the House.   Pinchback frankly defended himself for trying to preserve a hold on the Senate by asking whether any gentleman would have been so patriotic and considered the

dignity of this House so far above that of the Senate as to have said, "I will not take the seat in the Senate, I will take the

---

[1] *Record*, 43 Cong., 1 Sess., 4695.   Spoken by Sypher.
[2] *Ibid.*, 4697.   [3] *Ibid.*, 4698.

seat in the House." If this House is composed of gentlemen
of that character, I am forced to admit that they are more
disinterested patriots than I have yet found in my brief
political career. The rule adopted by all those I am acquainted
with has been to take the best office they could obtain.[1]

And he gratuitously advised the Senate:

Sir, I demand simple justice. I am not here as a beggar.
I do not care so far as I am personally concerned whether you
give me my seat or not. I will go back to my people and come
here again; but I tell you to preserve your own consistency.
Do not make fish of me while you have made flesh of everybody else.[2]

His blatant conceit is somewhat startling,[3] while his
morals were, to say the least, erratic when he could say:

I had a good many friends under Warmoth in office and was
comfortably housed myself. I concluded that I would drive
along with him until I could get a convenient jumping-off place.
I wanted also to see what his plans were so as to defeat them. Oh!
I could tell you a tale that would harrow up your very soul.[4]

Sheridan's speech, if a bit flowery, was dignified and

---

[1] *Record*, 43 Cong., 1 Sess., Appendix, 431–2.   [2] *Ibid.*, 432.
[3] "I have a clear and unimpeached party record. From the first day
when you have clothed me with the right to vote to the present, I have
voted at every election the straight Republican ticket. And what is more
than that, I have done that in Louisiana which few men have done in any
portion of this country; I have shown on several occasions that I held party
success above personal interest. . . . Chandler asked me how it (the
Republican party) could be saved, and I told him that there was but one
way on earth; that was for me to take my life in my hands and start for
New Orleans, and if I got there before Governor Warmoth, I could save it.
. . . I knew the dangers I should encounter, but was brave enough to risk
it. . . . It is but another dastardly attempt on the part of these men to
deprive me of my right and the people of Louisiana of a vote in this House,
because I am unwilling to be cheated by these false Republicans, and too
manly to be used as their tool. . . . I shall not blame you." *Ibid.*, 432–4.
[4] *Ibid.*, 434.

made an intelligible plea for justice for the white men of the South, when he cried:

Let it not be written, let it not go down in history, that we struck chains from the limbs of four millions of black people only to bind them upon the limbs of eight million white people. I believe that the black race of this country should have every right that we possess.   But I do not believe they should have any more.   Not for them, as has been the case in Louisiana, should armies be invoked to destroy the sanctity of the ballot and silence the voice of the people.[1]

The report of the majority of the Committee was adopted. The last notice taken in the House was on June 20 when it was voted to require McEnery to bring the returns of the election of 1872 before the Committee of Elections on the first Monday of the following December.[2]

The credentials of Pinchback and McMillan, presented to the Senate January 7 and March 3 of 1873 and laid upon the table,[3] were taken up and referred to the Committee on Privileges and Elections on one of the first days of the next session.[4]   There were arguments by counsel on each side before the Committee, and on one side, printed briefs,[5] but no testimony was taken.   December 15 Morton, on behalf of the Committee, asked to be discharged, referring the whole matter to the Senate, as the Committee was evenly divided upon the question.[6]   But on the same day he offered a resolution, since these credentials were regular, to seat Pinchback, subject to contest.   The debate began the 16th and soon became general over condi-

[1] *Congressional Record*, 43 Cong., 1 Sess., Appendix, 437.
[2] House Journal, 43 Cong., 1 Sess., 1263.
[3] The credentials of McMillan and those of Ray, both presented by West, had been referred on January 22, 1873, to the Committee on Privileges and Elections. *Globe*, 42 Cong., 3 Sess., 766. It was the presentation of McMillan's claim for the long term which was now tabled, March 3. *Ibid.*, 2147.   [4] Dec. 4. *Record*, 43 Cong., 1 Sess., 57.
[5] On the statement of Morton. *Record, ibid.*, 190.   [6] *Ibid.*, 188.

tions in Louisiana.   Morton, the ever-ardent champion of Kellogg, formally opened the debate, which hinged on the *prima facie* right of Pinchback to be seated.   He attempted to demonstrate material improvements for the Kellogg régime and to show that the body electing Pinchback to the Senate was the valid legislature.[1]   But January 20 he himself moved that Pinchback's credentials be referred to the Committee with instructions to investigate his personal character.   He had heard charges of improper conduct[2] by Pinchback in connection with his election which he did not feel at liberty to withhold from the Senate.   To go on with the original motion would be an assumption on his part to determine the question, which responsibility rested with the Senate.[3]   This motion was never disposed of, disappearing after February 2.   But the credentials of McMillan, whom the McEnery legislature had sent back to Washington to fight for the full term, were recommitted on January 27.[4]

In an elaborate speech, occupying the greater part of two days, January 29 and 30, Carpenter gave notice of an intention again to introduce another bill for a new election.[5]   It

[1] *Congressional Record*, 43 Cong., 1 Sess., 223.

[2] Pinchback had accepted money as a salve for his wounded feelings in withdrawing from the Senatorial contest in favor of one Norton, which he, as a matter of fact, had used corruptly to secure his own election, no doubt supposing that "as the end in view was in either case the triumph of good men," the means used would be justified. *Nation*, Feb. 5, 1874.

The *Republican* printed with great·gusto the story of how, during his residence at Washington, his Spanish type of looks misled several young society belles to accept the statement that he was a Brazilian attaché and to evince great anxiety to meet him.   Feb. 14, 1875.

[3] Sen. Jour., 43 Cong., 1 Sess., 164.   *Record*, 774.

[4] *Record*, 43 Cong., 1 Sess., 941.

[5] *Ibid.*, 1036–58.   Carpenter was pledged to the people of Louisiana. He had been in New Orleans in May, 1873, and in a public speech he had promised that if they would stop violence and submit to Kellogg until Congress met, he would try to secure a relief bill of the Senate.   *Ibid.*, 3034.

was a long, logical argument to prove that Congress had, by its action on the Presidential vote, declared that the Kellogg government never was elected, as the election had been a monstrous fraud; that Congress had power to pass such a bill; that the bill did not controvert State rights and it pointed out that Congress held the right to determine the manner of its interference. He dismissed, as too late, the proposition to seat Pinchback on a *prima facie* case.[1] He summed up the case against the Lynch Board in these words:

All these questions from the right of a Senator of the United States down to the right of every parish officer in Louisiana, are to be settled by a false return, proved false in every court that has ever investigated it; known to be false by every man who has examined it; proved false by the very men who made it, and known by the Senator himself to be an unparalleled fraud; and that false canvass has estopped the State courts, and the State courts estop us, and everything is concluded by a fraud which is confessed on all hands and laid bare by an investigation of a committee of this body.[2]

Without waiting for the bill, Morton replied at once,

[1] His attack on executive interference was tolerant. "I do not say it (the proclamation of May 22) was issued in violation of any act, because no act forbids it to be issued. I say it was issued without any authority of law. There was no case made before the President which authorized him to interfere. Nothing was shown to him establishing the fact that there was an insurrection in that State against the government of the State. We must have a case, not of domestic violence, but a case of insurrection in a State against the government thereof; and I say no such case was shown. Therefore, I say, there was no authority for issuing that proclamation." *Record*, 43 Cong., 1 Sess., 1050.

[2] *Ibid.*, 1055. It is interesting that when the Louisiana case came before the Electoral Commission in 1877, Carpenter served as counsel against the acceptance of the votes for Hayes, although he had voted for him, because the one calamity greater than the accession of the Democratic party would be to keep it out by fraud and falsehood. *Record*, Electoral Commission, 72.

attacking it on the score that it was desired by neither Republicans nor by the best part of the Democrats, by colored people, nor by the business men.   The men who were moving in the matter were those who had covered Louisiana with blood,[1] the assassins of 1866, 1868, and 1873.   He then followed with a lurid account of the Colfax Massacre.   Since 1866 there had been a constant series of murders in Louisiana, until it was patent that the life of a colored man was of no more account than that of a mad dog, and yet not one murderer had paid the penalty of his crime.[2]

The next day[3] his speech was intended to answer the arguments of Carpenter.   The first proposition of the latter had been that, according to the returns, the McEnery ticket had been elected by some nine thousand majority; his next that the unlawful interference of Judge Durrell had installed the Kellogg government illegally; and the third, that McEnery had not been elected at all, as the election had been an organized fraud.   This presentation of the case ought, Morton felt, to satisfy the Kellogg supporters, but left the Senator not one inch of ground on which to stand.   After dwelling at great length on the murders, he solemnly admonished the State that the murder business must stop.[4]   While refusing to defend wrongs committed, he presented the history of Louisiana

---

[1] He declared that Warmoth and McEnery, whom he characterized as "the Governor whose criminal pretensions have caused bloodshed and murder," were both on the floor of the Senate during this debate, engineering for a new election.   *Record*, 42.

[2] *Ibid*, 43 Cong., 1 Sess., Appendix, 41–3.   He had prepared this part of the speech while at Hot Springs with R. P. Hitt.   Foulke, II., 286–7.

[3] Feb. 2.

[4] "I say to the people of Louisiana, unless they would have a fatal blight to fall upon their State, withering its every interest, blasting its reputation and prospects, they must stop this murder business.   The blood of the innocent cries to Heaven, and makes barren the soil upon which it is shed. The people that instigate murder must perish.   God has declared it in his

as a vindication for the mass of the Republicans and warned Carpenter that the bloody scenes of Mechanics Institute or Colfax might be renewed in New Orleans and that

those who encourage them, who give them ground to believe that that government will be overturned, however good may be their intentions, will have a fearful load of responsibility to carry, if these things again happen. I know very well what was the effect in New Orleans and in Louisiana of what was said upon this floor last winter, and I know what joy, what exceeding joy, was carried to the hearts of these men by this movement on foot now for a new election. I am informed who are moving in it, who are controlling the secret springs: and I hope for the sake of the people of that State, I hope for the sake of the people of the Union, that this agitation will cease.[1]

The debate turned into a personal quarrel between Morton and Carpenter, in which the former lost none of his usual vindictiveness.

Frelinghuysen, believing there was grave question as to the right of Congress to order a new election, preferred to recognize neither Senator, but to wait until the next November, when a regular election would possibly create a legislature which the central government could recognize.[2]

February 5, Carpenter fulfilled his promise with a bill for another election,[3] almost identical with that of the

---

Holy Word, and throughout all the history of mankind. The land that has been sown in blood will spring up with the poisoned teeth of the dragon. . . . People of Louisiana, you must not, you cannot, tolerate these crimes. Innocent blood contaminates like the plague. If the people of Louisiana tolerate these crimes, connive with the murderers, and shelter them from punishment, they must perish with them." *Record*, 43 Cong., 1 Sess., 47.

[1] *Ibid.*, Appendix, 48. [2] *Ibid.*, 1110–1.

[3] *Ibid.*, 1215. It was printed as Senate Bill No. 446.

previous session. But only on March 4 was he able to carry his motion to postpone all pending business so that the Senate could proceed to its consideration. [1] But that consideration was limited to a patient hearing of his long speech, which pointed out logically that if the results as to Presidential electors were void, it followed that the election of State officials, subject to the same objections, had also been declared void by Congress [2]; and that the bill under consideration was constitutional under the clause which guaranteed to every State a Republican government. He met the argument as to expediency [3] and pointed out, almost as a prophecy, the opportunity for contest which it afforded at the next Presidential election. [4] And there the matter rested until April 14, when, against serious objection, he succeeded in again bringing it to the fore. [5]

West, as was to be expected, did not care to run the risk of a new election, asserting that he was sick of returns when one set was a fraud, the other all guesswork. [6] Morton on April 16 in a speech of much force urged the danger of Congressional interference. Four days later it was Bayard who replied to Morton by offering a substitute amendment recognizing the McEnery government, [7] which he vigorously defended.

[1] *Record,* 43 Cong., 1 Sess., 1952.

[2] *Ibid.,* Appendix, 87. See 86–99 for able marshaling of new arguments.

[3] "There are two sides to this question when you look to expediency. Non-interference is far more dangerous than interference." *Ibid.,* 96.

[4] "We cannot expect so decisive a result of the next presidential campaign. And it seems little short of madness to adjourn the difficulties now attending the state government of Louisiana, which are almost certain to be revived in the count of votes for the next President." *Ibid.,* 98.

[5] *Ibid.,* 3033, 36, 59.

[6] Starting in a lofty tone, he soon fell into mere partisan abuse. *Ibid.,* 3090.

[7] For the amendment in full see *ibid.,* 3189.

The wrong which has been done, you partly may undo. No one can question that there has been the invasion of a state by the armed forces of the federal government. Withdraw your troops. Call off your dogs. Set the state free to speak her own mind and live under her own laws. That is all. . . . Sir, if collision should ensue, if blood should flow, it is better for a people to lose many of those they value most than to submit to such a wrong as that under which Louisiana groans today.

And in a lofty tone he warned the North:

Believing the cure for present evils and disorders to rest in a revival of the proper public sentiment, and especially in the dominant section, in the populous and wealthy states of the North, I beg them to consider the effect upon themselves and upon their own prosperity of thus permitting the lingering spirit of hostility engendered by a civil war to control their action or tinge their legislation in respect to that portion of the country with whom they were some years ago at strife.[1]

But Bayard addressed, for the most part, empty benches. Few of the administration party were present, many of the Democrats absent.[2] To such a degree were Senators uninterested, that on one occasion eight men graced the benches.[3] Sherman apparently voiced the feeling of the Senate when he held it best to pass in silence what had occurred there, as Louisianians would soon have an opportunity at the polls to redeem their government if it had fallen into the hands of usurpers.[4] And so Pinchback was again ignominiously shelved, together with the new election bill, when further consideration of unfinished business was postponed on April 28.[5] Morton had enforced his will, but Pinchback was not seated.

[1] *Record*, 43 Cong., 1 Sess., 3199.   [2] *Ibid.*, 3193.
[3] According to Senator Hamlin, *ibid.*, 3302.   [4] *Ibid.*, 3034.
[5] *Ibid.*, 3436. He had long before suffered complete eclipse, for the discussion had been transferred to the question of a new election.

When Congress met again in December, 1874, the Louisiana question, after the exciting events of the summer and autumn, naturally claimed its early attention. The President drew attention in his annual message to the "unsettled condition of affairs in some of the Southern States." After briefly reciting the events of September 14 and of the November election, he vigorously defended his interference, which he declared "repugnant to public opinion, to the feelings of those, who, from their official capacity, must be used in such interposition, and to him who must direct." But at the same time, he unmistakably defined his position: "While I remain Executive all the laws of Congress and the provisions of the Constitution, including the recent amendments added thereto, will be enforced with rigor, but with regret that they should have added one jot or tittle to Executive duties or powers."[1] And he suggested that Congress create a committee to learn whether the alleged wrongs of the colored citizens be "real or manufactured" for the occasion.

The House promptly[2] ordered the creation of a committee of seven on that portion of the President's message relating to the South. The full committee ordered a sub-committee of three to New Orleans on December 22 to make an investigation.

The personnel of this committee merits notice. Foster and Phelps, both Republicans, had seemed to be ardent party men, while Potter was a zealous Democrat.[3] Foster was born in the Black Swamp of Western Ohio in 1812 of Scotch-Irish stock. His educational training had been

---

[1] *Record*, 43 Cong., 2 Sess., 6.

[2] Dec. 9, *Record*, 43 Cong., 2 Sess., 31. The speaker announced the appointments December 15.

[3] Potter was a leading member of the Judiciary Committee which was investigating Durrell and ascribed the Louisiana muddle to that gentleman, according to the *Picayune*, Dec. 31, 1874.

limited to the public schools and an academy which he had been obliged to leave at an early age to aid his father in his store at Fostoria, though he later secured private instruction. Succeeding at the age of nineteen to the business, which he enlarged and modernized, he acquired a wide circle of acquaintances and became a sort of patron-saint to the countryside. If any one were in need of money or in distress, or if any one were promoting a charitable enterprise, he sought out "Charley Foster." He was forty-two years of age when he first ran for Congress, but so great was his personal popularity that he won the election in a Democratic district in 1870 and for three succeeding terms.[1] He quickly won the confidence of the House by his work on committees and his ability at debate.

Different in every way had been the training of Phelps, scion of a distinguished Connecticut family, though born in New York. Wealth had given him every educational advantage; nor had he slighted his opportunities, for he graduated from Yale second in his class and won valedictorian honors from Columbia Law School. Although he entered upon active practice, he was forced to devote his time to the vast estates left him by his father, which he looked upon as a trust. Coming of a line which had served in public office,[2] it was not unnatural that he should win an election to Congress in 1872 by a large majority, where he had, already within two years, made a brilliant record as an orator and independent thinker by a bold attack on the Civil Rights Bill. He was noted as one of the few men to whom the House would always listen.[3]

[1] See White, *National Cyclopedia of Biography.*

[2] One of his ancestors had represented his town thirty successive terms in the Connecticut Assembly. See the accounts in White's and Appleton's *Cyclopedias.*

[3] Based upon White's *Cyclopedia*, Appleton's *Cyclopedia*, and the *Nation* for June 21, 1894.

But, if of dissimilar training, the two men had alike the qualities of honesty and moral courage, for it took courage to condemn the policy of their party and their President.   Both had the capacity of seeing both sides of a question and of reading men, so that when face to face with the Louisiana witnesses, they could discriminate between truth and falsehood.   The *Nation* regarded the trioₐ̆ as honest, fair-minded and judicious men as could have been selected from the whole House.''[1]

The sub-committee determined to limit their investigation to the recent election and to confine themselves to certain parishes, selected by the Radicals as typical of Conservative misconduct.   At their sessions, which continued through eight days, they were attended by counsel from both parties.   They examined ninety-five witnesses besides taking a large amount of documentary evidence.[2] In view of the urgency in the politics of Louisiana, the committee decided not to wait to print their evidence but to report at once certain conclusions to which they were all agreed.[3]   The people of the State of Louisiana, in their opinion, did fairly have a free, peaceable, and full registration and election, in which a clear Conservative majority was elected to the lower house of the legislature, of which majority the Conservatives were deprived by the unjust, illegal, and arbitrary action of the returning-board.[4]   No general intimidation of Republican voters, in their opinion, was established.[5]

[1] Jan. 21, 1875.   It later declared that if forty such men could be sent to the Senate, the better half of the American people would heave a sigh of relief.   Jan. 28.

[2] Some 1500 pages.   Such was the interest that people fairly camped with the committee.   [3] Jan. 15.

[4] House Repts., 43 Cong., 2 Sess., No. 101, 8.

[5] "No colored man was produced who had been threatened or assaulted by any conservative because of political opinion, or discharged from employment, or refused employment; of all those who testified to intimidation

21

No witness, we believe, succeeded in naming in any parish, five Republicans who supported the Kellogg government who were not themselves office-holders or related to office-holders or those having official employment, while arrests upon affidavits of alleged threats of discharge were frequent.[1]

On the general condition, though they did not attempt any recommendation, their conclusion was equally strong and independent.

The conviction has been general among the whites, since 1872, that the Kellogg Government was an usurpation. . . . With this conviction is a general want of confidence in the integrity of the existing State and local officials;—a want of confidence equally in their purposes, and in their personnel —which is accompanied by the paralyzation of business and destruction of values. . . . As the people saw taxation increase and prosperity diminish—as they grew poor, while officials grew rich—they became naturally sore.   That they love their rulers cannot be pretended.[2]

Never before had the Southerner had so sympathetic a treatment as when the report declared:

What they [the Conservatives of Louisiana] seek is peace and an opportunity for prosperity; to that end they will support any form of government that will afford them just protection in their business and personal relations.   In their distress they have got beyond any mere question of political party.   They regard themselves as without government and without power to form one.[3]

---

there was hardly anyone who of his own knowledge could specify a reliable instance of such acts, and of the white men who were produced to testify generally on such subjects, very nearly all, if not every single one, was the holder of an office. . . ."

[1] House Repts., 43 Cong., 2 Sess., No. 101, 5–6.

[2] *Ibid.*, 6–7.   This report, as well as the second, was obviously written by Foster.   [3] *Ibid.*, 9.

They found the White Leagues composed of ordinary political clubs, neither secret nor armed, except in New Orleans, where it was composed of respectable citizens and property-holders, leagued for self-protection only.

The report produced a profound impression on the North.[1] It was quite unprecedented in Reconstruction History that men of both parties on a Congressional committee should present a unanimous verdict on a partisan question—and that favorable to the opposition party. It furnished great strength to the Conservative party in Louisiana, especially when the Democrats had been made conscious by the outburst after January 4 that public opinion in the North believed peace could be secured only through home rule. Under it the Conservatives showed more vigor of opposition than ever.[2] But to the Radicals it was, in very truth, a wet-blanket, thrown by the hands of those who were supposed to be their political friends. Naturally, the Republican press tried to minimize its effect by treating it lightly. "The sub-committee planted themselves down here and examined about all the White League who offered themselves and as few Republicans as they could get along with, and finally, posted off to Washington no wiser than they came."[3]

Stern partisans[4] felt that something must be done to

[1] The *Republican* gave the chief credit for the document to Potter and his Democratic counsel in the city, condemning some portions as literal excerpts from the Democratic brief to the Committee. This paper found a certain satisfaction in pointing out that Potter had voted against the Civil Rights Bill and was guilty of owning a half-interest in the New York *Tribune*. Jan. 12.

[2] The *Picayune* regarded it as "the ablest and most comprehensive statement of the Louisiana case that has yet appeared," and avowed that it could not have been produced in the State. Jan. 17.

[3] *Republican*, Jan. 12.

[4] In an interview, widely published, Morton criticized it severely in his usual sarcastic manner. He held it false as to the Leagues, of whose

counteract the damaging effect of the report, and so Hoar, chairman of the Committee, Wheeler and Frye, all good Republicans, accompanied by one Democrat, Marshall, proceeded on January 22 to New Orleans for another investigation.[1] This committee remained there eighteen days, conversing with many people and collecting a vast amount of testimony. The formal committee report, submitted February 23, presented, as usual, majority and minority opinions. The elaborate minority report, written by Hoar and signed also by Wheeler and Frye, set forth with minute detail the acts of violence and bloodshed in the State, the political massacres and barbarities committed upon defenseless negroes and Republicans, "so cruel and barbarous as to excite astonishment in any people making the least pretense to civilization."[2] The White League was declared to be a military organization, designed to put the whites into power, who, they felt, would refrain from the use of no instruments to attain it. In view of the facts, they did not hesitate to declare that the election of 1874 was "neither full, free, nor fair."[3] They showed credulity remarkable in statesmen, as Rhodes points out,[4] when they accepted Sheridan's

---

brutality and murders there was abundant evidence. But he did not fear that the legality of the board could be impeached by a superficial examination of a few days. Foulke, II., 296–7. The report was not in accord with Republican sentiment, but there was no purpose to criticise it harshly, though the papers ridiculed it and abused the three members of the Committee.

[1] Their arrival was hailed with satisfaction by the Radicals, with consternation or mockery by the Democrats. The *Times* said, Jan. 12: "Ye committeeman has become so numerous that we no longer regard him with other awe than that with which the enthusiastic countryman gazed on a flock of crows nine miles long. If we had our own way, we would say, less committee, if you please, and more bona-fide relief." Jan. 12, 23.

[2] House Repts., 43 Cong., 2 Sess., No. 261, Part i., 9.

[3] *Ibid.*, 19.

[4] Rhodes, VII., 125–6.

figures of the number killed between 1866 and 1875, "as
far short of the truth,"—especially when one notes how
his number had swelled from 2140 of the dispatch of
January 10 to 3500.[1]

But Hoar's respect for the truth forced him to add that
78,524 out of 87,121 negro voters were reported as illiterate
and adds: "These masses of illiterate voters must of
necessity to a very large extent be instruments in the
hands of others, who can influence their passions or excite
their fears,"—involuntary testimony for the Democrats.
They united with the Democratic members in reporting
that the returning-board, "in canvassing and compiling
said returns and promulgating the result, wrongfully
applied an erroneous rule of law," but illegal also was the
action of the legislature in admitting the Conservative
members.   But a new election was not desired so that
the only alternative was recognition of Kellogg, whose
government was a fact and had been recognized by the
President.

While the four members of the first sub-committee
and Marshall of the second committee differed in their
conclusions as to the election,[2] they could agree on two
recommendations: One to recommend to the Louisiana
House immediate steps to place the persons rightfully
entitled in their seats, and the other, a recognition of

[1] Nor should one fail to see Nordhoff's opinion in 1875 that since
1870, except in Coushatta and Colfax, most of the murders in Louisiana
had been non-political, 48.   See also his table, compiled not from official
returns—"the government being too busily engaged in stealing"—but
from county clerks and coroners from thirteen parishes.   From 1868 to
1875 there had been 313 murders, mostly negroes by negroes, instigated
by whiskey and jealousy, 55.   Major Merrill's black report was offset
by the report of Captain Morrow, commanding at Shreveport, dated Jan.
25.   *Times*, Jan. 27.
[2] They dissented emphatically from any accusation of unfairness in the
election as a false assumption.

Kellogg as governor until the end of his term of office.[1]
Foster and Phelps did not oppose the recognition of
Kellogg, but neither did they wish "to be understood as
urging it," only believing that it might be less intolerable
than the present distress.   But to such recognition, Potter
and Marshall were utterly opposed.[2]   It will be noted
that the committee had already been asked to serve as
arbiters and that their solution was virtually approval of
the Wheeler Compromise.

Meanwhile debate in Congress had not waited for the
report of the committee.   The Democrats in the Senate
at once gave voice to their wrath.   On the day following
the stirring events in the Southern city, Thurman offered
a resolution that the President inform the body whether
any portion of the army had interfered with the organization of the general assembly of Louisiana, and if so by
what authority,[3] and grew greatly excited over the outrage to State rights.   Morton offered an amendment
that the President inform the Senate in regard to the
existence of armed organizations in Louisiana intent
on overturning the government by force.   "Let the
whole story come, . . . " he cried.   "We are always
safer in the presence of the whole truth than of a part."[4]

A debate, bitter and heated to fever-point, in which
all the leading Senators took part, was immediately
precipitated.   Thurman insisted that the time had passed
when a plain violation of the Constitution could be justified by the cry of Southern outrages.   During the preceding summer the outrage mill had been started with the

[1] House Repts., 43 Cong., 2 Sess., No. 261, 5.
[2] In their judgment, all that was needed, was to withdraw the troops.
Ibid., 4.
[3] *Record*, 43 Cong., 2 Sess., 238.   Considerable debate was provoked
over the mere form of the resolution, which was held to be discourteous
to Grant.   [4] *Ibid.*, 240.

Attorney-General as head-miller, but the people had rejected the grist and condemned this attempt to keep alive the fires of the late war and to stimulate hatred in one part of the country for the other.[1]

Saulsbury became sufficiently wrought up to say:

I say, if the facts be as alleged in the papers, if the statements intimated and suggested in the resolution of the Senator from Ohio be true, whether the other side of the Chamber be willing or not, to apply a remedy, the American people will find a way to deal with the question.   I hope the time has not yet come when any Cæsar may clothe himself in his robes or in purple and bid defiance to the American people. . . .   Why sir, if Cæsar attempts to wrap the purple about him, I say in the name of public liberty let the American people tear the robes from him.[2]

On the other side, Logan condemned his Democratic friends who "stand by and sustain them in these horrible and damnable crimes" as no better than the perpetrators,[3] while Edmunds assured Senators that the people would not see thousands and tens of thousands of their fellow-beings made the victims of oppression and assassination and every species of wrong, because they wish to assert their constitutional rights.[4] Morton wanted to know why these fifteen hundred soldiers came to be in New Orleans,—if the streets of that city for the last three months had run with blood.   Statements were published and then "came ten thousand times ten thousand lies, denying them, or excusing them, or justifying them, until the public mind was confused and confounded by the innumerable lies."   Men who would murder, would lie, commit perjury, forgery, and arson, and every minor crime to cover up their guilt, and he wanted to know

[1] *Record*, 43 Cong., 2 Sess., 249.   [2] *Ibid.*, 242.
[3] *Ibid.*, 243.   [4] *Ibid.*, 248.

whether murder were to become an established institution in this country.[1]

Debate did not spare Sheridan nor Grant. Said a Senator from Maryland:

Grant may not be Cæsar, he may not be a Cromwell, he may not be a Napoleon; but he possesses today the power of all three. . . . I tell you that this body is not higher in responsibility, is not greater in degree, than the Legislature of a sovereign State, and the regular soldier that enters there under the order of the President of the United States whether to organize or disperse that legislature is competent to march into either body here, and the day may come, unless the pure spirit of American liberty still survives, when amid troubles and disorder and violence some aspiring Cæsar, Cromwell, or Napoleon, at the other end of the avenue may require the arrest of some or the dispersion of all the members in both Houses of Congress, and the regular Army, taught as it is now, will do it if ordered.[2]

Or hear Bayard's burning attack on Sheridan:

Sir, if these things [Bill of Rights] were read by that officer, surely he must have forgotten them, or else have the more guilty audacity to ride rough-shod over them. If he has forgotten, let him now be taught anew. Let us see who is the stronger. The issue cannot come too soon. If this cavalry officer [and he reminded Senators that Sheridan had been trained at public expense] with whatever of renown he may have gained with his bloody sword, shall be stronger than these guarantees of personal liberty which we supposed were secured to us, let us know it now. We cannot have the issue raised too soon or too distinctly stated. I ask the Senate and the country to listen to the tone of this officer, and see . . .

[1] *Record*, 43 Cong., 2 Sess., 251. Thurman's retort was apt: "It will as long as it is to the interest of the Republican party to say that it is the case." He was promptly asked if he meant to say that the Republicans had committed these murders, a query which he disdained to answer.

[2] *Ibid.*, 312.

who shall say he is even fit to breathe the air of a Republican government..'.

There stands the constitution of Louisiana and of the United States. . . . Overthrown and cast down by the furious lawlessness, by the unlawful ambition of these two officials whom I have named, the creature and the creator. Look at it, Senators! Look at it, people of the United States! Contemplate the picture of the dispersed assembly; read the protest of the peaceable and orderly men rejected by brute force from their lawful places in the Assembly, and then say whether party passion or sectional prejudice can constrain you to approve it or prevent you from grave and deliberate condemnation of the act and of those who have committed it. [2]

Before the resolution came to a vote, Schurz offered a resolution that the Committee on the Judiciary inquire what legislation was necessary to secure to the people of Louisiana the rights of self-government. This resolution he supported with a carefully prepared speech which made a deep impression on the Senate. [3] After a concise statement of the facts of January 4, he said:

Nobody respects General Sheridan more than I do for the brilliancy of his deeds on the field of battle; the nation has delighted to honor his name. But the same nation would sincerely deplore to see the hero of the ride of Winchester and of the charge at the Five Forks stain that name by an attempt to ride over the law and the Constitution of the country and to charge upon the liberties of his fellow-citizens. The policy he has proposed is so appalling, that every American citizen who loves his liberty stands aghast at the mere possibility of such a suggestion being addressed to the President of the United States by a high official of the Government. . . . How long before a soldier may stalk into the national House of

[1] *Record*, 43 Cong., 2 Sess., 332.   [2] *Ibid.*, 331.
[3] The *Nation* pronounced it a fitting termination to his Congressional career.

Representatives, and, pointing to the Speaker's mace, say, "Take away that bauble."

Even Republicans were moved as he solemnly charged Senators:

Turn back, turn back in your dangerous course while it is yet time. In the name of that inheritance of peace and freedom which you desire to leave to your children, in the name of the pride with which the American lifts up his head among the nations of the world, do not trifle with the Constitution of your country, do not put in jeopardy that which is the dearest glory of the American name. Let not the representative of the people falter and fail in the supreme hour when the liberties of the people are at stake.[1]

Nobody objected to Schurz's resolution, yet so surcharged were the feelings of Senators that the debate continued. Language of the most violent character was uttered by Senators usually calm and dignified. One member, who had not spoken in three years, felt it his duty to ask to be heard on the question.[2] The purpose seemed to be more to afford men an opportunity to declare their positions than to reach any legislative conclusion, for no final action was taken on it. One object, on the part of the Radicals, may have been to counteract the effect which the military interference had produced on the public mind. Certainly the excited state of mind was not confined to the Senators. The galleries were crowded every day. Repeated outbursts of applause for both sides subsided only after repeated reproof from the chair and motions to clear the galleries had been pressed.[3]

---

[1] *Record*, 43 Cong., 2 Sess., 371.   [2] *Ibid.*, 532.
[3] *Ibid.*, 308–9. The interest manifested was greater, it was declared, than over any measure since the Ku-Klux bill was up for discussion. The subject seemed, as Thurman said, to be "one to make a man's blood run fast; it is a subject to make the nerves thrill in the body of any man who ever loved liberty or had the least idea of constitutional law." *Ibid.*, 339.

Two days after Schurz introduced his motion, January 13, the President sent to the Senate the documents called for, together with a message,[1] setting forth the violence in Louisiana, which reflected the position already taken by Morton.[2] It proved to be a long defensive document and necessarily touched upon all the events of recent Louisiana history. Of the events of January 4, he disclaimed any knowledge prior to the morning of the 5th.[3] In Sheridan's defense he said:

General Sheridan was looking at facts, and, possibly, not thinking of proceedings which would be the only proper ones to pursue in time of peace, thought more of the utterly lawless condition of society surrounding him at the time of his dispatch and of what would prove a sure remedy. He never proposed to do an illegal act, nor expressed determination to proceed beyond what the law in the future might authorize for the punishment of the atrocities which have been committed, and the commission of which cannot be successfully denied.[4]

In his own defense he wrote the following paragraph:

I have deplored the necessity which seemed to make it my duty under the Constitution and laws to direct such interference. I have always refused except where it seemed to be my imperative duty to act in such a manner under the Constitution and laws of the United States. I have repeatedly and earnestly entreated the people of the South to live together in

[1] Rumor had whispered that the tone of the message was defiant, but Grant had evidently been startled by the public clamor and had modified it to prevent a breach in the cabinet, it was said. *Record*, 43 Cong., 2 Sess., 523. Gossip gave the credit to a different group from Grant's habitual advisers: Carpenter, Edmunds, and Fish. Merriam, *Bowles*, II., 236.

[2] The Indianapolis *Sentinel* noticed this striking similarity, but preferred Morton's speech in Sep. 1874. Foulke, *Morton*, II., 295.

[3] Richardson, VII., 311. It is indicative of the rancor of the times that Saulsbury on the floor of the Senate congratulated the President on the conciliatory and fair tone of this document which seems to us so tense with feeling.   [4] *Ibid.*, 312.

peace and obey the laws; and nothing would give me greater pleasure than to see reconciliation and tranquillity everywhere prevail, and thereby remove all necessity for the presence of troops among them.[1]

But since this condition did not exist, he declared that no White League would be allowed to persecute or murder Union men. He concluded with an earnest appeal for action by Congress, "so as to leave my duties perfectly clear in dealing with the affairs of Louisiana."[2]

And still for five days longer the Senate chamber rang with denunciations, on the one hand, of Grant's tyranny and, on the other, with defense of that "modest, retiring, and indomitably brave man"; with blood-curdling tales of murder, and with eulogies of the South. Schurz's resolution, postponed January 18 to make way for the Appropriation Bill, was resumed on the 22d and discussed daily at great length until February 1 when it finally disappears from the records.

The Louisiana question came up again this session in the form of a resolution to admit Pinchback as a Senator. Another reëlection by the Louisiana assembly on January 13 had been duly brought to the attention of the Senate on the 22d by Senator West. On February 8 Morton reported favorably for the Committee on Privileges and Elections.[3] This action inaugurated a long debate, opened by Morton on February 15 with a speech in which he relied on precedent to justify seating Pinchback. In a futile attempt to settle the question the Senate remained in session from noon of February 17 until half after four of the next afternoon. But, although that body was very

---

[1] Richardson, VII., 313.   [2] *Ibid.*, 314.

[3] This action provoked a brief sharp debate, as it was held that only four of the nine members of the committee were present at the meeting at which action was taken on this question. *Record*, 43 Cong., 2 Sess., 1063.

thin at certain hours of the night, the Democrats were unwilling to let the question come to a vote.   At last, about 3 o'clock in the afternoon, the weary Senators disposed of it by ordering it to lie on the table,[1] some fifteen regular Republicans voting with the Democrats.

Meanwhile, notice of the absorbing question had also been taken in the House.   On January 6 a resolution was presented for a new election in Louisiana, which immediately precipitated a sharp debate, affording opportunity for one member to denounce Sheridan as a tyrant.[2]   This was followed the very next day by a resolution of confidence in the President,[3] to which, however, objection was made. On the 11th Cox introduced a resolution, condemnatory of the intervention of the military, which demanded the immediate withdrawal of the military force of the United States.   Here, as in the Senate, feeling ran high, and denunciations of Sheridan and Grant lacked nothing in bitterness,[4] while the Louisiana question kept interjecting itself into the debate on the Civil Rights Bill[5] and on the Army Appropriation Bill.   One member thought the President would come short of his duty if he did not remove Sheridan; another that "no Tudor or Stuart did

---

[1] This action was influenced, no doubt, by the fact that it was generally understood that the Senate was to be recalled in special session.   For an account of how frenzied Pinchback was when he learned that he had again been pushed aside, see the *Times*, February 23.   *Record*, 43 Cong., 2 Sess., 1583.

[2] It also intruded itself into the other debate on the 5th.

[3] *Ibid.*, 313.

[4] *Ibid.*, 1143.   "He has disgraced the name of Ireland," one member said of Sheridan; "he has disgraced the United States, his adopted land. The spirit that actuated Emmett, Grattan, and a host of others is foreign to his nature; and I believe that all liberty-loving sons of Erin will disown him and brand him traitor to the sacred cause of liberty, for which so many brave Irishmen have shed their blood."

[5] As a part of the excitement of the time, may be noted the intemperate language into which Brown was betrayed, for which he was publicly censured.   *Ibid.*, 992.

more or worse"; another asserted that Sheridan had "forgotten the first duty of a man and a soldier, he has forgotten his love of truth."[1]   But, in general, the House evidently felt it improper to conduct a formal discussion on the question while one of its committees was investigating.[2]

During the very last days of February the Committee on Elections reported in favor of seating Lawrence, a McEnery Representative, instead of Sypher.[3]   A minority of five concluded that they could not afford to affirm the right of either to a seat, predicated upon the system of frauds in the election and canvass.   Accordingly, the last day of the session Sypher was unseated and Lawrence sworn in.[4]   March 1, Hoar, acting upon the Wheeler Compromise, was able to press through a resolution, carefully drawn so as not to offend the *de facto* faction, neither the *de jure* faction, which recognized Kellogg as governor, and a recommendation to the Louisiana House to put the rightfully elected persons in their seats, thus securing in this house the acceptance of the Wheeler plan of adjustment.   Thus was the action of the House also inconclusive, recognizing Kellogg, but seating a representative of the other government.

Not enough that the Louisiana question had consumed about one-half the time of the Senate during the regular session, almost the whole of the extra session of March was devoted to Pinchback.   February 17 the President issued his summons for a special session to begin on March, 5.[5]   Without awaiting the President's communication,

---

[1] *Record*, 43 Cong., 2 Sess., 289.

[2] The speech on this subject on Feb. 10 seems a detached attack on the administration.

[3] House Repts., 43 Cong., 2 Sess., No. 269.   [4] *Record*, 2235.

[5] The comment of the *Times* as to how expensive Pinchback had proved to the Nation is, at least, suggestive: "The time spent in debating him

Morton offered a resolution declaring that the Kellogg government was the lawful government of Louisiana and that whatever assistance was necessary to sustain it should be given by the Federal power. This motion was tabled. At the same time he again presented his motion to seat Pinchback,[1] which he supported the next day with a long and careful speech.[2]

As stated by one Senator, the discussion had been continued so long and had been so exhaustive that the subject was threadbare. And yet a very large number of leading members spoke, all at first opposing the admission. Debate started calmly on the legal phases of the question, Merriam controverting Morton's interpretation of a *prima facie* case. But it soon took a wide range, including the election of 1872, with Morton as usual ringing the changes on the murders and violences.[3] Several sharp altercations between Thurman and Morton did not tend

has cost the Government directly several thousand dollars, and indirectly many times more by taking time from legitimate business and thus defeating needed legislation; it has cost the State of Louisiana its levee appropriation and the people of the south-west the defeat of the Pacific Railroad Bill; it has cost the much abused newspapers a pretty bill for dispatches," March 18. He was indeed a National subject, a target for poker stories and tales of ill-gotten wealth.

[1] Evidently his doubts as to the dishonesty in Pinchback's election had been put at rest. This was forcing the matter on the Senate in a quite unnecessary way.

[2] For the benefit of new Senators, he presented the history and legal aspects of the case. He urged it as a *prima facie* case, insisting that the integrity of the Senate required that applicants presenting credentials in due form, should be admitted until ousted by an investigation; secondly, the Senate was bound by the decisions of the Supreme Court of the State, recognizing Kellogg as governor and the body which elected Pinchback as the legislature; thirdly, it was bound by the President's recognition of Kellogg and his legislature until Congress should reverse such action.

[3] "You must take into consideration the fact that they had been hunted like mad-dogs from plantation to plantation, had been murdered at every step in every town and at every cross-roads &&." *Record*, 44 Cong., 1 Sess., 85.

to lend dignity to the debate.[1]   After a charge against the Democrats of partisan action, Morton showed that he had none too dull an eye for party advantage when he stated the reasons for Democratic opposition.

A vote to reject Pinchback is a vote against the legality of what is known as the Kellogg government. . . .   The next House of Representatives will be Democratic.   Among the very first resolutions to pass that body, I predict, will be a resolution recognizing McEnery as the governor of Louisiana, recognizing the McEnery government, and calling upon the President to recognize it, and if the Senate has in advance rejected the Kellogg government by refusing to receive a Senator elected by it, I ask what ground the President has left to stand upon?[2]

It was found that the opposition to Pinchback was so strong that the resolution giving him his seat could not be passed and so West, after an evening session prolonged almost to midnight on March 16, startled his party by declaring that he was not willing to submit the claims of his colleague to the test of a vote, as he knew that many of the new members would refrain from voting.   He, therefore, moved the postponement until the next December.[3]   And against the objections of Thurman

[1] The latter asked whether the Supreme Court had not decided in many cases to follow the decisions of the State courts upon actions arising under the constitution and laws of the State.   Thurman replied that the Senator "had been so long from the bar that he has got rusty, prodigiously rusty, or he would never make such bold assertions as that."   In a very few minutes Thurman charged Morton with ignorance greater than he had supposed. Morton became exasperated, and when Thurman proceeded to read an extract, the former offered to continue the reading.   But Thurman replied, "If the Senator wants to read for the purpose of enlightening himself, it will take more time than I can spare."   Morton's retort was equally caustic, "I want to read enough to send back the charge of ignorance where it belongs."   *Record*, 44 Cong., 1 Sess., 45–6.   [2] *Ibid.*, 85.   [3] *Ibid.*, 90.

and Logan, the friends of Pinchback carried it through.[1]
By a close vote the Senate again recorded its failure to
grapple with the question. The fact that he was not
admitted made him ugly and sore,[2] a feeling shared by his
following, which may explain some features of the next
election.

But though the Senate would not accept Pinchback, yet
they were in favor of sustaining the President in his recognition of Kellogg. At a Republican caucus, March 5, it
was decided to bring in a resolution approving the action
of the President in protecting the Kellogg government,[3]
which motion was admitted immediately after the vote
on Pinchback was taken. The debate of three days' dura-
tion which followed was confined to the Democratic
Senators, but did not prevent the stern rejection of
Thurman's several efforts to add an amendment excluding the Kellogg legislature nor the adoption of the
resolution.[4]

The Pinchback case came up once more for consideration in February of the next session when Morton offered
his last argument in the mulatto's behalf, when he considered the personal charges against him and challenged
the production of any evidence to prove them.[5]   But the

---

[1] The practical advantage of postponement over a definite rejection is
obvious: it would prevent the Democrats, now in a majority in the Louisiana House, from electing a Democratic Senator.

[2] House Misc., Doc., 45 Cong., 3 Sess., No. 31, Wash., 809.   He was also
ugly about some school money. On Pinchback's return to Louisiana, a
large group of adherents gathered in Exposition Hall to condole with him.
Picayune, March 26.

[3] Foulke, *Morton*, II., 300.

[4] *Record*, Special Sess. of Sen., 1875, 148. What the President's friends
wanted was the original form, which added that "he should continue to
recognize the existing government," but the Republicans could not be
brought to support it.

[5] *Ibid.*, 886-8.

22

opposition was not to be overcome. And so, on March 8, Edmunds's amendment that he be not admitted carried by a very close vote[1] and the tedious contest was finally closed.[2]

[1] The vote stood 32 to 29. *Record*, 44 Cong., 1 Sess., 1558. In July Pinchback was offered some solace in the form of pay for the time he had lost. *Ibid.*, 4401.

[2] The country, according to the New Orleans *Times*, drew a sigh of relief to have the interminable Pinchback case finally settled. March 9.

CHAPTER XVI

The Wheeler Compromise

THE picture of the economic condition of the State had been steadily growing blacker. Trade and business had in a great measure been driven from the streets and wharves of New Orleans. The spirit of enterprise had been broken and capital refused to be employed when it was liable to practical confiscation. Citizens from every profession, every walk of life, and from all parties testified unanimously that the economical and political condition was, to quote the phraseology of one of them, "pitiable beyond all precedent in modern history."[1] There was no immigration to the State; what little there was, left it again; there was a general lack of confidence in the government and utter depression.

Machinists and engineers, competent in their professions, were glad to accept positions as firemen or at even lower employment. In the midst of the busiest season, the administrator of improvements stated that he had received over three thousand applications for work from men of all classes—merchants, clerks, professional men—pleading for any work that would give their families bread.[2] The young men, and as many of the older as could, were leaving the State. A newspaper declared

---

[1] House Repts., 43 Cong., 2 Sess., No. 101, Part ii., 143. Before the sub-committee there was only one person, the president of a bank, who found the financial condition sounder than it had been for years, but even he retracted this statement later. *Ibid.*, 268.   [2] *Ibid.*, 36.

339

that there were more than six thousand houses and stores to let in the city,[1] which could be had for the taxes; and the terrible financial robberies which had been perpetrated on the city's means, combined with the unprecedented taxes, had proved so severe and disheartening, that the population of New Orleans had decreased thirty thousand in the last two years.[2]

The delinquent taxes amounted by this time to $4,100,-000 or three and one-half mills of the fourteen levied. Men did business on credit and then were unable to collect their obligations.   One jobber testified that where he had formerly sold goods to the value of a quarter of a million dollars, he could now scarcely scrape up $20,000 worth of business.[3]   An estate which could have sold for $1,000,000 in 1867 and netted seven per cent showed in 1872 taxes and insurance which exceeded the entire rental by $540. The story of one of the most important and useful members of his community, rendered desperate, is worth repeating. One piece of property after the other had gone for taxes, until he said to the sheriff : "This property which you are advertising is the last possession of my mother and sisters, and their only support.   I warn you that on the day you put it up at auction, I am going to attend the sale with my double-barrelled shot-gun."[4]   And when a shoe-maker of Algiers was prosecuted for non-payment of his license, he said, "I owe $400 for leather which I cannot pay; you insist on your money; here are two pairs of shoes.   Sell them and give my family tickets to the soup-house."[5] The distress reached high-water mark in the early months

[1] A citizen testified to the committee that one-half the buildings in the city would accommodate the business and residents.   The only portion where this was not true was Camp Street and its vicinity.

[2] *Record*, 43 Cong., 1 Sess., 3268.   Quoted from a newspaper.

[3] House Repts., 43 Cong., 2 Sess., No. 101, Part ii., 239.   A Republican of Wheeling, Va.   [4] Nordhoff, 59.

[5] *Times*, April 28, 1875.

of 1875, when the extent of suffering, as depicted by the *Times*, was beyond the conception of the most penetrating. Hundreds of strong men were on the verge of beggary; the family of a prominent professional man subsisted for weeks on the remnants from the tables of friends; there was death for lack of proper food; sheets were deposited with grocers for bread.[1] The taxes on a small vacant lot owned by a negro were five dollars and the day the property was sold by the tax-collector, there was no bread in the house.

It is not hard to understand why resentment burned in the breast of every Conservative when we find proof of such highway robbery as came to light. Their legislators revelled, many of them for the first time in their lives, on Brussels carpets which cost four dollars a yard, padded with the most expensive paper lining, it may safely be asserted, which ever reposed under carpet, fifty cents a yard; spit into spittoons which cost one dollar apiece; and stretched their feet on walnut desks which cost three hundred and seventy-five dollars each.[2] He must lave himself with soap which cost thirty-five cents a bar, straighten out his curly kinks with a brush and comb which cost five dollars, brush his shoes with seventy-five cent brushes, drink from a thirty-five cent tumbler; dip his gold-mounted pen into a "fancy" inkstand, which cost the State ten dollars; and write his letters on heavy monogrammed stationery, while the very dust that fell from his heels had to be gathered in extraordinary dust-pans for which the taxpayers squandered seventy-five cents apiece. And it must be confessed that the item of eight serving-trays, called waiters in those days, at a cost of

---

[1] *Times*, April 28, 1875.
[2] A visit to the State capitol at Albany is sufficient to convince any Northerner that the Southern carpet-bagger did not have a monopoly on corrupt practices.

four dollars each conjures up visions of a banquet table at which some of the heavy reams of paper had been translated in process of entry into champagne bottles and cigars. [1] It could hardly be expected that it would sweeten the disposition of the indignant taxpayer to see his former slave driving in a stylish equipage drawn by prancing steeds, a diamond stud blazing in his vivid scarlet tie, to the legislature. [2] To show what grand totals such munificent profits would yield to the business houses which gulled the Assemblymen, some bills might be summarized for the brief period of December 29 to January 27. Pens, pencils, and erasers cost two hundred and ninety-eight dollars, paper only two thousand, four hundred and twenty-two dollars, and mere ink one hundred and eight dollars. [3]

The story of the finances of New Orleans is one steady downhill race. By leaps and bounds the debt had almost doubled since carpet-bag government began—had reached

[1] Note the following itemized Senate bills:

2 Reams Ruled Enrolling Paper at $80	$160.00
24 Boxes Steel Pens at $2	48.00
36 Erasers at 50 cents	18.00
96 Inkstands at $1	96.00
36 Sponge Caps and Sponges at $1.50	54.00
96 Bottles Mucilage and Brushes at 75 cents	72.00
15 Date Calendars at $1.50	22.50
3 Silver plated Call Bells 1 at $10, 2 at $6	22.00
12 Papers of Pins at 25 cents	3.00
1 Pair Extra Large Shears	10.00
2 Cork Screws at $1.25	2.50
3 Doz. Parlor Matches at 75 cents	2.25
4 Mops at $2.50	10.00
36 Candles at 10 cents	3.60
1 Gas Lighter	6.50

Sen. Jour., 1875, Extra Sess., 26–7. As early as 1869 the *Picayune* was complaining of the plate glass mirrors before which the legislators disported. February 7.

[2] Nordhoff states that he saw just such sights as these, 43.

[3] Sen. Jour., 1875. Extra Sess., 26–7.

$25,000,000 to be exact. The burdens and maddening restrictions can be no better described than by quoting the governor:

The debt of the city built up during a series of years of mal-administration of city affairs, aided by unwise legislative enactments, is now so great that the annual tax required to keep up the interest payments[1] has become an almost unsupportable burden upon the property of a large class of worthy, law-abiding citizens who endeavor to pay their taxes when due, and an excuse to other citizens, generally of greater means and less respect for law, to refuse the payment of any taxes at all.

The expenses of the city for a considerable period have annually exceeded its revenue, and the volume of its bonded and floating debt has thus increased year by year with accelerating rapidity.

In the meantime there are many compulsory expenditures of an oppressive character imposed upon the city by legislation. . . . The commerce of the city, which forms so essential an element in the general prosperity of the State, is hampered by many exactions, some entirely unnecessary, others needlessly oppressive or misapplied. Heavy wharfage dues are exacted by the city, from all vessels trading with this port, yet few of the wharves and landings, except those maintained by private enterprise, are kept in sufficient repair to satisfy even the moderate requirements of a great commercial port. An unnecessary tax, yielding no advantage to the State or city, is levied on emigrants arriving at this port, thus discouraging immigration.[2]

By the last of February city officials were realizing the absolute impossibility, even with the most rigid economy, of providing for the current expenses.[3]

[1] Interest on the bonded debt was nearly $1,500,000.
[2] A great number of boards of inspectors drew their incomes from these taxes, where one salaried officer could do the duties. Sen. Jour., 1875, 7–8. Ann. Mess.
[3] All sorts of plans were suggested to meet the crisis: bankruptcy, a

The condition was no better on the plantations.   One of the largest agriculturists in the State was able to win from a plantation, equal in fertility to any in the world, which had cost him $700,000, not counting the sugar-refinery upon it, worth $100,000, only a bare subsistence—and his taxes.[1]   His annual visit to the capital in 1875 brought only discouragement, as merchants declined to advance money, doubting his ability to plant.   Lack of supplies forced the planting of land in food-stuffs; transactions in rice, sugar, coffee, and grits exceeded those in any twenty other articles.[2]   An agent for a property assessed at $400,000 reported that the owner was compelled in 1874 to send $6000 above the revenue of the estate for taxes.[3]

Hear the wail that went up from one of the city papers:

---

lottery scheme like the European Bond Plan, the sale of the water-works for fifty years to a company of bondholders, or the appropriation of the interest funds for the city.   On May 18 about three hundred property-owners assembled to evolve some plan of solution and formed the Property Holders Union, the practical aim of which was to reduce taxation for all purposes for the city to 1½%, for the State to 1%.   The Union did some effective work during the remainder of the year in watching the pay roll; in offering constitutional amendments; in conferring with the State central committees; in drafting a revenue bill; in directing representatives how to vote on important measures.   But by early December the city had reached the point of bankruptcy.   An injunction has been served by the United States Circuit Court enjoining it from any payments until the interest on certain bonds was satisfied, a step which left the city without money for the most ordinary expenses—for street-lights, scavenger and drainage purposes, and water protection.   But the court on December 15 set aside this seizure of the scanty funds of the city by a few creditors and recognized the condition which compelled the city to "ask creditors to help the movement to relieve the people."   *Times*, Jan. 12, Dec. 16, 22; *Bulletin*, May 14.

[1] Though the estate was adapted to the growth of rice, sugar, and cotton, as well as tropical fruits, and had one hundred acres of bearing orange trees, he expressed great doubt whether he could sell it for the cost of the refinery.   *Record*, 43 Cong., 1 Sess., 3268.   [2] *Times*, July 13.

[3] *Ibid.*, July 17.

The people of New Orleans, and indeed of the whole of Louisiana have been enduring for six long years privations and sufferings that no other people in the United States have ever endured. Our property has no salable value, our working-men are without employment, our merchants without customers, houses and stores vacated in every street, $40,000 to $50,000 *f. fas* in the hands of the sheriff, for uncollected city taxes, and thousands of properties advertised in the official journal to be given away by the tax-collectors for State taxes[1] —our State taxes being three times what they were when the Republicans came into power in 1868 and our city tax one per cent more than in 1868, although property is not worth one-half what it was then, and with the laws for collection increased in severity and those for rents relaxed so that it is almost impossible to collect rent.[2]

But perhaps the picture can be drawn no more graphically than in the words of Bishop Wilmer, whose calling took him to all parts of the State and whose testimony is stamped with liberality, fairness, and insight:

It is hardly necessary to add my testimony to what has been heard by the Committee, that the State of depression and embarrassment in the country is almost without precedent, without any parallel in any civilized country. Our ruin is almost complete, our people are depressed, are almost in desperation.

He emphasized the exodus from the State and added:

It is also due to the unsparing depredations to which they are exposed, and to their utter lack of power to bring the culprits, whoever they are, to justice. I think, even where

---

[1] The *Times*, on February 16, devoted 21 columns of fine print to advertisements of sheriff's sales for taxes. It would deprive one hundred and two families of homes.

[2] *Ibid.*, January 25, 1875. The above is hardly a fair sample of the grammar usually found in the *Times*.

the crops have failed, it would have been possible for our people to have sustained themselves by raising live-stock, poultry, vegetables, and everything of that kind, but there seems to be no encouragement for them. The universal sentiment is that they cannot raise anything because they cannot keep it; it is stolen from them.[1]

The importance of this last point, especially in the rural districts, should be emphasized. Negroes, accustomed to dependence and sharing, and virtually shielded by the judges from all punishment, took to filching and stealing fruit, vegetables, and poultry so generally that the raising of these articles had to be given up. The writer was given a graphic picture by a woman who had visited as a child in the country, especially in the St. Mary sugar region, of how unsupportable the negroes became. No white woman dared to go unescorted or without a pistol; they never left the plantations.[2] In a visit to Hale Sypher's plantation, who was trying to raise Southdown sheep, she knew how the negroes stole and killed all the small stock on the place. At night she could hear the horses neigh and resist when the negroes borrowed them for all-night jaunts. Salt was given out for the meals, but food came to the table without savor; buttons, added to a dress for decoration, were cut off in process of laundry-

---

[1] House Repts., 43 Cong., 2 Sess., No. 101, Part ii., 251. It is on this statement that Sheridan is said to have based his "Banditti" message. Of weight also is the opinion of an attorney, who had resided in the city since 1841, "I think that the material interests of the city and the State of Louisiana have been reduced to a point of depression which it is difficult for a person who resides here to conceive of. I think that values in this city and State have been almost annihilated," and attributed the condition to the misgovernment. *Ibid.*, No. 261, Part iii., 688.

[2] Negro pretensions knew no bounds. In a public speech a colored county clerk declared his intention of having a white wife from one of the best families in the parish.

ing. Such boldness would not have been risked in slave days, and it only ceased when punishment began to be meted out. The hanging of a negro in St. Mary after 1877 had a salutary effect.[1]

Even allowing for the natural loss incident to the slow moving of crops caused by bad navigation at the mouth of the Mississippi and the divergence of trade from the southwest to St. Louis by the new railroads, the root of the depression undoubtedly was, what every intelligent citizen indicated—the vilely-corrupt government.[2]

Of course, scurrilous attacks[3] were made on the head of the administration, many merited, a few unjust. It was pointed out that promptly after Kellogg assumed office he had appointed to lucrative positions relatives of the three Supreme Court judges who had seated him[4]; that confidence in his word had been shaken by violated promises and false subscriptions, whereby he sought to garb himself in the cloak of generosity[5]; that, while he freely exercised the veto power,[6] he was far from consist-

[1] Miss Marion Brown, Vice-Principal of the Esplanade Avenue Girls' High School.

[2] Nordhoff found many who would vote to make Grant President for life, as then, "We should have at least equal protection and could appeal direct to Cæsar for justice and against robbery." He adds, "It is not pleasant to hear such words from an American," 68.

[3] See the *Picayune* of Nov. 7, 1874, where it coarsely commiserates with the earth-worms that cannot feed upon their brother-worm, "Billy Pitt," as it familiarly terms the governor, who was recovering from a recent illness. [4] *Globe*, 42 Cong., 3 Sess., 1746.

[5] It was understood that he subscribed $1000 for the Shreveport sufferers, but it was learned later that it was public money. A witness thought he would not be believed on oath by half a dozen men in the city. House Repts., 43 Cong., 2 Sess., No. 101, Part ii., 247.

[6] For the year 1875, he vetoed 26 House bills, 11 of the Senate. House Jour., 12; Sen. Jour., 46, 1876. Three of the worst laws passed over his veto: purchase of the state-house, the election amendment, the funding of the Levee Company debt,—a theft of nearly $2,000,000. Between 1868 and 1871, $4,500,000 had been spent for levees and still there were none worthy the name. See Nordhoff, 58-9.

ent in its use; and that he had grossly abused the pardon power.[1] Evidence could be adduced which looks like complicity in underhand dealings. Complaints were audible concerning rent for an unused armory for the "City Guards," which had been a myth on paper since his inauguration. An investigating committee endeavored to secure the attendance of the governor to explain the use and expenditure of the sum of $10,935.79, drawn by him for militia purposes during 1874, but "failed to secure his attendance."[2] His appointments were certainly no improvement over Warmoth's and were made use of to bolster up the machine.[3] He put in three colored men as police jurors who could neither read nor write; one white man of such infamous character that even Republicans protested. Under them the parish tax soared as only in Louisiana taxes could soar.

On the other hand there is no question but that he took office under such difficulties, to quote his own words, "as few men have been called upon to encounter," and that no Republican, elected as was he, could have won the good-will of the opposing faction.[4] He fell heir to all

[1] He had pardoned 84 criminals within about a year, among whom were persons convicted of poisoning, murder, rape, burglary, assault with intent to kill, perjury, and bribery of witnesses. Nordhoff, 56; House Repts., 43 Cong., 2 Sess., No. 261, Part iii., 652. Sometimes criminals escaped merely by his failure to sign their death-warrants. An embezzler was pardoned on the score of his political influence!   [2] Sen. Jour., 1875, 118–9.

[3] In many parishes all the white Republicans and officeholders belonged to a single family. House Repts., 43 Cong., 2 Sess., No. 101, 7. One John Leet was appointed harbor-master who never went to his office except to draw his pay. When he was removed after three years, Kellogg made up a purse for him of $150 a month. House Misc. Doc., 45 Cong., 3 Sess., No. 31, 914–5.

[4] Says Nordhoff, "I have been amazed to see how all white men and many blacks to my own knowledge—whether rich or poor; whether merchants, mechanics, or professional men; whether Americans, French, Germans, Irish, or Italians by birth; absolutely all except the officeholders and their relations unite in this feeling of detestation of their rulers," 43.

the hatred which had been accumulating against his predecessor which even found vent in several attacks upon his life in broad daylight.[1]   Nordhoff probably does him justice when he calls him weak:

I believe that Governor Kellogg has a sincere wish to do right; but he has no force of character. . . .   He lacks the iron grip which is needed to bring reform. . . .   The good Kellogg only drifts and hopes—he is drifting toward the United States Senate.   But he fatally impedes reform; allows things done which embitter men and make them hopeless of reform.[2]

The subject of corruption in legislation has been worn threadbare.   Let it suffice to say that, under Kellogg as under Warmoth, nearly every bill was a swindle, even harm-less-looking measures which have seemed too insignificant to merit mention.   Ferry monopolies, granted to members of the legislature, were often located at points where fer-ries already existed; county seats were removed to mem-bers' farms; new parishes created to insure the reëlection of certain members; petty villages incorporated to authorize officials, not of the villagers' choice, to draw fees and sala-ries for needless offices.[3]   Everywhere the honest citi-zen suffered.   The Shreveport Savings Bank and Trust

[1] *Republican*, January 29, 1875.   Recall the attack on Warmoth in 1874.
[2] His weakness is admirably illustrated by a speech made in the Senate. "I have no complaint to make or urge against our State Executive; he has, I may say, uniformly appointed every man to office whom I have seriously or urgently asked him to appoint." *Republican*, Feb. 20, 1875.
Nordhoff tells how he complained that the superintendent of instruction had appointed two notoriously corrupt men to office on a parish school-board. "I asked him how he came to permit such wickedness. He replied, 'The colored Senator Blunt demanded it; Brown weakly gave in to him. I am sorry—but what am I to do?'" 67.
[3] Nordhoff says that he knew small towns which had never been ruled by officers of their own choice. The governor appointed all. *Ibid.*, 62.

Company, for instance, in return for a paltry $500 a year, had the sole right to erect water and gas works and to run a ferry across the river, although the city had a gas company and good ferry, which had been a source of revenue, and had no pressing need of water-works. Among the incorporators were six State officials![1] If one were to collect a list of the acts passed since 1868, the bare titles of which betrayed their transparent purpose as graft, it would cover half a dozen pages.[2]

The governor's annual message in 1875 pointed with pride to the fact that the receipts for the year ended nearly equalled the expenses; that the rate of city and State taxation had been largely reduced; that for the first time in many years, not one dollar had been added to the debt —in fact that it had been decreased by over a million dollars by the funding bill.[3] The executive admitted that the fees of tax-collectors were still exorbitant and declared that "by the employment of unnecessary clerks and pages and by excessive appropriations for contingent purposes the expenses of the year were double what they should

[1] *Cotton States*, 45.

[2] One Southern witness believed that if it were left to an intelligent jury of honest Republicans from the North, the State officials, with scarcely an exception, would be convicted, banished from the State, or sent to the penitentiary.   House Repts., 43 Cong., 2 Sess., No. 101, Part ii., 246.

[3] But the Congressional sub-committee should be heard: "This measure aroused great hostility . . . because it gave to the funding-board, whose powers seem to be absolute and without review, discretionary authority to admit to be funded some six millions of debt alleged to be fraudulent." *Ibid.*, 7.   Of all the debt created after 1865, the State did not realize over fifty cents on the dollar, nor was the amount expended for the benefit of the State more than half the amount.   It is not amiss in this connection to call attention to the Lottery Company, authorized in 1868, which by 1875 was composed of a few men, most of whom were living in New Jersey.   On a capital of $1,000,000 they were thought to make yearly three-fourths of a million dollars.   They had established shops and dens around the markets of the city, which demoralized the laborers, especially the negroes, but their agents were all over the State.   Nordhoff, 60.

have been.[1] But nothing could avail against the fact of large delinquent lists.[2] From November, 1871, to November, 1873, over eight hundred tracts of land in St. Martin Parish were actually sold for the taxes. But pity changes to wrath when we read in the auditor's report for 1874 that twenty tax-collectors had defaulted for almost $200,000. It was said that in many cases they received greenbacks but turned in scrip. Several collectors even admitted to Nordhoff that they bought up parish scrip, as they could get a judgment which forced the judge to levy a special tax to pay them.[3] Rings were sometimes formed in the parishes, composed of the officers, their relatives, and, occasionally, of coöperating Democrats, to buy up these obligations and cause judgment to be enforced. So great became the distress in 1875 that it was absolutely impossible to sell land for taxes.[4]

The condition of the parishes as to debt and corruption was utterly deplorable. Let it be remembered that the large proportion of parish officials were negroes. In 1875 there were, according to Nordhoff, but four or five honestly governed parishes in the State: Tensas was one, where there had never been any disturbance or pretense of intimidation since 1868, for the Republicans who had come in from the North were honest and sensible, and where they had paid a debt of $190,000, where there were good roads, bridges, and schools together with low taxes.[5] But in

[1] Sen. Jour., 1875, 10.
[2] During this year $14,000 was turned over to A. J. Sypher by the tax-collector to take to New Orleans. But as it was not paid over, the citizens soon made inquiries and tried to have Sypher and the collector indicted. The latter was only given additional time! *Times*, June 13. In a suit against taxpayers one official cleared $40,000 in fees in one day! The following August the *Times* assailed the corruption in a series of daily attacks. It showed that the office of sheriff could be worth $100,000 yearly, even in a bad year.   [3] Nordhoff, 63.
[4] House Repts., 43 Cong., 2 Sess., No. 101, 8.   [5] *Cotton States*, 55.

most parishes a large fraudulent debt had been created in 1870–1 for the most part. Certain cases may be cited as illustrative. Before the war in Plaquemines there was no debt with $6000 in the treasury; in 1875 the parish owed $93,000, while taxes to the amount of $25,000 had been collected every year since 1868. And yet there were no roads, schools, nor levees to represent the money.[1] In Nassau so much scrip was issued that in two or three years it sank to fifteen cents on the dollar but was always receivable for parish taxes. In Natchitoches $24,000 worth of parish paper was issued in twenty months to paupers, when it was universally known that one of the paupers had been dead two years, and it was not believed that one-half the paupers ever saw the warrants. Two warrants for $500 each could not be explained by the clerk. It was common to allow $3000 to $4000 to tax-collectors per year.[2]

Complaints of the courts on the score of inefficiency and of the sale of justice were universal. The judges were utterly disreputable men. "I know men who have good suits," declared a witness, "but they will not bring any action in the courts, because they have no confidence in the integrity of the judiciary."[3] Nordhoff had pointed out to him a parish judge, utterly ignorant of the law. While making a campaign speech, he was accused to his face of taking a bribe of ten dollars, which his accuser claimed to have paid.

The whole parish bar believed that he sold justice, and still the negroes elected him.[4] A parish judge, who acknowledged that he had for two years retained $7500 of parish money, had repeatedly refused to have juries drawn in order

[1] Nordhoff, 51–2.
[2] House Repts., 43 Cong., 2 Sess., No. 261, Part iii., 539.
[3] *Ibid.*, No. 101, Part ii., 218.   [4] Nordhoff, 53.

to shield confederates; yet Kellogg appointed him district judge.[1]

To meet this common evasion of justice, the law endeavored to compel the drawing of juries. Another judge of East Baton Rouge, who was not recognized by any decent man, was also a member of the police jury, chairman of the finance committee—in which role he approved his own bills against the parish internal revenue officer—and member of the school board. He and his confrères took $37,500 to run the parish, and none of them ever owned a cent there.[2] In Natchitoches in 1872 the grand jury indicted an officer for embezzlement. The parish judge, a personal friend, neglected to draw a jury, but the matter came before a district judge where a negro jury returned a verdict for $40,000. Thereupon, the legislature divided the district; the governor appointed as judge of the new district the same personal friend who had before protected the criminal. It was only slightly encouraging that the people later drove that judge out of the county. The tax-collector of that parish, who was also driven out, appeared in the list of defaulters, and acknowledged to Nordhoff that he had been in partnership with a Democratic member of Congress to buy up depreciated warrants which the parish must redeem at par. Both men held office in 1874, the judge being further rewarded with the treasurership of the school funds, though he had not entered the county since July, 1873. The son of the other continued as deputy collector and deputy treasurer, offices which

---

[1] Nordhoff, 54. The same writer tells of one case where no jury was drawn, because the judge himself feared indictment for gross misapplication of funds. Natchitoches.

Business was neglected. A clerk of court was known to go to New Orleans to stay for six or eight weeks while business might wait. Judge Breaux told the writer that it took months to get a case on the docket.

[2] House Repts., 44 Cong., 2 Sess., No. 156, Part i., 78–80.

2

should serve as checks upon each other.[1]   Even the highest administers of justice were tainted.   The Federal Supreme Court, passing upon the Louisiana Railroad case in 1874, where property on which the State had expended $2,000,000 was bought by the very persons who defeated a sale for a higher price and retained the purchase money, said of Ludeling, chief justice of the Louisiana bench:

It is impossible to characterize this agreement as anything else than a gross fraud. . . .   It is a flagrant breach of trust on the part of Horne, and it was a fraud in Ludeling, with knowledge of the trust Horne had undertaken, to persuade him to violate his instructions and sacrifice the interests of his constituents, himself becoming a party to the violation.[2]

And Ludeling, in the face of such condemnation, was still allowed to trail the ermine in the mire.[3]   In view of such demoralization on the bench, it can scarcely be a surprise to learn that juries, when drawn, consisting almost exclusively of negroes, were partial, unjust in their decisions, and wholly in sympathy with the guilty parties.   The negroes on many police juries were totally illiterate; yet they controlled the parish taxes, roads, bridges, and all county matters.   They were called upon to pass upon intricate cases of commercial law which puzzled white men.   They seemed to see the absurdity themselves, for a negro criminal always asked for a white jury.   To Bishop Wilmer there seemed "to be no par-

[1] Such duplication of office was far from uncommon.   Some of the legislators of 1875 were judges, some tax-collectors, one secretary of state.
[2] Jackson vs. Ludeling, 21 Wallace, 629.
[3] Nordhoff thought "he was the right man in the right place," and it was part of a general system when he decided in 1870 that "courts are not permitted to go behind an enrolled, authenticated, and promulgated public statute, to inquire into the motives which may have influenced the members of the General Assembly in enacting it," 47.

ticular disgrace attached" to conviction and a term in the penitentiary.[1]

In the light of these facts, one feels inclined, not to condemn the disorder,[2] but rather with Nordhoff to wonder "that society has not gone entirely to pieces." He became persuaded that the white population possessed unusually high qualities when he saw that,

in spite of an incredible misgovernment, which encouraged every vice and crime, which shamelessly corrupted the very fountains and sources of justice, and made the rulers a terror to the peaceably-inclined—in spite of this, order and peace had been gradually restored and are now maintained, and this by the efforts of the people chiefly.[3]

In some parishes, where the whites, despite every obstacle, showed vitality, they accomplished results.[4]

Opposition there naturally was to the sickening immorality and total inefficiency in the educational system. In 1874 the cost of education was $36 a head in the city, and $24 in the country, when the total school revenue had been only $700,000—too high, especially when the income was lost or improperly diverted. The bare reports emanating from Superintendent Brown's parlor at the statehouse, furnished with a magnificence suited to a "Turkish pasha," present the facts clearly enough. There had

[1] House Repts., 43 Cong., 2 Sess., No. 101, Part ii., 251.
[2] An elderly man tells that more than once he had taken his life in his hand to deal with ruffianly young men. There had been one conviction in his parish in five years, and that offender was pardoned.
[3] *Cotton States*, 17.
[4] Shreveport proposed in 1874 to issue bonds for $100,000 to improve the streets. The Taxpayers Association defeated this, offered to undertake the same work, if allowed to raise money in tax receipts. It did the work for $36,000. The police were demoralized by being paid in depreciated scrip; the citizens secured an unsalaried police and the city became at once orderly. In 1874, Conservatives were elected, and the scrip rose from 40 to 90.

been mismanagement of the school funds at Concordia Parish[1]—a delicate way of hinting at the embezzlement of some $30,000 by the Senator of the district; in Morehouse similar mismanagement had deprived the children of schools; but Carroll had been the most unfortunate of all, as not only had the warrants on the accumulating fund, amounting to $26,444, been absorbed, but also the quarterly apportionments, and yet the schools were closed in July, 1872. No less than $30,000 were spent in the parish and yet the schools were open less than a year![2] Of St. Tammany, Brown reported that the schools "have remained closed during the year, the former treasurer of the board having absconded with about $1200, leaving a heavy debt."[3] Likewise in Tangipahoa, he reported a misappropriation of funds. Mahoney and Butler, a controlling portion of the board in Plaquemines "could not resist the temptation to use the funds for private and partisan purposes."[4] In addition fictitious claims were allowed and paid to fictitious persons. In Shreveport after 1872, $40,000 was reported in the treasury, but nobody ever saw any statement of its disposition; in St. James the board had burned the records, while the president fled the State while on bail for fraud.[5]

The school system had become part of the political machine, as members of the legislature were usually members of the local boards. This system did not make for competent school directors; often they were unable to write their names. Inevitably the character of the teachers suffered. A Senator, as president of a board, would select colored men for teachers, as they made pliant tools! A

---

[1] These facts are taken from the superintendent's report for 1873.

[2] House Repts., 43 Cong., 2 Sess., No. 261, Part iii., 936.

[3] *Ibid.*, 937. In 1873, 101 schools were built, 864 in operation and 57,433 pupils were enrolled. Supt.'s Report, 1870–3.

[4] *Ibid.*, 937–8.   [5] Nordhoff, 52.

good colored Republican complained that in his parish there were many more colored schools than white, but that most of the teachers were incapable men or lazy, or sometimes, drunkards. "Their work is to talk up the man who appoints them."[1] Teachers were even known to sublet their schools at one-fourth the amount of their salaries.[2] They were often densely ignorant, as said before.

Naturally such incompetence on the part of the teachers could not command the respect of the pupils. In Natchitoches Parish, the white lads had things their own way: they drove the black children away, later the teacher himself.[3] Such independence was not at all unusual. In December of 1874 the girls of the "Up-Town High School" on Chestnut Street in New Orleans refused to accept their diplomas at the hands of "Nigger" Brown, and never did receive them until 1877.[4] On one occasion when he visited the school, all the girls left. The school lads dared assert themselves against Pinchback, where he was most vulnerable. Though there was a negro school in the district in which he resided, he was determined that his two sons should attend the silk-stocking school of the city at Magnolia and Carondelet Streets, and so they were daily escorted to school by a policeman, and just as regularly run off by the white lads at recess. One boy, upon being admonished by his White Leaguer uncle to leave the boys alone, explained the social situation with true Southern logic, "They're good enough niggers, but they're niggers."[5]

[1] Nordhoff, 52. Confirmed by men of both colors.
[2] House Repts., 43 Cong., 2 Sess., No. 156, Part i., 145.
[3] House Repts., 43 Cong., 2 Sess., No. 261, Part iii., 320-1.
[4] On the authority of a member of the class, a leader in the revolt. The affair caused great excitement.
[5] On the authority of Miss Marion Brown. For an interesting account of the school quarrel with the board, which came to a head in September of this year and resulted in a general demand for the resignation of the

The debt, despite all efforts to veil the truth by funded bonds, had been increased under Kellogg.[1] Money was so scarce that even Supreme Court judges were compelled to wait for their pay at the doors of the treasury. In the metropolis the fire department had gone unpaid for months; the teachers and police were many months in arrears. But that is scarcely strange when we recall that the city defaulted on her interest both in December and January, 1874–5.[2]

Therefore the situation which the sufferers in Louisiana faced early in 1875 may truly be termed desperate. The efforts at peaceful revolution had been rendered a failure by the returning-board; efforts at violent overthrow of the corrupt government had been promptly crushed by the relentless arm at Washington; another trial at the ballot-box could save them only after another two years of ruinous radicalism; hope of relief from Congress, in the light of the fruitless debate of the two past sessions, was vain. Was there no other possible solution? There remained one method untried—compromise.

There had been previous efforts which had come to naught. During the session of 1873 the Kelloggites had offered a compromise: 45 Fusion Representatives and 10 Senators in consideration for acknowledgment of all the Kellogg officers in office, but the Committee of Two Hundred had rejected it.[3] As early as July of that year action looking toward arbitration had been broached by McEnery—and refused.[4] But now the first step in 1875

---

negro board—there was only a small minority of whites on it—see the *Picayune* of Sept. 18, 30, Nov. 7, and *Times* and *Bulletin* of those dates.

[1] On the showing of Graham, House Repts., 43 Cong., 2 Sess., No. 101, Part ii., 244.   [2] *Ibid.*, 36.   [3] *Picayune*, April 22.

[4] "I have been informed," wrote McEnery, "that you recently declared that in order to settle the present trouble, you were willing to submit the returns to a board of five citizens." He thought Kellogg could initiate

came from Kellogg, who, possibly weary of the strife, longed for some definitive settlement.[1] Dr. Southworth, eager for some honorable solution, approached Kellogg, and, in order to forestall the outbreak of January 4, secured from him, December 30, the statement, "If the Congressional Committee on Louisiana affairs, recently appointed, can be induced to consider and propose a plan for the immediate and final settlement of our political difficulties, I will accept and abide by the plan." The plan was for McEnery to write a similar letter to a political friend, but the latter failed to respond to the idea. Southworth then read the letter to the Committee, and urged their coöperation, but without success. On January 2, Kellogg renewed the subject to the Committee in a letter which was published in the papers the following day. He concluded with a renewed promise to abide by their decision.[2] Foster seems thereupon to have submitted the proposition to all concerned. And on January 5 came the statement of the five chief officials of the other faction,[3] headed by McEnery, expressing their willingness to submit the whole question of the election of 1872 to the Committee before they should leave the State. That body asked each side explicitly if it would accept the decision as final, to which proposition the two leading Conservatives assented on January 6.[4] In the course of his examination before the

---

the necessary measures for such a purpose and outlined a plan for a board to consist of two members chosen by Kellogg, two by himself, the fifth by the four first chosen, before whom he offered to place the returns. See *Times* of July 5 for his letter. Kellogg seemed no more anxious to run the risk of a new election now than he had when the idea was suggested by the New York *Herald* in Sept., 1874.

[1] Dec. 17 Kellogg urged the early arrival of the Select Committee. He seemed to want a complete investigation of the legislature. *Times*, Jan. 3, 1875. [2] See *Republican* for full letter. January 3.

[3] McEnery, Graham, Penn, Ogden, and Lusher.

[4] *Times*, January 7.

Sub-committee, Governor Kellogg expressed the same intention and his belief that his associates ought to consent, but through the press, Antoine declined to submit to such an agreement.[1]

But the opportunity was propitious. From that moment rumors of compromise settled into open discussion.[2]   Southworth continued to interest himself, opposed the compromise, but wished a full settlement left to the Committee.[3] A reporter of the *Times*, which paper was pressing the adjustment, interviewed a number of business men, all of whom seemed to favor such a move.[4] Many interviews occurred between the prominent men of the different parties; the Conservatives for a time seemed to feel that they must solve the problem themselves, but they had reached a crisis beyond any mere difference of opinion.   The return of the Conservatives to the Hahn Legislature and an early election had been remedies suggested, the latter of which had been urged by the Republican legislature in caucus, January 14. Up to January 20 there was no indication of a disposition among the Radicals to submit the controversy to the Committee; the Republican press was inclined to scoff at it and preferred a military territory.[5] Finally,[6] in caucus on Janu-

---

[1] House Repts., 43 Cong., 2 Sess., No. 101, Part i., 10. He feared that Kellogg was trying to go to the Senate and would agree to leave the Conservatives in power. *Picayune*, January 8.

[2] The general plan seems to have been foreshadowed as early as January 6, as shown in an issue of the *Times* of that date.   See also issues of the 7th, 13th.   [3] See his letter in the *Republican*, January 9.

[4] Issue of January 8.

[5] "The whole matter, however, is too absurd to merit notice, were it not for the prominence given it by one of our contemporaries yesterday in the editorial columns." *Republican*, January 7. The *Picayune* also opposed it as the "climax of fatuity and madness," and held it better to resist the military.

[6] It was said that Hoar opened the way by asking the Conservatives on what terms they would return to the House, *Times*, Feb. 9.

ary 23, the Conservative members returned by the board and others claiming to have been defrauded, in reliance "on the integrity and fairness of the four gentlemen members of the Congressional Committee," agreed to ask that body—in advance of any investigation, let it be noted—"if the task is not considered too onerous" to take the returns of 1874 and declare what members were fairly elected.[1]

Confidence was felt in this group of men, but more especially in Wheeler. Born in New York in 1819, he was now of mature judgment and had held a prominent place on nearly all the important committees and was considered one of the most conservative of the Republicans, commanding the respect of both parties.[2] Since his arrival in New Orleans he had been waited upon by the most important business men in the city and urged to arrange some settlement.[3] Hoar, too, was known for his opposition to sectional strife, while his speeches on Southern affairs had always shown moderation.[4]

The Republicans in caucus on January 24 opposed submission, as they felt that that would be surrender, especially for those whose seats were doubtful.[5] But the McEnery leaders the next day expressed their entire willingness to accept the Sub-committee as arbiters and to abide by their decision, on condition that their opponents did the same.[6] They believed that the Committee would

[1] For the resolutions see the *Annual Cyclopedia,* 1875, 457. Note that this is the Hoar Sub-committee which had come to the State for a second investigation. The favorable report of the first group undoubtedly weighed with the Conservatives.

[2] It was at first desired that Wheeler act alone, but he was unwilling to assume so much responsibility. *Times,* January 12.

[3] *Republican,* February 18. When he asked these men why they did not share in the movement for a compromise, the reply was that it would ruin their business.

[4] *Times,* January 30.   [5] *Picayune,* January 25.

[6] House Repts., 43 Cong., 2 Sess., No. 261, Part iii., 944.

assume the burden because of the urgent necessity, both to the State and the Nation, to end the scandal in Louisiana.

After various informal consultations at the St. Charles Hotel between the Committee, as individuals, at which Frye was the chief spokesman, and various leaders on both sides,[1] Wheeler submitted the outlines of a plan of adjustment to the Democratic caucus on the evening of February 5. It promised (1) To submit the claims to the Congressional Committee and to abide by its decision; (2) Democratic Senators were to agree to attend the Kellogg legislature to secure its adoption; (3) The legislature further was to agree, as a whole, not to disturb the Kellogg government or to try to impeach the governor.[2] The caucus sat until late in the night in the effort to secure unanimous consent, but the vote was hopelessly divided— 37 to 28.[3] McEnery did not approve, and Wiltz was said to have resigned; but the caucus agreed that every member must abide by the action of the majority.

Misapprehensions before the terms were definitely known and wild report led to great excitement on the morning of the 6th. People did not wait for the correct account. The *Bulletin* cried: "Give us the names of the traitors," by which flattering title were designated the supporters of the measure. In an extra on February 7 it demanded, in the name of the white people, recognition and safety "from the deep damnation of this fatal act." But the *Times* rose to their defense in the hope that the

[1] Hoar laid emphasis on the point that they were acting only as individuals. The Radicals felt very secure, as telegrams were coming from the North, urging compromise upon Kellogg.

[2] Later worded: "That no factious proceedings will be taken with respect to the legality of the present government."

[3] The writer has been unable to decide which of the numbers given here by various authorities is correct, though the relative proportion is the same in all.

rumors that they had "sold out" would turn out to be as "unfounded as unjust,"[1] while the *Picayune* presumed that the knowledge of the terms as actually laid down would dispel the sentiment that they had betrayed the party.[2]

A great indignation meeting, called by McEnery, Ogden, and twenty other Conservative leaders, was held on the evening of February 6 at the Clay Statue for the execration of those who had "sold out their constituents."

We desire [declared the card] to hear from your own lips whether those men represent you truly, whose action last night in legislative caucus we deem a betrayal of your rights and liberties, and an ignominious surrender of the cause, not only of Louisiana, but of American liberty.[3]

The attendance surpassed all expectations. For an hour before the appointed time, people had been gathering, until around seven thousand people were assembled, among whom were twenty-five of the Committee of Seventy, and two of the Congressional Committee. The speakers were continually interrupted by cries of denunciation, such as "Hang them," and calls for the names of the "traitors." The chairman's query reveals the principle back of their anger: "We want to know whether this cause, so long maintained, and in which we have suffered so much, is now to be frittered away on the altar of bargain and sale." "No, no! Hang them. We'll stand it two years more," came back the reply. Judge Kennard in a brief speech stated the position of the

[1] February 7.

[2] See also its strong defense, February 7 and 8, of the terms as "restoring the results of the recent election."

[3] See the call in the supplement to the *Times* of February 7 and in the *Bulletin*, Evening Edition, February 6, copied in House Repts., 43 Cong., 2 Sess., No. 261, 687–8.

Committee of Seventy: As long as the Democratic victory of 1874 was not recognized, the Representatives could not listen to any proposal without dishonor. McEnery made the marked speech of the meeting, in which, while not impugning the motives of the gentleman who presented the compromise to the caucus, he denounced it as an act of great folly and virtual surrender. Though differing from the majority of the caucus, Wiltz defended them as honest in their convictions. But the mob was not to be appeased; names of members who had voted for the measure were held up to execration. Resolutions repudiating any recognition of Kellogg, directly or indirectly, as "base and treasonable," or any action which in effect would condone the unparalleled "infamy done to the people of Louisiana by the Federal military power on the 4th of January" were adopted.[1]

The Committee of Seventy met to condemn the compromise and appoint a sub-committee to investigate. Resolutions instructed it to inform the caucus that the compromise or any other compromises having the effect of recognizing the legality of the Kellogg government or impairing the rights of the people as they stood on the 4th of January would be disastrous to the people of this State.[2]

A still larger number of the Radicals were dissatisfied, for they had never formally agreed to such arbitration. The invitation issued by the legislature on January 3 and February 5 to the Conservatives to return had not aimed at compromise, its sole purpose being to show the people that the Radicals were anxious to perform their duties.[3] And they resented Kellogg's assumption of control over the legislature.

[1] *Times*, February 7, Supplement, and *Republican*, February 7.
[2] *Bulletin*, February 8.
[3] House Jour. 1875, 122. Kellogg in a telegram from "Many students of Amherst College" was urged to stand firm.

At a Conservative caucus the day after the acceptance
of the compromise the matter was reconsidered and a
committee directed to ask of the Congressional Committee
in anticipation of the Clay meeting, a modification of
terms.   The Committee deferred its departure two days
in the hope of securing unanimous acceptance.   These
two groups were closeted long and late and reported a
slight change.   At a third secret caucus, a stormy all day
and night session on February 8, a new proposition was
drawn up by a vote of 59 to 7,[1] in which the phraseology
was varied so as not to place Conservatives in a false
light concerning the recognition of Kellogg.   In its
essentials it provided that the election of 1872 was not
to be included, and that the House was to be organized on
the basis of the Committee award.   The Conservatives
were to sign an agreement that, while not opposing or
recognizing the legality of the Kellogg government, they
would not disturb the executive because of his past acts,
so long as he was sustained by the President.   This plan
was to be submitted to the members of the Congressional
Committee in New Orleans to be by them in turn submitted to the full Committee in Washington for action.   The
caucus did not adjourn until half after one in the morning,
when the new plan was taken to the St. Charles Hotel.[2]
Wheeler telegraphed his refusal of these terms from
Mobile.

The compromise was the all-absorbing topic of conver-

---

[1] This session was as stormy as had been the meeting at the Clay Statue.
They felt that McEnery had been unjust and denounced the mass meeting
as impolitic.   The reading of the *Bulletin* charge of bribery was interrupted: "It is a lie, a vile slander."   Friends refused to greet members who
had sustained the measure.   On the authority of several men who witnessed such slights.

[2] The *Times* reports an audience with Wheeler before daylight, though
other accounts state that the terms were handed Wheeler just as he was
leaving for the station.

sation in all circles. The Radicals were elated, but the
Conservatives were not alarmed.[1] The attitude of the
Democratic press was, at least, divergent. The *Bulletin*
was "more than glad to know that no compromise can now
be effected, and that we are in a position to demand
our rights."[2] The Shreveport *Times* was very violent.[3]
The *Bee* frankly feared that the Conservatives "could
not hold good for two more years" but still declared
unswerving opposition to the proposition and to every
arrangement of that kind.[4] Of the same opinion was the
Courier des Opelouses.[5] Ward clubs adopted strong
resolutions, insisting on an explicit denial of the legality
of the Kellogg government.[6]

Rumors began to be heard immediately of a renewal
of the compromise negotiations. They were based upon
fact, for scarcely had Wheeler set foot in Washington before he had a telegram asking if the original terms were
still open. His reply declined individually—though he
did not presume to speak for his colleagues—to renew any
proposition.[7] Several Democrats had already departed
for Washington soon after their ultimatum to Wheeler in
order to present their cause there. Even Lieutenant-

---

[1] *Times*, February 12. The *Picayune* thought there was no essential
difference in the two plans.   [2] February 6.

[3] It is interesting to observe a change of heart on the part of this hotheaded editor thus: "The revolution must come, and we believed it better
that the American people should confront Grant and his 20,000 soldiers in
1875, than that they should confront Grant and his 300,000 or 400,000
soldiers in 1876. But our people have decided and we stand with them.
Jan. 29." From this acquiescence he advanced to the position of one of the
most zealous promoters of the compromise. He was even sent to Washington to further its interests. House Repts., 43 Cong., 2 Sess., No. 261, Part
iii., 868. Wheeler is reported as saying that his compromise must have
the support of the most radical White Leaguer in the State, and he sent
for the editor of this sheet.   [4] February 11.

[5] Quoted in the *Bee*, February 11.

[6] *Times*, February 11.   [7] *Republican*, February 18.

Governor Penn arrived at the capital on the 20th.   The
Radicals promptly sent attorneys Field and Ray, together
with Marshal Packard.

During the critical period the Democrats were guilty
of unwise remarks, such as that "Kellogg would not last
three days after they had control of the House."   To
three of the committee, who secured a protracted interview
with the President, on February 22, he expressed his deep
anxiety to have the matter adjusted and referred them
to Wheeler.   They found that individual indisposed to
accept any modification of his original proposition.   The
four Committee men agreed to undertake arbitration only
as individuals, after an agreement to abide by the decision
had been signed by a majority of the Democratic caucus,
including all who claimed seats, especially those thrown
out by the returning-board; and under the condition that
only those who signed would be considered.   The fact that
it was reported that the full Committee was to canvass the
returns, caused a change of feeling.   Strong pressure was
brought to bear on the caucus; telegrams from leading
Democratic Congressmen and business men in all the
principal cities urged acceptance.   Kellogg favored the
basis, but McEnery held true to his former position,
challenging the power of the caucus to make such an
arrangement for the people so far as the election of 1872
was concerned.[1]   The committee at Washington, after
consultation with friends of all parties, in and out of
Congress, felt "constrained to advise its acceptance,"
finding the hope of conservative Republicans and Democrats delusive, and that "nothing better can be obtained."[2]
Even Louisiana's strongest friends, Senator Gordon of

[1] He declared that if such power were exercised, it would be but an
addition to the sad chapter of usurpation of authority against which their
people had gallantly struggled for the past two years.   *Times*, February 24.
[2] *Ibid.*, Feb. 26.   For Burke's full report to the caucus, see issue of Mar. 2.

Georgia, Potter, and Phelps, had urged acceptance. Finally, after a long debate, the caucus reluctantly voted for the compromise on February 24 by a bare majority of one—34 to 33.[1] Forty-four names were signed to the pledge required.[2] With the signature were coupled two conditions: that the full Committee serve as arbiters, and that an extra session late in March should be called to pass reform measures.   A long list of merchants indorsed the action of the caucus.   But not since the beginning of the war had the better element of the community been more evenly divided upon any political question or with more intensity of feeling.   Inasmuch as opposition had already manifested itself in the other party, Wheeler assured the Conservatives, that "should the whole power of the Government become necessary to force a compliance, it would unhesitatingly be used."[3]

Efforts were made to bolster up hostile feeling, but the mass meeting at St. Patrick's Hall on February 26, though large and representative of every shade of sentiment, was moderate in temper and betrayed no marked enthusiasm.   There was no denunciation of caucus members, although speeches of repudiation were made and resolutions adopted, declaring they would never acquiesce.[4]   Several societies[5] and ward clubs[6] sent in

---

[1] "In announcing this acceptance, we desire to state that it is given under protest, and that we have been reluctantly forced to the conclusion that no other terms would be obtained.   It is evident, if rejected, the people of Louisiana had either to submit directly to an undoubted usurpation, or to plunge the State into a condition of anarchy, in which event they were warned the strength of the Federal forces would be used unrelentingly by the Federal authorities."   *Times*, February 26.

[2] One paper states 45.   *Annual Cyclopedia* gives the above number, 1875, 458.

[3] Letter of Wheeler to Leonard, editor of Shreveport *Times*, New Orleans *Times*, March 7.   [4] *Times*, February 27.

[5] Mechanics Benevolent Society, White League of St. Martinsville, *Republican*, February 18.   [6] *Picayune*, February 28.

protests, but the Committee of Seventy, though condemning it on March 1, indicated some change of sentiment by a refusal on the part of individual members to vote. Parish papers, especially, were averse to the movement. The Tangipahoa *Democrat* regarded compromise as a "fatal finality, to be swallowed as the best terms obtainable. But hatred to the usurpation is a vital, breathing, living, immortal principle in our people which is not dead and cannot die."[1] La Fourche repudiated it. Again March 1 and 2 the subject filled the columns of the papers. Only tardily, March 16, did the Radical House request the Select Committee, appointed December 15, to visit the city and inquire into the present condition.[2]

The comments in the North were favorable to adjustment. Hundreds of private letters and messages from business men North and South poured in at Washington, urging this peaceful settlement[3]; congratulations and predictions of good commercial returns were showered on the State.[4] Capital and business promised once more to return to the empty stores and wharves. The editorials in the State press breathed the spirit of peace and a determination to make the adjustment work. There lay their only salvation. The *Picayune* came out for it[5]; but the *Bulletin* and *Bee* were uncompromising to the very end, the latter regarding it as a "submission, pure and simple."[6] Naturally, the terms could not entirely please either party: the Conservatives felt that they were getting less than they were entitled to by the election of

---

[1] Quoted in the *Republican*, March 9.
[2] House Jour., 1875, 58.　　　　　　　　　　[3] *Republican*, February 26.
[4] *Times*, April 21, *Picayune*, April 15.　　　　　[5] February 24.
[6] As late as March 23 it printed, "Out of this proposal grew the riddling, double-dealing, obscure, indefinite, Wheeler Compromise proposition, which was full of loop-holes for trickery, fraud, coupled with a compulsory recognition of the usurper Kellogg as Governor of Louisiana." It was still unreconciled April 15. See the *Bee*, February 27.

24

1874, the Radicals, that they were forced to make a pure gift.

The papers which had played their famous part before the returning-board the preceding November saw the light once more in Mr. Phelps's office in New York. Work began March 12, all the Committee men present, except Mr. Frye,[1] who arrived late. The sessions were secret, although counsel for each faction was occasionally called in from an adjoining room, for consultation. Packard's presence with a number of colored men in New York can scarcely be explained except as an attempt to place obstacles in the way of adjustment.[2] The investigation was completed March 15, when the Committee had passed on nineteen contestants with the result of seating a Conservative majority of eight in the House. The relative balance of parties then stood sixty-three Conservatives as opposed to forty-seven Republicans in the House; twenty-seven Republicans to nine Conservatives in the Senate. They did not pass on the treasurer, which action meant retaining Dubuclet,[3] while the election in Grant Parish was referred back to the people. The decision was in most of the cases unanimous.[4]

The winter session of the legislature had meanwhile passed into history. "After the subsidence of the revolutionary proceedings," with which terse statement the journal dismisses the important events of January 4, "the organization of the House was proceeded with by the election of Michael Hahn as Speaker."[5] It had had a hard struggle for existence with McEnery men absenting

---

[1] There was much debate as to whether the whole Committee should serve, the Republicans holding that as the addition of a new condition.

[2] The *Times* accused the other party of trying to stir up trouble.

[3] The final decision on this question came up in regular suit.

[4] For the text of the award, see McPherson, *Handbook*, 1876, 201.

[5] House Jour., 1875, 1.

themselves so that already on the third day, the House lacked a quorum. Able to transact business only irregularly without a quorum, the House was sufficiently discouraged, January 22, to suggest adjournment *sine die*.[1]

It is impossible to see how this body surpasses any of its predecessors in morality: it did not reduce expenses, despite a parade of virtue through investigations and resolutions of retrenchment; neither did it pass other legislation of a notable character. It could not even be said that standards of honesty or conduct had improved.[2] Stormy sessions occurred when members threatened to resign. Seven members were indicted for bribery by the grand jury in May; the same dishonesty in vouchers to men unheard of before, payment of unitemized accounts for contingent expenses, with which we are only too familiar came to light again.[3] The habit of extravagant cost clung to both bodies—there were the same wearisome rolls of special sergeants and unnecessary clerks. Party greed became more glaringly revealed than ever before.

The list of measures, important for good or ill, is short.[4] Of these, the appropriation bill and those incorporating new towns consumed by far the major portion of the time. The general appropriation caused a profound sensation. Rushed through by arbitrary rulings of the speaker *versus* the finesse of the Conservatives during the bedlamite confusion which invariably ensued during the last session, it afforded opportunity for Hahn and Antoine to charge that the measure published in the *Republican*

---

[1] The Senate moved to adjourn *sine die* February 5.

[2] It was during this session that a member dared the speaker to seat him, whereupon, the latter heartily replied, "If the speaker seats the Gentleman, he will seat him so that he will not get up again." *Picayune*, February 17.

[3] *Times*, May 2, July 13, 23. Reporters of six papers received the usual $500. Contingent expenses were $92,000, but then large bills almost as large were unpaid.   [4] Only fifty-three in all.

March 30 was not the one passed. This gave birth to
counter-charges, in which Kellogg became involved because
of his favoring the compromise.¹ He weakly saved his
political scalp by signing the one testified to by Antoine.
One of the bills most violently assailed was that appropriating a quarter of a million dollars for the purchase
of the St. Louis Hotel for the state-house.² The resolution which, to quiet all doubts, reëlected Pinchback to
the Senate for the term to end in 1879 is worthy, perhaps,
of passing notice.³ The election law was again amended
to assure the presence of three commissioners at each
poll; a supplemental funding bill, including the dishonest
debt to the Levee Company, was severely attacked,⁴
but after being declared void by Judge Hawkins, the
Supreme Court found it constitutional.⁵ A new city charter for New Orleans, costly and clumsy, failed under the
governor's veto.⁶ No careful reader can agree with the
Republican that the laws were the "purest in the annals
of the State, for the last generation," nor that members
had shown devotion to the State.⁷

At first the Conservatives met daily, supported by the

---

¹ The opponents held that Antoine and Hahn had themselves changed it
in order to attack Kellogg. *Picayune*, March 30, Extra; *Times*, March 31.

² Session Laws, 1875, No. 6. It passed over the veto, as Kellogg regarded
the price as too high. One need not be confused about this building, if it
be recalled that it served as the state-house between two periods of hotel
existence. (The building still stands, a great interesting ruin.)

³ House Jour., 1875, 21.

⁴ *Times*, May 25. The funding act of 1874 cost the State $13,549.42.
House Repts., 43 Cong., 2 Sess., No. 261, Part iii., 934.

⁵ *Times*, July 31.

⁶ This would have done away with the bureau system. Nordhoff says
that Kellogg kept this bill as a whip without signing it. Merchants became so alarmed at the danger, that they petitioned against it. The
governor gave them to understand that if they would unite to prevent the
election of Wiltz as speaker at the extra session, he would veto it. *Cotton
States*, 50–1.   ⁷ March 4.

subscriptions of merchants.[1]   But on March 2, the last day but one, eight Conservative Senators created surprise but no sensation by taking their seats in the Radical Senate, though they protested that "William P. Kellogg has never been and is not the legal or *de jure* Governor."[2]

It only remained to put the compromise into execution. Strenuous exertions were made by a class of Republicans to prevent the extra session on the cry of impeachment.[3] But the summons went forth March 24.   The body, which was to convene on April 14 for ten days, was invited not only to adjust the political difficulties, but to give their consideration to taxation and the revenues of the State. As usual, New Orleans loomed large as a subject for legislation.[4]   McEnery did his part by retiring on March 26.   Preliminary caucuses of both parties were held April 12 and 13 to decide on a program and   found the Conservatives a unit to carry out the compromise.   But the opposition, long-smoldering in the Radical House, burst into flame[5]; men offered the pretext of utter distrust of the good faith of the Conservatives.   Probably a majority, among whom were the negroes who were afraid of losing their seats, were opposed to the compromise.[6]   Anti-compromise men nearly succeeded in seating new members; and some motions, looking toward impeaching Kellogg for his vigorous defense of it, appeared.[7]   Packard

[1] Up to February $100,000 had been subscribed.

[2] Sen. Jour., 1875, 151.

[3] Their organ urged Republican Senators not to assemble except under certain conditions.

[4] Its financial condition and government, relief from port charges.   *Cf.* Gov. Message, Sen. Jour., 1, 7–8.

[5] Note that thus long after the Congressional Committee had done its work, Radical opposition became outspoken.

[6] Nordhoff tells how they held on to office.   A Radical, when asked why he opposed compromise, replied with a pathetic quaver, "It means that I shall go out," 63.

[7] One newspaper on the 24th had a canard of such action.

opposed it at first[1]; Pinchback opposed it constantly by underhand methods "as sure to denationalize the Louisiana question"[2]; West fought it until silenced by Sheridan; but the President favored it, and Republican leaders in National politics were anxious for it, as relieving Congress of an apparent deadlock. Kellogg met with the representatives in the rotunda of the capitol to explain the award. Bidden to a conference with the State Central Committee and with Wheeler, who had come down to New Orleans on April 13 to assist in the execution of the award, the caucus listened to the explanation of the Congressman, and was urged by the Central Committee to conform. To avoid endorsing it, Pinchback[3] and Hahn broke the quorum; but at the evening session such a resolution carried with but one negative vote.[4]

On the morning of April 14 popular interest, without undue excitement, manifested itself around the statehouse. Not only were the lobbies thronged, but the adjacent streets. The Republicans met in caucus in a quiet and orderly session, where there was some division of sentiment, but as a body they took it for granted that the adjustment would be voted through. About noon the Conservative caucus passed into the hall. Thirty-one Senators are recorded present at the same time that Hahn was calling the House to order. It had not been a part of the program that the Conservatives should take their seats until the award had been confirmed, but, owing to a misunderstanding, those whose seats were not contested—thirty-five—were sworn in,[5] and a committee

[1] *Picayune*, March 1.
[2] Spoken by a henchman. Nordhoff, 64; *Picayune*, March 2.
[3] It was said that Sheridan was also finally able to squelch him.
[4] *Times*, April 14.
[5] La. House Jour., 1875, Extra Sess., 1–2. Wheeler was in the building during this interesting session, but did not appear in either assembly.

was sent to inform the Senate of the readiness of the
House to transact business. The twelve men who claimed
membership but who had been excluded by the returning-
board were referred to the Committee on Privileges and
Elections. The following day that committee reported
in favor of their admission in place of those who had
been seated. In accordance with the award, the report
was adopted and the Conservatives given seats.[1] Eight
of the men unseated were colored.[2] Thereupon House
Resolution No. 1 passed, forming a part of the Wheeler
Adjustment, by a vote of 89 to 18[3]; its acceptance by the
Senate on April 17 with only three dissenting votes consummated the compromise.[4]

Then in order came the governor's message. The
praise which the *Times* bestowed upon it of "a creditable
performance" seems to be merited.[5] He understood the
object of the session to be "to give effect to an adjustment
of past political differences" and at the same time it
"presents an opportunity to restore peace, order, and
confidence. We know how great blessings these things
are, for we have been so long deprived of them," he
added suggestively.[6] He then rehearsed the subjects
which seemed to him pressingly to require legislative
action.

The third day witnessed the settlement of the contest
over the speakership. There was much acerbity within

---

[1] The vote was not unanimous: 89 to 15.

[2] The spirit breathed by a negro in his farewell remarks toward the man
replacing him offers evidence of Democratic assertions. He was proud to
yield to his old master and held it a good thing for the State that a man of
his character should be admitted. *Times*, April 16.

[3] *Ann. Cyclop.*, 1875, 457; Session Laws, No. 1.

[4] Sen. Jour., Extra Sess., 20.

[5] But pessimistically, "If we get half the good things recommended
therein, the message will mark a new era in the history of our State."
April 17.   [6] Sen. Jour., Extra Sess., 9.

the Conservative party over this honor.   Although the
Bee[1] probably represented the sentiment of the greater
part of the business community when it insisted that the
honor and dignity of the party prescribed the renomination of Wiltz, he had lost the support of the wing
which stood for compromise, and which, under the leadership of Leonard, had determined to defeat him.   Leonard
did not hesitate to accept the help of the Kellogg wing,[2]
while Wiltz tried to enlist Pinchback in his support.
Although the latter was therefore accused of bribery,
Nordhoff thought there was no corruption, no promise
except a fair share of places to the negroes.   This view
is borne out by the fact that Wiltz always displayed a
high sense of honor.   But Pinchback abandoned him, possibly at the instigation of Sheridan, as Nordhoff thought,
or at that of Kellogg,[3] with the result that Estilette, a
man of little personal presence and slightly deaf, praised
by his bitterest opponents as a man of amiable intentions
but constitutionally a "trimmer,"[4] was seated by a
large majority.   Wiltz's speech of congratulation was
not free from bitterness.[5]

The principal subject on April 19 was the ousting of
four Republicans who had not been returned by the
board, but seated soon after that party came into control.
The Conservatives held that as they were seated while
the award was pending, they were not included in it.
Although excitement ran so high that the party threat-

[1] April 13.
[2] It was understood that the better class of Republicans would coöperate
for thorough reform.
[3] It was said that Kellogg sent for twenty Republican negroes and
ordered them to support Estilette. *Times*, April 17.
[4] Nordhoff says he seemed incapable of a direct course.   But see the
praise bestowed on him as a true representative of adjustment in the *Picayune* of April 17.
[5] *Times*, April 17.   The vote stood 66 to 37.

ened disorganization, the Conservatives unseated them on April 20.[1]

And therewith the ground would seem to be cleared for action. But by April 21 the governor's patience was exhausted and he sent in an extra message urging attention to the crying evils. Even the *Times* suggested caustically that until "candidates who manifest a nominal desire to serve the people and a blind fanaticism in serving themselves, learn to grasp this first principle of political duty, they had better retire to private life."[2] Bribery had become so chronic that this body could not hope to escape the taint.[3] As the limit of the session drew near, indignation at the dilatoriness of members was loudly voiced. A group of mechanics visited the House on April 24 to deliver a severe but well-merited arraignment.[4] Each side tried to blame the other. The Republicans blamed the Democrats for trying to do in ten days "without due deliberation" what the Republicans were willing to devote seventy days to doing. The *Bulletin* threw the onus on the Radicals:

Even the gentlemen who favored Compromise because they

---

[1] Of course, the *Republican* charged violation of faith, April 21, 22. "It rendered all but partisan legislation impossible, destroyed the hope of better days and less bitter feeling, and defeated every effort the compromise was to promote." Wheeler in the New York *Times* declared they were not included. He held that the House was to be that returned by the returning-board, and not what it was when the Conservatives voted to accept the award.   [2] April 22.

[3] See *Times*, April 17 and July 25.

[4] "Hour by hour the session had been frittered away, chiefly in the vain endeavor to accomplish a narrow-minded and bigoted partisan success, to gain offices, or secure the dispensation of patronage. Scarcely a man of any political party has been found of sufficient magnanimity to forget party affiliations and stand forth as the champion of true reform and measures of relief. . . . Recently the struggle was for rights; do not forget that with the people the great struggle is now for daily sustenance." *Times*, April 25.

were led to believe that the Republicans would act in good faith, and that Kellogg would use his best endeavors to accomplish some good, are now fain to confess that they have been bitterly, cruelly deceived and that so far as the Republicans are concerned, they never intended to accomplish anything except the quieting of Kellogg in his seat.[1]

The *Times* felt the failure of the session a severe disappointment, the more annoying because unnecessary. "One hour less devoted to inconsequential talk and devoted to these bills, would have secured the passage of at least the most important of them."[2]   The *Bee* had stoically never awaited any other result from a compromise which had only recognized a usurpation.[3]

But the palpable truth remained that very little legislation of any kind had passed until the last twenty-four hours, when the rushing through of a very large number of bills proved that a "long session is not essential to the passage of bills."[4]   But they were chiefly appropriation bills and those for the relief of taxpayers.   The reduction of the cost of the metropolitan police; the restriction of the publication of the statutes and journals to the official organ; provision for testing at the instance of any taxpayer the legality of any item of the debt[5]; and prohibiting the Board of Liquidation from funding the questionable debt were bits of the reform legislation for which the State was clamoring.[6]   Economy could not be especially placed to their credit, for the ten days of the session cost the State $117,362 for mileage and per diem,[7] while the reporters for seven papers received $525 each for ten days.[8]

The completion of the process of adjustment seemed

---

[1] April 25.
[2] April 25.
[3] April 25, May 1.
[4] Caustic comment of the *Times*.
[5] Session Laws, No. 11.
[6] Session Laws, No. 12, 3, 8.
[7] *Ibid.*, No. 2.
[8] Sen. Jour., Extra Sess., 1875, 58.

attained when gratifying reports began to come in from
the parishes.   By May the press was saying that by
common consent the acrimony of the past years had been
dropped.[1]   A   prominent   gentleman   from   St.   Mary
Parish, who had at first strenuously opposed compromise,
was optimistic concerning the change for the better in
his locality.   Hints of an increasing business activity
were heard by September, while good crops that year
improved the situation for the planter.   Peace and relative
prosperity seemed to be the rewards of adjustment.[2]

[1] *Times*, May 23.
[2] *Times*, May 23, Sept. 1; *Picayune*, Sept. 29; *Republican*, Oct. 13.

CHAPTER XVII

Repudiation of the Wheeler Compromise

T HOUGH the Conservative members of the Assembly had formally pledged themselves to the Wheeler Compromise and the people generally had acquiesced, there was a wing, aggressive if small, which was irreconcilable. The Committee of Seventy, immediately after the acceptance of the conditions, announced, "on behalf of the Democratic-Conservative people of Louisiana, our unalterable resolution to continue to oppose the Kellogg Government and to prosecute the Louisiana cause before the Congress and people of the United States."[1]

In compliance with petitions for reorganization of the Democratic party, as it was alleged, the Central State Committee, with a generous representation from city and country,[2] met quietly on August 19 but deemed it inexpedient to call a State convention. It was willing, however, to adopt a resolution urging parish assemblies to instruct their representatives to vote no supplies until the existing unjust legislation be repealed.[3]

Notwithstanding this resolve, rumors of a convention persisted. Booth and Vorhies seemed to be the prime

---

[1] *Picayune*, March 2, 1875.

[2] Some seven parishes and every ward in the city but one was represented. It was thought that the project of a convention in November was defeated by the country members. *Ibid.*, August 21, 23.

[3] *Ibid.*, August 22, and the *Times*, August 21, accused them of striving for an extra election.

380

movers, basing their action on the plea of getting into line with the National Democratic party. Party leaders were not too dull to see that this but veiled the reopening of the question of compromise. Of course, the Republicans assailed the idea caustically: "The program of the Democracy means nothing except the spoils for themselves and civil war for the rest of the public. The Conservatives do not like this bill of fare." At first Democratic papers tried to discount the rumors as mere suspicions of "egregious folly and bad faith" and did not regard it as reasonable to suppose that the people would countenance its violation now. [1] While the *Times* did not think it would occur, it pointed out the consequent evil results. [2] Democratic leaders there were, like Eustis, who felt that the reopening of the question could only benefit the Republicans; like Judge Egan, who felt that a convention ought not to be forced until time had elapsed for the subsidence of recent asperities. [3] From observation of the country press, [4] the *Picayune* was persuaded that a fair statement of public opinion would declare any political attempt a "pestiferous mistake and impossible of good." [5] As was to be expected, the editor of the Shreveport *Times* was as strong against repudiation as he had been for the compromise. "It will be seen," he declared, "that however the Democratic and Conservative papers of North Louisiana may differ as to names, they

---

[1] *Picayune*, August 23.   [2] August 22.   [3] *Picayune*, August 23.
[4] The Alexandria *Democrat*, Natchitoches *Vindicator*, Mansfield *Reporter*, Minden *Democrat*, Bossier *Banner*, Richland *Beacon* were all quoted by the *Republican* as adverse. October 2 a mass meeting at Lafourche protested vigorously against the call. "The general impression seems to prevail that the decision of the Central Committee ought to have settled the question of a convention and the minds of the people allowed to remain free from harangues and political disputes among themselves," according to the Minden *Democrat*. Quoted by the *Republican*, Oct. 7.
[5] August 25.

are almost a unit in opposition to the action of the self-constituted body of men who have taken the Democratic party into their special keeping."[1]

But calls for a convention in November began to make themselves heard. The Second Ward Club as early as September 2 felt that "since the fusion at Baton Rouge had left the Democratic party without organization, the party should be consolidated to overthrow Radical rule."[2] By the middle of September even the *Picayune* admitted that there seemed to be a general movement in the parishes toward a reorganization of the party,[3] but followed it with an accusation of unworthy means to bring about those calls.[4] It is noticeable that they came largely from Republican parishes. On his own authority, though forty-six men added their signatures, Marr acceded to this general demand, while his address suggested, as befitted a non-official document, not nominations, but resolutions only.[5] But certainly the chief leaders of the party condemned the project for its elements of political disturbance and for its intrusion on the interests of business. Lieutenant-Governor Penn, Phelps, Marks, and Burke all apprehended that the question of the compromise would be raised.[6]

By the last of September the city clubs were actively espousing the cause, strong in their claim that the action of the legislature could not bind the people. The Second Ward Club indorsed the call; a First Ward Club, hastily

---

[1] Quoted by the *Republican*.   [2] *Times*, Sept. 3.   [3] Sept. 17.
[4] It was held that communications were sent out to the country, urging the formation of clubs and the passage of resolutions favoring the idea. Sept. 26. It might be noted that September 13, 1875, the Chicago *Tribune* outlined a Conservative plot to break up the compromise and dispose of Kellogg after January 1, 1876.
[5] The *Republican* tried to dispose of it as an autocratic act of Mr. Marr.
[6] *Picayune.*, Sept. 29. This paper interviewed all these men besides others and printed their adverse opinions.

organized September 24, did the same thing[1]; the Third Ward and Ninth Ward Clubs declared themselves in favor early in October. The purpose is practically unveiled in a letter of Representative Ellis to one of these clubs: "Understand me, that we do not seek to unsettle the status of the members of the Lower House of the Legislature as fixed by that adjustment." But he did deny that the compromise settled the election of 1872.[2]

Parlor P of the St. Charles Hotel on October 21 was the scene of a second and full session of the State Central Committee. More than forty members debated in a protracted meeting the question of a convention for the first Wednesday in January. Here the anti-compromise men were in the ascendant. Though the call issued disclaimed "any intention to revive the question of the Wheeler Adjustment, so far as it has fixed the status of the present House of Representatives," it declared it the sense of the Conservatives that "all constitutional means should be taken in Congress for the recognition of the McEnery government" and that the resolution should be forwarded to their Congressmen. Parish committees were to call parish conventions at an early date. The election held on December 30 for members to the convention passed quietly, the voting being without incident to disturb the peace.[3] By the middle of December the "Bourbon" Democrats, as this wing was termed, had secured an organ, called simply the *Democrat*,[4] which

[1] *Times*, Sept. 25.

[2] *Picayune*, October 13, gives this letter in full.

[3] The *Republican* felt that "the people have almost ignored the call of the parish committee to vote, while a majority of those who voted gave their suffrages against the originators of the scheme." Jan. 1. The *Picayune*, however, conceded that the voting had been very lively most of the day. Dec. 31.

[4] The organ of these "Last Ditch Democrats" in the parishes had been the *Delta*.

declared its position in its issue of December 28 in the candid statement that those who favored the Wheeler Compromise were guilty of dishonor.[1]

The convention was the principal theme of conversation January 4. No one seemed to know the program—except that delegates to the National convention would be chosen. Such a body of representative men as the five hundred delegates had not gathered in the city in years, as the planting interest was well represented.[2] The group was called to order by Marr at St. Patrick's Hall on January 5. Early in the session Congressman Ellis made it clear that the purpose of the convention was to secure such an investigation of the election of 1872 as would seat McEnery—the repudiation of the compromise —by pledging the Louisiana Representatives in Congress to support a resolution looking to the overthrow of the Kellogg government.[3]

The second day saw the adoption of a platform of seven planks and a memorial to Congress. After declaring the primary test of a Democrat to be unrelenting opposition to the usurpation, the platform advocated abolition of useless offices, reduction of taxation, together with immovable opposition to fraudulent obligations, reduction of printing and police expenses, and hearty opposition to all monopolies. The last plank reaffirmed Democratic faith in the gold and silver standard.

The memorial tried to prove by several specious arguments that the people did not by the Wheeler Compromise acquiesce in the usurpation, because the legislative mem-

---

[1] *Times*, Dec. 29. It was not so severe on the new paper as might have been expected. See also the *Bulletin*.

[2] The *Republican* tried to discredit them as of "no great influence in the financial affairs," a few planters but many lawyers. "From the petition the mercantile and labor interests were excluded." Jan. 8.

[3] *Times*, Jan. 6.

bers did not intend to yield the claims between the governments, because the claims of the two governments were
never submitted, since evidence was not taken as to the
earlier election,[1] and because the adjustment

expressly withholds approval of the Kellogg government and
cannot bind the people who were not parties to it. [Speaking
for themselves,] the people do solemnly affirm that they have
not acquiesced, and never will acquiesce, in the Kellogg usurpation; that it is as repugnant to their wishes, and interests, and
sense of justice as it was on the day of its lawless establishment
over them by force; that they recognize as the only government
elected by the people of the State or entitled to their support,
respect, or confidence, that of which John McEnery and D. B.
Penn are the official heads[2]; and they affirm that they have
been patient and silent since the adjournment of the last
Congress in the hope and belief that the present Congress
would listen to their grievances and grant the proper relief.[3]

The time was regarded as especially propitious for a
petition to Congress—the eve of an election; Democrats felt
they were sure of a favorable reception in the Democratic
House, and felt that the Senate could not afford to delay
action, because the contest would probably be a close
one and the Republican party be seriously injured should
the Senate continue silent on the Louisiana case.[4]   The
final appeal, if unavailing, did not lack fervor:

[1] *Annual Cyclopedia*, 1875, 460–1.
[2] The *Republican's* arguments are rather forced when it saw no other
meaning in this issue than to win back pay for the Democratic claimants to
office.   It bid for Conservative support: "They may await the guarantees
of the Republican party before signing the indentures and accepting the
handicuffs of the dictatorial Democracy."   January 9.
[3] *Annual Cyclopedia*, 1875, 461.
[4] Spirit of a speech by Wickliff, *Republican*, Jan. 7.   There is a ring of
sincerity in the declaration by one member that Wheeler had assured him
he did not mean to restrict the people as to the legality of the governorship.
25

To you, the President and Representatives, we, the people of the State of Louisiana, do present our grievances and ask you—in the name of our common country, in the name of our common civilization, in the name of the sacred memories that cluster round this centennial year—in the name of liberty and justice—that you blot from our national history this shameful record of usurpation and of crime committed against our State, and permit it no longer to remain a precedent for the overthrow of other States.[1]

The convention closed its labors by the election of four delegates and four alternates to the National convention and by provision for the appointment by the president of the convention of a new State Central Committee.[2] The Democratic press had ceased its opposition: the *Picayune* commended the convention for its temperance and unanimity,[3] while the *Bee* frankly approved the reopening of the subject.[4] But Congressmen Gibson and Levy felt it their duty to declare that many friends of Louisiana in Congress had indicated an unwillingness to open the case.[5]

The Conservatives were early in caucus for the legislative session of 1876. Beginning November 23 nearly all the members[6] met weekly to define as far as possible their

---

[1] *Times*, January 7.

[2] Louisiana was not the only State to act early. Conventions were in session at the same time in Texas. *Times*, January 8.

[3] January 6, 7.

[4] "Au lieu de demander à ceux qui ont voté et accepté le compromise de violer leurs engagements, la convention doit protester au nom du peuple contre l'atteinte qui a été portée aux droits de ceux des élus du peuple qui non pas été advis à sieger. Enfin, elle doit constater que le compromis n' a jamais, dans l'intention de ceux qui l'ont voté, eu d'autre object que de regler le droit de sieger des représentants et sénateurs élus en 1874 et rejetés par le bureau de retours." January 5.

[5] *Republican*, January 7.

[6] Among them were six or seven country members who came to the city expressly for this purpose.

course in the present session with regard to reform measures.   A number of bills were soon selected and routine
business decided upon.[1]   It became clear that the proposed reorganization of the House by the Republicans
would be opposed by all the Conservatives.   Thereafter,
the caucus met every day but with extreme reticence as
to the business transacted.   The Republican caucus, on
the other hand, seems to have met first on December 29
and to have felt that it must pursue a defensive course.

The first day of the session attracted an immense
throng of lobbyists, politicians, and applicants for clerical
positions on committees, who were scattered along the
banquettes on St. Louis and Royal streets.   The lobby
was occupied in surmising the probable policy of each
party, some asserting that the Conservatives had all
arranged to reorganize the house at roll-call, others that
the Radicals would oppose every measure and delay the
apportionment.[2]

The annual message, unusually lengthy and comprehensive, touched upon practically every subject of interest
to the State.   The matter of most vital importance, the
finances, received full treatment.   The satisfaction expressed with the funding law of the preceding session is
natural:

[1] *Times*, Nov. 24.   A committee was directed to present a careful estimate of traveling expenses from every parish in the State and to study a
reduction of police expenditure.   The *Bee* shows how fiercely determined
the people were upon the reform of the registration and election laws
January 2: "Nous espérons donc que les démocrates ne recontreront
q'une faible résistance de la part des radicaux à l'adoption des mesures de
réforme les plus urgents, les plus indispensables.   Ce qui sortira de cette
sesson de 60 jours, nous ne saurions le prévoir, mais les radicaux feront sage-
ment de ne pas se refuser à voter des lois propres à assurer l'exactitude de
l'enregistrement, et la liberté et la sincerité des élections."   Jan. 2.

[2] The speaker refused to appoint committees until he became satisfied
that the Conservatives would have a fair representation on the Senate
committees.   *Times*, Jan. 2.

During the whole term of forty years over which the new bonds run, the debt cannot be increased beyond the point to which it has thus been limited.   The appalling contingent debt, over $21,000,000 in amount, never actually incurred, but standing on the statute books a constant source of danger and uncertainty, has been buried beyond resurrection. . . . No power can hereafter tamper with the credit of the State. The rate of taxation is limited.   The legislature is restricted in its expenditures to the revenues which that rate of taxation will yield, and the revenues of each year are to be devoted exclusively to the expenses of that year.[1]

Kellogg tried to make out a reduction of the debt of over four million dollars during the past year; a reduction of expenses by nearly a million and a half; a reduction of taxes by one-third.   He criticized the system of appraising and assessing; he found a tendency to discriminate unfairly against the city, as assessments in the city were arbitrary, while in the country they were lax.   He believed an equalization of values would add a large sum to the assessment rolls of the State and to that extent lighten the taxes.[2]   He also recommended three amendments— one, to reduce all salaries fixed by the constitution; another, to reduce the per diem of members to five dollars a day, mileage to five cents a mile; and a third, to reduce the session to thirty days.[3]   But it is difficult to join in his optimism when he says, "They hold out to us, I venture to think, the prospect of a future more prosperous, more peaceful, more thoroughly in accord with the great principles of Christianity, civilization, and human progress than the State has ever yet enjoyed."[4]

Ten days of the session were absolutely wasted without

---

[1] La. Sen. Jour., 1876, 4-5.   [2] *Ibid.*, 19.
[3] Sen. Jour., 1876, 20.   But all his protestations and recommendations for reform were simply, to the *Bee*, "un leurre, une fourberie," since he had the veto.   Jan. 6.   [4] Sen. Jour., 1876, 5.

any work accomplished. On January 11 the two houses succeeded in appointing their committees and the deadlock seemed broken. But despite the hammering of the press, the apparent hurry and bustle of business, no results were achieved. "If we had elected a battalion of officials to play the elegant, and air their social accomplishments, and develop the art of dumb-show, the present General Assembly might be termed a success."[1] As late as January 22 the standing query was, "When will the legislature get to work?" Fourteen days before the time of adjournment the *Times* accused it of not having passed one act of material relief,[2] and attacked the whole Senate "ring," whose theories could all be boiled down to loot.[3] The *Democrat* and *Picayune*[4] confined their attacks almost exclusively to colored Republicans, while the *Republican* put all the blame on the other party.[5] But it may be said that the House settled down to business January 24 with the introduction of a long list of bills. By February 3 twenty reform bills had been offered.

There was no dearth of measures, though the actual number passed was only ninety-five. Attention turned at once in the Senate to the coming election in an act apportioning the State into Senatorial districts, and fixing the number of Representatives from each district. This bill proved such a stumbling-block that it was determined to introduce bills pending action on this measure and to set investigating committees to work.[6] A committee found great irregularities in the Police Board in the appointment of deadheads for political purposes—

[1] *Times*, Jan. 19.   [2] *Ibid.*, Feb. 12.   [3] Feb. 6.
[4] "Absolute or even-handed justice was not to be expected from so partisan a body," according to the *Picayune*.
[5] Feb. 24, March 2.
[6] Charges of bribery which had been made against Lowell, Dewees, Ray, and several others were ordered examined. House Jour., 1876, 25; 60–1.

at least one hundred and fifty useless men drawing pay—
and so hoped that the "present odious Board should be
abolished forever."[1]   The Finance Committee was directed to investigate the mayor and administrators of
New Orleans.[2]   Even the election of West to the Senate
was raked up because of charges in the New York *Tribune*,[3]
and declared "legitimate and honorable."[4]   But such
an investigation of Pinchback was voted down.[5]   The
apportionment question ultimately was settled only by a
caucus on January 22 when the Conservatives agreed to
let the Senate remain unchanged, and to concede to the
House one hundred and nineteen members, one less than
the constitutional limit, a rearrangement which gave more
Republican districts.

One of the subjects which came up for early action
was the election of a United States Senator.   In an open
letter to McEnery, McMillan had resigned early in December "as the struggle of the people had been determined
against them."[6]   This led to an argument between them
in the press and to McEnery's appointment of Marr,
though the Senate had already accepted the withdrawal of
McMillan's credentials.[7]   The House on January 11 elected
J. B. Eustis Senator, and then invited such members of
the Senate as were willing to act with it to meet in joint
session.   Neither the lieutenant-governor nor the secretary
appeared, although twelve of the Senate, among whom
were three Republicans, joined with seventy-eight of the
House in declaring Eustis elected for the term beginning
March 4, 1873.[8]   But forty-four of the House protested[9]

---

[1] Sen. Jour., 194–7.   [2] *Republican*, Feb. 19.
[3] January 28; Sen. Jour., 279.   [4] January 31.   [5] January 31.
[6] *Times*, December 11; see the same paper for a statement of McEnery's
position.   [7] Vote of 30 to 28.
[8] House Jour., 36–7.   Oddly enough, Blackburn, a Republican, acted
with the Democrats and served as presiding officer in a spirit of compromise
"to forget the past."   [9] *Ibid.*, 34.

and the governor refused to issue a certificate, consenting only to certify to the proceedings. Eustis, armed with a copy of the proceedings, went to Washington to claim his seat. Of course, the hostile press regarded it as "another revolutionary measure, based on the violation of the Wheeler Compromise."[1]

Probably the most important bill of the session was the election bill. A strong effort to dispose of the returning-board and vest in the secretary the work of consolidating the vote was made in the House, despite the expressed fears that it "would provide for making the shot-gun policy of conducting elections more effective, and reduce the penalties for intimidation and violence at the polls to a minimum with the least possible percentage of chances for conviction."[2] The Senate, even against some opposition in its own ranks, promptly passed a substitute with a returning-board more objectionable than the one existing, as it was to consist of five members, three appointed by the governor, two by the House.[3] On the ground that the Wheeler Compromise committed the Assembly to a policy of reform, the House declared that a persistence of the Senate would be a violation of the adjustment which would absolve it from all obligations.[4] The remarks hurled back and forth grew very sharp. A Democrat declared, "Give us war; we are ready for it." Another warned Senators that if the board were not abolished, "ten thousand negroes would be killed." Another turned

---

[1] *Republican*, January 14.   [2] *Ibid.*, Feb. 3.
[3] See the debate as reported in the *Republican*, Feb. 4. Robertson, colored, refused to vote for it, as he knew the people of his district were opposed to it. The men who offered the substitute were reported as saying that they had not anticipated the violent construction placed on it by the Democrats, but intended it only as a "bluff" for a conference. *Ibid.*, Feb. 5. See comments of the *Times* and *Bulletin*.
[4] For the returning-board clauses, see *Republican*, Feb. 5, House Jour., 135.

with disgust and loathing from the contemplation of the scandalous action of the Returning-Board of 1874 in their management of the returns of that year.   I, by my vote, do not intend to place the rights that properly belong to every American citizen in the hands of members composing a returning-board.[1]

While one Republican thought that victory had perched on the Republican banners and that that party could not be defeated, another was opposed on the ground that the board "is not held for the purpose of benefiting the Republican party or any other party, but in the interest of a ring power in order that they may feed on the fat of the land." And so, the House returned the bill with this important feature struck out.   To this the Senate would not concur, and when a committee of conference failed,[2] it was apparent that no reform was to be accomplished here.[3]

Other measures meriting passing consideration were several amendments: One limiting the expenditure of each session to $175,000 and members to $5 a day, one requiring the governor to sign all bills in five days or within twenty days after the session, one abolishing parish courts, one reducing the governor's salary to $6000, and one cutting off all perquisites from the treasurer, attorney-general, or district attorneys.   As had become usual now, legislation of vast importance was rushed through during the last hours without being printed, or referred to a committee, but half-understood by either party.   In this group were a new charter for New Orleans, and the Premium Bond bill.[4]   To the credit of the Assembly, be it added, it appropriated the sum for its own

[1] *Republican*, Feb. 4.   [2] House Jour., 1876, 224.
[3] This was later to furnish an excuse for the impeachment of Kellogg.
[4] *Times*, Feb. 24, 1876.

expenses from the funds for that year and made an encouraging decrease in the printing-bill. [1]

Actual repudiation of the compromise did not come until the eve of the adjournment. This was by no means an unexpected move on the part of the Democrats. That such action was regarded as a possible contingency is sufficiently evidenced in a precautionary act offered by the Republicans during the last days of the preceding session when it was clear that a compromise would be effected. It provided for the manner of filling the offices of governor and lieutenant-governor relative to the suspension of either. [2] We have seen how the Bourbon wing refused to accept the adjustment at all, and how the movement for a convention was regarded as a threat. Very early in the session one can find covert accusations of violation and consequent right of repudiation. No later than February 3 the *Picayune* declared that "unless reforms are passed, the tacit conditions of the compromise will have been violated." It affected Democratic feeling not at all that the *Republican* denied such tacit agreement as "idiotic." [3] In explicit language the *Times* a few days later[4] urged that the results of broken faith be forced home upon the Republicans, but only after the Senate had wantonly disregarded its pledges of reform. The Bourbon organ on February 12 openly avowed that it was "distinctly and unalterably in favor of the impeachment of *de facto* Governor Kellogg and *de facto* Lieutenant-Governor Antoine," should the scalawag and negro senators insist on retaining the returning-board as a part of the election law. [5] Such plain talk was not lost on the *Republican* for it rejoiced the same day in a legal snag, which the "would-be

---

[1] Session Laws, 1876, No. 19, 16; House Jour., 55.
[2] Feb. 24, Sen. Jour., 1875, 122, and Mar. 1, House Jour., 124.
[3] February 4.   [4] February 5.   [5] The *Democrat.*

impeachers of Governor Kellogg have struck."[1]   But by February 19 rumors of impeachment were rife on the streets.   On that date the *Bulletin* declared: "We do not believe that impeachment would succeed; but it is nevertheless the duty of the House to proceed as if it would, and thus throw the blame for failure upon the Senate."   The *Democrat* lashed the House on: "As soon as the House awakens to a proper sense of its duty and formulates its charges of felony against William P. Kellogg —and we can hardly permit members to doubt that such action will soon be taken—that individual must step down and out, or else be put out,"[2] and declared that it would rather see Antoine in the chair than "a contemptible carpetbagger," representing nothing but the "insatiate greed of his fellow adventurers and conspirators."   Again in varied phrase, a few days later, it urged impeachment "while there is yet time and obtain the respect of the people, if it cannot secure fully their liberties."[3]

A House committee, which had been appointed at the extra session of 1875 to examine into the accounts of the auditor and treasurer, reported about the middle of February that sums to the amount of nearly $200,000 had been drawn from the interest fund without warrant. But it found the treasurer less guilty than Kellogg, "the originator of the whole scheme," or Hawkins, or Dibble, the acting attorney-general.[4]   And it concluded by recommending Kellogg and Dubuclet for impeachment, Dibble to be addressed out of office.

[1] *I. e.*, the lieutenant-governor could not be suspended by a resolution of impeachment.
[2] Feb. 19.   The *Republican* looked upon these fulminations as merely "necessary as a campaign issue."   It did not expect a trial.
[3] February 23.
[4] House Jour., 1876, 200.   This was, it was alleged, a violation of Act 3, 1874.

On the 26th of the month, [1] a majority of the committee
of seven, which had been appointed to examine the charges
against Kellogg, reported that subsequent to the 14th day
of April, 1875, he had "been guilty of many and divers
high crimes and misdemeanors in office, against the laws,
constitution, and people of the State of Louisiana."
The report produced the liveliest excitement and was
discussed the whole day. The Republicans astutely
realized the exact situation, and not a point in parliamentary tactics which could delay the issue escaped them. [2]
One member wished the committee discharged, as he was
assured that the business men did not want such action;
it was a design to promote strife and create turmoil,
especially in the coming election, a scheme in accordance
with the Bourbon declaration that at all hazards Radical
rule in Louisiana must be broken up; he held it a violation
of the spirit and letter of the compromise. The Conservatives, however, held that it was the Radicals who had
broken the compromise. The former had favored it for
the sake of the reforms, but when they asked what measures had passed that were the consideration of adjustment,
the echo came—nothing. "We are asked to condone his
offenses and put him back once more. I say never, never,
never! We will deal with unscrupulous men without
scruple. It is not necessary to go back of the compromise. Since then the governor has gone on as before." [3]
Another declared that compromise was held as an estoppel
against all prosecution of violations of law. At the vote
it would be found that this was not a Bourbon measure;
that no one had any intention of violating any part of the

---

[1] *Annual Cyclopedia* says Feb. 27, 1876, 482, but the journal gives the
26th.

[2] The Republicans were rather puzzled just then at the object, for there
had been no hint of impeaching Antoine.

[3] See the speech of Kidd, *Republican*, February 27.

compromise, but only to show that the governor had been guilty of crimes since its adoption. One Levisse revealed the nature of the investigation as a farce. He declared that not a witness had been examined, and that the chairman brought the report in finished form to the first meeting. And he warned members against thought-less haste. Lowell declared it a Star Chamber proceeding, originated, tried, and judged in caucus.[1] A Republican who tried to prevent the presentation of the articles and complained of predetermined ruling caused a commotion and was forced to apologize.

The resolutions were passed at five o'clock on February 28 by a vote of 61 to 45. The committee of five which was directed to prepare the articles appeared with its resolutions at five forty-five at the bar of the Senate, which immediately organized as a court with Ludeling in the chair,[2] allowing the committee until seven o'clock —less than an hour—to prepare and present the charges. But the House had adjourned to March 1 to prevent the delivery of the message of the Senate,[3] in which case Kellogg would be suspended until the next Assembly, as the Democrats denied the right of the governor to call an extra session merely to try the case. But, when the Senate sat again as a court at seven o'clock, although the board of managers appeared without the authority of the House, the Senate dismissed the impeachment and acquitted the governor by a vote of 25 to 9,[4] knowing

[1] See the fiery speeches of Wiltz and Booth in the *Republican*, February 29.

[2] Kellogg had appeared by counsel immediately and asked that the court require specific articles. Sen. Jour., 1876, 289.

[3] Wiltz indignantly denied this charge of the Senate and held that the House had remained in session one and one-half hours after the Senate was notified, condemning, in his turn, the "indecent haste" of the other body.

[4] For impeachment proceedings see Sen. Jour., 1876, 80–1, and the *Times* Mar. 3, for Kellogg's defense.

that it was a political conspiracy of the Democratic party to effect partisan purposes without any regard for the public government, and that the resolutions contained in the formal articles of impeachment were either false or frivolous.[1] Indignation among Democratic Senators ran high.

The House, nevertheless, on the next day proceeded to adopt all the fourteen articles,[2] to report the facts of the case, and send the committee to notify the Senate of their action, only to be informed of its adjournment as a court. It then wreaked its vengeance on the Senate in an entirely futile series of resolutions, declaring the Senate disqualified from sitting in judgment on the trial and "that this House can proceed no farther in the premises and are powerless to resent this outrage upon right, justice, and decency, and can only refer the matter to the people of the State for their consideration."[3]

The feeling with regard to impeachment was by no means unanimous even within the ranks of the opposition. Many of the business men disapproved of renewed disturbance—a petition against the trial appeared; and the Democrats at Washington were strongly opposed on account of the approaching election. Even the *Times* had this to say: "The House gets up an impeachment, foolish and frivolous in design and unspeakably feeble in execution; and the Senate trumps up a trial and acquittal as monstrous, so arbitrary and so scornful as to shock and startle every reasoning mind."[4] The *Picayune* held that the Democrats should be sure of their charges and

---

[1] La. Sen. Jour., 281. Parts of this message were held so disrespectful that the speaker refused to allow them to be entered on the journal. Phelps states that Kellogg had admitted that he had approved certain temporary diversions of the interest fund, but only at a time of great public need and without the loss of a dollar to the State.

[2] For all the charges, see impeachment proceedings.

[3] House Jour., 325.   [4] *Times*, March 1.

evidence.[1]   The *Democrat* still sought means of wresting victory from defeat by urging the impeachment of Antoine and Anderson in order that the Democratic speaker, Estilette, might become acting executive.[2]

The *Republican* struck a much higher note than usual when it appealed to the Wheeler Compromise as a bar to impeachment, for it was "the agreement of high-minded gentlemen that they would henceforth bury party bickerings and address themselves in the future to considering measures for the public good and discharging the duties for which they were elected,"[3] and was quite just when it objected to a snap judgment of the governor at the last hour without time for the Senate to try the charges.[4] No doubt the Democrats were annoyed that the legislature had no reforms to show.   No doubt they could convince themselves that the compromise had implied agreement to pass such reform legislation.   But by what logic should the governor be impeached for the sins of the Assembly? And so the impartial reader will probably see with the *Times* "no statesmanship in these proceedings."[5]

On February 25, in the midst of the impeachment excitement, the governor issued a call for an extra session of the Senate for ten days, for the purpose of considering any executive or other business that might be brought before it, or for the purpose of sitting as a court of impeachment, if necessary.[6]   And so the Senate met immediately after the expiration of the regular session March 2 with but five absentees.   Democratic Senators evidently opposed obstacles, for the journal shows a resolution to the effect that that body was not legally in session, as the governor was without authority to summon it.[7]   Fifty additional sergeants and as many as "the president

---

[1] February 27.   [2] March 2.   [3] *Republican*, February 22.
[4] *Ibid.*, February 27.   [5] March 3.   [6] Sen. Jour., 283.
[7] This resolution was later expunged from the journal.

deemed necessary" were authorized,[1] action seeming to indicate that trouble was anticipated. The message harped upon delinquent taxes and the necessity of devising a way to force the wealthy citizens to meet their obligations.[2] With frequent adjournments and short executive sessions the session glided quickly by. The question of a successor to Pinchback was agitated on March 12.

Attacks against the inefficiency of the Assembly continued until well into the summer.[3] The Republican Senators presented an explanation to the public which asserted that all Republicans stood ready to pass reforms while the Democrats frittered away the entire session in an effort to gain partisan advantage, and had abandoned unfinished work at the very end in a foolish attempt "to seize the State government by a revolutionary *coup d'état*."[4] Charges against the legality of some bills were made, such as the railroad aid bill for a five mill tax, and the act chartering the North Louisiana Railroad, since it did not pass the Senate. Probably the *Times* hit the nail on the head in the statement that the coming campaign "was a matter of more engrossing interest to our legislators than the welfare of the People."[5]

[1] Sen. Jour., 1876, 284–5. The executive proceedings were not published.
[2] *Ibid.*, Extra Sess., 10.
[3] See *Times*, July 3.
[4] *Republican*, March 2.
[5] *Times*, March 3.

CHAPTER XVIII

Louisiana a Storm Center in the Election of 1876

THE manœuvres for the most exciting election in our history opened appropriately in what was to prove the pivotal State. It will be recalled[1] that even in 1875 the Bourbon wing of the Democratic party had pressed through a State convention—for local objects, it is true; that they had so far succeeded as to bring together a group of politicians in early January, 1876, when the election wheels were set in motion by the appointment of delegates to the National convention at St. Louis, and by the creation of a State central committee.

This committee in its address of February 10 struck the key-note of the campaign in the following words:

> The people, for whom this committee speaks, are resolved, in this centennial of their liberties, to test the relative strength of intelligence and ignorance. They will use no violence, but all the means in their power will be employed to defeat the further rule of the vicious and ignorant in this State. . . . What remains to be done, is the perfection of the Democratic-Conservative organization in all parishes of the State where action has not been taken.[2]

And it urged the Conservative legislators to exhaust every means to prevent the passage of an election bill

---

[1] See preceding chapter.   [2] *Annual Cyclopedia*, 1876, 483.

establishing a returning-board with any power "which will enable them to defeat the will of the people as expressed at the ballot-box."[1]

The Republicans met at New Orleans on May 30 and 31 to select delegates to the National convention. The principal matters, as admission of contesting delegations and the appointment of a Committee on Credentials, were discussed in caucus for an hour before the doors of the convention were opened. When the body was called to order, it was found that the colored delegation outnumbered the white as two to one. Great difficulty was experienced in the preliminary work, for there were a dozen competitors for even the humble post of doorkeeper. A perfect babel of voices—for the best lungs seemed to carry the day—rendered the transaction of business under parliamentary forms impossible. Outside the bars, the house was filled, the galleries crowded, while the windows, forty feet above the floor of the hall, were a curious mixture of rusty boots and sandals. Members smoked and sweltered.[2] After considerable time spent in clearing the hall and in adjusting contesting delegations the convention slowly got to work and selected as delegates at large old war-horses—Packard, Kellogg, Pinchback, and Brown, thus evenly dividing the honors between white men and black. In the evening came a lengthy set of resolutions, recognizing the centennial, submitting certain measures of National policy, and urging just support for National works of internal improvement. Delegates were left free in the choice of President but a decided hint was added in a very hearty indorsement of Grant and Morton.[3]

As in the Conservative address, so here we have a clue

[1] *Annual Cyclopedia*, 1876, 484.
[2] Although the account of a hostile paper, it is probably not far from the truth.   [3] *Times*, June 1.

26

as to the lines along which the campaign might be fought
in the resolution,

That the assassination of many hundreds of prominent
Union men . . . the massacre of thousands of inoffensive
colored citizens, the relegation of nearly all the Southern
States to the control of the disloyal elements whose treason
brought about the war . . . indicate grave national dangers,
which demand the enactment of additional laws to secure to
every citizen the inalienable rights of life and liberty.[1]

Within less than a month the party assembled again to
nominate candidates for State offices. The rivalry within
the party had resulted in two slates: a Kellogg-Packard
combination *versus* a Warmoth-Pinchback alliance. The
first round for Warmoth had been fired in the Homer *Iliad*
in June, 1875, when it was declared that Louisiana might
have a worse governor and the Republicans a worse
candidate.[2] Warmoth, unwilling to renounce his old
power, set to work upon a most active and open canvass.[3]
The opinion seemed to prevail, according to the *Times*,
that he would go into the convention with more strength
than any other candidate, but insufficient to win the
nomination, as the entire strength of the State adminis-

---

[1] *Annual Cyclopedia*, 1876, 484. Hahn had dwelt upon this subject in
his speech the second day. On June 17 a group of about one thousand
Radicals gathered to indorse Hayes and Wheeler, the colored element
constituting about one-half the number. Warmoth was greeted royally;
the telegram to Hayes bore his name.

[2] The *Times* alleged bribery, June 15, while the *Republican* explained it
as a "gratuitous compliment to a gentleman, as much sinned against as
sinning, who might be allowed another and more favorable chance." June
17. But seventeen days later the latter tried to ruin his chances by printing a telegram from a New York broker who had canceled his order for
State consols, because of Warmoth's prominence in the convention.

[3] In June he was devoting his time to the city. "His headquarters on
St. Louis Street are constantly invaded by a crowd, and he is kept constantly advised of what is going on in the different wards." It was generally known that Grant opposed him. See *Times*, May 25, June 20.

tration was being used against him.[1]   After some doubt as to whether Kellogg meant to enter the lists again, he came out June 23 with an explicit statement that he was a candidate for neither the governorship nor senatorship.[2]   A general party caucus on the evening of June 26, at which Pinchback announced his own candidacy, excited much comment.   But the strongest name in the field was Packard's, despite his protestation that he did not want the office, for thirty or more delegates from the country came pledged to his support.   The Warmoth men worked with more discipline but only one ward[3] voted as a unit in his favor at the election of delegates on June 21.

Delegates began to arrive in the city as much as five and six days early to attend the caucuses and pull wires. On the day before the opening of the convention, the temperature stood at fever heat.   Near the state-house, the streets and banquettes were filled with a motley crowd of not less than a thousand persons, the colored element largely in the majority.   In the preliminary discussion Stamps was opposed to Pinchback for temporary chairman.

At the formal opening at Mechanics Institute on June 27 by Flanders, a Packard man, it was apparent that a spirit of insubordination and disorder was rife, due to the impression that in factions so nearly equal in strength, any advantage would need to be won by hard work.

---

[1] During the convention the *Picayune* expressed the fear that he might be foisted on the State by the Central Committee after the nominee, by preconcerted plan, had resigned.

[2] *Times*, June 24.   He eventually threw all his strength for Packard, though a henchman stated to a committee in 1878 that he never intended that Packard be nominated.   House Misc. Doc., 45 Cong., 3 Sess., No. 31, 916.

[3] Disorder had appeared already in the preliminary ward caucuses, where all who could had crowded to the platform to champion someone.

Stamps and Pinchback both took seats at the secretary's desk. Two hundred and twenty-three delegates answered the roll, with forty contestants present. The Warmoth party occupied the center of the hall, every movement directed by the ex-governor's leaders with the keenest interest. The fight over the temporary chairmanship lasted until nearly five in the afternoon, for the administration party insisted on a *viva voce* ballot in order to hold their men in line. When the first vote was taken on the method of balloting, the scene was said to beggar description. The yelling was so loud that it was impossible to hear anything ten feet from the platform; a dozen men were on their feet at once, while leaders moved hither and thither to direct operations. A majority of one for the closed ballot proclaimed a victory for Warmoth. For fifteen minutes the convention went wild. When the ballot for temporary chairman was announced, it seemed as if the Warmoth party had lost their senses[1]— men jumped upon chairs, threw their hats to the ceiling, yelled at the top of their voices, hugged each other, and wrestled with one another in their delirium. In his speech upon taking the chair, Pinchback declared that he was no man's man and should appoint the committees to give satisfaction to both sides.

The group lost nothing of its discordant spirit by its transference to the St. Charles Theater, where it gathered the second day, stronger, freer, hotter than ever. On the third day the Committee on Credentials reported, allowing the contested wards to Warmoth in nearly every case. The chairman instantly moved the adoption of the report together with the previous question. Action was taken so quickly that the house hardly realized what had occurred. But in a few moments every person was

[1] The *Times* pays Warmoth the tribute of saying that if money was used, it was too quietly to be detected.

on his feet, the lobby yelling, while one-half the delegates were trying to get the attention of the chair, and calling loudly for the minority report. The uproar was heard until men came running for squares from all directions and shut out the light in the windows.[1] Packard showed his usual moderation by urging order and Pinchback his violence by insisting on finishing a speech which assailed Kellogg and the Republicans.[2] It even became necessary to summon the police to eject some contestants who engaged in a free fight. The hostile faction attempted to force Stamps into the chair, thereby precipitating a scene of pandemonium in which pistols were drawn.[3] Even a conference of the leaders and candidates failed to produce definite results the fourth day, but did coerce Pinchback into deference to a motion for reconsideration on the credentials. But still the seven hours of that day were wasted in howling and disputing over the same question, until the convention degenerated, as Pinchback in his disgust declared, into a mere mob.[4] There was even danger of the crowd seizing the hats from the tellers when they attempted to count the votes.[5] Ugly feeling ran so high that on July 1 one of the delegates was seriously wounded while striving to gain admission to the hall.

On the fifth day all factions desired peace to save the

---

[1] Pinchback elevated his feet to the table with the remark, "You might as well take it easy, for you've got to stand it."

[2] He taunted Kellogg with the intention of carrying his influence over to the Democracy unless the convention bowed to his will.

[3] The idea of ousting Pinchback had undoubtedly been mooted in administration caucus June 30, according to the *Times*, July 2.

[4] Even the *Republican* was driven into disgust: "Nothing was done all day but howl, raise silly points of order, bully the chair, and each other, and listen to two or three windy orations from as many demagogues." It declared that the Democracy could not behave much worse. July 1.

[5] *Times*, July 1.

party from ruin.[1] A compromise among the leaders, admitting certain delegations on a half-vote, made possible a permanent organization, which continued Pinchback as president and appointed a Committee on Platform. This committee recommended the reconvening of the convention to renominate for governor or lieutenant-governor in case of a vacancy.[2] After indorsing the Cincinnati platform and the candidacy of Hayes and Wheeler, it defined its position on financial questions as approval of the funding-scheme, reduction of the debt, and the resumption of specie-payment.[3]

By the sixth day[4] the body had settled down to more orderly procedure and to the business in hand. On the first vote for governor, Packard led with Warmoth a close second. After the second ballot Warmoth settled the issue by withdrawing in Packard's favor amid pro-longed cheers.[5] Antoine was made the nominee for second place by acclamation; and Brown put forward again for superintendent of education. The work of naming the lesser candidates proceeded slowly on the last day in a depleted body, for candidates for each position loomed up by the dozen. The slate as completed showed Honoré for secretary, Johnson for auditor, Hunt for attorney-general, and Warmoth nominee for Congress from the first district, where a strong Republican majority insured election.[6] Pinchback retained the honor of chairmanship

---

[1] The mob, though shut out, broke in. The *Picayune* had not greatly overshot the mark when, on July 1, it predicted work for the coroner.

[2] There seemed to be constant fear that Warmoth might slip in through the resignation of a black-horse candidate or through election by the Central Committee. [3] *Times*, July 2.

[4] The writer is dependent for the account of July 2–6 on one-sided reports only, as the files of the *Republican* are missing. This is also true of the Democratic convention from July 23–6.

[5] *Picayune*, July 4.

[6] He later withdrew, but Packard manœuvred with him until he became a nominee for representative from Plaquemines Parish.

of the Central Committee, while Kellogg was rewarded with a position among the Presidential electors. On the whole the arraignment of the *Picayune* is none too severe:

> The scenes enacted within the week at the St. Charles Theater would be sufficient to cover any party with infamy were they presented to any other section of the Union but the South. . . . There ignorance and ruffianism ran in high and unrestrained riot, and every act and every utterance betrayed a fixed and brutal disregard of the interests of good government.[1]

The comments of the adverse press on the nominees[2] are interesting. Hear the *Democrat's* opinion of the man who headed the ticket: "Adding the prejudices of birth and sectional hate to the venom of party greed and personal ambition, S. B. Packard is, perhaps, the most complete personal and political representative of U. S. Grant that the hideous phantasmagoria of the past eight years has produced."[3] Or just as bitter, the *Picayune*: "We reject Packard as a mediator; we reject him in every capacity which implies confidence, respect, or toleration."[4] And later, "He is only known in Louisiana as a Federal officeholder who has done his utmost to secure the interference of the General Government in our State affairs, whenever it was necessary to secure the success of his party."[5] But the *German Gazette* declared, "His most violent and bitter opponents acknowledge that he—Marshal Packard, of the whole Radical clique which for eight years has ruled the State—has been one of the few, per-

---

[1] July 6.
[2] The *Bulletin* describes Antoine as formerly an excellent barber, subsequently a chevalier d'industrie in Shreveport, and since 1872 "Mr. Warmoth's bland and suave Lieutenant."   [3] July 6.
[4] See also the *Picayune* of March 1, 1875, July 4, 1876.   [5] *Ibid.*

haps the only honest one."[1]   The description by Nordhoff
has the value of coming from an outsider:

> The strongest and probably the most dangerous politician
> in the State on either side is the United States marshal,
> Packard.   He is reputed to be a man of unflinching courage,
> strong will, and no scruples.   His body is large and somewhat
> heavy, and his mind does not move rapidly.   His single idea
> is to keep Louisiana in Republican hands, and his only method
> is to mass the colored vote.   To him is due largely the color
> line. . . .   A part of his strength lies in that he is believed
> pecuniarily honest.   He has a little the air of a fanatic, but
> he is in reality an extremely adroit and unscrupulous politician
> who tolerates no rival near his throne.[2]

There was no gainsaying the fact that his nomination
produced a great deal of dissatisfaction in the party—so
much that it was debated among leading Republicans
whether it were not best to protest against it.[3]   It caused
some defection within the party, for Pinchback and
Warmoth both abandoned the State shortly after the
convention, though both held office on the Central Committee,[4] while Sypher retired to his plantation.

The Democratic nominating convention was fixed for
July 24[5] at Baton Rouge.   Among a number of candidates for governor, Penn seemed in the beginning to have
the strongest support, especially among the commercial men,[6] but his executive committee pledged itself

---

[1] July 4, 1876.   [2] *Cotton States*, 64.
[3] According to Morey and Sypher, House Misc. Doc., 45 Cong., 3 Sess.,
No. 31, 822, 808.   Morey believed that with another candidate there would
have been no bulldozing in Ouachita Parish.   *Ibid.*
[4] An Election Committee, created to take its place, really threw the management of the campaign into the hands of Jewett, as secretary of the
committee.   *Ibid.*, 1457.
[5] This date had been selected as early as April 21 by the Central Committee.
[6] See *Bulletin* of July 9, *German Gazette* of that date, *Times* of July 10,
all urging the claims of Penn.

to support the nominee of the party. But already by July 14 the delegates of southern Louisiana were speaking of General Nicholls of Assumption Parish as a man who could carry the nomination, showing clearly that the issue would lie between a city or country representative. The ardor, however, seemed dampened by his positive refusal to appear as a candidate. But it soon became apparent that no representative of the Bourbon or narrow Democrats, as Vorhies, Wiltz, Ogden, or McEnery, could rally the independent or other aggressive factions of the party to his banner.[1]

Promptly at noon the chairman called the body to order, secured the appointment of a temporary chairman, and appointed the committees on Credentials and Organization. Prolonged debate over some contested cases deferred the report of the first-named committee until the third day, when the disputes were settled only by admitting two delegations on half-votes,[2] and the contestants from the second city ward. The permanent chairman was then promptly selected. As a body, it was a most earnest and intelligent assembly.

The all-absorbing topic, the nomination for governor, led to numerous prolonged caucuses, and all sorts of rumors of changes. The country delegates in their caucus on Sunday night before the convention had seemed united

---

[1] See the *Times* of July 18.
Several bloody scrimmages, and the scratching and splitting of the ticket at the ward elections of delegates, did not augur well for the harmony of the convention. *Ibid.*, July 20.

[2] The color question came into play through a charge against one faction of receiving colored votes; whereupon the other faction charged the presence of a negro in the opposing delegation. The first faction refused to accept a half-vote on a threat of withdrawal. Marr tried to hold the convention to action consistent with its promises to accord negroes all civil and political rights. Still the city delegation voted almost solidly against admitting the delegation with the negro member.

upon only one point—the desire for a country executive. At the actual voting on the third day, Wiltz led on the first three ballots, McEnery withdrawing in favor of Nicholls after the second ballot. But before the result of the fourth ballot was announced, East Baton Rouge changed its vote to the Nicholls faction, whereupon the nomination was made unanimous amid great enthusiasm. With manifestations of satisfaction, Wiltz was given second place on the ticket. The former was greatly affected in his speech of acceptance. He declared that if elected, he would enter office, untrammeled by any clique or faction, that he would enforce the law without regard to race or color, and would give office to no man for supporting him, at the same time condemning fraud of every kind.[1]

General Francis T. Nicholls, a member of one of the most prominent families of the State, was born in 1834. Graduation from West Point had been followed by service in the Seminole War, artillery service in the regular army, and outpost duty in California. He changed the nature of his work to law in 1856 by resigning his commission, but entered Confederate service, naturally, at the outbreak of the Civil War. Rapid advancement brought him to the rank of Brigadier-General. He sacrificed an arm under Stonewall Jackson and lost his left leg at Chancellorsville. At the close of the war, he resumed his law practice in Assumption Parish, where already by 1876

---

[1] *Times*, July 27. Nicholls had insisted that he did not want office and refused to listen to the first five or six men who approached him. Finally, friends secured a tacit consent to present his name if the convention could not agree on anyone else after several ballots. But his supporters felt that he must be announced the first day. After the nomination, he called Judge Breaux, who was present as a delegate, aside and said, "See what trouble I am in." Wiltz's friends were adroit enough to make the nomination unanimous in order to secure him second place. *Times*, July 20. Personal statement of Judge Breaux.

he had won a high position.[1] He had the respect and confidence of Democrats and Republicans alike, of white men and of many negroes. He was no politician, but his incorruptibility, his fearlessness and firmness, combined with great innate modesty, appealed to everyone.[2]

At an evening session of the convention on the same day the Committee on Platform reported a severe arraignment of the Republican party for corruption, misrule, and violation of the spirit and letter of the constitution in fomenting dissension between the races; it declared the party in favor of a peaceful election,[3] but added a demand for the protection of the colored Conservatives in the free exercise of the franchise; recognized the finality of the war amendments; and declared for reform, pledging the party to an economical administration, to a curtailment of expenditure, and reduction of taxes to the lowest limit "commensurate with necessary expenses and the preservation of the public faith."[4]

The ticket was completed on the fourth day with the nomination of H. N. Ogden for attorney-general; W. E. Strong for secretary of state; Allen Jumel for auditor; Lusher for superintendent of schools. McEnery was recognized with the office of elector-at-large.[5] The convention closed with a resolution urging the State Congressmen to use every means in their power to secure an appropriation for levees; and with a commendation of McEnery's administration.

At the chief landings all along the river, Nicholls and Wiltz received ovations, the choice arousing considerable enthusiasm, even in New Orleans. The press extolled the former's exemplary character and eminent abilities,[6]

---

[1] *Cyclopedia of National Biography.* Judge Breaux said of him, in speaking to the writer, "I never knew a more upright character than he."
[2] *Ann. Cyclop.*, 1876, 485.   [3] *Ibid.*
[4] *Ibid.*   [5] *Times*, July 28.   [6] *Picayune*, July 27.

while large ratification meetings in the parishes brought out evidence of party loyalty. Especially was the gathering at Lafayette Square on August 10 a fusing of business men, politicians, and voters to the number of fifteen thousand. Ward clubs marched about the square under the light of flaring torches and rockets to the sound of fife and drum and the National salute. About six hundred colored voters were conspicuous by their participation.[1]

The *Republican*, after first hailing Nicholls's nomination as a blow to the "Last Ditchers,"[2] soon called attention to the fact that he owed his nomination to Confederate sentiment[3]; that not a Whig or negro had found a place on the ticket; and that it would sound the recall of all the White League armies and bulldozing frauds of Louisiana.[4]

The campaign opened early[5] and was, on the whole, far more peaceful and freer from disorders than the most sanguine had dared to hope.[6] Some outbreaks, arising late in 1875 and early in 1876, were local and seemed a closed issue until the doubtful outcome of the election dragged them once more into the limelight before investigating committees.

During 1875 and the year following, property owners formed companies and were active in suppressing the thieving by negroes, which had become intolerable. At

---

[1] See the *Times* of August 11 for a full account.

[2] July 28. It thought it easier to defeat Nicholls than any other man named, except, perhaps, McEnery.

[3] The Mansfield *Reporter* objected because he had been a Confederate general.

[4] July 26. And it insisted that Nicholls's departure for the Federal Senate would leave Wiltz governor.

[5] The formal opening of a series of rallies in the capital might be placed on August 19, though skirmishing had been going on for months.

[6] "Many have apprehended that the approaching campaign in this State would be unusually vindictive, bitter, and, perhaps, bloody." *Times*, May 7.

first, they were known as Regulators, but by July of the campaign year they were being organized throughout the parishes into a more compact organization as rifle clubs of thirty to fifty members, equipped with a good rifle or pistol, and well-mounted, and were designated by Radicals as White Leaguers under another name.[1]   As usual, they attempted a defensive position by asserting that associations of armed Republicans had been formed among the freedmen as the Union Stop[2] and Councils of Freedom.[3] Before long the Radicals had fastened on the Conservative companies the invidious name of "Bulldozer."[4]   The purpose, as stated by the head of the organization in Ouachita, was for "the mutual protection of ourselves

[1] The majority of the House Committee of Congress took such a view.

[2] *Republican*, June 24, 29; *Times*, August 11.   One Logwood admitted that negroes carried pistols constantly.   Sen. Repts., 44 Cong., 2 Sess., No. 701, 39.   It was even asserted that negroes were banded together to kill white people.   House Misc. Doc., 45 Cong., 3 Sess., No. 31, 589, 305.

[3] The *Republican* ridiculed the *Times* and *Picayune* for thus advertising ward clubs.

[4] The *Times* published an interesting etymology of this word: "To recover backsliding blacks to the Republican party, secret societies were formed. Notice was served on a suspect to come to a certain point to take an oath to the Union Stop.   On the third refusal he was brought in and whipped with a bull whip.   In obstinate cases, a bull's dose of several hundred lashes on the bare back was administered.   After being exposed, Radicals applied the term to any intimidator."   Nov. 16.

For another version, I am indebted to Conerly, Pike County: "It arose with Louis Waggoner, a blacksmith in Clinton, East Feliciana, who, irritated with someone at the inception of the organization of the Bull Whippers, remarked, 'Tam him, I'll bulldosch him.'   The word then grew to bulldoze, and lastly bulldozer."

The following definition by a Democrat may throw additional light on this interesting character: "To have been a bulldozer, it was necessary to have been a native desperado, a reckless character, an unscrupulous local politician, willing to stuff a ballot-box or shoot a nigger, or, for that matter, a white man, in order to get an office.   They were always a millstone about the neck of the Democratic party, and, as Kellogg always admitted, their performances were a Godsend to the Republican party."   House Misc. Doc., 45 Cong., 3 Sess., No. 31,935.

and all others who might require that protection," including the negroes who might "come with us in the election," as it was known that they feared to desert the Radicals.[1] It was only quasi-military, held the leader, as there was no order-book.   The membership varied, probably, in the different parishes, but consisted in general of propertyholders and good citizens, according to J. R. Brooke, one of the principal Republican witnesses.   He testified that the regulators included nearly the whole white population —all the most reputable—and, in some cases, negroes. Not only were Republicans often members, but in many instances, chief officers.[2]   It was insisted that they were rarely out with their arms, unless accompanying a sheriff; that if they attended Republican meetings, arms were not in evidence[3]; that they rode during the day only as a patrol under orders of the chief[4]; that their political complexion was due to the fact that whenever any criminal became the object of punishment, he claimed to be the victim of political persecution.

On the other hand, we find testimony from apparently sincere men,[5] who declared that it was the action of the common class of white people, "to scare people for political purposes."   Ludeling, hardly an unprejudiced witness however, gives hearsay evidence of "both white and colored, that the members of those clubs had been riding about the country at night, visiting the cabins of Republicans and threatening them with violence, if they did not

[1] Dr. Aby.   Sen. Repts., 44 Cong., 2 Sess., No. 701, 787–8.

[2] Especially true in West Feliciana.   House Repts., 44 Cong., 2 Sess., No. 156, Part i., 15.

[3] Ibid., 46–7.

[4] Testimony of Dr. Aby, Sen. Repts., 44 Cong., 2 Sess., No. 701, 788. In West Feliciana nine clubs, exclusively Democratic and white, were reported.   Sen. Exe. Doc., 44 Cong., 2 Sess., No. 2, 11.

[5] Such as Morgan of West Feliciana, who spoke in just and affectionate terms of his old master.   Sen. Repts., 44 Cong., 2 Sess., No. 701, 2351.

attend democratic meetings and join democratic clubs, and in some instances inflicting injuries upon their persons."[1] The Republican minority of the House Committee found all the turbulent and dangerous element embodied in them; found that they descended to the inhumanity of shooting to death without provocation, hanging at will and burning out of house and home harmless negroes.[2] The truth, as usual, probably lies somewhere between the extremes. Undoubtedly the appearance of armed men riding over the country, as one negro said, "took more effect than anything else"[3]; undoubtedly the planters did feel the need of some organization to preserve order, to punish and stop the stealing and crime[4]; but just as undoubtedly, they probably could not resist the temptation to wield political pressure, sometimes aggravating the very evils they intended to correct; in their zeal to drive out incompetent officials, Democrats might possibly have expelled only the Republican leaders of the negroes.

No one who has traced the repeated comments in the Republican press through that year could fail to see the preparations for overturning the election, should the face of the returns show a Democratic victory. In

---

[1] Sen. Repts, 44 Cong., 2 Sess., No. 701, 856.   E. L. Weber held before the Mississippi investigating committee that the clubs must rob and plunder to subsist. Sen. Repts., 44 Cong., 1 Sess., No. 527, 1567-71.

[2] House Repts., 44 Cong., 2 Sess., No. 156, Part ii., 6.   The evidence of their terrorism becomes at times humorous, as when Logwood was intimidated by hearing a band "rid" by at night and sing:

"A church to keep I have,
A God to glorify,
If a nigger don't vote for us,
They shall forever die."
Sen. Misc. Doc., 44 Cong., 2 Sess., No. 14, 97.

[3] Ibid., 95.

[4] The case of whipping a negress for cohabiting with a white man, who went scot-free, is less laudable than pursuing a desperado from Texas. House Repts., 44 Cong., 2 Sess., No. 156, Part i., 39-40.

January the *Republican* was printing in double type,
"The Week's Record of Outrages," "The Ku-Klux in
Absolute Control,"[1] and declared that these measures
were part of a system.   In February the same paper was
convinced that a "spirit of violence exists in the Red
River districts which commands its followers, like the
fiery cross, to obey under penalty of political destruction."[2]
The Port Hudson affair afforded it an opportunity for
drawing a very black picture of terror among the blacks,
their homes abandoned, their summer labor lost, their
families destitute, and the parish abandoned by hundreds.[3]
In the next issue it admitted that the rioters were adventurers and roughs, but blamed the whites for that state of
affairs.[4]   By July it had worked itself up to such a pitch
that it could discern another civil war impending.[5]   A
month later its full cannon was trained against the regulators.   In its issues of August 6 and 9 it printed affidavits
of violence from East Baton Rouge, given before a State
investigating committee.   Throughout that month and
the next some allusion appeared almost daily.[6]   It refused to believe the Democratic assurances of good will
and proclaimed a "Shotgun Campaign."[7]   It seized upon

[1] *Republican*, January 21.   [2] *Ibid.*, February 24.
[3] *Ibid.*, June 30.   Yet blacks increased twenty per cent in Ouachita,
1870–5; twenty-four per cent in the State as a whole.
[4] At times the charge was made that Democrats invited ruffians in to do
their dirty work for them.   Sen. Repts., 44 Cong., 1 Sess., No. 527, xxvii.
[5] "It will begin in this campaign.   It will enter the electoral college.   It
will present such cases of violence and fraud that the nation will not submit
to a claim of victory resulting from such proceeding."   July 16.
[6] August 9 it promised more concerning Baton Rouge and the Felicianas.
See August 22, 30, 31, Sept. 10, 12, Oct. 12, 19.   Oct. 3 appeared a heinous
story of coercion.   The following on October 5 made good capital: "A
Republican at Bayou Sera Convention said, 'If I had come in here with a
nigger's skull tied to the pommel of my saddle, I might have stood a
chance!'"
[7] Antoine insisted that he had proof that many Republicans had been
obliged to hide in the swamps to save their lives.

the pretext afforded by the Dinkgrave murder to send a citizen north to investigate, who found the Republicans of Monroe completely terrorized, "the greater part of the colored people having left for the woods, or wherever they could secure safety."[1]   The nearer the election approached, the blacker grew the picture:

We have had the affidavits of negroes, maltreated until inhuman cruelty could devise no additional punishment, that the Democrats of East Baton Rouge and the Felicianas have determined to crush the Republican majorities. . . . The result is shown that in these parishes colored men are driven into the Democratic clubs and mass meetings, and will be as helplessly driven to the polls unless protection is afforded.[2]

And when it ran out of Louisiana outrages, it printed gory tales of bulldozing in Mississippi.[3]

The Democratic press, while admitting a state of unjustified terror,[4] insisted that the campaign had "been planned with negro massacres as a necessary feature in order to afford an excuse for the use of troops," and that the disorders were part of a scheme to provoke retaliation and bloodshed.[5]   It urged significantly, "Let us determine not to be provoked."   A committee later stated that testimony established the fact "that prominent Republicans considered the killing of a black man as equivalent to $50,000 of a campaign fund for the party."[6]

[1] The report lacks the earmarks of truth, and is highly inflammatory. Sept. 10.   See this book, p. 432.   [2] *Republican,* October 1.
[3] *Ibid.,* Sept. 29.   It is also worth noting that Northern Republicans were alert for weak spots in the Southern armor as is attested by the suggestion of the chairman of the Indiana committee to the editor of a Hoosier paper, speaking of Southern outrages, "I suggest you give them as great prominence as possible in your paper from this time until after election." *Record,* 43 Cong., 2 Sess., 305.   [4] *Times,* September 13.
[5] *Ibid.,* Sept. 3.
[6] House Repts., 44 Cong., 2 Sess., No. 156, Part i., 14.
    27

It was early felt by both sides that the climax of the reconstruction struggle was involved in this campaign.[1] And so everyone was urged to the most strenuous exertions, and dire pictures of calamity held up in case of victory by the opposing party.[2] More Conservatives seem to have participated than had done so since before the war; the old line Whig Association, which included business men who had before taken little part in politics, took a hand[3]; the strictest of the Bourbons, who, although opposed to radicalism, had lived outside of politics, came out from their long retirement[4]; many who had disdained to stand an hour among the roughs and negroes to vote, had been compelled by poverty to stand with the roughs for work, until they were glad to register in order to force the roughs and negroes out of office[5]; while the better class took control of the convention and campaign. The party pledged itself from the very beginning to a vigorous campaign[6] and to the attainment of negro co-operation by peaceful means.[7]   The *Democrat* summarized

[1] Note the prediction of the Bossier *Banner*, Oct. 1, 1875: "We think it too soon to inaugurate a campaign that, judging from the signs, bids fair to be one of the most exciting that has ever occurred on this continent." The *Times* felt that no election that has ever occurred in the State, not even that on secession, was "fraught with weightier consequences than the election now before us."   July 21.   [2] *Republican*, June 23.

[3] *Times*, August 22.   [4] *Ibid.*, June 3.

[5] *Ibid.*, July 21.   The *Picayune* said July 10 that more business men were interesting themselves than it had ever known to do so.

A story was told of a railroad president, who had never had anything to do with politics, organizing a negro club and bringing members on cars to many meetings.   House Misc. Doc., 45 Cong., 3 Sess., No. 31, La., 593.

[6] One can hardly reject the testimony of Gauthreaux, Head of the Democratic Registration Bureau, when he says that Judge Dibble, Chairman of the Republican Committee, called him foolish to work so hard, for "no matter how the election went, no matter how large a majority we received, even if it was 20,000, we would be counted out by the returning-board."   *Ibid.*, 1054, Washington.

[7] So well did the Democrats achieve their purpose that Sypher admitted, after conversing with men who made the canvass with Packard, that

well the actuating spirit: "The idea is peace at all hazards, and perfect, thorough, universal organization in every neighborhood, for the purpose of preserving the peace."[1]

There had been, ever since the franchise was given the negro, a small nucleus of colored Democrats.[2] There is no doubt but that the Democratic side worked hard to gain over colored men to their ticket, while there is considerable evidence that their opponents made but little effort.[3] Colored men were made officers in white clubs, the former master as president seated beside his former slave as vice-president; colored preachers and leaders were invited to speak to white Conservatives, were sent out to canvass for the party and to organize other clubs[4]; negro voters were enrolled in the same clubs with Conservative whites to protect them from Republican intimidation; and negroes formed clubs of their own. Merchants and planters seemed to think that the great effort should be made in this campaign to break the color-line.[5] Old-

---

Republicans had been treated generally with kindness and courtesy. House Misc. Doc., 45 Cong., 3 Sess., No. 31, Wash., 809.

[1] Sept. 12. For a good résumé of Democratic methods, see testimony of Ex-Governor Wickliffe, *ibid.*, 548, La.

[2] In Vernon Parish a supervisor testified to 75 or 80 negro voters, who lived on terms of substantial equality with the whites and had always voted the Democratic ticket. Only two Republican votes were cast in the parish. House Repts., 44 Cong., 2 Sess., No. 156, 139. Also House Misc. Doc., 44 Cong., 2 Sess., No. 34, Part iiii., 1–2, where the speaker in a colored community had not known of any Republican votes until the election—two then.

[3] Testimony of Lieutenant Gerlach, House Repts., 76. Gerlach had never been an active partisan of any party.

[4] They thus established some fifteen clubs with a colored membership of a thousand voters in West Feliciana. House Misc. Doc., 45 Cong., No. 31, 555, La. See also House Repts., 44 Cong., 2 Sess., No. 156, Part i., 49–50. A lawyer tells of a Democratic club where with marked success members agreed, each to be a committee of one to get negro members. House Misc. Doc., 44 Cong., 2 Sess., No. 34, Part vi., 208.

[5] *Times*, August 25. See the testimony of Powell, House Misc. Doc., 45

fashioned barbecues were prepared at which they took their places, white and black alternately; there were parades, the scenes sometimes resembling old-time camp-meetings, in which the negroes joined with loud hurrahs.[1] The Seventeenth Ward Democratic Club and the Fossil Guards asked all colored men to join. Where the leaders of the colored race go, the masses generally follow; and so we find that they crowded to Democratic meetings, carried banners in the processions, hallooing louder and taking as much interest as any white man.[2]

There is no doubt but that these dramatics and merry-makings appealed to the negro,[3] but not without force was the argument presented through the channel which usually reaches the heart—the pocket-book. It was presented to the black, in personal conversation, especially by the planter, that the Republicans, who had proved dishonest and corrupt, were ruining them; that the interests of the races were identical; that what influenced the fortune of the planter affected the laborer on his land; that their school-money had been misapplied; that they were grossly and unnecessarily overtaxed; that, if the parties who had deceived them were retained in office, it was the negroes' fault. One man testified that he made a deep impression on the negro by showing him that he was taxed $22 on a horse valued at $60; $7 on a cow worth $25[4]; $13 on a piano worth $40; $9.65 on a cow

Cong., 3 Sess., No. 31, La., 550; of Leake, 554–5; of Burke, Wash., 1004; of Roberts, 898.

[1] Sen. Repts., 44 Cong., 2 Sess., No. 701, 393; House Misc. Doc., 45 Cong., 3 Sess., La., 555.

[2] Evidence of Wickliffe, House Misc. Doc., 45 Cong., 3 Sess., No. 31, 548–9. Wash.

[3] One negro remarked that it seemed like one long holiday. House Misc. Doc., 44 Cong., 2 Sess., No. 34, Part iii., 82.

[4] House Repts., 44 Cong., 2 Sess., No. 156, Part i., 49. See also testimony of Col. F. P. Stubbs, House Misc. Doc., 44 Cong., 2 Sess., No. 34, Part vi., 183.

and calf worth $30. They were disabused of the false impression concerning their superior numbers, dinned into their minds by the Republicans, and shown that they "could not resist the whites."[1]   Another telling argument was used: when they were ill, they invariably called in Democratic doctors; in litigation came to Democratic lawyers; in domestic troubles turned to their old Democratic masters; why not in politics?[2]

The arguments fell on the more willing ears that negroes were already restive and dissatisfied with the government[3]; with the robbery of the money for public education and the failure to provide instruction for their children, and with their losses in the Freedmen's Bank.[4]   The whites

---

[1] House Misc. Doc., 45 Cong., 3 Sess., No. 31, La., 550, Powell of West Feliciana.   A lawyer said that the result was won by personal persuasion.

[2] *Ibid.*, 555.

[3] It is scarcely possible that the following reasoning is sound: "Their leaders held no social position there, and I rather inferred that they (the negroes) were ashamed of them and wanted to associate themselves with what they thought were the gentlemen of the parish."   This witness tried to show that they held the balance of power.   Powell, *ibid.*, 550.

One negro of East Baton Rouge testified that they "talked together as they were all going to destruction," that they had been discussing it for four years and had advised with white Democrats.   Another declared he heard men talk when they were jogging along on the road and in the grog-shop; they all pretty much said that they must have a change and that they were going to try the Democrats and see if they would do better. House Repts., 44 Cong., 2 Sess., No. 156, 68.   One was willing to join the Democrats "to take down that stealing."   *Ibid.*   The *Times* records many cases of negroes turning Democrat, though the writer regards this newspaper evidence of very little value.   It is included rather to show the tactics of the times than as proof.

[4] A clever cartoon appeared in the *Democrat* of September 24.   Before the steps of a building placarded "Office to Let—Carpetbaggers not wanted," stands a negro kicking a white man off the steps.   In the hand of the latter is a carpet-bag lettered S. B. P., Maine.   Another on October 8 presented a bank teller's window and grating, separating a carpet-bagger from a row of negroes, who are depositing money in a box, above which stand the words, "Place the proceeds of your Honest Toil in this box, where they will be perfectly safe."

promised longer school terms, higher wages, and lower taxes.

Another cause of negro conversion to the Democracy was the unpopularity of the State or, more often, parish ticket with the negro leaders.[1]   An address to the colored citizens from one of their own number, dated September 14, urged them in the interest of peace and good government and for the sake of their own welfare to vote for the Democratic candidates.   They were assured of the fullest protection and equality under the law.   Indeed, the Democrats fairly outrivaled the Republicans in promises of equality in hotels, theaters, street-cars—social relationships.[2]   In reply to a letter from a colored club in New Orleans, Mr. Nicholls pledged himself as follows:

The laws should be general in their operation and any law directed against a class or race in the community would meet my most determined opposition.   No such attempt, however, will be made, for independently of the constitutional barriers which would stand in the way, the Democratic and Conservative sentiment of the whole State is united against such action.   To disregard and go back upon the pledges which I have given on this subject would be to disgrace me before the country.

Pressure there probably was, some from merchants,[3] more from planters, in making advances to negroes who

[1] House Repts., 44 Cong., 2 Sess., No. 156, 33; House Repts., 43 Cong., 2 Sess., No. 101, Part ii., 30.   A candidate for sheriff, one of the chief witnesses before the returning-board, it might be added, had been removed from office by a judge of his own party for incompetency, and two indictments for extortion in office were pending at his renomination.   House Repts., No. 156, 33.   Such cases could be indefinitely multiplied.

[2] According to Sypher, House Misc. Doc., 45 Cong., 3 Sess., No. 31, Wash., 816.

[3] The *Times* openly printed, "We hear of merchants who have kindly but solemnly warned those who depend upon them for patronage, that their opposition to General Nicholls or the ticket of which he is the head, will be a signal for the termination of all business relations."   October 30.

expressed sympathy with Democratic policies.[1]   A witness
put a very radical speech into the mouth of McEnery,
supposed to have been made at Monroe, which scarcely
needs his card of denial.[2]   But more telling as an argument of Democratic coercion is the confidential circular
of the State Committee.   The *Picayune* held that it had
been openly distributed to delegates to the convention,
but the public generally saw it first in the *Republican*
of August 5.[3]   It urged the formation of ward clubs, the
avoidance of gloomy forebodings in conversation, and the
assumption of Democratic victory in the election as a
foregone conclusion, as "we have the means of carrying
the election, and intend to do so, but be careful to do or
say nothing that can be construed into a threat or intimidation of any character."   It urged the presence at every
political meeting of the opposite party of several men to
"take notes of the proceedings, and especially of any
threats on their part against the white people, or of any
appeal made to the negroes by any white man of an
incendiary character."   It recommended frequent meetings of all clubs to proceed on horseback to the central
rendezvous, as that "would impress the negroes with a
sense of your united strength."   The suggestion of the

[1] There is probably some truth in the assertion of a Democrat that if such
pressure from employers were to annul an election, few would ever stand
the test.   It is highly probable that the planters felt as one was represented: "If you don't go with us, you'll be sorry for it some day or other;
we are the people who give you bread and meat and land and everything to
work with and we will take the state one day."   Sen. Repts., 44 Cong., 2
Sess., No. 701, Part ii., 347.

[2] He was quoted as saying of Packard, "He ought to be killed, and it is
lucky for him and probably for me that I have no such power; but if I had
I would kill him.   But someone ought to kill him; someone ought to put a
bullet right here" (indicating his temple).   *Ibid.*, 221-2.   It would seem
that McEnery did make some violent speeches, more or less purposely
misunderstood.

[3] To be found in Sen. Exe. Doc., 44 Cong., 2 Sess., No. 2, 37-8.

preparation of affidavits at each poll that there had been no intimidation by the Democrats is susceptible of two interpretations.

Occasionally country papers indulged in wild talk. "The white people now have no recourse left them but must accept the issue as made by the negroes themselves and fight it out on the color-line. It is the height of folly to attempt to pursue the policy we have inaugurated," declared one paper.[1] The Morehouse *Clarion* fulminated: "The white people retaliated by hanging four or five of the ringleaders. This is the right way. . . . We hope the radicals of Morehouse will not force the people to resort to any such extreme measures."[2] And thus the Vienna *Sentinel* of Lincoln Parish on August 19: "The promoters of these murderous principles are well-known and well watched, and the halter for their necks is already greased."[3]

Evidence of success seems not to be lacking when negroes themselves testified to four hundred of their race turning Democratic[4]; nor when we find three hundred negro members enrolled and present at a Fifth Ward mass meeting; nor when we read of twelve hundred Zouave uniforms for colored Democrats sent to Bayou Sara; nor when we read the following resolution of a colored Conservative club:

The object of this meeting is in the interest of the Conservative party. When we say interest, we mean we are ready to take part with them in their interest. We intend to campaign with our party in the coming election. We intend to support the candidate that may be put in the field and

---

[1] Minden *Democrat*, quoted by the *Republican*, October 5.

[2] Quoted in Sen. Exe. Doc., 44 Cong., 2 Sess., No. 2, 28. June 26.

[3] Sen. Repts., 44 Cong., 2 Sess., No. 701, xii. These unfortunate words were the ones quoted in Congress before the Electoral Commission.

[4] House Misc. Doc., 45 Cong., 3 Sess., No. 31, La., 307.

intend to remain with them as long as they act square with us.[1]

It was estimated that from 5,000 to 17,000 negroes allied themselves with the Democratic ranks.[2] The majority in the country clubs may have been colored, as claimed by a prominent Democrat,[3] though in town the majority was undoubtedly white. In East Feliciana there were eight hundred and sixty-three negroes in the clubs of that party. Mr. Palmer of the Congressional Committee said in December, after conferring with more than three hundred negroes of different parishes, that Nicholls had gained the confidence and respect of the colored people to a greater degree than any other politician in Louisiana.[4]

And yet it would seem, that while the negroes would gladly feast on roast ox at the barbecues, don the gay-colored uniform of the Zouave, seat themselves in proud dignity beside prominent white men on the campaign platform, and halloo where hallooing was expected, when it came to election day, many were found steadfast to the party which had given them their freedom. Appreciable accessions there doubtless were, but the numerous thousands of converts, evidence for which appears in the records, would probably not be claimed to-day even by Louisiana Democrats.[5]

The generous period allowed for registration extended from August 28 to October 28. It was based upon a

[1] *Times*, November 29, 1875.
[2] House Repts., 44 Cong., 2 Sess., No. 156, Part i., 147. The latter estimate is, in the writer's judgment, undoubtedly too high.
[3] Opinion of Powell, who held it true of every club in the country except one. House Misc. Doc., 45 Cong., 3 Sess., No. 31, La., 550.
[4] *Ibid.*, Washington, 1087.
[5] Based upon the replies of as many Democratic survivors of these days as the writer has been able to consult.

false census of 1876,[1] made by a man of bad repute, named Jewett, who had been employed unofficially for that special service by the Republicans.   It appeared that there were 20,025 more adult colored people in the State than white, but the Federal census of 1870, the accuracy of which had never been questioned, made the number of adults of the two races about equal, while all the causes which should have varied this relation, as shown by vital statistics and naturalization records, had operated, according to the House Committee of the Forty-third Congress, rather for the increase of the white than the black population.[2]   Another fact tends to discredit that census; namely, that 24,-300 of the adult blacks were returned from the parish of Orleans alone, while the entire colored population was 57,-647—such a proportion of males as never existed in our western mining camps.[3]   Furthermore, the negroes, with all the election machinery in their favor, were able to cast only 13,000 ballots.   But despite the fact that the Conservatives cried for a thorough revision of the registration,[4] no correction was made.

Naturally, the Conservatives clamored for Democratic representation among the registrars—one clerk in each registration office—and just as naturally in vain.   Antoine replied that the appointments were almost all made by August 23; that where able Democrats had been presented

[1] A committee of the State Assembly found the census so incorrect that it refused to base the apportionment upon it.

[2] House Repts., 44 Cong., 2 Sess., No. 156, 5, grants a possible excess of colored over white voters of nearly 1000.   Leet, whose testimony is questionable, it is granted, held that St. Tammany, where he was registrar, showed a decrease of colored voters.   House Misc. Doc., 45 Cong., 3 Sess., No. 31, 917–8.   According to this census, whites had increased four per cent, blacks, fourteen per cent.

[3] Sherman blindly accepted this proportion, counting the negroes solidly Republican.   Sen. Exe. Doc., 44 Cong., 2 Sess., No. 2, 7.   He estimated 92,996 whites, 115,310 blacks.

[4] *Times*, August 23.

they had been appointed[1]; that removals would be made where there was clear assurance that such action would help in a fair election. The request was renewed September 2, and again refused. Absolute strangers[2] were appointed supervisors in some of the more important parishes; some twenty held positions in the custom-house, post-office, or on the police force; many were themselves candidates[3]; several were under indictment; while some commissions had been issued in blank to the Republican candidate or representative of the district.[4]

That crooked work was intended in the registration, the Conservatives held to be proved by the circular letter to all the supervisors from party headquarters, which declared that the registration and vote of the full Republican strength was expected of all supervisors. The covert bribe in the following exhortation suggests encouragement of fraud: "Your recognition by the next State administration will depend upon your doing your full duty in the premises, and you will not be held to have done your full duty unless the republican registration in your parish reaches 2200 and the republican vote is at least 2,100."

[1] Yet Kellogg claimed that he appointed a clerk for the Democrats in every case. House Misc. Doc., 45 Cong., 3 Sess., No. 31, 657. A list of 350 Democratic names was presented but Pitkin found that every man was a White Leaguer and he did not want men "who had recently deluged the city in blood." But two days before election he was able to find 35 men who were not Leaguers. *Ibid.*, 413.

[2] Sometimes even non-residents of the State, as Clover in East Baton Rouge, who had held office in Mississippi until March, 1876. Then he was a caller for a gambling-tent on the wharf until August 27. House Misc. Doc., 44 Cong., 2 Sess., No. 34, 63–4; House Repts., 44 Cong., 2 Sess., No. 156, Part i., 148.

[3] House Misc. Doc., 45 Cong., 3 Sess., No. 31, Wash., 1052. Kellogg himself filled the position of supervisor and clerk.

[4] So disreputable were some of these men that Kellogg disowned their appointment. House Repts., 44 Cong., 2 Sess., No. 156, Part i., 6. For a long list of such supervisor-candidates see House Misc. Doc., 45 Cong., 3 Sess., No. 31, Wash., 1052.

It closes significantly. The results once obtained, "your recognition will be ample and generous."[1]

Complaints of unfairness appeared as early as August 29, but moderation was counseled and a sub-committee created to keep lists of all voters denied registration, as well as of fraudulent enrollment.[2] All the old subterfuges, with which we have become familiar in the preceding elections were resorted to. Neither were the tactics to defraud East Feliciana of her vote new. Anderson, a notorious vagabond and politician, had himself shot at, when he found the parish going Democratic, or was shot by Republicans, as the result of a conspiracy by Kellogg to get rid of him, and to have no election. Under the plea of intimidation, he then fled the parish.[3] The Democrats, anxious for an election, hired him to go back, but his absence of ten days had deprived five hundred Democrats of registration.[4]

Mutual fear and jealousy were manifest. The chairman of the Democratic Committee implored all citizens to be patient under provocation, seeking for injuries only legal remedies, for the "outrage mill is the main capital of the Republican party."[5] At the close of October the

[1] House Repts., 44 Cong., 2 Sess., No. 156, Part i., 5.

[2] It was the duty of such committee to report the registrations daily, which were then canvassed. Fraudulent registrations were made the subject of affidavits, each signed and sworn to by two citizens, upon which they based their demand to have the names struck off. The Democrats claimed to have found 25,000 false registrations. House Misc. Doc., 45 Cong., 3 Sess., No. 31, Washington, 1051.

[3] House Repts., 45 Con., 3 Sess., No. 31, Washington, 5–6.

[4] One witness stated that Kellogg, after many fruitless promises to the Democrats, hired Jenks to prevent Anderson's return, but that the latter escaped. Ibid., La., 85, 87, 128, 180; House Repts., 45 Cong., 3 Sess., No. 140, 30–1. A witness said of Anderson, "I think he is a man who would be liable to shoot at his own coat in order to make political capital of it." One witness held that it was "the original program, calculation, or intention of Kellogg, from the beginning of the campaign, to have no election there." House Misc. Doc., 45 Cong., 3 Sess., No. 31, 927.

[5] Times, September 24.

Committee vainly sought equal representation on the Board of Revision and sought to have members of their party at the polls on election day.[1]   On the other hand, an attempted robbery of registration documents at the state-house October 24 gave the Republicans an opportunity for accusation.   What was known as the Sewing Machine Swindle[2] debarred some eight thousand Democrats from the polls, hundreds of whom had lived all their lives in the spot registered.   About twenty-nine thousand of these circulars were sent by mail to the registered Democrats, the carriers instructed, if the persons to whom they were addressed were not found, to return the circulars.[3]   Policemen then inquired, more or less carelessly, in the same houses for the persons.   Arrests were issued against eleven thousand persons for false registry[4] and some thousands of names, many the oldest and most respectable in the city, struck off on the Saturday night preceding election.   A Federal commissioner held only five of thirteen hundred cases for further consideration, but the rest could not get a hearing.[5]

[1] See *Times*, October 26, for Kellogg's reply.

[2] It seems that there was a Southern Charm Sewing Machine manufactured in Alabama, but since the firm consisted of Blanchard, Catlin, and Jewett, and had its offices in the state-house, it looks suspicious.

[3] Gauthreaux may be quoted: "I have it from a clerk in the post-office that the instructions were, not to be particularly anxious to find the parties." If a circular were directed to No. 132, and the man had moved next door, it was marked "Not found."   House Misc. Doc., 45 Cong., 3 Sess., No. 31, 1054-5.   Representative Ellis was struck off.

[4] Two to three hundred of these warrants were indorsed, "Not found"; yet the fees for them were collected. *Ibid.*, 1433.   This device did probably detect some illegal Democratic registrations.   Burke virtually admitted this. *Ibid.*, 1002.

[5] House Repts., 44 Cong., 2 Sess., No. 156, Part i., 148.   The Central Committee felt that it was a scheme to stir up violence on the eve of the election and so urged submission to arrest.   Some had moved and taken out new papers according to law. *Times*, October 27.   One page of the *Picayune* was covered in fine print with the names of the Democrats struck off, Nov. 3.   The party did everything possible to restore the names.

This action naturally stirred up intense feeling[1] and yet quiet was preserved.

In the arrangements for the election, State Supervisor Hahn tried to be fair, ordering that the names submitted by the Democrats must be appointed unless they were objectionable on the score of character, but that to them should be assigned the checking of the names from the poll-list, while a Republican must invariably receive the ballots.[2]   He also allowed each party an equal delegation of challengers at the polls.

A disturbed condition had begun to be manifest in East Feliciana early in 1875.   That parish borders for twenty miles on the Mississippi, while Clinton is distant only a few miles from the disturbed Mississippi counties, where an exciting election was in progress.   In July a number of minor officers fled from the parish—the recorder, sheriff, and Representative, because it was believed that they had incited a negro uprising.[3]   On October 7 a large body of armed horsemen rode into Clinton, interrupted the court, forced the negro sheriff to resign, and threatened the judge.[4]   On October 14 came news of a further disturbance.   The mayor reported that as John Gair was being taken by the sheriff and a posse to Clinton under accusation of poisoning Dr. Saunders, he was seized by a party of masked men and shot on the road.   The sister-in-law, who was supposed to have administered the potion, was hung in the court-house square.   Antoine promptly issued a

[1] The *Democrat* waxed vehement, publishing an extra headed, "The Plot Disclosed. The Damnable Infamy of the Radical Managers. A full and Reliable Exposure of the Manner in which Democrats and Conservatives are to be Disfranchised." (Nov. 5.) But it urged in the same issue, "Preserve the Peace and work till the election is over."

[2] House Misc. Doc., 45 Cong., 3 Sess., No. 31, Wash., 1075.

[3] Denied by the officials. The sheriff returned the next day.

[4] The full story is found in the governor's message, House Jour., 1876, 95–6.

proclamation, ordering the dispersal of all disorderly bodies and summoning all good citizens to assist in the restoration of order.[1] A mass meeting at Clinton on January 22 of citizens of both colors demanded the resignation of the parish officials in order to put an end to lawlessness.[2]

In West Feliciana there occurred a murder which gained some notoriety. Gilbert Carter was betrayed to an intended victim as the leader of a plot to organize a colored club, sworn to kill certain white persons together with their families. The negroes, quick to take the alarm, did not hold their rendezvous and so the whites, who had gathered to surprise the negro club, arrested Carter at his cabin. In trying to escape he was killed.

In March, race feeling broke out in East Baton Rouge. At a public meeting in which colored citizens participated, the sheriff, parish judge, and tax-collector were called upon to resign. Within a few days the governor called the attention of the district-attorney to combinations of lawless persons, requesting him to institute proceedings against those concerned in the recent disturbance. But the latter knew of no such combinations, for the action had been publicly taken and the officials induced peaceably to resign.[3] The killing of the Myers, father and son, on April 12 in the same parish seems more obviously a case of "bulldozing" Republican leaders, and yet the Democrats produced some evidence that the testimony of the wife was inspired.[4]

Early in May a certain Twitchell, said by the *Times* to be undoubtedly one of the worst, as he was one of the

[1] House Jour., 1876, 98; *Times*, Oct. 15. The Clinton *Patriot-Democrat* shows the spirit of the whites defiant. The *Republican* was less violent than usual. See its editorial of October 16.

[2] *Times*, January 27, 28.

[3] *Annual Cyclopedia*, 1876, 485.

[4] Sen. Exe. Doc., 44 Cong., 2 Sess., No. 2, 278–9, for Anne Myers's account.

ablest, politicians in the State, [1] was shot down by a masked assassin at Coushatta. The explanation of the *Times* was his failure to pay a bribe, which he had offered in order to suppress a poll at an election. [2] The riot at Port Hudson on the 17th of June, in which shots were fired, was useful for newspaper artillery. [3] Kellogg took advantage of these occurrences to send a sensational telegram to Washington on May 17, thus securing an extension of the Mississippi investigation, then in progress, to Louisiana. [4]

But the outbreaks which were most serious in their consequences occurred in Ouachita. By July, Dinkgrave, a Radical leader, had organized clubs in every ward but one. Feeling was tense; Democrats crowded around and interrogated the speaker at Republican meetings, while negroes shot into white men's houses and were talking of organizing rifle companies. On the afternoon of August 30 he was murdered on the river bank by a person on horseback, unknown to his companion. The assassin was within thirty yards when he fired and fled. Although pursued by the sheriff and rifle clubs, he made good his escape. The Democrats labored to make it appear that the murder was occasioned by a personal quarrel with a Wimberly family of Texas and held that all testimony of any value was "opposed to the idea of his death for political reasons." Republicans just as assiduously circulated a statement that his death was due to his boldness and influence in organizing the Republican party. [5] An uprising was planned by leading Republicans;

[1] May 4, 1876.

[2] May 10. It was quite right in anticipating that political capital would be made of it.

[3] The *Times* held that it was concocted by the *Republican*, June 26.

[4] Sen. Repts., 44 Cong., 1 Sess., No. 527, iv.

[5] Ludeling, a relative, gave that as his opinion and that of his intimate friend. Sen. Repts., 44 Cong., 2 Sess., No. 701, 855. The Senate report sweeps such a theory aside. For his whole testimony see *ibid.*, 854–64.

orders were sent out to the country, summoning the negroes to Monroe, as "the war had begun." Large numbers of armed negroes did assemble in the various parts of the parish, especially the island, threatening to burn Monroe and to kill the white people. The prompt assembling of the rifle clubs enabled the white people to persuade the negro mob to disperse without the discharge of a gun.[1] The leaders in the uprising fled, and their flight tended to shake the confidence of the colored people. That it did materially injure the Radical party is true, but the testimony is also strong that many colored converts had joined the Democrats three weeks before Dinkgrave's death.[2] It is readily comprehensible also why white men on the island, where the proportion of white men to black was as one to ten, should have felt it incumbent to patrol the district for several nights.[3]

Just on the eve of the election occurred several revolting murders and whippings in Ouachita, one of which evoked attention out of all proportion to its significance. On the Saturday night preceding election, a party of men, some of whom their victim claimed to have recognized, rode up to the cabin of Henry Pinkston. When he refused to appear in response to their summons, they broke in the door, seized and gagged him, meanwhile knocking his wife to the floor when she attempted to interfere; gashed him,

The evidence of Democratic rejoicing over his death does not constitute proof that his death was a political murder.

[1] Only McCleod was shot for refusing to halt at command. See Aby's testimony, Sen. Repts., 44 Cong., 2 Sess., No. 701, 788. McCleod's own story presents him as the aggrieved party. House Repts., 44 Cong., 2 Sess., No. 156, Part i., 41–2.

[2] See testimony of Colonel Stubbs, House Misc. Doc., 44 Cong., 2 Sess., No. 34, Part vi., 183.

[3] Dr. Aby's orders called for men of sobriety and discretion to watch for symptoms of a recurrence of the affair. Sen. Repts., same session, No. 701, 789–90.

28

making a sound "just like cutting in new leather"[1]; and concluded their work by shooting him seven times until he ceased to breathe. Some of the party then reëntered the cabin, killing in the wife's arms a babe, which was later thrown into a pond, assaulted her, and gashed her with an ax on the neck, thigh, and breast until she, too, was left for dead. Eliza, who seems to have been a synonym for vileness and falsehood,[2] won credence for her story by displaying her own gashed body before the returning-board. The Democrats made every effort to show that Pinkston's death had occurred at the hands of a negro, with whom he had had a fight some months before,[3] but it would seem rather the work of an armed group of men.[4] The fact that the men whom Eliza accused of the murder did not appear before the board was regarded by the Senate Committee as going far to corroborate her story, but it should be noted that several of them sought in vain to submit proof of their innocence to the board.[5] Certain weight must be allowed to the fact that the affidavit first filed by her at Monroe was suppressed and another, accusing different persons, substituted; that some of the men accused were able clearly to prove their absence miles from the scene of the murder[6]; and that

[1] Eliza embellished her tale, horrible enough at best, with loathsome, fictitious details as Gibson pointed out. *A Political Crime*, 163.

[2] She had been driven away from a plantation at the request of the other negroes. And her own testimony shows her lewd and vulgar in the extreme. Sen. Repts., 44 Cong., 2 Sess., No. 701, 909. For other evidence of her bad character see Sen. Repts., 44 Cong., 2 Sess., No. 701, 517–36; House Repts., same session, No. 156, 44–6. She even tried to implicate her employer. No. 701, 914.

[3] House Repts., No. 156, 46; Sen. Repts., No. 701, 515.

[4] The evidence of a neighbor speaks of hearing a number of horses. *Ibid.*, 623.

[5] According to General Palmer, who had at first been greatly shocked by the story. House Misc. Doc., 45 Cong., 3 Sess., No. 31, 1089. One, a physician, came the next day to dress her wounds.

[6] On the showing of the House Committee.

her testimony had been so effectually impeached in the courts of Morehouse Parish that the Republican attorney refused to call her as a witness.   Her employer, who had good reason to know her, thought that she had killed the child herself.[1]   And so one reads with considerable sympathy the charge of the Democratic Committee that "this wretched creature, this miserable prostitute, has become a saint in the political calendar of the Republican party of Louisiana."   And her testimony is weakened, when the day before she was theatrically produced before the returning-board, borne in by two stalwart negroes and attended by a woman with restoratives, she had been seen to walk down a steep and difficult staircase in the custom-house unattended.[2]

It seems not unreasonable to infer that that same gang of ruffians, who had visited the Pinkston cabin, were guilty of the other acts of violence which were committed that same Saturday night in the neighborhood: Two Republican negroes were severely whipped; the daughter-in-law of one of them abused and whipped instead of her husband, who had taken the precaution to spend the night in a cotton-field; another negro killed and his disemboweled body cast into a bayou.[3]   The truth will now

---

[1] Though bluff and rude, his evidence rings sincere.   Sen. Misc. Doc., 44 Cong., 2 Sess., No. 14, 116-8.

[2] Morey thought that even the visiting statesmen valued the political effect of this dramatic scene (House Misc. Doc., 45 Cong., 3 Sess., No. 31, Wash., 823), while Emil Weber gave it as his understanding that "they understood this matter of Eliza Pinkston was a put-up job to make political capital in favor of the Republican party." *Ibid.*, 621.   Kenner testified that Wells said, "You don't suppose that I am to be humbugged by any such nonsense as that." *Ibid.*, No. 42, 386.   And a rumor seems to have been industriously circulated shortly after her appearance of her death from her wounds.   An affidavit retracting her first evidence appeared in the New York *Herald* the last of June, 1878, but was evidently unfounded, as no such retraction was produced before the investigating committee.

[3] Sen. Repts., 44 Cong., 2 Sess., No. 701, xix.

probably never be known concerning these outrages, but the ugly facts remain and constitute evidence of a very disorderly state of affairs in a parish where they could occur.

But the worst weapon which the Democrats placed in the hands of the Republicans was the charge of armed pickets on the roads to Monroe on Sunday, November 5. Dr. Aby declared that he had been informed that negroes were to come to the election armed, and that he had known for weeks that arms were being deposited in Monroe. From Thursday to Saturday large numbers of blacks had been coming into the city with guns on their shoulders. The whites became excited, whereupon the mayor issued a proclamation, forbidding armed men in the town.[1] The political motive in picketing the roads was undoubtedly to thwart the Republican scheme of polling this entire vote in the four boxes located in town—an unusual number—in order to throw out the outside boxes, where the bulk of the Democratic vote was, on the plea of intimidation. But it might also very well prevent election officials from going out to the polls.[2] All pickets were withdrawn before daybreak of election day.

As the day of election drew near, the enthusiasm of the masses exceeded all bounds. Mass meetings were of daily occurrence[3] and nightly parades cheered Nicholls and Wiltz. The picture drawn by the *Times* may be regarded as true:

The anxiety everywhere felt, but more particularly among Conservatives, who freely express their views, is simply in-

[1] For this proclamation see Sen. Repts., 44 Cong., 2 Sess., No. 701, xxviii.

[2] The Senate Committee collected many such illustrations. It must also be pointed out that there was nothing illegal in having the negro vote all polled in Monroe.

[3] The campaign brought out some clever cartoons in the *Democrat*. See issue of Oct. 26.

tense. . . . Every influence which can be brought to bear to control even a single vote has been exercised. . . . Never, perhaps, in the history of New Orleans, has a canvass, without necessarily implying a breach of the peace, or any disturbance whatever, assumed a graver aspect.[1]

But on the whole the State had been unusually quiet, so quiet that there were less than a thousand Federal soldiers located in five parishes which had been reported restless.

Election day passed without riot or the slightest disturbance in New Orleans, without reports of intimidation or violence from the country except in Ouachita and Concordia Parishes.[2] Even the congregating of negroes about the polls or the arrest of repeaters[3] could not provoke any outbreak. There was scant need of the thirty-five hundred marshals scattered throughout the State, eight hundred at Federal expense.[4] Business was generally suspended in the city so that it was quieter, except around the polls, than on Sunday. Even the Republican press testified to the quiet.[5] One parish after the other reported

---

[1] October 30.

[2] House Repts., 44 Cong., 2 Sess., No. 156, Part i., 150.

[3] An interesting device was made use of to detect repeaters. A man at each poll put a spot of red paint on the shoulder of each suspect as he voted, so that he was easily detected at another poll despite duplicate papers. House Misc. Doc., 45 Cong., 3 Sess., No. 31, 801. Fish-hooks were also attached to the clothing.   [4] *Ibid.*, 451.

[5] "Of the election in the parish of Orleans and the great majority of other parishes of the State of Louisiana it may be said with exceptional truth that its marked characteristics have been peace." *Republican*, Nov. 12. See also the *Democrat* of Nov. 8, which denied the presence of a single drunkard on the streets; or the *Picayune* of same date, which declared it the most peaceable which ever occurred there. Of a thousand witnesses before the Congressional Committee not one swore to actual violence at any poll. House Misc. Doc., Wash., No. 31, 454. After two and a half years Trumbull still thought it as fair as was usual there. The most that Wells could cite as evidence of intimidation at his precinct was the fact that

a quiet and orderly election. The entire vote proved very large,[1] exceeding, even in the parishes where intimidation was charged, any previous vote.

As the popular vote began to indicate a Democratic victory, there was much jubilant enthusiasm and the Democratic papers exulted rather too boldly.[2] But already by November 9 it was apparent that the result was in doubt, and National interest was focused on Louisiana[3] because of the uncertainty there. The very slowness with which the returns were made operated for the Republicans.[4] That party rose to the occasion and on that date the official organ printed under the headlines, "A Tale of Shame and National Disgrace," what it termed the "crowning act of perfidy, cruelty, and fraud on the part of the Louisiana Democracy." It should be stated that the *Republican* had the day before charged violence and intimidation in the country, but they assumed tremendous proportions when Louisiana proved the pivot on which swung the National election. Kellogg telegraphed on November 11 to the New York *Herald*, claiming proof of bulldozing to the extent of invalidating

---

the sheriff took his revolver to the poll.   House Misc. Doc., 44 Cong., 2 Sess., No. 42, 244.

[1] 15,000 greater than ever before it was said.   Even in West Feliciana reached the largest vote ever polled there.   House Misc. Doc., No. 31, 608.

[2] See issues of Nov. 8 and 9 of the *Picayune, German Gazette*.   Monroe held a torchlight procession on Nov. 11.   Even the *Republican* admitted defeat. See Kellogg's cry, "We are after all beaten," *ibid.*, 592; Weber's evidence, 626.

[3] The story of the election in its National bearings is not regarded as pertinent to this story.

[4] Up to midnight, Nov. 10, the secretary of state had received official returns from only 88 of the 119 polls in the city, from only three-fourths of the parishes.   Indeed, the Republicans were envied because of the fact that their forethought made it possible for them to know the substantial result as early as Nov. 13.   The Central Committee had asked nearly all supervisors to send duplicate returns to the committee.

the vote in five parishes, which showed a Democratic majority of six thousand.[1] He declared that those parishes were

patrolled by the White Leagues, reinforced by armed bodies from Arkansas and Mississippi; that most of the Republican leaders had been driven away or murdered. . . . Numbers of the negroes had been intercepted by the White League pickets, their registration papers destroyed, and, in some cases, the holders terribly beaten.[2]

All day long, and up to a late hour in the night, the committee rooms and the streets and banquettes in front were crowded by an eager throng of information-seekers. Not less than twenty thousand citizens endeavored during the day to catch a crumb of news. The community realized the gravity of the situation. The excitement was rivaled only by that which prevailed at the beginning of the war. The papers fiercely demanded acknowledgment for the party with which each affiliated.[3] The *German Gazette* saw a Republican dangling at every lamp-post unless the Democratic ticket were counted in, while the *Republican* calmly reviewed the relative strength of the two parties for war.[4] The *Democrat* thought that if the Radicals tried to steal Louisiana, "there will be fun,"[5] and main-

---

[1] The parishes named were Ouachita, East Baton Rouge, Morehouse, East and West Feliciana. *Times*, November 9. See Map IV.

[2] *Ibid.*, November 12.

[3] Yet note the exhortation of the *Times* on November 12 against any rash act which might "not only jeopardize our own rights, but precipitate the whole country into turmoil." New Orleans was more self-controlled than New York, where street-fights occurred. Naturally, the fierce temper of the Northern papers, which were copied by the New Orleans press, did not tend to lower the temperature. See the New York *Tribune* and *Herald:* " We beg the New Orleans Republican managers remember that their previous frauds are well-known here in the North, and that as men already detected and exposed in kukluxing election returns, they need to be conspicuously fair."   [4] November 11.   [5] November 10.

tained a bold claim of victory in each issue. And the Conservatives boldly asserted that with the past experience of its citizens, the whole power of the government could not maintain a chief magistrate in Louisiana who had not been fairly elected.

On November 10 Grant endeavored to cool the fever by instructing General Augur to be vigilant to preserve peace and order and to see that the legal board was unmolested.

Should there be any grounds of suspicion of fraudulent count on either side [he wisely said], it should be reported at once. No man worthy the office of President should be willing to hold it if counted in or placed there by fraud. Either party can afford to be disappointed in the result. The country cannot afford to have the result tainted by the suspicion of illegal or false returns.[1]

He then asked several prominent Republicans to go to New Orleans to witness the canvass of the votes by the returning-board: John Sherman, Stoughton, J. H. Van Alen of New York, Hale of Maine, Garfield, Parker, Kelley, Clark, and Wilson.[2] At the request of the National Democratic Committee several of the most prominent Democrats also went to the Louisiana capital in an effort to prevent frauds: Palmer, Trumbull, Randall, Bigler, Stevenson, J. Lee Carroll, more than twenty in all,[3] arriving November 13, one day after the Republicans.

[1] *Annual Cyclopedia*, 1876, 486.

[2] Several others were later associated with them, General Lew Wallace among others, until the number reached twenty-five. Even these eminent men were not above criticism. It was pointed out that several were intimate friends of Hayes, one his choice for speaker. Later the fairness of their judgment, their probity, was assailed. Hardly a man escaped untainted.

[3] Already on November 10 the *Picayune* knew of the departure of these Democrats, and it was then that the *Republican* reviewed the strength of each party for war.

The coming of the Northern men, on whose fairness they relied for a fair count, brought a strong feeling of relief, like the quiet "after a delirious fever" as the *Times* phrased it.   Gossip was somewhat hushed, and those compelled to attend to details moved languidly through the streets.   Partisans were not so demonstrative.   The confidence of the Conservative papers in the power of the statesmen to prevent frauds is almost touching,[1] while the Radical organ, until it learned that Republicans also were coming, saw only an intention to disregard the laws of Louisiana, and evidence in "this intimidating intervention" that the Democrats would not acquiesce in any adverse decision of the ballot.   But the issue would depend in its final analysis upon the returning-board.

[1] "But if it be inspected by these informal, but trusted commissioners and by them pronounced correct, whomsoever it may favor, the country will at once and peacefully accept the verdict as the true one." *Times*, November 11.   See also Nov. 12.   Sherman declared that when he arrived in New Orleans he found far less excitement in respect to the count there than in Ohio.   *Recollections*, I., 554.

CHAPTER XIX

The Decision of the Returning-Board

NOVEMBER 15 the visiting Democrats presented to the visiting Republicans, "in view of the unhappy controversies which have heretofore arisen over the Returning-board," a request that the two delegations might confer in "order that such influence as we possess may be exerted in behalf of such a canvass of the votes actually cast as by its fairness and impartiality shall command the respect and acquiescence of the American people of all parties."[1] But the men addressed, while also desirous of an honest count,—which they knew no reason to doubt,—declined the conference solely on the ground that they were there as private citizens and could not supersede or modify any laws of the State; that any effort to influence any officer would be condemned by every State as improper interference with local administration.[2] The Democrats resented the imputation, and

[1] Sen. Exe. Doc., 44 Cong., 2 Sess., No. 2, 31.
[2] *Times*, Nov. 17. For the full reply see *ibid.*, 32. Garfield later defined their status as witnesses with no official character whatever, simply individual citizens to witness a public transaction and inform themselves of the actual facts. Yet Garfield occupied a room in the custom-house, interviewed and took part in the examination of negro witnesses, even drafted some interrogatories to draw out more fully the testimony which they had "given rather in brief," and would even have advised pressure to make the witnesses stand firm, "if I thought they needed any strengthening." House Misc. Doc., 45 Cong., 3 Sess., No. 31, Wash., 790, 792, 797, 1087. Lew Wallace also expressed a wish to see the injured witnesses and so Pitkin ordered them brought to the office, a step leading to a charge of corrupt

442

so the only result was a somewhat acrimonious exchange of notes.

It would seem that the Republican statesmen organized promptly by making Sherman chairman, and keeping a regular record of all meetings and resolutions. A committee was appointed to examine the Louisiana election laws. All testimony relating to one parish was given to one member, and when he was satisfied that votes there should be rejected, he so advised the whole group.[1] Five of their number, varying from day to day, were detailed to attend the sessions of the returning-board.[2]

That body was made up, as we know, of four men,[3] whose reputations, to say the least, were vulnerable. Kenner had for a long time been a servant in a gambling-house, from which he had been discharged, it was asserted,[4] for stealing, whereupon he opened a faro bank and a house of ill-fame a few doors from the state-house. Anderson, poor at the end of the war, had acquired considerable wealth as a Senator, to which still clung the unsavory odor of interested, corrupt legislation.[5] J. M. Wells, a native Louisianian, was a defaulter to the State, while holding a claim of nearly half a million dollars against the government, based upon rebel property not entitled to reimbursement. He held the lucrative office of surveyor of the port.[6] Cassanave, a negro undertaker, though by all

---

offers. House Misc. Doc., 45 Cong., 3 Sess., No. 31, Wash., 417. But Garfield denied emphatically any plan to get up affidavits or throw out parishes.   [1] *Ibid.*, 790–1.

[2] *Ibid.*, 790.   [3] See above, Chapter XIII.

[4] He admitted his guilt, but by confession escaped punishment. House Misc. Doc., 44 Cong., 2 Sess., No. 34, Part ii., 597–8.

[5] See House Repts., 44 Cong., 2 Sess., No. 156, Part i., 7. This legislation was that encouraging navigation. See Chapters II and III. There was some question as to his eligibility, as he was a candidate for reëlection. He was willing to acknowledge his competitor elected though he did not hold himself precluded from serving on the board. Sen. Misc. Doc., No. 14, 23.

[6] House Repts., 44 Cong., 2 Sess., No. 156, Part i., 7.

odds the most honest member according to the Cincinnati *Inquirer*,[1] was too ignorant to be well-informed on the nature of his work and in his testimony showed "such indifference to the obligation of an oath as warrants the conclusion that he would be a willing accomplice in any rascality by which he might profit."[2]   With this description should be compared the white-washing which Sherman applied:

Wells was a Union man from the time the war broke out, and although he suffered greatly by it in the loss of property, he never faltered in his devotion to the Union cause.   His experience in public life has been great and varied, and his capacity to discharge the duties assumed cannot be questioned.[3]

Anderson he found "widely known and highly respected throughout the State."   Cassanave was a "man of intelligence, excellent character and business habits," not dependent on nor seeking office, a well-educated citizen.   Kenner he described as "intelligent and active," for some time in charge of the Commissioner's bureau.[4]

[1] Nov. 18.   See also opinion of Palmer, House Misc. Doc., 45 Cong., 3 Sess., No. 31, Wash., 1085.

[2] A partisan view, of course.   No. 156, Part i., 7.   But before a later investigating committee, he was vague, couldn't "recollect" much of anything, didn't know whether the board threw out 1500 or 10,000 votes.   See House Misc. Doc., 44 Cong., 2 Sess., No. 42, 189.

[3] And this is the same man of whom he wrote Stanton in 1867 as follows: "I say now unequivocally that Governor Wells is a political trickster and dishonest man. . . . His conduct has been as sinuous as the mark left in the dust by a snake."   Sen. Exe. Doc., 40 Cong., 1 Sess., No. 14, 213-5. For other opinions see Harper's Weekly, XX., 988; Sen. Exe. Doc., 44 Cong., 2 Sess., No. 2, 6; House Misc. Doc., Same Congress, No. 34, Part ii., 507-9; *ibid.*, No. 42, 143-63.

[4] See Sherman's report, Sen. Exe. Doc., 44 Cong., 2 Sess., No. 2, 6.   In another place he is able to write, "I have formed a high opinion of Governor Wells and Anderson.   They are firm, judicious, and, as far as I can judge, thoroughly honest and conscientious."   House Misc. Doc., 45 Cong., 3 Sess., No. 31, 772.

These men organized formally as the returning-board
November 16 in their room at the state-house, which was
filled by the distinguished visitors from the North, a
committee of five representing the Democratic State
interests, Judge Spofford, representing the State and
parochial tickets, and reporters from all parts of the
country. The Democratic representatives asked for open
sessions and the opportunity to offer evidence against
charges of violence. President Wells granted the latter
request, but the former only at sessions where contested
cases should come up.[1] On the 18th the board invited a
committee of five from each visiting delegation to attend
its sessions "in their capacity as private citizens of eminent reputation and high character"—that is, as spectators
and witnesses of the proceedings.[2]

On the 20th the board adopted its rules, which the
Times stigmatized as the quintessence of unfairness.[3]
Uncontested returns should be canvassed first; in contested cases all motions and arguments should be in
writing; no returns might be inspected except under certain restrictions[4]; nor could either party make or answer
any objections to them; the board might go into secret
session at the request of any member to consider arguments; no *ex parte* affidavits should be received as evi-

[1] The Democrats justly complained that those who were familiar with
local matters were thus excluded, while the visitors had no familiarity with
the localities or with the facts. The local counsel were allowed to take
copies of the papers, but there was very little opportunity for it.

[2] Sen. Misc. Doc., 44 Cong., 2 Sess., No. 14, 13. Kellogg stated that he
had advised this action to several members of the board, while Senator
Matthews held that it was at the suggestion of the Northern visitors. But
it was interpreted to mean only at the opening of the returns, Anderson
naïvely saying that he recollected no request of theirs to be present at
executive sessions. House Misc. Doc., 44 Cong., 2 Sess., No. 42, 177.

[3] *Times*, November 25.

[4] Wells allowed copies of the returns. He said that later he invited
Democrats to inspect them.

dence except as a basis for investigation[1]; but returns by officers were to constitute *prima facie* evidence.[2] The Democratic counsel at once offered a resolution for open sessions, maintaining that "entire publicity is the only antidote to the poison of suspicion." But the refusal was emphasized by promptly excluding all but the members of the visiting committee for an executive session.[3]

On November 21 the board canvassed eleven parishes, deferring five in which contests appeared.[4] If there were no protests among the papers, the returns were sent to a private room to be tabulated in secret by clerks whose past records were no surety for honesty.[5] If a protest were found, they were laid aside for later secret consideration. By November 27 the canvass of the uncontested

[1] The method of procedure was as follows: each party presented interrogatories to witnesses, those witnesses were examined outside before some officer, and their testimony brought in. Thus the evidence consisted of depositions and *ex parte* affidavits.

[2] Protests were filed against several of these rules, but especially against Rule 9, which forbade *ex parte* affidavits as evidence. Democratic candidates and Federal supervisors protested against these rules. The board later exercised the privilege of changing its rules and received over 200 pages of such testimony for Kellogg, but again reversed its ruling when McEnery offered *ex parte* evidence in contravention. Sen. Misc. Doc., 44 Cong., 2 Sess., No. 14, 19.

The full proceedings of the returning-board are published in Sen. Exe. Doc., 44 Cong., 2 Sess., No. 2, 39–145.

[3] Ray, Republican counsel for the party and the board, was alone admitted to the secret sessions. The comment of the *Nation* is fair: "If the men who composed the returning-board of Louisiana had been of well-tried and acknowledged probity, Republicans could not have been too anxious, even then, to throw the strongest light of publicity upon all their actions." March 8, 1877.

[4] Sen. Misc. Doc., 44 Cong., 2 Sess., No. 14, 29.

[5] It was said that five were under indictment in the criminal courts of the State, but Jewett declared that he had been exonerated from the charge of perjury, while McCormack denied ever being indicted for murder. House Repts., 44 Cong., 2 Sess., No. 100, Pt. iii., 15 and 17. Into the hands of these men fell the fate of all but the governor and electors, as all canvassing was left to them without the check of a single Democrat.

parishes was completed and the board devoted itself to hearing testimony and arguments until the afternoon of December 2, when it went into secret session to complete its work. From December 2 to 5 was but scant time for the studying of forty-five hundred pages of manuscript testimony[1] and the investigation of charges of intimidation, especially when three whole days were devoted to one parish, Ouachita, in which case several persons were orally examined before the board—notably Eliza Pinkston.

The Democratic charge of partisanship against the board seems well-substantiated.[2] Efforts for representation were unavailing. As early as November 10 the chairman of the State Central Committee appealed to Kellogg to force the reorganization of the board so that at least two members and one-half of the clerks should be of the other party, so that "no one will hesitate to accept their decisions as final."[3] As no answer was returned, a copy was sent to the board on the 16th, claiming representation as a matter of right. On the 17th, in the face of continued silence, formal request was

[1] Sen. Exe. Doc., 44 Cong., 2 Sess., Nos. 2 and 14, 167 ff. Trumbull said that no testimony had been read at any session at which he was present prior to December 1. Before they met, Pitkin was said to have sent the following telegram: "Louisiana safe; our northern friends stand firmly by us; Returning-board will hold its own." House Repts., 45 Cong., 3 Sess., No. 140, 40. Gauthreaux said that this reply was simply a knowing laugh at the idea that the board would read anything that was submitted to it. House Misc. Doc., No. 31, Wash., 1064.

[2] It is rather difficult to see how Sherman could feel that the board acted openly and fairly, though he clearly says so. Sen. Exe. Doc., 44 Cong., 2 Sess., No. 2, 2. It is interesting to note that he did not later change this opinion. "As to the action of the returning-board in Louisiana, I feel bound now, after a long lapse of time, to repeat what was reported to General Grant by the Republican visitors, that it made a fair, honest, and impartial return of the result of the election." Sherman, *Recollections*, II., 557.

[3] *Times*, Nov. 11. They also wished Republicans of like moderation and conservatism.

made for the appointment of Dr. Hugh Kennedy, known
for his union and conservative views, to fill the vacancy.
November 18 the Democratic counsel filed a plea against
the jurisdiction of the board over the Presidential vote
because, among other reasons, it was not properly constituted.[1]   But the board summarily overruled this protest without affording a chance for discussion[2] under the
specious argument that the law had been originally complied with, thus relieving it of all further responsibility to
change the board "to suit shifting political organizations."[3]
On the 21st it was learned that the board manifested ignorance as to the vacancy, and so the Democracy indicated
once more the empty place caused by Arroyo's resignation.
Again on the 22d, 23d, and 24th the request was renewed.[4]
Finally, November 25 a half-answer was wrenched from
the unwilling lips of Wells:

I have just stated that we have not come to a final determination, because we have never had any idea that it would
not be filled, but that the board differed in opinion regarding
the gentlemen you have proposed. . . . If we are to act
harshly we might say that you have no claims on the board for
representation as you have forfeited them by the resignation
of Mr. Arroyo.[5]

And he put them off with the promise to try to agree
on an individual.[6]   But the entire canvass was made by
Republicans only.

[1] Another reason was that two of the nominees for elector were ineligible,
as they were both holding office at the time of election.   *Times*, Nov. 21.
[2] The Democratic House and Senate committees insisted long on these
arguments as grounds for rejecting the electoral vote.   Sen. Misc. Doc.,
No. 14, 4.
[3] *Ibid.*, 17.   [4] *Ibid.*, 40, 50, 51.
[5] *Ibid.*, 56.   The board was quite impervious to the hammering of the
press.   "This country calls and requests them to step down."   *Times*,
Nov. 13.
[6] Wells declared that there was a lack of confidence in the Democratic

The partisanship manifested itself in a dozen other ways. The entire clerical force was Republican. Democrats were not allowed to know the order of investigation nor the exact date on which contests would be considered, although they regarded it as highly important, since it took five or six days to bring witnesses from the upper parishes.[1] Democratic counsel also insisted that they ought to be supplied with copies of all protests on file, be allowed to inspect accompanying affidavits, and be able to order the subpœna of witnesses.[2] But no Democrat saw a protest until after November 23, no *ex parte* affidavit until about November 24. When toward the close of the month, the Democrats requested night sessions of the board, it refused peremptorily.[3] It was arbitrary in its rulings at times. When the Conservatives asked to be present at the tabulation, the following conversation occurred:

"What action will your honorable body take on that application? Wells—Have you anything further?

"Nothing, except that we would like your honorable body to act. Wells—The application is refused."[4]

---

politicians. Cassanave had no objection to a Democrat, though he did not think it his duty to get one on and did not know whose duty it was. He said that two members objected to Kennedy but that the question was never put to a vote. Anderson thought it unnecessary to make such a motion, and none of the members were disposed to resign. But Shellabarger declared that Wells had told him that the position was tendered to several men and refused. *Record,* Electoral Commission, 100, House Misc. Doc., 44 Cong., 2 Sess., No. 42, 185, 40–1.

[1] Sen. Misc. Doc., 44 Cong., 2 Sess., No. 14, 30. It was impossible to disprove the charges against De Soto, dated Nov. 25, on this account.

[2] Wells evaded and insisted that they should have their witnesses ready. *Ibid.,* 30.

[3] "We will not do it *positively;* we will have to do less talking," decreed Wells. "You have given the whole day to the Republican party," charged the Democrats. Wells retorted, "We will give *you* a whole day, if you have as good a case on your part." *Ibid.,* 113.

[4] *Ibid.,* 51–2.

29

But worst feature of all, perhaps, was the refusal to order in certain boxes of returns, which Democratic counsel reported on November 23 as still retained in the possession of supervisors, after their arrival in the city; and refusal to receive those of Franklin Parish, known to have Democratic majorities, which had been lying in an express-office ten days, on the flimsy pretext of the charges, [1] even after the Democrats had offered to defray the costs.

During the sessions of the board more than three hundred witnesses, nearly all Republicans, were summoned to New Orleans by the marshal at a cost of ten thousand dollars to the National government. The witnesses testifying were generally unknown to the officers by whom the oath was administered—usually the Federal commissioner—nor was their identity proved to such officers. The affidavits and other testimony were often prepared by Federal soldiers and employees detailed for the purpose by Packard, [2] and yet such testimony was made the alleged basis of action by the board. And the value of the evidence of dazed, ignorant negroes, summoned from the fields for the first time in their lives to a crowded city, marched past cordons of police, and placed before a corps of stenographers, should not be overrated. [3]

[1] Wells's solicitude concerning the costs hardly rings true: "The members of the board are unwilling to risk their own means for the public, if there is no assurance that they are to get back what they expend, or if they are to be paid back in warrants at 30 cents on the dollar." Sen. Misc. Doc., 44 Cong., 2 Sess., No. 14, 57.

[2] A policeman testified that 20–30 police were so employed up to a day or two before the board closed its sessions. House Misc. Doc., 45 Cong., 3 Sess., No. 31, 1074. See also the testimony of the clerk Muhlerin that they were manufactured in the polling-room, almost any names being used. House Misc. Doc., No. 42, 316. Kenner himself would not say that more than 1000 of the 10,000 votes rejected were votes cast against the voters' will. He admitted that there had not been one man before the board who swore that he voted contrary to his conscience. *Ibid.*, 249, 97.

[3] There is doubtless something in the House report that "they supplied the answers, and that persons standing around supplied more," and that

This evidence began November 22 and continued until one hundred and fifty-seven men were examined—those confined chiefly to Ouachita Parish.

The general charge of the Republicans that the Democrats had chosen certain Republican parishes for scenes of intimidation in the belief that other parishes would carry the State, even should the former be rejected,[1] would hardly constitute grounds upon which the returning-board could act. And so it produced protests against the fairness of the election. The Democracy attempted to show that these protests and affidavits were often filed late,[2] after the election had originally been declared fair—in fact, that but one protest in the whole State was made within the time prescribed[3]; that protests by supervisors, unsupported by the affidavits of witnesses, had been accepted; that, on the other hand, such allegations not reported by supervisor or commissioner, as required by law, had been given validity; that some parishes were excluded on the bare protest of Marshal Packard[4]; that

---

they might be expected to put their mark where told to. The dense ignorance is well-attested by the examination of Thornton, House Misc. Doc., 45 Cong., 3 Sess., No. 31, La., 527; of Legadie, 530–2; of Armistead, 298; of Green, 51. Legadie, when asked a year later what ticket he had voted, replied, "I couldn't tell you now to save my life." Finally he concluded that he didn't vote at all, but went to the poll and had as "much fun as anyone," 528–9.

Duncan says, "When a man is hungry you know, why it (a dollar) would make his memory right smart then," 318.

[1] Sen. Exe. Doc., 44 Cong., 2 Sess., No. 2, 4. It was asserted that they had thus selected East and West Feliciana, East Baton Rouge, Morehouse, and Ouachita, with the largest negro vote. It was also pointed out that geographically they had chosen well to pretend border ruffianism from neighboring States.

[2] The De Soto returns were received Nov. 18, but affidavits were found inclosed, dated Nov. 25. Sherman looked uncomfortable when this fact was brought out. House Misc. Doc., 45 Cong., 3 Sess., No. 31, Wash., 1060.

[3] Ibid., 574.

[4] He tried to embrace the sixteen parishes which had not been protested and concerning which there had been no controversy. Ibid., La., 109.

many statements had been changed; and that some
affidavits had even been forged.   Witness after witness in
1878 denied their affidavits.   One denied making the
statement which there appeared and asserted the very
opposite of a free election[1]; another declared that names
given by a man beside him were inserted[2]; another that
he had not been sworn[3]; another that he had signed,
under threat of losing his mileage, a statement which he
knew to be false[4]; a fourth that he was drunk when
induced to sign and that the statements in many material
regards were not true.[5]   One of the clerks testified to
substitutions and alterations "to make it as strong as
possible."   He skipped parts in reading the affidavit to
the witness and could not remember a single case where
Woolfley read over a deposition.[6]   This testimony should
be accepted for what it is worth, as the writer frankly
admits that in such a maze of assertions and denials,
bribery and counter-bribery, and false testimony contra-
dicted and retracted, the truth is well-nigh hopelessly
buried.

Other supervisors than Anderson and Weber, as Grady
of Ouachita and Grant of Morehouse,[7] first testified to a
free, full, and fair election, and were then induced to
make supplemental charges.   One Kelly of Richland
Parish stated that great pressure was brought to bear
to procure those charges.[8]   He delivered his returns on

---

[1] House Misc. Doc., 45 Cong., 3 Sess., No. 31, La., 530, 492, 507.

[2] *Ibid.*, Washington, 1077.   [3] *Ibid.*, 446.   [4] *Ibid.*, La., 446.   [5] *Ibid.*, 126.

[6] *Ibid.*, 583.   Many so testify—523, 320, and Washington, 1077.   The
fact that many of the protests were burned after they had served their
purpose is damaging.

[7] *Ibid.*, Washington, 1445–6.   See Jewett's admission that on the night
of Nov. 24 he met in the post-office the supervisors from Webster, De Soto,
Bossier, and Red River parishes, from whose statement of facts he drew up
Ferguson's and Grady's protests, 1442, 1446.

[8] House Repts., 45 Cong., 3 Sess., No. 140, 33.

November 13 without protest.   But after a second subpœna to appear in New Orleans, he filed his statement
November 30, alleging intimidation at certain polls.[1]
It appeared that his protest was expressly made on report
to him and not from personal knowledge[2], and had been
drawn up by Kellogg.[3]

In 1878 Anderson swore to a story the reverse of that to
which he had testified two years earlier.   He revealed
or pretended to reveal a Republican conspiracy to afford
a pretext for casting out the Felicianas[4] by preventing
Republican votes.[5]   He held that the election had been
fair, although he refused to sign the returns until he got
to Baton Rouge,[6] but that he had been urged to prepare
a protest which he had at first refused to do; that an
effective, if untrue, protest had been prepared for him to
sign and was signed, under the influence of liquor, as he
claimed, but left by him incomplete; that he and Weber
had secured a written promise from Sherman of reward
from the party.   But when he found that Sherman and
Matthews would not reward him properly, as he thought,
he began to make the party trouble, played fast and loose

[1] The above facts appear from his own testimony to the House Committee.
But see Sen. Exe. Doc., 44 Cong., 2 Sess., No. 2, 459–81.   A very few
specific acts were alleged.

[2] When asked if he believed the facts sworn to, he said, "I doubted
a heap of it.   I know he reported a lie, for he afterwards voted the Democratic ticket."   House Misc. Doc., 45 Cong., 3 Sess., No. 31, La., 178.

[3] Jewett claimed to have the original document and sought to use it as a
whip over Kellogg.   Ibid., Washington, 1413, 1421.

[4] It is worth noting that a Federal captain said there had been no force
or intimidation there.   Ibid., 1087.

[5] Some testimony corroborates this plot, as word was being spread about
the Saturday preceding election for Republicans not to vote.   Ibid.,
La., 139.

[6] Even thus early he was dealing with both sides.   It would seem that
he received a draft for $350 from the Democrats to sign the returns with-
out a protest.   This would explain the delay, as the Democrats refused
to pay it at Clinton.   Ibid., Wash., 164.

with both sides,[1] and made public the charge implicating
Sherman in dishonest negotiations.[2] It was demonstrated
to a Congressional committee that about November 23
these sealed-up returns of supervisors were opened in the
presence of the secretary of the Republican committee
and new protests inserted.   In one or more, interpola-
tions were made, seven or eight days after the same were
sworn to, of new matter by which votes might be thrown
out.[3]   Into other packages were inserted new protests of
vague and indecisive character.[4]   Returns from Claiborne
Parish were unaccompanied by any protest from the
supervisor, but a later affidavit, sworn to November 18, by
parties who could neither read nor write, was filed with a
subsequent report on November 24, charging that two
hundred and fifty negroes were prevented by threats from
voting at Poll 3.[5] Late protests appeared also for West
Feliciana and for Ouachita.[6]

[1] Burke frankly related that Anderson tried to sell his evidence of a
conspiracy to the Democrats for $5000, an offer accepted but lost for lack
of funds.   House Misc. Doc., 45 Cong., 3 Sess., No. 31, Washington, 1007.

[2] Anderson's testimony may be found in *ibid.*, 1–62, 161 ff.   Sherman
denied any such relations.   It is not deemed necessary to sift the evidence
or discuss the question of the Sherman letter here, though it might be
added that a careful reading of all the evidence has convinced the writer
that Sherman was not guilty of the charges made against him.

[3] *Ibid.*, 1444.

[4] House Repts., 45 Cong., 3 Sess., No. 140, 100; House Misc. Doc., 45
Cong., 3 Sess., No. 31, Wash., 1444–5.

[5] It is a singular fact that when Claiborne Parish was called, Wells required it passed on the grounds of a contest.   When Judge Palmer asked
how he knew, Wells replied that in some instances the protest was sent with
the returns, sometimes separately.   One is at a loss, as was the committee, to see how any fair officer could have ordered Claiborne passed
because of a contest, when no papers contesting were then filed.   House
Repts., 44 Cong., 2 Sess., No. 156, Part i., 23–4.

[6] *Ibid.*, 83, Nov. 14; Ouachita, filed Nov. 21.   In this case returns were
not received by the board until Nov. 24 so that the Democrats had no
chance to meet the charges, since the board adjourned the hearing of
 estimony Nov. 29.

Then the value of *ex parte* evidence is open to challenge. In the case first mentioned, a majority of the Congressional committee were disposed, from the testimony of three prominent citizens, to believe the affidavit, signed with a cross, "untrue in fact, and possibly a manufactured paper,"[1] as there had been but very little interest in the election. Even more incriminating were three affidavits from Vernon, which purported to have been made three days before the returns were received by the board, signed by three marks. Certain members of the Congressional committee were wholly unable to obtain information about these three men and so came to the suspicion "that they have no actual existence"[2] and were created to favor certain local officers. One poll in Caldwell Parish was rejected although there was no protest of any kind, solely on the testimony of one Robinson, received December 1.[3] Moreover, such *ex parte* statements can always be easily procured in every community.[4] A Congressional committee thought that offices "applied for if not promised" were productive of altered affidavits,[5] an opinion which was sustained by the patent fact that nearly all engaged in the business received lucrative posts.[6]

[1] House Repts., 44 Cong., 2 Sess., No. 156, Part i., 26. [2] *Ibid.*, 139–40.

[3] The Democratic members of the sub-committee summoned seven witnesses who disproved the statements of Robinson, whom they represented as a worthless negro politician. *Ibid.*, 27.

[4] Especially when the election of a President with all his patronage depended on it. Worthy of credence is the testimony of Capt. Hale and Lieut. McCawley, Sen. Doc., No. 2, 330–420.

[5] One Morgan testified that he knew personally of an instance where answers were struck out because "it was a pity he couldn't lie a little for the party," and alterations made which gave a different character. He also heard it said of one answer, "they could fix it afterward." House Misc. Doc., 44 Cong., 2 Sess., No. 34, Part i., 87. He quoted Anderson as saying, "They may beat us voting, but we have the best of them in the count," 88.

[6] House Repts., 45 Cong., 3 Sess., No. 140, 100. A list of the positions of every minor official interested in the election, extending to the minute-clerk, police, and relatives, makes interesting reading. All, except one, a

Votes were cast out for technicalities, and yet other irregularities excused. Some were rejected because they were cast outside the judicial district; one poll in Iberia, because the commissioners did not indorse each certificate[1]; two polls in Webster because the tally-sheets were not footed at the polling-place, and because the commissioner was aided by a substitute, as the regular person fell ill; over three hundred votes of Orleans because careless figures made the number uncertain, though the tally-lists showed the number clearly; another poll because the commissioners' statement was not handed in within one day, and yet it was publicly announced that such failure did not constitute ground for rejection[2]; other wards were ruled out on "general intimidation."[3] But the board did not feel it incumbent to refuse returns brought personally by a supervisor to New Orleans and retained in his possession for ten days[4]; and it did count 2500 ballots bearing the names of only three electors as for the entire eight; in fact, in almost no case was the law with regard to the filing of protests complied with.

And so we find two diametrically opposite views possible: one, the Democratic Senatorial view, which regarded it as indisputable that the board had "no jurisdiction to inquire into and reject the returns from any voting place

---

supervisor, who was killed, were comfortably housed in the custom-house as inspectors, surveyors, weighers, laborers, etc. Anderson, alone, suffered. After assigning him to Funchal, Hayes felt obliged to revoke the commission on account of his character. For the full list see House Misc. Doc., 45 Cong., 3 Sess., No. 31, Washington, 1463-4. Gibson, *A Political Crime.*

[1] House Repts., 44 Cong., 2 Sess., No. 156, Part i., 153-4.

[2] Sen. Misc. Doc., 44 Cong., 2 Sess., No. 14, 34.

[3] The Congressional committee says tersely, "The only proof against these wards seems to have been that they gave 375 Democratic and only 83 Republican votes."

[4] When examined, he could not recollect anything clearly. House Misc. Doc., 44 Cong., 2 Sess., No. 34, Part i., 72.

on account of intimidation, unless the foundation for such rejection is laid at the time and in the manner provided by law "[1]; and the Republican view, as voiced by Howe, who found it strange if the legislature had charged such a duty upon the board, and should have "prohibited them from discharging the duty in every case where the commissioners carelessly or willfully refused to discharge the duty devolved upon them."[2]

Two days before the electoral college was to meet, rumors were rife that one or more of the members of the board were for sale—and this when it was known that one vote would change the Presidency. But it was not until February 1 and 2, as the electoral vote was about to be counted at Washington, that the revelations of one Maddox caused a great sensation. Additional evidence came to light in 1878. It would appear that Wells was trying to run with hare and hound. An effort at bribery by a Democrat is undoubted. Kenner, a Democrat of good reputation and standing in New Orleans, had several interviews with Wells concerning the political situation, beginning November 19, in the course of which, after allusions by Wells to his poverty and the necessity for compensation which would enable him to retire to his home, Kenner urged him to state his price. After additional interviews and a consultation with Anderson, $200,000 in greenbacks was stipulated. But there the matter dropped.[3]

[1] Sen. Misc. Doc., 44 Cong., 2 Sess., No. 14, 9.
[2] Sen. Repts., 44 Cong., 2 Sess., No. 701, Pt. ii., viii.
[3] It is regarded as immaterial to our purposes to go into the question of whether Wells invited the offer by allusions to his poverty, as Kenner asserted, or whether Kenner flatly offered it, as Wells asserted. In any case, it is clear that a bribe was entertained by both sides. See Kenner's testimony, House Misc. Doc., 44 Cong., 2 Sess., No. 42, 377. At a chance meeting after the promulgation, Wells replied to an expression of surprise at the result on the part of Kenner, "What could I do? You had no money." The evidence seems in favor of Kenner as he was of "Highest reputation,"

Immediately after this failure or temptation, as we accept or reject Wells's version that Kenner offered the bribe, he seems, however, to have entered into another negotiation. Maddox, a claim agent in the Treasury Department, succeeded in renewing with Wells an acquaintanceship of ante-bellum days. According to Maddox, Wells felt that his life was in danger, so that he did not see how he could finish his difficult task, although he wished to serve his party, unless he were compensated for it, and concluded with the request that Maddox see prominent men in Washington in order to assure the former of protection and the money necessary to satisfy him.[1] But Maddox won no friendly hearing with the President or other prominent Republicans, and so he turned to the Democrats, representing himself as a Republican in sympathy with the South and assuring them that the vote of Louisiana could be secured to Tilden for a million dollars.[2] But here too he met rebuff. Wells denied any conversation with Maddox or any knowledge of the corrupt transaction, calling him an "unmitigated liar." But he had intrusted to Maddox a letter of warning which he had written Senator West:

Millions have been sent here and will be used in the interest of Tilden and unless some counter move, it will be impossible for me or any individual to wrest its destructive results. The gentleman presenting this is fully aware of the moves, and if you will allow, will communicate freely. See our friends and

---

even according to Ray, House Repts., 44 Cong., 2 Sess., No. 100, 12, while Wells had no standing in the community.

[1] House Misc. Doc., 44 Cong., 2 Sess., No. 42, 144. It is difficult to weigh the value of Maddox's testimony, as about as many testified to his probity as against it. *Ibid.*, 278, 280, 281, 330.

[2] It was understood that Wells wanted $200,000 for Anderson and himself each, some small amount for the colored members. *Ibid.*, 145. See memorandum of Maddox, 138.

act promptly or results will be disastrous. A hint to the wise.[1]

His explanation that he feared that the people, under the influence of the money sent from New York, would do bodily harm to the returning-board and destroy the returns,[2] is hardly convincing. In his examination before a Congressional committee, he evaded the issues cleverly and doggedly and took refuge in anger when hard pressed,[3] but his replies do not ring true and only convince the reader of his guilt.

It had been suggested, meanwhile, according to Maddox and Wharton, that Packard[4] promise Wells one of the most valuable offices in the State. But Wells wanted a bribe of money and the payment of certain worthless warrants. This story was uncontradicted but cannot be relied upon because of the character of the chief witness. Still Wharton was rewarded with the second most lucrative Federal office in the State, and the bribe was offered, Saturday or Sunday at the very crux of the case.

Meanwhile the board worked in secret all day Sunday[5] and Monday, December 3 and 4, promulgating the official

[1] House Misc. Doc., 44 Cong., 2 Sess., No. 42, 180. The word "productive," which appears in the documents, is, Wells explains, incorrect.

[2] Ibid., 204. He insisted that the resentment with the board was due to no other cause than money. Maddox withheld the delivery of this letter, for his own purposes.

[3] Field forced him to admit that he did know the outcome before the canvass was completed and that the face of the returns gave Tilden the majority.

[4] Packard denied any conversation with any of the members of the board, and, indeed, the report only states that he hinted at what he had done in the past for Wells.

[5] Dec. 3. A scanty and incomplete record of the secret sessions is to be had from Kenner's Memorandum, printed in House Mis. Doc., 44 Cong., 2 Sess., No. 42, 126–8, where the polls rejected are enumerated with the alleged reason. Judge Palmer heard Sunday evening that the board had reached a conclusion for Hayes.

returns in the *Republican* on the morning of December 6.[1] The number of votes actually cast was, according to their count, 160,964; the returns as made by the election officials to the board showed a majority of 6300 to 8957 for Tilden electors.[2] But the board gave majorities ranging from 3437 to 4800 in favor of Hayes, casting out votes to the number of 13,211 for Tilden and 2412 for Hayes electors.[3] And so a Democratic majority of 7639 was converted into a Republican majority of 3437. It declared Packard and Antoine, together with the entire State ticket and four of the six Congressmen, elected. The Senate was declared to consist of 19 Republicans and 17 Democrats; while 71 Republicans and 43 Democrats with 3 Independents should make up the House.[4] To attain this result, all the polls of East Feliciana[5] and Grant Parishes, against only one of which any testimony had been taken, were rejected, also polls from twenty-two other parishes, sixty-nine polls in all, amounting to 19,436 ballots,[6] while 2500 ballots, bearing the names of only three electors, were counted for the entire eight. In addition, it was charged that alterations were deliberately made, for which the way had not been paved by affidavits, true or false. The most conspicuous example cited was

---

[1] Members swore that the canvass was not completed until 8 P.M.; yet a reporter had heard at 3 o'clock that the certificates for the electors had been made out. Electoral Commission, 62–3.

[2] The figures vary as usual but the difference is not essential. I have followed the Morrison report. But see Sen. Exe. Doc., 44 Cong., 2 Sess., No. 2, 8, and also the Palmer letter, Electoral Commission, and *Cyclopedia*, 489.

[3] The Democrats held that certain polls with large Democratic majorities were omitted so that the actual majorities were still larger. Sen. Repts., No. 701, li.   [4] *Ann. Cyclop.* 1876, 489.

[5] Rejected because no Republican ticket had been sent—evidence of intimidation.

[6] Ouachita lost 7 polls, Monroe all but 4, Claiborne 1, Catahoula 2, Caldwell 1.

Vernon Parish, where the transposition of two polls from the Democratic to the Republican side was ultimately betrayed by the clerk, Littlefield, who claimed to have done the work at Wells's command in order to elect a Republican attorney and district judge, and who failed to burn the original paper.[1] Of course, Wells denied all knowledge of the transaction, but his explanation that the blunder had crept in through the clerks is lame.[2] None of the other members of the board seem to have been implicated in this affair. The Republicans accused Littlefield of compiling the error into the returns purposely in order to cast a doubt on their correctness.[3]

Some delay in the count had occurred on November 27, as it was discovered that the program for casting out the votes of the bulldozed parishes, as predetermined, would elect Packard, but defeat two of the Hayes electors, because of imperfect electoral tickets in several cases, of lost tickets, and of a ticket improvised in Plaquemines by local politicians which bore the names of only three electors. And so the count was suspended[4] in order that messengers could be sent to gather additional protests. It may be observed that these affidavits bore in every instance date on or subsequent to November 27.[5]

With the promulgation the board printed its usual accusation of intimidation, charging throughout Ouachita a "systematic intimidation, murder, and violence

---

[1] Littlefield's statement at some points is quite unsupported.

[2] House Mis. Doc., 44 Cong., 2 Sess., No. 42, 213. Here as always, the maze of contradictory evidence buries the truth. It seems that Littlefield betrayed the story to a Democratic uncle and to a Republican who thought the information worth $100,000.

[3] House Repts., 44 Cong., 2 Sess., No. 100, Part iii., 5.

[4] Jewett admitted that figures were calculated to show the result in case certain parishes were rejected and that polls were selected with regard to how the protest would affect the returns. House Misc. Doc., 45 Cong., 3 Sess., No. 31, 1443.

[5] See the list given, *ibid.*, Wash., 591–2.

toward one class of voters, white as well as black, of such a character as to have scarcely a parallel in the history of this state."[1]   The next day the *Republican* printed the results of the parish and city elections.

On December 5, McEnery, as governor, certified that he had, in the presence of Attorney-General Ogden and a judge of Orleans Parish examined duplicate returns of the commissioners of election at each poll and found the Democratic electors chosen.   The Democratic Committee on Returns certified to the same result, as obtained by the compilation from sworn duplicates and copies of original consolidated statements of supervisors.   It published also the full State ticket.[2]

While the returning-board was settling the result behind closed doors, a battle royal was going on outside in the papers.   Such admonitions to the board as the following appeared: "Your lives are not worth half a cent. Millions of people will rise *en masse*, if you do not make truthful returns; you will all otherwise be cut up into mince-meat."[3]   Distrust of the board was voiced in the North, by such papers as the *Nation*.[4]   November 29 the citizens of New Orleans, pastors and bank presidents, appealed to the Nation, deprecating the impression produced on their fellow-citizens, and the great injury done to the business interests of the State by hasty military proclamations and the sending thither of troops.[5]

---

[1] *Times*, Dec. 9.   All the members of the board were indicted in 1878. Anderson was sentenced for two years but finally released as the offense was not covered by statute.   [2] *Picayune*, Dec. 6.

[3] Copied in the Sen. Misc. Doc., 44 Cong., 2 Sess., No. 14, 54.   A threatening letter enjoined the board to count the votes fairly; otherwise the signers had taken a solemn pledge to execute every member of the board. Anderson declared they did not regard such things, so common were they. *Ibid.*, 27–8.   [4] See issue of Nov. 23.

[5] *Times*, Nov. 30.   See also *Republican* of Dec. 1, which ridicules the invocation of "Benefit of Clergy," as it calls it.

The finding of the board was known and discussed on the evening of December 5 and caused irritation, although it was just what was expected by almost everyone, as the *Times* and *Republican* united in saying.[1] But the *Democrat* was in "no degree dispirited." It declared itself

for peace only so long as the best interests of the country are identified with peace. There sometimes arise emergencies in which peace only encourages and abets usurpations and lawlessness. Our second wish is that the country may have peace; our first is that the constitutional government of the Republic may be preserved and that the American people may remain free.[2]

And it indulged in the prophecy that Nicholls would be governor before spring. The *Picayune* looked to the National Congress "to repudiate from the electoral college so foul a reproach upon the Republic, and to blot this crowning infamy from the history of the country."[3] December 6, Nicholls issued an appeal to the people of the State, commending their orderly conduct and urging them to refrain from violence, to hold every feeling, passion, and resentment subordinate to the great work of redemption, which he felt was near at hand.[4]

December 5, Kellogg issued certificates to the Hayes electors, who met the next day at four in the afternoon in the state-house to cast their votes. As there was some little difficulty over the eligibility of two of the electors, who had resigned government positions only on November 10 and 19,[5] they conveniently absented themselves, until

[1] Dec. 6. The *Times* declared that the result was received with "ominous calm," Dec. 7.   [2] Dec. 7.   [3] Dec. 6.
[4] *Annual Cyclopedia*, 1876, 491.
[5] Brewster was surveyor-general on a salary of $2000 and perquisites; Levisee, commissioner of a circuit court up to November 19. Brewster admitted that he had resigned November 14 to take effect November 4. A Congressional Committee was unable to secure Levisee's presence. House Repts., 44 Cong., 2 Sess., No. 156, Part i., 19–20.

the vacancies were filled by their own appointment,
whereupon they immediately appeared and cast their
ballots for Hayes.[1] As one elector cast his ballot, he
declared that he had been offered $100,000 to vote for
Tilden, but he valued even more his right to help elect
Hayes.[2] The electors disregarded the constitutional
provision which required them to vote for President and
Vice-President by distinct ballots[3] and to certify to their
vote by separate lists.[4] When Anderson, who had been
chosen official messenger, delivered his certificates to
Vice-President Ferry, the latter called his attention to
the fact that the envelope was not properly indorsed but
allowed Anderson to retain it to have it rectified. Anderson then began to have doubts concerning the regularity
of the contents, and when he had shared them with the
Republican leaders in New Orleans, it was decided that
new certificates were the only safe procedure. Accordingly, new ones were signed December 29, antedated
to December 6, with two forged signatures, for which
Kellogg was held responsible.[5]

The Democratic electors resolved December 5 to accept
certificates from McEnery, an action which had the
approval of the leaders in the city. The following day

[1] House Repts., 44 Cong., 2 Sess., No. 156, Part i., 20. But the election
law of 1870 provided for the filling of vacancies by popular election.

[2] *Republican*, Dec. 7.

[3] Levisee says that they used but one ballot for both nominees. For
proceedings in the electoral college, see House Misc. Doc., 45 Cong., 3
Sess., No. 31, Wash., 80, 95, 128.

[4] The certificates were as regular as the Democratic certificates from
Florida, Louisiana, and South Carolina, and the Republican certificate from
Oregon, implying separate ballots. See Electoral Commission, 287, 293,
299. But the forged certificates were substituted in process of printing so
as to come before the commission, and Morton was careful to move that
the votes of No. 1 (original) be counted. Morton had been told of the
forgery. Foulke, II., 470.

[5] The actual forgery seems to have been done by a minor official, House
Repts., 45 Cong., 3 Sess., No. 140, 50–63, House Misc., No. 42, 180.

they met in the hall of Representatives, although Kellogg objected to its being crowded with a large political assemblage, and cast their ballots for Tilden and Hendricks.

If reports could have thrown light upon the question, the country should have been duly illuminated, for there were no less than seven reports. The delegation of visiting Democrats were first in the field on December 6 with the report which they submitted to A. S. Hewitt, chairman of the National Committee, known as the Palmer-Trumbull report. It took the ground that the board had no jurisdiction over the votes of electors, as they were elected under the law of 1870, which provided for the canvass by the governor in the presence of the secretary, attorney-general, and a district judge, since the law of 1872 made no provision for the electoral canvass; that the returning officers were unworthy of confidence; that they had violated the law in refusing to fill the vacancy in their own number and in the manner of conducting the canvass so that the result from first to last was a fraud; and that its result was arbitrary, illegal, and entitled to no respect whatever.[1] In stirring language it asked whether the will of forty millions of people, constitutionally expressed, should be "thwarted by the corrupt, arbitrary, and illegally constituted returning-board in Louisiana, whose wrongful action heretofore, in all respects similar to its present action, has been condemned by all parties."[2]

Sherman's letter to the President, signed by ten other Republicans, was transmitted by the latter to Congress

---

[1] *Ann. Cyclop.*, 1876, 492. This report with its extended array of facts was published in all the leading papers about December 10–12. This eventually reached Congress in the form of a petition, signed by but five members, as the others had left Louisiana upon being excluded by the board. Sen. Misc. Doc., 44 Cong., 2 Sess., No. 12.

[2] Sen. Doc., No. 2. With this report is found the record of the returning-board and the testimony taken by it.

the same day as the Democratic report appeared.   Emphatic language was not wanting to convince the public.

Organized clubs of masked, armed men, formed as recommended by the central Democratic committee, rode through the country at night, marking their course by the whipping, shooting, wounding, maiming, mutilation, and murder of women, children, and defenceless men, whose houses were forcibly entered while they slept, and, as their inmates fled, the pistol, the rifle, the knife, and the rope were employed to do their horrid work.   Crimes like these, testified to by scores of witnesses, were the means employed in Louisiana to elect a President of the United States.[1]

And they concluded that complaint should not be made if political success thus attained by violence were denounced by judicial tribunals as illegal and void.[2]

Immediately after the convening of Congress, committees were sent to Louisiana by both houses to make investigations.   The House Committee held its first session, December 12, while the Senate Committee began work only six days later.   The board refused to be investigated and protested against the demand of Congressmen for its archives in order to review the action of a State tribunal, consenting only to copy its records at the expense of the committee.[3]   Both committees were divided into several sub-committees to prosecute different branches

---

[1] His reasoning to show that a Democratic majority of 4000 odd in five parishes with 13,244 colored population proves intimidation is specious but not conclusive.   Sen. Exe. Doc., 44 Cong., 2 Sess., No. 2, 8.

[2] Ibid., 9.

[3] The *Times* waxed indignant at this "cool impudence," and rather cleverly termed it "the most flagrant assertion of state rights heard for some years," which would carry them back to the doctrine in vogue before the war.   Dec. 13.   This attitude was attributed to support from Grant, *Times*, Dec. 17.   The board delayed and thwarted the copying of the returns in every possible way; the telegraph company refused to produce messages.

of the inquiry. Numerous witnesses were examined in New Orleans and in various parishes, the committees even continuing the examination in Washington during January and February.[1] Majority and minority reports were made late in the session by both committees, in which a strictly party view of events was presented and strictly partisan conclusions reached. The Republican members of each group were convinced of the fairness and legality of the action of the board, while the Democratic members found evidence equally convincing of the falsification of the result by the board.[2] So far did partisanship hold sway that five Republican members of the House Committee felt obliged to protest against and deny any jurisdiction to inquire into the late election in Louisiana for the purpose given.[3] It will be sufficient to oppose to each other the two following antagonistic conclusions. First hear the majority report of the House:

Taken altogether, the acts and doings of said board force upon your committee the conclusion that it entered upon the canvass and compilation of the votes cast at the recent election with a prearranged purpose to change the result, and fraudulently declare the result in favor of Hayes and Wheeler; that in the accomplishment of this unlawful purpose, the

[1] The House Committee was in session in New Orleans, Dec. 12–21, 26, and Jan. 2; in Washington, Jan. 22–3, 29–31, Feb. 9. The Senate Committee from December 18 on.

[2] The Democrats of the Senatorial Committee do admit that "excesses were committed of the most grievous character, in which the colored men were tortured to make them confess their guilt, as most of this thieving was charged to have been committed by the colored people. . . . It is extremely difficult, in an impartial review of the testimony taken by the sub-committee, to determine what acts of outrage and violence are to be accounted for solely as the result of lawlessness and crime to which we have referred, or whether, in the heat of the political canvass which followed, there was not . . . some political element." Sen. Repts., 44 Cong., 2 Sess., No. 701, lxiii.

[3] House Repts., 44 Cong., 2 Sess., No. 156, Part i., 2.

members of the board did not hesitate to commit any act of official perfidy necessary to the end to be attained.[1]

And so it formally concluded that

the Democratic electors received a majority of the votes actually and legally cast at the recent election . . . and that the vote of that State cannot be counted for Messrs. Hayes and Wheeler without the confirmation and approval of the illegal and fraudulent action of said returning-board.[2]

And then the majority report of the Senate Committee: ".That very gross intimidation was employed in the parishes examined there seems no room to doubt.   And that such intimidation very materially and very surprisingly changed the result of the election, there seems no room to doubt."[3]   Naturally, the minorities in each case took the opposing position, the Senatorial minority covering in a long discussion much the same ground as that covered by the majority report of the House Committee.[4]   But the matter was not allowed to rest even there.   In June, 1878, the fairness of the decision was again challenged and the participation of the visiting statesmen in the action of the board investigated.   And so over two hundred witnesses were examined and some three thousand additional pages of testimony contributed to the documentary depositories.   Even after that brief interval the temper seems more judicial and impartial, though misrepresentations appeared constantly in the press.   The majority attempted to rest

---

[1] House Repts., 44 Cong., 2 Sess., No. 156, Part i., 9.   [2] *Ibid.*, 20.

[3] Sen. Repts., 44 Cong., 2 Sess., No. 701, xli.–xlii.

[4] The House minority were less restrained than their fellow-Republicans in the Senate: "The mode of action to overthrow free choice was fearfully alike in all these parishes; it was one sad, weary, and monotonous repetition of inhuman cruelty, one melancholy and systematic crushing-out of free thought, free speech, and free action by audacious crime."   House Repts., 44 Cong., 2 Sess., No. 156, Part ii., 16.

their conclusions "rather upon such known and patent facts and the attendant circumstances than on the confessions" of any of the participating parties.[1] And yet their decision reads:

Men who thought the welfare of the country depended upon the continuation in power of the Republican party would naturally have been disposed to consider almost anything justified to retain it there. To us it seems impossible that the flagrant and atrocious conduct of the Returning-Board was not realized above all by the men of most political experience, or that the most dangerous and outrageous political fraud of the age was not assisted and advised by those who next proceeded to take possession of its best fruits.[2]

It has been left to this point to weigh the charges of intimidation.[3] The exact truth cannot be ascertained. Witnesses retracted, altered, denied former statements until frequently testimony becomes quite worthless. For instance, one Lapierre testified that he was not allowed to take the tally-sheets to his ward nor act as his conscience dictated; yet he later voluntarily testified to a peaceable election.[4] A creole supervisor who understood English poorly was induced to suppress his first statement in order to allow another made, which omitted two polls. He testified later that his statement had been materially misrepresented as translated by Republican officials.[5]

---

[1] House Repts., 45 Cong., 3 Sess., No. 140, 4–5. It is conspicuous that no member of this committee complained of any unfairness in respect to the conduct of the investigation.

[2] *Ibid.*, 47.

[3] Except for the brief consideration of the disorders on pp. 430–6.

[4] Compare House Repts., 44 Cong., 2 Sess., No. 156, Part i., 64, and House Misc., Doc., 44 Cong., 2 Sess., No. 34, 73.

[5] House Repts., 44 Cong., 2 Sess., No. 156, Part i., 155. These instances could be greatly multiplied. See the case of the sheriff who swore that he had no recollection of any whipping, though such an account appeared in his own statement. *Ibid.*, 103.

Doubtless, some of these retractions were inspired by revenge or a hope of reward, as in the case of Jenks and J. E. Anderson of East Feliciana, and in the case of Weber, who endeavored to bribe and persuade the negroes of his vicinity to retract their testimony in order to support his retractions.[1] The Republican minority of the Committee of 1878 even tried to establish the falsity of these retractions, their contention based on the contrast in manner of the negroes between the first time, when answers were clear and confident, and the second time, when they seemed "to be doggedly denying the truth" and affecting stupidity.[2] In the light of such conflicting evidence, it seems not worth while here carefully to sift the evidence, collected in some nine thousand pages of testimony. The Republicans produced witnesses throughout the parishes where intimidation was charged, but more especially from the colored parishes, to prove coercion.[3] But it savors of *opéra bouffe* when a witness charges that he saw Republicans "a crying there" because not free to cast the ballot they wished to,[4] and when such harsh epithets as "orang-outang, monkey" and suggestive verses are cited as evidence of intimidation.[5] The usual story of negroes marched in line to the poll to deposit Democratic ballots was forthcoming and denied.[6] Likewise, the Democrats piled up affidavits that tended to show no intimidation;

[1] Claim of Dula, House Misc. Doc., 45 Cong., 3 Sess., No. 31, La., 342–4, that Weber had offered him $500 to change his testimony; St. Martin declared that he saw money given to every one of the negroes, *ibid.*, Washington, 1214; Weber was quoted as having been promised $10,000, 1233. Even Stenger of the Congressional Committee was not exalted above accusations of knowledge of the fraud. *Ibid.*, 1208.

[2] House Repts., 45 Cong., 3 Sess., No. 140, 87.

[3] Sen. Repts., 44 Cong., 2 Sess., No. 701, 2343.   [4] *Ibid.*, 2344.

[5] Where the bullet enters,   Where the knife is thrust,
    The flesh will quiver, and   The blood will flow. *Ibid.*, 153.

[6] See also Sen. Exe. Doc., 44 Cong., 2 Sess., No. ii., 226–7, 220–1. House Repts., 44 Cong., 2 Sess., No. 156, Part i., 65.

assertions by negroes that they had voted the Democratic ticket of their own will, that Republican negroes had been able to cast their ballots without interference.[1] They also secured the testimony of Federal officials and army officers to the absence of intimidation, of which the most notable was that of Lieutenant Gerlach.[2] They did not fail to point out that in all the testimony admitted for Hayes, but sixteen affidavits by colored men alleged intimidation, and that when pressed, such testimony was frequently only hearsay.[3] They asserted that outrages were committed by blacks on blacks; produced about four hundred and seventy-three affidavits signed by negroes from Ouachita that their action in joining the Democrats had been voluntary[4]; pointed to the fact that witnesses who swore to intimidation very generally voted the Republican ticket. They held that a scheme to exclude the Democratic majority was carried out in Grant and East Baton Rouge; and that if Ouachita were bulldozed, all the polls—not merely the Democratic—should have been rejected. And they made their usual counter-charges—control and abuse of the election machinery,[5]

[1] See evidence of David Jones, House Misc. Doc., 44 Cong., 2 Sess., No. 34, Part iii., 35; of Rev. Plunket, 42; of Burnet, who believed that negroes who alleged fear of bulldozers did so for effect, 83; of Sandidge, House Repts., Part vi., 213; of Brigham, 198; of Polk, 215; Todd, 208; of Ferguson, Part iv., 186; of Duncan, Danford, Niles Smith, Crocket in Sen. Exe. Doc., 44 Cong., 2 Sess., No. 701.

The following figures speak for themselves: To 49 witnesses whom the Republicans produced, the Democrats opposed 527 in West Feliciana; to 51 in Ouachita, 727; to 63 in East Baton Rouge, 457; to 26 in East Feliciana, 1196. House Repts., 45 Cong., 3 Sess., No. 140, 39.

[2] House Repts., 44 Cong., 2 Sess., No. 156, Part i., 76–7.

[3] House Misc. Doc., 45 Cong., 3 Sess., No. 31, La., 360, 390. One tender-hearted negro refused to give names on the plea of ill-manners. *Ibid.*, 360.

[4] But see Sen. Repts., 44 Cong., 2 Sess., No. 701, 600–3.

[5] The Republican party had the marshals send for witnesses, and as a Democrat pointedly remarked, "A man can tell more lies in an hour than can be disproved in a day."

corruption in the election officials and deputy marshals,[1] fraudulent registration and ballot-stuffing; dishonesty in tally-sheets,[2] and encouragement given to the board in the presence of the visiting statesmen.[3]

And so the conclusion would seem to be that the Democratic party, fearing the acts of intimidation of their supporters would be seized upon by the Republicans to reject their votes, had come to the determination not to have any bulldozing in the suspected parishes during the campaign of 1876, but to rely upon conciliatory means to win over the negroes, with which peaceful policy was doubtless mingled a certain constraint due to the intimidation of previous elections.[4]   But the Republicans had predetermined that the votes in those parishes, to the number necessary, should be rejected, depending on the protests of supervisors which were always forthcoming in a State where disorders, more or less political, were frequent and where Republican officials were easily intimidated.[5]

---

[1] Let the description of one suffice: He lived on the wharf, lodged nowhere, and had no particular employment; got one hundred and fifty negroes in the club-room and kept them there the night of December 6; supplied them with Republican tickets, and at 7 o'clock carried his poll.   House Repts., 44 Cong., 2 Sess., No. 156, Part i., 6–7.   Those who served from patriotic devotion, as Packard claimed some did, are hard to find.   Even the few Democratic appointments were not satisfactory.

[2] It was regarded as telling proof when several Republicans refused to accept office—Long of De Soto, a legislator; Carr, a sheriff; and a justice of the peace.   *Times*, December 15, *Picayune*, December 29.

[3] The writer cannot agree with Rhodes that but for the presence of the visiting statesmen, the returning-board would have made a fair canvass, for their action in the canvass of 1874 would indicate no regard for public opinion and they had all to gain with nothing to lose by the attempt at a return for the Republicans.

[4] The writer cannot feel that there is conclusive proof of a Democratic plot for bulldozing in the five suspected parishes, though she admits the possibility of the murders in Ouachita being political.

[5] This opinion, it will be observed, coincides very closely with that reached by Butler, who can hardly be accused of partisanship for the ex-Confederate.

CHAPTER XX

In Statu Quo

TENSENESS of feeling did not relax during December, neither North nor South. The New York *Herald* recommended impeaching Grant. The Democrats of Louisiana had telegraphic assurance from Indiana that there were half a million men ready to demand the spoils of war or blood. By the middle of the month it was said at Washington that there was general apprehension of trouble in February. There was stagnation in business and deep apprehension pervaded the whole country. To the New York *Herald* it seemed patent

that we are drifting further from shore and into deeper water every day. We may expect tempestuous times until the fourth of March; and if even then a satisfactory peace comes, it will be more than present indications justify us in expecting.[1]

The *Daily Bulletin* of the same city even hinted at war. Though the Louisiana papers indulged in occasional outbursts of feeling when they had "no doubt the people of this country would wade through leagues of trouble" until every citizen could stand "the peer of every other man in the nation,"[2] there was general quiet throughout the State, due, undoubtedly, to the feeling that the scene of conflict had been shifted from the State to the National capitol.

[1] December 15.   [2] *Times*, December 18.

We cannot determine the national contest by any action of ours [admonished the *Times*], while we might prejudice the case of Tilden and our own future status by the employment of such forcible means as would undoubtedly be resorted to were the case simply and solely our own.[1]

Never for one moment did Nicholls concede the possibility of defeat. In the last days of the year he defined his position.

Peacefully, fairly, legally elected your Governor by over eight thousand majority of the votes of both races in the State, I announce to you my fixed determination to assert and maintain my right to that position, and I know that you are equally determined that I shall do so. I shall be prepared to do my whole duty, and I shall expect the same from every citizen of Louisiana.[2]

So accustomed were the people by this time to ruptures in their legislature, that they took for granted such a condition in 1877 and discussed quite calmly the chances for success of each faction.[3] But no serious disturbance seems to have been apprehended. All sorts of rumors were afloat: that the Republicans had barricaded the state-house and would allow only returning-board members to enter; on the other hand, that the Democrats meditated seizing the house by force; that Warmoth wanted the Democratic members present on the first day, but the extremists preferred that the Democrats keep out of the legislature altogether; that Republicans would rely on the troops; and that the White League had been ordered to assemble at four o'clock on New Year's morn-

---

[1] *Times*, December 18. Note how poor a prophet this paper proved: "Hayes could not if he would, go into office, on the electoral vote of Louisiana and then turn his back on Packard. For him to admit the election of Nicholls, is to concede his own defeat and fraudulent tenure of office." Dec. 28.　　[2] *Picayune*, Dec., 29.　　[3] See *Times*, Dec. 31.

ing. Speculations concerning the speakership were rife. Conservative sentiment might be described as one of watchful waiting.

Party caucuses were numerous and almost unprecedentedly early.[1] As a number of Conservative legislators were already in the city by December 25, they assembled that day formally but did no work. Republicans of both houses met in their respective caucuses, December 29, in order to arrive at an understanding about their organization. The plan of the Democrats was formulated in caucus on New Year's eve when every member was present but was kept a profound secret. The Republicans, in order to control the situation, lodged and breakfasted at the state-house, which was barricaded and defended by armed police officers, assigned to their positions at six o'clock, while squads of police kept the people from collecting in front of the state-house. All entrances were closed but one, access to which was gained through two rows of police. The Republicans in caucus that morning settled definitely upon Hahn as their choice for speaker.

A small committee was sent from the Democratic caucus, in session from ten o'clock to eleven fifty-five to ask the governor that all Democrats claiming election be admitted and that armed men be removed, in return for which concession the promise was given that there should be no disturbance. The governor was warned by the clerk of the House that he should refuse to call the roll unless the barricades and armed men were removed. A great crowd collected outside the Democratic caucus in Royal Street, crowding the balconies of the adjacent buildings.

All the Democratic members at five minutes before twelve, attended by a large crowd, proceeded down Royal Street to the state-house, the police along the line of their

[1] The Republican Senators held a meeting as early as Dec. 14.

advance slowly retreating before them. The crowd cheered and applauded as they approached, while Republicans who had ventured forth hurried to get into the fortress. All but those recognized by the returning-board were denied admittance. Bush, the Democratic leader, called on the clerk to clear the obstructions, and demanded the removal of the forces—a request which was peremptorily refused, of course. They then retired after the reading of a "solemn protest"[1] against this invasion by the executive of the rights and privileges of the legislature and against the military occupation of the state-house,[2] declining to enter the legislative hall, until it should be opened freely.[3] Followed by two thousand people, they then marched in a body to St. Patrick's Hall, where the clerk appeared, because his demand for the withdrawal of the troops had been refused, at about half after one to call the roll. He declared sixty-two members[4] present and a quorum. Colonel Louis Bush was almost unanimously elected and sworn in by the oldest member present. Minor officers were elected and routine work begun by the election of a joint committee of the House and Senate to draft an address to the people, setting forth the reasons for the action of that day.[5]

The Conservative Senate was called to order by Senator Robertson, who moved that in the absence of Antoine, they elect a temporary president. Nine hold-over and eleven[6] new Senators responded. After Wiltz was made president, the customary committee was sent to notify the governor of their organization and to protest against

[1] Directed (1) against the invasion of the executive, (2) against military occupation of the state-house. House Jour., 1877, 12.

[2] La. House Jour., 1877, 12.

[3] For the full account of this day's proceedings see *Times*, Jan. 2.

[4] House Jour., 1877, 4. Forty held certificates from the board, twenty-two had none.   [5] House Jour., 12.

[6] The *Picayune* says 11, differing from the *Annual Cyclopedia*.

the presence of military forces in the building adjacent to the state-house.

Meanwhile the sixty-eight deserted Republicans in the state-house were honoring the roll-call of one Souer, acting-clerk by request of the secretary of state.[1] Hahn and Warmoth were candidates for the speakership, the latter "to emancipate the House" from the dictatorship of the governor, he declared. Hahn's fifty-three votes readily elected him, whereupon he made the usual speech, regretting that so many members had seen fit to absent themselves, when there was such need of able counsel. Organization was completed and a call upon Grant for aid against domestic violence passed.

Antoine called the Radical Senate to order. With eleven hold-over Senators and eight new ones, he declared a quorum and authorized permanent organization by the election of officers. The arrest of two Democratic Senators, who were serving as a committee to notify the governor of the Patrick Hall organization, caused a flurry of excitement. Before the close of the day, summary action filled two contested seats and passed two bills; one condemnatory of the "illegal assembly at St. Patrick's Hall," and one calling on the President to preserve the peace.

Kellogg's annual message came to the Republican houses in regular course. He began with a characteristic defense of his administration: he tried to show an eighty per cent reduction of State taxes, a limiting of the parish taxes; a reduction of the cost of government by almost half; and pointed to helpful financial amendments, and appreciation of the consols. He could not resist a fling at Conservative-

---

[1] One member responded because he regarded that as the proper place, but objected to the revolutionary measures of the House. Two members might fairly be called independents. Of the other five Republicans declared elected one had refused to accept election. *Picayune*, Jan. 3.

ruled New Orleans: "The fact is indisputable that the agricultural districts of the State are rapidly gaining in prosperity, while the City of New Orleans, the chief center of turbulence and political discord, is daily declining in wealth." His presentation of the race question could hardly be termed fair. He felt that the acute political situation had become a question for the Nation to decide —whether the violent and illegal means which had been systematically put forth in that and other Southern States to prevent the will of the people should prevail. He no longer felt any need to conciliate the Democrats:

There can be no mistake as to the attitude of the opponents of the Republican party in Louisiana toward the constitutional amendments. It is clearly cut and well-defined. The proof does not rest upon evidence of violence in any one or more parishes, or at any one election. It is legibly written all over the history of the State since the termination of the war.[1]

January 2 saw significant and similar work performed by both legislatures. The committee of the Patrick Hall body, which had waited upon Kellogg the first day, reported to the Senate his refusal to see them, whereupon Wiltz was ordered to telegraph the facts to Grant. The canvass of the recent election by both houses in joint session in the presence of a lobby of fifteen hundred people then followed in regular order. Upon the refusal of the secretary of state to deliver the returns to this body, the speaker stated that he had duplicate returns from the secretary recognized by the *de jure* government, and so the canvass proceeded from the face of the returns. It appeared that Nicholls was elected by 84,487 votes as opposed to 76,477 for Packard; Wiltz by 84,242 as opposed

---

[1] *Republican*, January 3, 1877. It is probably to the last paragraphs that the *Picayune* referred when it called it "remarkable for extravagant assumptions and for abundant misrepresentations."

to 76,471 for Antoine. The president of the Senate, accordingly, made the usual proclamation, and a joint committee was created to arrange for the inauguration.[1] Similar action in the state-house[2] produced exactly opposite results. It was found that Packard was elected over Nicholls by 74,624 *versus* 71,198 votes, and that Antoine had won over Wiltz. The House then proceeded at once to active legislation, crowding through a relief bill by suspension of the rules.[3]

The third day of the session saw the Conservatives housed in Odd Fellows Hall. There was talk of compromise, but also of trouble. All the State offices were strongly guarded and no one permitted to enter but by permission.[4] In the Republican House contests were received and filed, and an effort made to declare all seats unoccupied by January 6 permanently vacant. A bill to appropriate $200,000 for the militia of the State was considered so important that it passed through all its stages in one day.[5] To get rid of a Democratic judge, a civil superior court was created to replace a regular district court.[6] The Senate of that faction hurried through an act to authorize the governor to assume charge of the capitol buildings, and to empower him to maintain peace and order in their vicinity.

By the fifth day of the session the Democratic House had progressed so far as to appoint its standing committees

[1] *Times*, January 3, 1877.
[2] Two additional members were sworn in that day so that the number reached 63. At the count of the vote for governor there were 89 members present.
[3] For January 3, see the accounts in the *Times*, *Picayune*, and *Republican*.
[4] The *Times* declared that the office of the secretary looked like a camp, January 4.
[5] Already vouchers of this House had begun to decline. They were worth thirty-five cents on the dollar on January 7. *Times*.
[6] See the official publication in the *Republican*, January 5.

and to take up an appropriation bill, and to issue an address to the people. After recounting the history of the recent election, it declared that there no longer existed in the State a Republican government, due to the usurpation of the board and of the Federal bayonets, and so invited all people without reference to color or politics "to stand by the legitimate government elected by them in November." It urged them to frown upon the illegal body holding forth under the shadow of the military in the barricaded state-house; to withhold taxes from the collectors of this spurious organization, and in the meantime wait and forbear, "for the day of deliverance is near."[1] And by January 6 the Democratic organization was feeling its strength sufficiently to become more aggressive. It adopted unanimously a resolution declaring the pretended canvass of votes made by the body, styling itself the returning-board, null and void, and directing the judiciary committees of the House and Senate to present an act providing for a proper canvass. The Committee on Qualifications reported adversely to the leader of the other House and swore in a contestant in his place.[2]

Meantime, also, the excitement had calmed down so that there was comparative quiet, though not perfect order. According to the *Picayune*, the crowd in front of the state-house had become less each day. As the dread of an attack from the Conservatives decreased, the Republicans on guard relaxed their vigilance.[3] The former knew that their government commanded the moral and material support of the people, and were determined, actively but not forcibly, to put their government in motion, and to prevent any violence except that which came from the Radicals.[4]

[1] La. House Jour., 1877, 11–12. [2] *Ibid.*, 12. [3] *Times*, January 5.
[4] This was the view telegraphed by Burke to Representative Gibson,

Two days later came the double inauguration at their respective halls. It was a day of deep but not boisterous excitement. All business was suspended, except the patrolling of the city by the people's police, but it was an orderly populace that thronged the streets. At one o'clock occurred the installation of Nicholls and Wiltz in the presence of ten thousand people massed on the square in front of St. Patrick's Hall. In the space adjacent to the flag-wreathed balcony were seated the Senate and House together with distinguished members of the clergy and bar. The enthusiasm of the crowd, when Nicholls entered his carriage, led it to replace his horses by one hundred men who eagerly drew the vehicle to St. Patrick's Hall. The two executives appeared on the balcony to take the oath of office to the accompaniment of cannon. In his inaugural the governor expressed his determination that the fraud should be thwarted. He struck the keynote of his theme when he cried:

Self must be sunk, and the general good alone serve as the guide to the civil and political action of each citizen. Laws operating equally upon the whole people, without distinction of race, color, or condition, must alone be found on the statute books, and these laws should be thoroughly, fairly, and impartially executed. I shall devote [he declared] every energy to the great work of restoration, and to securing an efficient administration of public affairs, with the least possible cost to those upon whom the burdens of the State rest. Honesty and capacity will be required as absolute conditions to appointment, and every avenue by which the people can be injured will be carefully guarded to the limit of legal power.[1]

January 6, to present to Grant. House Misc. Doc., 45 Cong., 3 Sess., No. 31, La., 602. And this was their position, though they preferred rebellion to submission to Kellogg.

[1] *Times*, January 9. The *Republican* did not deign to notice Nicholls's inauguration.

31

At the same hour, within the safe barricades of the state-house, from which the public was excluded, Packard was outlining his policy in his inaugural address. It dealt with Federal protection, Republican principles and progress, domestic policy, immigration, schools, and municipal affairs. It rang all the possible changes on violence. He declared that he had received an undoubted majority of the votes fairly cast at the recent election and announced his purpose to invoke all the powers conferred upon him to enforce obedience to the laws and to secure an abiding peace for the State. The doctrine established by the constitution was laid down as the basis of guidance.[1]

Meanwhile the first manifestation of disorder made its appearance. An unfriendly crowd gathered outside the building to irritate the Republicans, and held them prisoners until late in the afternoon, despite the fact that Nicholls sent a written message, ordering the crowd to disperse. Some glass was broken and the effort to take baskets of bread into the fortified camp occasioned more laughter and shouts of derision. When a large squad of police took charge of the entrances and steps toward night, the crowd quietly left.[2]

But the next morning was seen the spectacle of men of all ages, hurrying on the streets, armed and determined.[3] The crowd increased and by ten o'clock many parts of the city presented a martial appearance. A State militia of

[1] *Republican*, January 9.

[2] See the *Times* and *Picayune* for January 9. The former tells how the dinner ordered by Kellogg was devoured by the crowd outside.

[3] Ogden had ordered the Crescent City White League to report at dawn Monday at Masonic Hall, whence they were to march to Lafayette Square at a later hour. This manœuvre had been kept such a profound secret that even the wives, awakened during the night by the mysterious actions of their husbands, could not comprehend the meaning, though apprehensive of danger. Told the writer by the wife of one of the officers.

six hundred men, the "Continental Guards," had been organized with Ogden in command, assisted by General Behan, Vaudry, and Penn.[1] In various quarters the militia assembled, the artillery congregating at St. Mary's Market with the field pieces, prepared to move to Lafayette Square. By half after ten the people's police entered upon their duties as metropolitan police, and at eleven-twenty the entire force, three thousand strong, marched from the square and formed into line. The purpose was to see that the Democratic Supreme Court should be permitted to take office, as the Republican chiefs had declared that the court would not sit. And the first change in possession occurred at that very point. The judges headed by Ludeling took their seats. The State militia marched downtown and Ludeling evacuated the building, as the police ostensibly there for his protection took a passive attitude.[2] In a very short time the Conservatives had possession of the other court-rooms of the parish, the police-stations, and State arsenal, leaving Packard only the state-house.

Affairs then assumed a warlike appearance in the state-house at the news that a large force of armed men were moving thither. The entire force of police within the building was formed along the corridors, armed with Winchester rifles. About one hundred and fifty colored militia were formed in line in the open space over the St. Louis Street entrance. The United States troops,

[1] It was said that such a militia had been organized prior to the inauguration. There were probably never more than 3000 men on duty at one time during these days, though 40,000 were available. Kellogg declared that when he left office affairs changed as quickly as you would shift scenes in the theater. House Misc. Doc., 45 Cong., 3 Sess., No. 31, 958, 644, Washington.

[2] Ludeling's court did not attempt to transact business after this date. The rumor had gone out that a conflict with the metropolitan police had failed and so the police defending Ludeling gave up without a struggle.

under orders to disperse illegal bodies, were ready to take the streets in a moment, but except for a few shots fired from the state-house, the peace was kept.[1]   The intense excitement did not prevent the transaction of business except in the immediate vicinity of the capitol.   Late in the evening after another parade, during which the columns were greeted with cheers from the multitude— even the negroes—the militia slowly dispersed, the specific program of the day having been consummated.[2] All day and until four o'clock of the afternoon of January 10 the Radical legislature was barricaded in the state-house.   The Kellogg police bivouacked in the building, regarding it as headquarters.[3]   But the Nicholls police were out in force to guarantee protection and prevent recovery of the courts and police stations by the Packard men.[4]

Ferocious as were the onslaughts of the Radical press,[5] even Kellogg and Packard admitted later that there was no armed interference.[6]   The Conservatives exerted every effort for peace and quiet.   Nicholls issued an address to the people January 9, urging them to retire to their own homes as there was danger in collecting in large bodies.

[1] Burke said later that they were ready for any sacrifice to avoid collision, but rather than return to Republican rule, they would have forced a military government.   House Misc. Doc., 45 Cong., 3 Sess., No. 31, Washington, 959.

[2] The above account is based on the reports given by the *Annual Cyclopedia, Picayune, Times,* and *Republican* of January 10, and upon the personal statements of General Behan.

[3] They had taken their guns to the state-house before daybreak of the 9th.

[4] *Picayune,* January 11.

[5] The headlines of the *Republican* on January 10 read, "Biennial Rising of the White League, An Army Massed in a Night, The State-House in a State of Siege, A Victory of a Day and Then—What?" It called it The Office-Hunters' Insurrection.   Jan. 13.

[6] House Misc. Doc., 45 Cong., 3 Sess., No. 31, La., 13.

I would be most profoundly surprised and disappointed should any citizen of Louisiana so far forget himself as to be guilty of any excess whatsoever. . . . The greater the wrongs to which you have been subjected, the greater to your credit, should you recognize and recollect your own simple and plain duty as citizens. Let no one be injured, however obnoxious he may be, and let the people of the whole country see that we are law-abiding, just, and moderate.[1]

Recognition of the Nicholls government by other bodies followed apace—by the city administrators in formal act on January 16[2]; by a declaration of sympathy and support from a large number of clergy and business men in the city; by numerous popular gatherings all over the State; by neighboring States and Democratic Indiana; but also by several Republican tax-collectors and by some Republican parishes. A favorable decision in the First District Court as to the legality of the commission of a district attorney signed by Nicholls on the ground that the returning-board had transcended its legal powers, tended to strengthen the claims of the Nicholls government.[3] And, finally, some support was won from the colored element by a legislative act, indorsing the assurances as to equal rights and impartial treatment of the two races given by Governor Nicholls in a speech at Baton Rouge.[4]

Even before the situation became acute, Kellogg had sought the aid of Federal troops to inaugurate the new State government. But Grant declined, as it would recognize one of two rival governments for the State

---

[1] *Annual Cyclopedia*, 1877, 456.

[2] It was resolved that administrators of finance and accounts be instructed to pay no accounts of municipal judges or officers save those commissioned by Nicholls. [3] *Ann. Cyclop.*, 1877, 456.

[4] *Ibid.* He declared utter opposition to class legislation. Passed unanimously, Jan. 16, *Times*, Jan. 17.

"even at the very time when a committee of each House of Congress was investigating the situation."[1] Marshal Pitkin declared in a message to Taft on January 6 that the "situation is hourly becoming more alarming and something must be done immediately," representing also that judges elected on the Democratic ticket were not recognized by Democratic lawyers.[2] But Taft replied that no actual violence against State authorities had been shown to justify a proclamation by the President to suppress insurrection.[3] On the day of the inauguration Packard importuned West, Sherman, and Morton to get the President to recognize his government soon or it "will prove fatal to our interests in the State."[4] Other Republicans tried to spur on action by assuring Morton that if the President adhered to non-recognition, "the Nicholls side will possess the whole city and entire State in forty-eight hours."[5] The marshal's report of the disturbances on the 9th brought a prompt order from Secretary Cameron to General Augur to inform the leaders that they must desist under pain of coming in conflict with the National government and military forces, but he carefully added that the order recognized neither side.[6] And so General Augur had, during the stirring events of January 9 and 10, confined himself to preserving the *status in quo* and preventing any disturbance. He requested from Packard written assurance that he would respect the President's wishes. In his reply Packard asserted the legality of his claim and charged the other party with violation of the existing status, but gave the pledge, " assured that the wrongs committed in the last eight days will be set right."[7] He

[1] House Misc. Doc., 45 Cong., 3 Sess., No. 31, La., 603.
[2] *Ibid.*   [3] *Ibid.*   [4] *Ibid.*
[5] *Ibid.*   [6] *Ibid.*, 603–4.
[7] *Ann. Cyclop.*, 1877, 456.

gave this letter to the press before it was received by Augur, whereupon he was sharply rebuked by that officer.[1] On January 14 Grant at last declared himself.

It has been the policy of the Administration to take no part in the settlement of the question of rightful government in Louisiana, at least, not until the Congressional Committees now there have made their report, but it is not proper to sit quietly by and see the State government gradually taken possession of by one of the claimants for gubernatorial honors by illegal means. . . . Should there be a necessity for the recognition of either, it must be Packard.[2]

This position caused a feverish excitement in the city. The wildest rumors and conjectures were afloat, and business, though apparently proceeding, was dull and neglected. Couriers of the United States army were seen flying through the streets from headquarters to the capitol and custom-house, while detachments of the sheriff's posse were now and then seen marching to the custom-house to strengthen that building against any attack the revolutionists might be mad enough to attempt.[3] At Fort Packard, as the Democrats sarcastically named the state-house, there was a large crowd, mostly negroes. Naturally in proportion as the Democrats were depressed, the Republicans were jubilant.[4] Upon the strength of this support, Packard issued a proclamation, "To the White Leaguers and their attendant Usurpers, The Supreme Court Cabal, etc." He ordered the body pretending to be the general assembly, the persons claim-

[1] For the text of this rebuke, see *Ann. Cyclop.*, 1877, 456.
[2] House Misc. Doc., 45 Cong., 3 Sess., No. 31, Wash., 962.
[3] *Picayune*, Jan. 15.
[4] See the *Republican*, January 16 and 17. "It is a pity to expend so much labor and show so much ignorance in compiling rumors, reporting what Tom, Dick, and Harry think or what they profess to think about it, and then have the whole turned into bosh by one simple dispatch from the President."

ing to act as Supreme Court judges, and all unlawfully assuming to act as executive and judicial officers, all persons having possession of the police-stations, and all illegally armed bodies to desist, disperse, and retire. All having State arms were ordered to deliver them up at once.[1] No attention was paid to the summons other than to strengthen the guard about the Supreme Court building. In his exultation Packard was even led to call upon General Augur twice for troops to reinstate the Supreme Court of his faction. The request, when transmitted to the President, was refused, as he wished to preserve the *status in quo* until the committees made their reports.[2]

The Nicholls government was steadily gaining in recognition and strength through the parishes. Nicholls issued some eight commissions to Ouachita officers on January 11, before Grant had requested no further changes, as officials had assumed office without violence. Grant acquiesced,[3] though a little later, under strong pressure, he decided a similar case in Natchitoches adversely to the Democrats.[4] And this relation of *status quo* between the two governments was maintained throughout the session.

A comparison of the two legislatures as to numbers, personnel, changes, and results now seems desirable. A study of the Packard legislature reveals the fact that the House once reached a maximum of 68, all the members admitted on returning-board certificates, 40 of them negroes. Though Anderson had admitted to the board his

---

[1] *Republican*, January 16.   [2] *Times*, January 17.

[3] The Republican organ kept up its courage by declaring, "With equal care and patience is the President acquainting himself with the exact facts of the revolution. Very shortly he will act and be found, as ever, maintaining the legal government." January 13. Again, "Packard will be recognized in good time." House Misc. Doc., 45 Cong., 3 Sess., No. 31, La., 609.   [4] *Ibid.*

defeat in the election he was willing on January 1 to accept
its decision, and so he helped to make the quorum in the
Senate.   But on January 10, when occurred the election
of a United States Senator, Pinchback, again a candidate,
secured the absence of Anderson, together with three
other Senators, in order to break the quorum.[1]   All the
votes at the joint session—though only sixteen Senators
were present[2]—were cast for W. P. Kellogg to duly reward
him for his part in the manipulation of the canvass.[3]
An effort was unsuccessfully made in the afternoon to
choose a Senator for the unexpired term for which J. B.
Eustis had been elected in 1875.   It proved too close a
race between Antoine and Pinchback.[4]   During the entire
month balloting in joint session continued with varying
candidates[5] and results.

It became impossible after January 10 to effect legislation because of the lack of a quorum in the Senate.   Several
contestants were admitted to seats in the House, originally
assigned to men in the Nicholls body; others were expelled
for continued absence and the governor requested to issue
his proclamation for new elections.   Members were not
allowed to leave the building for fear they would join the
Democrats, a fear justified by several defections.[6]   Already by the 11th two colored members of the House

[1] Anderson stated to an investigation that "for the trouble and expense
that I incurred in this, Pinchback promised to pay my expenses and gave me
$1000," out of which the former gave Morris $250 for guarding him.
But when pressed to explain his expenses, he could only point to dinners,
drinks, etc.   But in ten days a Senator supported by Packard secured Anderson's return, for which service he was to be allowed to fund $10,000 of
asylum warrants which he had bought up.   La., 225–6, House Misc. Doc.,
45 Cong., 3 Sess., No. 31.

[2] A quorum of both houses was held to be sufficient.

[3] On this questionable election, Kellogg was eventually seated.

[4] *Times*, Jan. 11.   That paper declares that a free fight broke out in the
hall during this vote.

[5] Warmoth, who had risen to second place, received but one vote on
Jan. 29.   [6] *Picayune*, Jan. 12, 1877.

had deserted to the Democrats,[1] one had resigned, and two had departed for their homes with no apparent purpose of returning. January 13 three Senators, who had been absenting themselves from the state-house, joined the Democrats.[2] And two colored Senators accompanied by Pinchback and a prominent representative of Ouachita went over to Odd Fellows Hall, after exacting Nicholls's assurance of the equality of all men before the law and the promise of his influence to advance the educational, political, and material interests of the colored people. Pinchback was allowed to make one of his characteristic flamboyant speeches, in which occurred the following striking statement concerning the Packard body:

For corruption and venality, for dishonesty, it has not its equal anywhere on the face of God's earth. . . . When I saw in the present pretended Senate of the St. Louis Hotel, and in the pretended House of Representatives, two monster rings demanding prices for every vote, this thing is too corrupt for me to stand by it any longer. I tell you that there can be passed in that body to-day, no bill, no law, and no measure without bribe.

In addition he charged that members had been purchased at two hundred and fifty dollars apiece to vote for Kellogg as Senator.[3]

[1] House Jour., 1877, 17–18.

[2] Nicholls scrupulously tried to learn whether Grant would object to such desertions, but his agents in Washington deemed it unwise to raise the question. House Misc. Doc., 45 Cong., 3 Sess., No. 31, La., 610.

[3] His speech awakens a suspicion of revenge. The *Republican* salved its chagrin at his defection in the following way: "When Pinchback took his small following into the Democratic camp, a weight was lifted from the Republican party of Louisiana, which more than once caused it to stagger and well-nigh fall. . . . The Republican party and government will continue to live, and must thrive all the better for such defections." Jan. 14. But the negro churches on the following Sunday held indignation

Enforced residence at the capitol building could not, obviously, contribute to the appearance of that building. The *Picayune* printed a nauseating picture drawn by a visitor who made his way through a file of policemen, haggard, unkempt, and disgusted at their confinement. He saw a file of about twenty men, guns in hand, behind a breastwork of books. The floor of the second story was strewn with the debris of meals; the air was thick with smoke; there was the smell of whiskey everywhere; groups of dirty and unkempt men in corners were trying to raise their spirits with cards, while others were drilling. The upper rooms were used as bedrooms. Rumors of small-pox victims, huddled in a remote room, were noised about.[1]

After January 14 the *Republican* did not print an official journal of the Senate,[2] while it strung out the House proceedings to make it appear an active body, though even a superficial reading shows that it was doing little work. Two printing bills, which Kellogg had returned with his veto, were considered; notice of bills was given; January 24 the committee reported on the bribery investigation[3]; it established a school bill with some features of economy and efficiency; and it busied itself with prohibitions on the sale of liquor and a bill to prevent the obstruction of

---

meetings, while Antoine, Brown, and all the colored Senators repudiated him to Morton and Sherman. The House indignantly appointed a committee to investigate his charges. *Republican*, Jan. 15.

[1] January 13. This picture was drawn by the hostile press, it must be recalled.

[2] It could only meet with the House to ballot for a Senator. The *Republican* printed the Senate proceedings from January 13–20 in its issue of the 21st, and then no minutes were printed until January 27. All Republicans were frankly discouraged; a feeling of uncertainty and dissatisfaction prevailed, and pressure had to be exerted to hold them together. Probably the visit of Hahn with a dozen members to the Democratic session on January 20 gave birth to the rumor of a stampede from the state-house. *Times*, Jan. 21. [3] Naturally, it found no evidence.

the government.[1]   It was apparent that the Packard
government was pining away.   On January 30 for the
first time there was no quorum in either house; while repeatedly after that date the House, too, had to adjourn.
The attendance in the House during February seldom
exceeded fifty, while the Senate outdid itself with eleven
one day and boasted two on February 28.   On March
1 the House continued in session without a quorum until
eleven-thirty at night when it adjourned *sine die*.   In
early January there had been as many as four hundred people shut up in the St. Louis Hotel, all told;
on March 4 there were perhaps one hundred and fifty.
It could be truly claimed that no government but that
of Nicholls was recognized outside the square of ground
on which stood the state-house, so that even the bread
that Packard's adherents ate passed in to them by
sufferance.

Note the contrast presented by the active, confident
body in Odd Fellows Hall.   In numbers there was no
question of a quorum: the House, with frequent accessions, never fell below sixty, and put on its roll the names
of all absentees, a step significant in itself.[2]   One of the
earliest acts of this body was a Declaration and Appeal
to the people of the United States, giving assurance of the
course to be pursued by Nicholls and his supporters.
It promised peace, free education, honesty, reduction of
the expenses and debt, and closed with an appeal to the
people to stay the hand of injustice and wrong, asking
it "in the name of what every American holds most
sacred—self-government, home-government"; and urging
them to revive kindly feelings and to establish good

[1] The *Times* found few in either house with any idea of their responsibility.   They looked to the executive for instructions.   January 24.
[2] *Ibid*., January 17.   Packard found only 42 legally in the House, 17 in
the Senate.   House Misc. Doc., 45 Cong., 3 Sess., No. 31, La., 23.

government by recognizing and sustaining F. T. Nicholls as the rightful governor of the State.[1]

By January 16 both houses were actively considering helpful reform bills. Beginning January 9, a ballot in joint ssssion was taken each day without result for a United States Senator, due to the pressure at Washington.[2] An entirely new tone in the Assembly was manifest in the determination to properly digest the various features of the general appropriation bill. It refused to rush bills through without due consideration—indeed one of the few bills passed under rapid suspension of the rules was one memorializing Congress for aid to protect the levees. The Committee on Retrenchment and Reform went to work at once to make a schedule of fair salaries.[3] The first bill reported was an amendment to the election law which replaced the notorious returning-board by a board of canvassers, consisting of the lieutenant-governor, speaker, and three Senators elected by the Senate from different parties.[4] Other important legislation was an effort to do away with unnecessary expenses in canceling official bonds, a law to provide for better management of charitable institutions, the fixing of salaries on a reasonable scale, the remitting of penalties for delinquent taxes paid by December 1, and the repealing of certain laws of 1869 and 1870.[5]

The method of securing funds for the support of the Nicholls government was novel. On January 2 a large committee of citizens agreed to coöperate in collecting five per cent of the State taxes and licenses in advance to maintain the Nicholls government, "as the liberties

[1] *Ann. Cyclop.*, 1877, 458.

[2] See the next chapter for explanation of this deferring of the election of a Senator. [3] *Times*, January 30.

[4] Session Laws, 1877, No. 1.

[5] *Ibid.*, No. 32. The excessive cost of printing was reduced, *ibid.*, No. 49.

and welfare of Louisiana depend upon the maintenance of that government."[1]   It proved a complete success, the taxpayers manifesting a decided readiness to pay twenty-five and even fifty per cent of the taxes.   In two days the committee was in a position to direct the president of the Senate and the speaker of the House that their orders on the treasurer would be promptly paid.[2]   Nicholls hesitated at first to appoint tax-collectors in order not to irritate Grant, and later in order to await legislation reducing the extravagant compensation, as he feared that such legislation might affect bonds given prior to its passage.   But by February 20 he felt strong enough to appoint collectors.[3]   The House passed a resolution late in the session, declaring that any attempt to gather the taxes by any other authority than the Nicholls government will "not only prove abortive, but lead to lamentable civil strife, if not bloodshed and actual war."[4]

The cost of the Assembly gave an encouraging promise of what Conservative rule could do.   The Senate drew from the treasury for its expenses only a little over $33,000,[5] less by about $7000 than the appropriation.

[1] *Times*, January 3.   The movement had the support of the Democratic papers.   See the *Picayune* for January 3.   The sum so collected was deemed sufficient for immediate purposes.
[2] House Jour., 1877, 10.
[3] House Misc. Doc., 45 Cong., 3 Sess., No. 31, La., 615–6.
[4] House Jour., 101.   February 24.
[5] Compare with the cost of the Senate for 1875—$58,000.   Sen. Jour., 1875, 8.   Extra session.

CHAPTER XXI

Restoration of White Rule

EARLY in January Nicholls came to the determination to make strenuous efforts through an accredited agent to secure non-intervention, and, then, if possible, to gain recognition for his government. Such a resolve grew out of information of constant efforts to misrepresent to Grant the condition of Louisiana, of constant prayers for interference in support of the Packard government; out of the report of a determination to force from Nicholls the election of two Republican Senators as the price of yielding up the State government.[1]

E. A. Burke was chosen for this important post. General instructions from Nicholls directed him to ascertain fully the state of affairs at Washington, the disposition of the National administration toward his State government; to ascertain definitely what demands would be made upon the governor or legislature; and to keep the governor advised as to all occurrences affecting the interests of his State government; also to represent the condition of affairs and the interests of his State to the best of his ability and to confer and act with the managers of the National Democratic interests at Washington.[2]

[1] According to the agent himself, House Misc. Doc., 45 Cong., 3 Sess., No. 31, La., 601–2.

[2] *Ibid.* The Louisiana Representatives, Ellis, Gibson, and Levy, were just as earnest and active in their efforts as Burke. The last named gentle-

495

Burke left for his post on January 15. His first efforts were naturally directed at Grant.[1] Representatives Ellis and Gibson had already been at work. During the period from December to February, the former had seen Grant more than fifty times. From the morose, non-committal man of the first interviews, he changed until he was the one who suggested the course of action which the Conservatives should pursue in order to accomplish the succession of the Nicholls government. To trace that change is the purpose of the next few pages.

Burke was of the opinion that Grant did not at any time, certainly not after January 8, think that the Packard government ought to prevail.[2] He believed that the policy of non-interference, which was finally adopted, first took shape in the mind of Attorney-General Taft on January 6 and was reflected in the President's telegram of the next day, which declined Kellogg's request for troops, —a thing which he had never done before[3]— and in the consistent refusal to recognize either government. This telegram, according to the advices of Louisiana Congressmen, was for party reasons—to prevent the falling to pieces of the Packard legislature.[4] But Grant determined to adhere to a position of *status in quo*, meaning, as he himself declared, simply that he would not decide which was the legal government; but that, on the other hand, the general sentiment of the people of Louisiana, representing the substantial interests of the State, should not control his activities in the administration to the prejudice

---

man thought that it was mainly due to Gibson's influence with Grant and Cameron that there was no interference on January 9. House Misc. Doc., 45 Cong., 3 Sess., No. 31, Washington, 1009.

[1] Burke said they generally communicated the intelligence they wished laid before Grant to Gibson. *Ibid.*

[2] *Ibid.*, 1012.

[3] *Ibid.*, 1013.   [4] *Ibid.*, 1016.

of his party.   He had no sympathy with the Republican party in that State, but he did not wish to interfere, and would not recognize Nicholls pending the count.[1]   Neither would he brook the violent seizure of the State by either claimant to the governorship.   Nevertheless, Burke and his confrères feared all through January and February that party considerations might cause a change of policy in the administration.   As March 4 and a change in the Presidency drew near, the great object for which the agent strove was the withdrawal of the troops before the question of a cabinet should come before the Republican leaders in the Senate to embarrass Hayes.   "We believed," declared Burke, "that when the issues were raised, when it came to a division of the patronage of the government, the dissensions would be increased and would jeopardize our prospects of peace in Louisiana."[2]   Burke's first interview with President Grant occurred on January 20 when the latter insisted that the *status quo* must be carefully observed.[3]   On the 22d the agent reported that the President accorded him free access, but that publication of interviews would irritate him.[4]

Questions of detail naturally arose.   January 23 Nicholls sought information as to Grant's interpretation of the existing status in reference to executive appointments. Packard held that if Nicholls's appointees took possession, even if quietly, it contravened Grant's orders, while Nicholls felt that his appointees were not precluded from resorting to the district courts to present their claims, though he should discountenance any attempt at force or illegal means.[5]   The immediate reply was the reiteration of a desire for no change.   While the President was then

[1] House Misc. Doc., 45 Cong., 3 Sess., No. 31, La., 614.   According to Levy's impression, written Feb. 18 at Burke's request.

[2] *Ibid.*, Wash., 1016.

[3] See Burke's report to Nicholls, House Misc. Doc., 45 Cong., 3 Sess., No. 31, Louisiana, 605.   [4] *Ibid.*   [5] *Ibid.*, 605–6.

32

favorably disposed, the Louisiana delegation felt that in case of necessity, Nicholls would be crushed to save Hayes.[1]   But the following day Grant rendered a decision on the question, definite and impartial, which would tend to operate to Nicholls's advantage: When both governors commissioned the same man, he should assume office; when but one commission was issued, and no contest was raised by the incumbent and there was no intimidation, that man should take office; when the governors commissioned different parties, the old incumbent should hold over.[2]   Similar local questions arose and were passed upon by Grant personally: in Natchitoches he insisted on an old incumbent continuing as judge until the questions at issue should be settled.[3]   It is probable, however, that Burke's opinion is correct that this apparent reversal of action—for it left a Republican in control—was due to strong pressure brought to bear on Grant, because of the tremendous party feeling aroused by the decision in the Ouachita case.[4]

Grant urged on Ellis the necessity for his faction steadily to preserve the peace. He spoke of the embarrassing position in which it would place him in case there were any outbreak, murder, or any violation of law. He voluntarily suggested how to collect taxes during rigid enforcement of the *status quo* by the anecdote of an Irishman, very fond of whiskey, who had joined a temperance society. On one occasion, when the druggist suggested a glass of whiskey instead of the soda which he had ordered, he refused: "I am a strict member of the temperance society, but if you'll put a little in it unbeknownst to me, it'll be all right."[5] Even the attempt on

[1] Telegram of January 23, House Misc. Doc., 45 Cong., 3 Sess., No. 31, La., 607.
[2] *Ibid.*, 608.   [3] *Ibid.*, 608–9. See above, p. 488.
[4] House Misc. Doc., 45 Cong., 3 Sess., No. 31, Louisiana, 608–9.
[5] *Ibid.*, 598.   One of the few jokes ever recorded against Grant.

Packard's life on February 15 when the tenseness was at its height, although creating great excitement at the capitol, and used for political effect on the Electoral Commission, seemed unable to ruffle the President's calm. And an ugly article in the *Democrat*, due to the report that Grant had recognized Packard, did not seem to touch him. [1] He calmly awaited whatever information Burke transmitted to him. [2] Ellis expressed the conviction that the policy which was afterwards adopted by Mr. Hayes was that which President Grant would have carried out but for fear of embarrassing his successor. [3]

Meanwhile Burke was exerting all his influence with the Republican leaders in the cabinet and Congress. His efforts may be regarded as having two phases: A Cameron phase, when the Republicans were insisting on Hayes and two Republican Senators from Louisiana; and a Matthews phase, [4] when they were satisfied with the simple inauguration of Hayes.

An important factor to reckon with was Cameron, Secretary of War. At first he had been hostile to the Democrats.

I remember calling upon him at the Continental Hotel a few days after the election [says McClure], and inquired of him whether he really meant to force the reversal of the vote. . . . He answered with perfect frankness that he had started in to do it . . . as the Republicans had no opportunity

---

[1] It proved that Chandler sent the dispatch which provoked the *Democrat's* wrath. House Misc. Doc., 45 Cong., 3 Sess., No., 31, La., 615.

[2] *Ibid.*, 612. Nicholls thought the attempt on Packard's life the act of a deranged person, who proved a stranger. Some believed that it had been preconcerted by the Republicans.

[3] *Ibid.*, 597-8.

[4] I use this as a convenient designation, though substantially the same proposition was made to Foster between February 18 and 23 and though other prominent men than those named were involved.

to vote in the South, and the only way to meet such frauds was by the strong power of the Government.[1]

But Burke secured an interview with him about February 9[2] at a private house, before any question of exacting a consideration had been determined on.   Cameron was by that time impressed with the conviction that the Nicholls government should prevail.[3]   The practical difficulties were touched upon and Burke assured Cameron that he could present a legal theory upon which the claim of Nicholls could be sustained, even if the electoral vote be given to Hayes, since under the laws the legislature was the sole power that had the right to count the vote for governor and lieutenant-governor,[4] though the returning-board could and did pass on the Hayes electors. The proposition was made that Burke have prepared a memorial, signed by Nicholls and the legislature, setting forth the facts and law in that respect, on which was to be based a bill or resolution to be introduced in Congress, looking to the separation of those questions and the recognition of Nicholls.[5]   The interview with Cameron was indefinite in some respects.   While it was understood that the selection of United States Senators would be exacted in case the Nicholls government were permitted to prevail, yet there was no agreement.   Burke found a

[1] *Our Presidents*, 265.

[2] Burke says between February 6 and 9.   House Misc. Doc., 45 Cong., 3 Sess., No. 31, Washington, 1008.

[3] The facts had been given to Cameron by Gibson, an old college friend.

[4] Burke said that he had been informed that Wells had so admitted at Washington before the count was terminated.   *Ibid.*, 1014.

[5] This subject did not appear to be fully understood in Louisiana, where it was feared the plan might alienate the National Democratic party, and the idea was finally abandoned about February 18 when negotiations with Matthews were begun.   *Ibid.*, 1010.   For telegrams on this subject, see *ibid.*, La., 610.   There is some evidence that Burke had a Nicholls-Hampton resolution in mind as late as February 27, to save Louisiana and South Carolina.   *Ibid.*, 610.

willingness in Cameron to negotiate, but further consideration was deferred, pending the action of the Electoral Commission and the absence of the former Secretary of the Interior at Columbus, apparently to consult Hayes.[1]

The suggestion of yielding the State in return for two Republican Senators seems to have arisen early. Burke says that he had had knowledge of the suggestion before he left New Orleans, as Governor Nicholls had been so advised by one of the Louisiana Representatives. He believed that they could have had at any time guarantees and assurances from parties connected with Grant for the security of their government, if they had been willing to yield up the Senators.[2] And West appeared to have information of such a determination, as he was eager to be selected as one of them, if such an arrangement were made.[3] Burke thought that Sherman was working with Cameron in reference to the Senatorship but later dropped that condition.[4]

We now reach the Matthews phase of the negotiations. The Electoral Commission had been created as a means of solving the terrible election muddle, and the count for President had been proceeding. Early in February before the decision on the vote of Louisiana had been made, Burke had had a casual conversation on the street with Senator Matthews, who, by personal request of Hayes, was acting with Dennison as Republican counsel, in which the latter had hinted at Louisiana affairs by saying that it would be to Louisiana's interest to understand the views of Hayes. Burke, unwilling to entertain the thought of

---

[1] House Misc. Doc., 45 Cong., 3 Sess., No. 31, Washington, 1010.

[2] *Ibid.*, 1012.

[3] West sought an interview with Burke February 13. As a matter of fact, West was careful to give the Packard government little or no aid in order not to offend the Democrats. *Ibid.*, 1011.

[4] *Ibid.* A denial by Gibson makes this point doubtful, probably untrue.

forsaking Tilden till all hope was gone, merely replied that it might be necessary to confer on the subject.[1]

On February 16 Louisiana was counted for Hayes by the Electoral Commission. As Senator Matthews and Burke accidentally met in leaving the Supreme Court Room, where the Commission had been holding its sessions, the latter remarked that it was about time for "that conversation."[2] By appointment they met that evening at Wormley's Hotel and discussed how Nicholls's government could be established. After Burke had made a full statement of the situation of affairs in Louisiana and the fixed determination never to submit to Packard, Matthews stated that he wished Louisiana disabused as to Hayes's policy toward the South. Although not authorized to enter into negotiations, he felt justified in saying that Hayes would not aid in the perpetuation of carpet-bag rule, but that rather it would be his aim to build up the material prosperity and restore fraternal feeling between the sections. The practical difficulties, such as the rights of the negroes and the inconsistency in receiving the vote of the State for Hayes, if Packard were thrown out, were discussed. Burke suggested the old solution, which had been submitted to Cameron; namely, that the legislature, and not the returning-board, had power to canvass the vote for governor.[3]

Burke submitted the substance of this interview to Gibson the following morning, with Matthews's consent, and on the 18th he put in Senator Matthews's hands a memorandum of points to which the Nicholls government

[1] House Misc. Doc., 45 Cong., 3 Sess., No. 31, Washington, 962.
[2] *Ibid.*, 963.
[3] Based on a memorandum made by Burke just afterwards. *Ibid.*, 1045. On the strength of this interview he telegraphed Nicholls that the rumor of Packard's recognition was without foundation, and that he was assured by high authority that things might be satisfactorily adjusted. *Ibid.*, 991.

would agree in order to reassure Republican leaders as to the course of the Conservatives, and to strengthen the hands of Matthews in argument with the Republican leaders. These four points were: 1. The acceptance of the civil and political equality of all men, and an agreement not to deprive the negro of any political or civil right enjoyed by any other class. 2. Enforcement of the laws rigidly and impartially, to the end that violence and crime should be suppressed and promptly punished. 3. Education of the white and black children with equal advantages. 4. The promotion of friendly relations between white and black citizens, upon a basis of justice and mutual confidence, and a promise not to engage in the persecution of individuals for past political conduct.[1]

At the time of handing over this memorandum, Burke stated that, while he was inclined to believe the assurances as to Hayes's intended policy, yet the latter would be unable to carry it out, if opposed by the strong leaders of his party, and that, therefore, the guarantees which were required should come from such party leaders as Sherman, Garfield, and Morton. When Matthews declared that he could not speak for them, Burke authorized him to warn his party associates that the Louisiana delegation would seek to jeopardize the Republican party.[2] What Burke had reference to was a scheme, which he had developed during the last few days, to stave off the electoral count until March 4 and so leave Hayes out unless the Republicans through their leaders would guarantee the withdrawal of Federal troops and so grant Democratic ascendency in South Carolina and Louisiana.

[1] For the original draft see House Misc. Doc., 45 Cong., 3 Sess., No. 31, Washington, 964.

[2] Burke testifies that he had conceived this plan before February 12. House Repts., 45 Cong., 3 Sess., No. 140, 108–9. Already on February 16 he asked Nicholls if he could guarantee the preservation of the *status quo* until March 4 if necessary. House Misc. Doc., same session, La., 613.

From that time he had little conversation with Matthews until February 26, except that about the 21st Matthews and Dennison suggested that mass meetings of loyal negroes through the parishes in support of the government might strengthen the cause.[1] And it is perfectly clear from an interview of Matthews with Chandler on February 20 that the former had made up his mind on the question. He asked Chandler to use his influence with Grant to prevent the recognition of Packard and said outright that it was the intention to recognize Nicholls.[2] But he also claimed that it would be arranged that the administration should not lose the Senators.

On February 17 it was decided by the Democratic caucus

that the count of the electoral vote should proceed, without dilatory opposition to the orderly execution of the Act of Congress creating the Electoral Commission, whose decisions shall be received and acted upon in accordance with the provisions of said law.[3]

Burke called on Hewett, chairman of the National Democratic Committee and ostensible manager for Tilden in the House,[4] on the Sunday morning following to learn why the party had abandoned his State. Hewett said that the party could not take the responsibility of plunging the country into anarchy, but decided to place the responsibility squarely on the Republicans. Burke replied that Louisiana had determined to endure it no longer, and that if Hewett and his associates thought there could be peace and quiet with Louisiana and Carolina under radical

[1] House Misc. Doc., 45 Cong., 3 Sess., No. 31, La., 616.
[2] Ibid., Washington, 534.   [3] Ibid., 970.
[4] Ibid.

rule, they had made a mistake; that while Louisianians were willing to do anything except sacrifice all that they held dear in order to avoid collision with the Federal forces, yet they were in possession of the only government that could protect life and property; that if there was an attempt to break down the Nicholls government, it would be resisted, and that it was for the leaders to consider whether a forcible resistance would not produce collision through the whole land. He then presented the point that those members who had supported the electoral bill in order to save the country from anarchy could, with the same consistency, join a movement to compel guarantees to save one State of the Union.[1]

And so Burke and his friends proceeded, despite the caucus resolution, to organize a body of Democrats to filibuster. From forty-one or two, who were standing out at first against counting in Hayes for other reasons, they swelled the number to one hundred and sixteen, able to defeat any action of the House.[2] In the ranks were to be found about sixteen Northern men. At the same time plotters interviewed all of the leading Republicans to whom they had access and sought to make such representations to them as would aid the cause: Wadleigh, Howe, Foster, Frye, Matthews, and Dennison.[3] In a word they took pains to let the intention be known to all Republicans of power, as well as Hayes.[4] And Burke

---

[1] House Misc. Doc., 45 Cong., 3 Sess., No. 31, Washington, 971. Although Hewett seemed deeply affected and conferred with Congressmen, there seems to have been no action.

[2] Leaders in the movement were Levy, Blackburn, Savage, Rice of Ohio, and Springer of Illinois. *Ibid.*, La., 601.

[3] *Ibid.*, Washington, 1008. Burke felt on February 25 that he could secure the short term Senator.

[4] Horne of Texas, a Republican friend of Burke's, sent daily bulletins to Young of Ohio, who promptly transmitted them to Hayes, thus keeping him informed of the intention to defeat the count. *Ibid.*, La., 617.

was laboring to preserve to the Democrats the ultimate choice of the long-term Senator. Just when the filibustering movement was at its height, February 22, and the count apparently to be defeated, an article, belligerent and unfair, appeared in the *Ohio State Journal*,[1] the editor of which was General Comely, a bosom friend of Hayes, to still further incite the filibusters.

> The late civil war [it declared] was termed in the South the "Yankee Radical War," and when reconstruction was inaugurated it was, in the eyes of this Southern Democracy, the organization of a Radical party on the sacred soil of the South —in their very midst! It was construed as a challenge. The war was commenced again, only in a different form, and has continued with gore but not glory for the Republicans in the South, until now our party in the States, though in some of them outnumbering the enemy, has gone down in defeat.[2]

It drew a dark picture of the result, had Kellogg called out the negro militia. It was promptly repudiated by Governor Young for Hayes and for Comely, who was ill, with the declaration that it did not reflect Hayes's views in the least,[3] but not before many men had joined the filibusters who had been disposed to accept the situation and accord Hayes an honest support. There were even rumors of a defection in the Senate, headed by Conkling, which favored a new election.[4]

But Charles Foster had made a speech in the House on February 20, which contained one indirect but significant paragraph, hinting at Hayes's Southern policy. The sentence in which he emphasized his lifelong acquaintance with Hayes but gave him authority as the mouthpiece of the new President.

[1] Represented as Hayes's organ.
[2] For the article in full, see House Misc. Doc., 45 Cong., 3 Sess., No. 31, La., 598–601.
[3] *Ibid.*, 601.
[4] *Ibid.*, 617.

Notwithstanding whatever else may be said to the contrary here or elsewhere, the people of all sections of the country may confidently expect from him not only fair but generous consideration. I feel certain that I shall be sustained by his acts when I say that his highest ambition will be to administer the Government so patriotically and wisely as to wipe away any and all necessity or excuse for the formation of parties on a sectional basis and all traces of party color lines; that thereafter and forever we shall hear no more of a solid South or a united North. The flag shall float over States, not provinces, over freemen, and not subjects. . . . It has been sneeringly said and for the purpose of stirring the wild passions of the human heart to bad actions, "that the South under Governor Hayes must submit to an unconditional surrender to the Republican party." No, sir, no such demand will be made. All that will be expected is the patriotic coöperation of Southern patriots in the great work of restoration through the Union, the Constitution, and the enforcement of the Laws.[1]

That very day Lamar, a Representative from Mississippi, told Ellis that Foster had betrayed the fact that he had made his speech after consultation with Matthews, Hayes's brother-in-law, who had urged him to say squarely that Hayes would have nothing to do with Packard. And Lamar urged Ellis to see Matthews at once concerning the possibility of assurances from Hayes that he would not maintain Packard in his domination.[2] Ellis telegraphed Nicholls for authority to go to Columbus in an effort to secure such assurances, but Burke, to whom he had imparted his information, differed from him, true to his instinct that the pressure should be exerted on the leaders

[1] *Record*, 44 Cong., 2 Sess., 1708.
[2] For letter see House Misc. Doc., 45 Cong., 3 Sess., No. 31, Washington, 973. Matthews said, when consulted, that if he were to speak, he would say just that, for it was the truth.

of the party[1] and that Hayes could give no personal guarantees.   As the two Louisianians were talking it over, Matthews and Dennison came up and asked Burke if he objected to an interview with Sherman.   A conference behind locked doors in the Finance Committee Room followed.   Sherman expressed apprehension over the danger of the electoral count being defeated, and asked Burke for suggestions, who, in reply, requested that friends of Hayes assure Grant that the removal of troops from Louisiana would not embarrass his successor.   Sherman threw up his hands, convinced that nothing could be accomplished with him.   But Burke assured him that he had that very morning had a very satisfactory interview with the President,[2] in which he expressed his view of the propriety of the Nicholls government prevailing, as the sentiment of the country was clearly against the further use of troops in Louisiana and declared that there would be no interference with the Nicholls government unless excesses should be committed; that he had not acted before, simply in order not to embarrass his successor.[3]

The three Republicans thereupon agreed to go to Grant the next day and urge immediate withdrawal of the troops; and successively guaranteed that Nicholls would be supported by Hayes if he were inaugurated.   On the other hand, to prevent the difficulty of two Democratic claimants in the Senate, Burke agreed that the long-term Senator should not be elected until March 10 at an extra session, allowing time for the cabinet to be confirmed, subject to the additional condition that Kellogg be not

[1] He telegraphed Nicholls from the hall of the Representatives to that effect.   House Misc. Doc., 45 Cong., 3 Sess., No. 31, La., 619.

[2] This was in the form of a dispatch to Nicholls, which Burke drew out to show the Republicans.   There is a confusion in House Misc. Doc., 45 Cong., 3 Sess., No. 31, Wash., 972, where a telegram of Feb. 20 is wrongly inserted.

[3] For the full telegram see *ibid.*, La., 618.

seated.[1]   Burke then suggested, as he was acting in conjunction with the Louisiana Representatives, the propriety of a consultation at which the men who felt that they represented Hayes meet those representing Louisiana, to preclude the possibility of misunderstanding.[2]   Accordingly the so-called Wormley Conference occurred that same night.   As Burke, Ellis,[3] and Watterson, a Kentucky Representative, who in some inexplicable way was to represent the interests of Carolina, entered Mr. Evarts's room[4] at the Wormley Hotel that evening, they found assembled: Matthews, Garfield, Dennison, Sherman, Charles Foster, and Chief Justice Carter, the latter retiring as they entered.   Matthews opened the discussion by asking the cause of the filibustering movement against the completion of the count and was told that it arose from apprehension as to Hayes's course.   Matthews thereupon gave an exhaustive statement.   He thought that he was familiar enough with the views of the Republican candidate to be able to indicate his policy.   Hayes was tired of the rule and plunder to which these States had been subjected; he despised the bad men who had been robbing them; he was tired of bayonet rule.   As evidence he displayed a letter from Hayes to Foster in which the governor thanked Foster for his speech of the 20th.[5]   Foster and Dennison gave the same assurance by reason of their familiarity with Hayes.   Burke, then turning

[1] For the full interview see House Misc. Doc., 45 Cong., 3 Sess., No. 31, La., 619–20.
[2] Burke said later that he wanted the committal in such form that if there were any violation, either by Hayes or the leaders, Louisiana would be justified if unfortunate events should result.   *Ibid.*, Washington, 1016.
[3] Gibson was ill; Ellis and Burke differ in their statements about the presence of Levy.
[4] Ellis incorrectly says, Matthews's room.   Garfield was criticized for his presence here, as he was serving on the Electoral Commission.
[5] Foster had already on Feb. 25 shown Burke this letter.   House Misc. Doc., 992.

to Sherman, who had volunteered nothing as usual,
pointedly wanted to hear from him, as he was popularly
"slated" for Hayes's cabinet.   The reply came emphatically: "The views expressed by Senator Matthews
are my views, and such, I believe, will be the policy of
President Hayes if he is inaugurated."[1]   Matthews's
solution of the practical difficulty of recognizing Nicholls
was then outlined—the starvation of the Packard government, in a word.[2]   Burke, for the Louisiana delegation,
read an agreement, which in substance was identical with
that handed Matthews on the 18th.[3]   Ellis then stated
that he would tell his friends that the time for filibustering had passed, that "we had every guarantee we could
have," that there should be no further factious opposition.[4]

The wires that evening of February 26 carried to the
anxious governor the good news: "We have been one
week organizing a force to compel guarantees securing
your government."   And then followed a brief résumé of
the terms,[5] calling for confirmation by the legislative
caucus.   It was said that the vote of Vermont was objected to on February 28 so as to gain a day in order to
get an answer from Hayes.[6]   The next day, under Burke's
appeal for prompt action, a joint caucus of the Nicholls

[1] House Misc. Doc., 45 Cong., 3 Sess., No. 31, La., 596.

[2] "If the time comes when the President must recognize either government, he will find one perfect in all its organisms and perhaps the shadow of
another government, but a something which amounts to nothing." *Ibid.*,
596.

[3] This agreement was incorporated in the resolutions of the Nicholls
legislature.

[4] For a full account of the Wormley Conference, see *ibid.*, 595–7.   Before
the 3d of March Burke had also a statement from Morton.   The occasion
for declaring himself publicly was furnished by Morton's Ohio friends by a
serenade.   His speech may be found *ibid.*, Washington, 1039.

[5] House Reports., 45 Cong., 3 Sess., No. 140, 110; House Misc. Doc.,
No. 31, La., 621.

[6] House Misc. Doc., 45 Cong., 3 Sess., No. 31, Washington, 999.

legislature agreed that the governor be informed that it was the sense of that body that the guarantees asked for could be freely given and that it would not elect the long-term Senator until the extra session.[1]   Burke promptly transmitted copies of his telegram to and from Nicholls together with the ratification by the caucus[2] to Matthews and his associates.   Therewith he considered the arrangement completed and gave to the Associated Press the statement that "it is ascertained that satisfactory guarantees have been given assuring the permanent establishment of the Nicholls government," together with the agreement on the other side.[3]

Oddly enough, additional guarantees, secured quite independently, were given to other Congressmen, which strengthened Louisiana's hands.   John Young Brown, Representative from Kentucky, went to Foster shortly after his speech of February 20 to request written assurances that if Hayes were inaugurated, he would restore home rule in Louisiana and South Carolina.   He agreed to give the desired assurances and said that he would request Matthews to sign it also.   On the 27th Foster handed Brown at his desk in the hall an unsigned letter in which the latter made some erasures.   In an hour Foster delivered the statement, signed by Matthews and himself, in which they assured him in the strongest possible manner of their desire to have Hayes adopt a policy of home rule and conciliation for the South.[4]

[1] House Misc. Doc., 45 Cong., 3 Sess., No. 31, La., 622.

[2] Although, on account of a clerical blunder, these guarantees appear in the record (*ibid.*, 622) identical with those given to Matthews, February 18, there was a slight difference, as Matthews had insisted on the substitution in the first article of the acceptance of the war amendments to meet the views of Morton.   *Ibid.*, Washington, 1035.   [3] *Ibid.*, La., 623.

[4] The letter was also addressed to Gordon of Georgia.   The prompt publication of this arrangement seems to have given it undue importance. *Annual Cyclop.* '77, 459.

March 1 Levy in a speech on the floor of the House advised his friends to cease the filibustering movement, with a frank statement that the "people of Louisiana have solemn, earnest, and, I believe, truthful assurances from prominent members of the Republican party high in Mr. Hayes's confidence that he will be guided by a policy of conciliation toward the Southern States and that he will not use Federal authority or the army" to force upon them governments not of their own choice.[1]   And so the ranks of the filibusters fell off about twenty-five on the first roll-call and the electoral count was allowed to proceed.   Although Hewett was deluded into thinking "that the count never would have been completed without assurances," Burke frankly admitted two years later[2] that he had become satisfied "that the movement would have failed," as many Representatives, who were willing to act with him long enough to compel assurances to save the Nicholls government, did not dare to assume the responsibility of the final defeat of the count.   On February 27 he urged Nicholls to prompt acceptance of the terms, as he did not think the arrangement could "be held together longer than to-day."[3]   There was from the first a strong inclination to sacrifice the National ticket, if thereby the State could be saved, especially as Hayes was personally popular.   In serving on a committee in the late '60's he had ridden over part of the State, and had made many friends among the planters and Democratic politicians, as a man of unusual fairness[4]— too fair to suit some of his own party.[5]

[1] *Record*, 44 Cong., 2 Sess., 2047.   It was not easy to win over all the filibusters, as, for instance, Springer of Illinois.   Indeed, a group which had opposed the count from the first were not won over and kept up their factious opposition to the end.

[2] Investigation of 1878, House Misc. Doc., 45 Cong., 3 Sess., No. 31, Washington, 990.   [3] *Ibid.*, La., 621.   [4] *Ibid.*, Washington, 875.

[5] As usual, the whole negotiation was charged by the Republicans as a

Although Hayes was properly very discreet and guarded, refusing to be trapped into an open statement, he was kept fully informed of every phase of the Louisiana situation and lent his complete approval to the assurances made in his name.   As early as December 4 Louisiana sought to learn his temper toward herself through Roberts, a Democratic editor of the *Times* of no great prominence who, through the editor of the *Ohio State Journal*, was able to secure a lengthy interview with Hayes.   In response to Roberts's "feelers," he merely declared that his letter of acceptance was no empty form of words; that the intelligence of any country ought to govern it; that he had always admired the Southern character and that the situation had not been fully appreciated at the North.[1] Although Roberts assumed that he had learned what he wanted, he could show no statement which hinted at bargain, so that his hopes were discountenanced by prominent Southerners, who felt that Hayes could never "unload" his party.   Bishop Wilmer also thought he had won an insight into Hayes's position.   He had gone to Washington to secure the recognition of Nicholls, if possible, and, at least, to represent that an attempt to install Packard would result in revolt, and had secured an interview with Grant on February 17.   Although Grant did not feel called on to do anything yet in the excited state of the public mind, he gave the bishop a personal letter to Hayes, which was presented on the 23d. What occurred at that interview never became public because Bishop Wilmer died before he could be summoned before the committee of 1878.[2]   Evidently he regarded

---

corrupt bargain, defended by the Democrats as an arrangement, provoking the usual investigation and differing reports.

[1] House Misc. Doc., 45 Cong., 3 Sess., No. 31, Washington, 880.

[2] House Repts., 45 Cong., 3 Sess., No. 140, 109.   He sailed for Europe about the time the committee of 1878 was organized, and died too soon after his return to be summoned.

33

Hayes's position as reassuring, for he sent a message to Burke to the effect that "the peace not to be disturbed in Louisiana,"[1] which was promptly interpreted to mean that the Packard government would not be installed.   And Sherman seems to have regulated his conduct with reference to Columbus, for he made a trip there about the middle of February just before the agreement was consummated, and again just after, about February 28.

In the last hour of his administration, Grant took the step to set Louisiana free and thus partially redeemed himself with the people of that long-suffering State.   After Burke had been advised[2] that Grant intended to issue orders enjoining the troops from any interference, the delegation urged upon Grant that it was within his power to wipe out all acerbities between himself and Louisiana; that instead of injuring the party, it would rather remove embarrassing questions for his successor.[3]   And so on the morning of February 28 Burke, Levy, and Ellis received his explicit assurance that he would withdraw the troops as soon as the electoral count was finished, together with the promise that he would so inform Kellogg and Darrell. The military order, they were given to understand, lay ready in the War Department.[4]   Although the weary struggle of useless filibustering went on, the dispatch to Packard, known as the Sniffin[5] dispatch, stating that the troops would be used only to protect life and property from mob violence, was prepared and dated March 1, but it does not seem to have been received by Packard

---

[1] House Repts., 45 Cong., 3 Sess., No. 31, La., 617.

[2] By Matthews to whom the statement had been made the preceding day.   It was also made by Grant to Roberts and Penn about this time, on which occasion he commended Nicholls as a manly fellow, whom he had known in the old army.   House Misc. Doc., 45 Cong., 3 Sess., No. 31, Washington, 889.   [3] Ibid., La., 631.

[4] Rumors of this change of policy promptly appeared in the papers. New York Tribune, March 1.   [5] President Grant's secretary.

until shortly after noon of March 2, after Sherman's dispatch to General Augur had gone forward. Secretary Cameron felt his dignity outraged, that the agents had sought the order from the President rather than from his office, and so he and Kellogg caused the instructions to be withheld at the telegraph office in Washington.[1] It is possible also that his action was prompted by pique that the arrangement for two Republican Senators had not been consummated.[2]

The long-awaited conclusion of the electoral count was reached at five minutes after four on the morning of March 2. About eleven o'clock Sherman and Dennison drove up to the executive mansion with the President-elect[3] for an interview with Grant. They came out before noon to make way for a cabinet meeting. In less than an hour Sherman sent Augur by telegram a copy of the Sniffin order for his "government and information."

Rumors of the President's intention had created the greatest excitement in Louisiana. The call for the extra session, set for March 2 and limited to fifteen days, was issued by Nicholls on February 28.[4] Packard also proclaimed an extra session. He had been warned, February 27, straightway the arrangement had been concluded, in a letter from Matthews, that under the circumstances

[1] Cameron told Bynum, a friend of Nicholls, that he had delayed the order, according to Roberts. House Misc. Doc., 45 Cong., 3 Sess., No. 31, Wash., 890. He had been friendly to the agents until they sought to trick him and then proved impervious to the pleading of Penn and Gibson. The reported opposition in the cabinet seems to sift down to him. *Ibid.*, 1012.

[2] Opinion of Burke, *ibid.* .

[3] Hayes had just arrived that morning. It was felt that this interview was about the crisis in Louisiana, but in view of Roberts's testimony, the writer cannot feel that Grant was concerned in delaying this telegram of March 1.

[4] House Jour., 1877, 117. There were present 19 Senators, as usual. It was issued in "view of the condition of public affairs and for the purpose of indispensable legislation."

it would be impossible for a Republican administration to maintain his title as governor by force of Federal arms, but added that it would be the duty of the administration to see that the negroes were protected and that staunch Republicans like himself should receive consideration and position in some appropriate way.[1]

On March 1 the rumor of Grant's order must have reached Packard's ears, for he wrote Grant an incendiary letter with a request for information as to whether the latter intended to withdraw the troops after the count was declared. He represented it as current belief that the White League was under orders to attack the state-house immediately upon the withdrawal of the Federal soldiery in order to leave no Republican State to be recognized.[2] Grant's reply was the Sniffin telegram. Still the Republicans tried to pretend that the rumored order was in their interest and so aroused Democratic apprehensions of a sudden dash by Packard to capture the Conservative State buildings, because of Nicholls's unwillingness to garrison them.[3] There proved reason for Nicholls to represent this anticipated violence as inspired from Washington.[4] Also the long delay of the President's

---

[1] House Misc. Doc., 45 Cong., 3 Sess., No. 31, La., 33. Packard gave this information to the *Republican* to print on March 16. He admitted later that he could not have maintained himself if the Federal troops had been withdrawn but he tells of an interesting proposition he made when he learned that the objection to his recognition was that Congress would not support the army in the South after July 1. If the United States would loan him 2500 stand of arms with ammunition and accouterments, consigned to Augur, he would undertake to maintain his government—with that much recognition. The Secretary of War did not feel authorized to grant it. *Ibid.*, 34.

[2] *Annual Cyclopedia*, 1877, 457.

[3] House Misc. Doc., 45 Cong., 3 Sess., No. 31, La., 626, Nicholls to Burke.

[4] See the message sent by Pitkin, March 2: "I have just left three members of the Cabinet, all of whom stated that the President's message to you in no manner changes or affects the *status quo*. Any aggressive course

order rescinding the *status in quo* made Nicholls uneasy and fearful that the instructions had been countermanded. Grant went so far as to revise and approve as "absolutely correct" the reply sent by the delegation to quiet the governor's apprehensions.   After reiterating the statement that Grant had sent a dispatch, they quoted him as having issued instructions to cancel all orders for the preservation of the *status quo;* as meaning to make the people of Louisiana as free in their affairs from Federal interference as the people of Connecticut, with no disposition to interfere with them any more than with the people of New York.   He had assured them that no posse to execute court process nor peaceable assumption of office would be interfered with. [1]   Still, despite sensational dispatches of White League preparedness, there was no demonstration by the Conservatives, nor the slightest danger of violence.   They appreciated Nicholls's plea that "this moment demands, more than ever, the exercise of combined firmness, moderation and devotion to principles."   He enjoined the maintenance of peace, observance of law, and proper regard for the rights of all, recommending the cultivation of good feeling and a spirit of harmony. [2]

Although Grant, in retiring from office, was indifferent to public sentiment, he was also doubtless aware of the greatly changed public opinion on Louisiana affairs. Nordhoff's book had had time to drive some facts

---

taken by Nicholls element will be promptly arrested. . . . Do not permit your friends to feel any disquietude because Nicholls's agents here dispatch empty fictions by the yard."   *Annual Cyclopedia,* 1877, 457.

[1] For full dispatch see House Misc. Doc., 45 Cong., 3 Sess., No. 31, La., 626–7.   Grant struck out the phrase, "assuming that the Packard government will disappear," as possibly obnoxious to his party.   Such explicit statements were avoided by every one.

[2] For the full proclamation see *Annual Cyclopedia,* 457.   It was issued in response to Burke's suggestion.

home.[1] In November of election year nearly all the Northern papers except the Chicago *Tribune* believed there had been intimidation; but the evidence against the board was clear, while Sherman's report had been manifestly partisan.   Hence, early in December, the Boston *Advertiser*, the most extreme of radical papers, was very gravely questioning the justice of the board.   It became felt that in so close a contest, the victor could not pursue any extreme policy toward his foe.   And the Republican papers were lavish in their promises that Hayes would allow the South to control her local affairs.[2]   Still it was felt that Hayes would have to tread a wary path in so delicate a matter.   Sherman cautioned Burke on March 3, "Tell Nicholls for me to go slow."[3]   Burke himself believed that as Hayes's government became organized, the Conservatives would be established, but urged gradual acquisition of strength through the courts.[4]

As Burke had been suddenly summoned home by Nicholls,[5] he sought a brief interview with the new President on the evening preceding the inauguration.[6] He pointed out the condition of affairs in Louisiana, and what they expected from the administration.   There was nothing further gained than the general assurance that his policy would be conciliatory, coupled with the request that opportunity be allowed to remove difficulties

[1] See the comments of the *Nation* on this work, Feb. 3, 1876, also the Independent's contempt for the Radical policy.

[2] Merriam, II, 289.   The *Nation* says April 5 that, since the outbreak of the war, there had not been a more rapid modification of public opinion.

[3] House Misc. Doc., 45 Cong., 3 Sess., No. 31, La., 630.

[4] *Ibid.*

[5] Penn, a close friend of Nicholls, was made confidential agent in his place and stayed through the inauguration.   *Ibid.*

[6] This was on Sunday evening, after Hayes had been sworn in privately, a step considered prudent under the circumstances, as the 4th fell on Sunday.   The official inauguration followed the next day.   *Ibid.*, Washington, 994.   Blaine, II, 59.

and to prepare the way.[1] In his inaugural the next day, Hayes made it evident that he intended to adopt a new policy on the Southern question. He had evidently determined to withdraw all National protection from the colored people of the South and to put the whites squarely upon their honor.[2]

The Louisiana assembly acknowledged the inaugural by a vote to coöperate in every effort to restore confidence and fraternal relations.[3] But as the weeks began to glide away without bringing the consummation of the bargain by Hayes, the contracting party on the other side became impatient. Brown of Kentucky, zealous for his sister State, issued a challenge on March 28 in the Louisville *Courrier-Journal*, by publishing for the first time the written guarantees of Foster and Matthews to him, demanding of the President conformity to "his own utterances and the promises of his friends." E. J. Ellis made public his recollection of the arrangements on the same day, but further exposure was checked by a publication by Burke, in which he held that the original parties were bound not to divulge anything concerning the arrangement except for violated faith, which had not yet occurred.[4] Finally, however, even Nicholls's patience snapped, and the Foster and Matthews letters were published about the time of the appointment of the commission.

The problem which had been causing delay was un-

[1] Burke's report does not say for what, but obviously for the withdrawal of the troops. House Misc. Doc., 45 Cong., 3 Sess., No. 31, La., 631.

[2] Hayes declared himself in favor of local self-government, and for a policy "which will forever wipe out in our political affairs the color-line and the distinction between North and South, to the end that we may have not merely a united North, or a united South, but a united country." Richardson, VII, 443, 444. The address did not give satisfaction to the Radicals, but was received with every mark of approbation by the more conservative of his party. Blaine, II, 595.

[3] House Journal, 1877, Extra Sess., 40, Sen. Jour., 34.

[4] House Repts., 45 Cong., 3 Sess., No. 140, 114.

doubtedly the difficulty of finding some way to recognize Nicholls without precipitating violence and without laying the administration open to criticism for abandoning Packard. The idea finally adopted was, doubtless, borrowed from the recent method of solving the Presidential election problem. But the first suggestion came about February 20 from Major Bynum[1]—a friend of Nicholls and an adroit politician, who had been present in Washington to safeguard the senatorships—to Foster to organize a Commission with a majority of Republicans who would understand what needed to be done. To meet the difficulty that there was no legal authority for such procedure, it was thought that if the Secretary of State could be induced to instruct the Commission, and if it went armed with the instructions of the President and cabinet, the Republicans might respect its extra-legal authority and yield to its influence.[2] The Commission was to appear to the country as going down to find out which was the legal government, although the result should have been predetermined. It was declined by various Republicans —friends objected to MacVeigh's acceptance—and the one Democrat, Brown of Tennessee, was persuaded only with great difficulty to serve. The object of the body was to settle some technical questions about the membership of the legislature. Though it was committed to no particular policy, it was expected that it would bring about the result of one government.

The plan was carried into effect, under much criticism,[3]

[1] Butler says in his report that it originated with W. E. Hoone, House Repts., 45 Cong., 3 Sess., No. 140, 114, but the writer found no such evidence, while she did find a statement that Bynum had suggested it. House Misc. Doc., 45 Cong., 3 Sess., No. 31, Washington, 902.

[2] *Ibid.*

[3] Burke was opposed. See *Nation* of March 29, 1877. No act of Hayes's, according to Blaine, did so much to create discontent within the ranks of the Republican party, nor did any other act give so much color of truth to

many feeling that Hayes should fairly shoulder the responsibility, and the following members appointed March
28:    General Hawley of Connecticut, Judge Lawrence
of Illinois, General Harlan of Kentucky, Ex-Governor
Brown of Tennessee, and MacVeigh of Pennsylvania.
Instructions for their guidance were drawn up by the
Secretary of State, April 2.[1]   They were not directed to
examine the recent election but to devote their chief
attention to a removal of the obstacles to an acknowledgment of one government.   If this should prove impossible,
they were next to endeavor to accomplish the recognition
of a single legislature as the "depository of the representative will of the people of Louisiana."   It concluded suggestively, "Your report of the result of this endeavor
will satisfy the President of the wisdom of his selection."
These instructions brought forth from Packard very
promptly an appeal to extend the scope of the Commission to inquire which of the local governments was
entitled to recognition.[2]

The men arrived in New Orleans, April 5, welcomed in
mass meeting by the Democrats, who expressed their
loyalty to the United States and satisfaction with the
avowed purposes of the President, reiterating also, however, their confidence in Governor Nicholls.[3]   The Commission at all times disclaimed any special authority
except as advisors, and practically the only result of which
they seemed desirous was a compromise.   They conferred

---

the charges of corrupt bargain with the South.   It was felt an unwarranted
and unwise act on his part to purchase peace for Louisiana by surrendering
her to the Democrats.   II, 596.   Hoar, II, 12, Sherman, *Recollections*,
I, 586, New York *Times*.   [1] *Annual Cyclopedia*, 1877, 460.
[2] April 5.   House Misc. Doc., 45 Cong., 3 Sess., No. 31, Washington,
834–5.
[3] Commented on favorably by the *Nation* as a dignified insistance on
their rights, an unexaggerated description of grievous wrongs.   April 12.
"This is not the language of banditti or ex-rebels, but of American freemen."

not only with the officials and legislators, but with large
delegations of business men, hundreds of all parties and
races.[1]　It soon became evident that they must try to
bring a majority of undisputed members into the Nicholls
Legislature, as there was no hope of that result in the
other body, even Packard declining to assist in such a
project as impracticable.[2]　Furthermore, the Conservatives showed throughout a spirit of coöperation.　Their
legislature, convened for but fifteen days, voted at once
to extend their session.[3]

It required fifteen days of negotiation and bargaining
before the Commission had secured a majority in the
Nicholls legislature.　They persuaded and advised Packard members to go over to the other body.　On April 17
they requested a consultation with the Packard body, to
which twelve members and two Senators responded.
MacVeigh stated the terms offered by Nicholls, which
insisted on the seating of three Democrats from New
Orleans, recognition of whom was requisite to give even
a show of legality to the Nicholls House.　While not indorsing the offer, he urged acceptance and attempted
to dissipate from their minds any lingering idea that the
troops would remain—even declaring that they would
be withdrawn the following Tuesday.[4]　This caused general consternation with results visible April 19.　Before
that date, there had been defections to the Nicholls

---

[1] According to their own claim.

[2] See the account of his meeting with the Commission.　He still insisted
on recognition and his ability to maintain himself.　House Misc. Doc.,
45 Cong., 3 Sess., No. 31, Washington, 837.

[3] La. Sen. Jour., Extra Session, 49; House Jour., 51.

[4] One account would seem to indicate some heat at this meeting.　Mac-
Veigh is quoted as saying:　"If you can make a fight here in Louisiana,
try it, but you will be wholly unsuccessful, and as they have the courts in
their hands, they will hang every one of you to the lamp-post."　House
Misc. Doc., 45 Cong., 3 Sess., No. 31, Washington, 459.

body,[1] but that morning there were not more than ten of the seventy-three members left at the state-house.[2] Money, legitimate and illegitimate, was undoubtedly employed to procure this result. Offers of pay and mileage for the full term—$8 a day—which they could not get from the Packard treasurer, looked attractive.[3] But it was also alleged that the sum of $15,000 was used to bribe the leaders to shift their allegiance. With this transaction there is no proof that the Commission was connected.[4] Very likely some of Nicholls's agents, while contemning the men they bought, did ask why they should hesitate to avail themselves for the good of the State of such venality.[5] The fact that the Louisiana Lottery Company was granted a twenty-five year charter, a hard bargain, which was kept when the Democrats came into power, would seem to indicate some evidence of the charge that that company came to the rescue of the impoverished Nicholls treasury, supplying the funds wherewith the Packard men were purchased.[6] Packard was offered the collectorship of

---

[1] March 28, 29, April 2, 6, 11, 12. Five Senators responded suddenly to the roll on April 5 to prevent the coming of another Northern delegation. Sen. Jour., Extra Sess., 1877, 111.

[2] See the resolutions of the Packard caucus of that date, condemning the Commission for interference in domestic affairs. House Misc. Doc., No. 31, Wash. 460.

[3] Such a measure had been passed early by the Nicholls body. Members were paid as fast as they came in.

[4] The charge of the German *Gazette* is probably to be entirely discounted, though it is difficult not to believe that they knew of the negotiations. But even it does not charge that the money passed through their hands. *Ibid.*, 461. [5] *Ibid.*, 462.

[6] McClure, *Our Presidents*, 267–9. This was not the only source of funds. It was said bankers and insurance companies advanced money, available later for taxes. House Misc. Doc., 45 Cong., 3 Sess., No. 31, Washington, 841. According to Sypher. The editor of the *Democrat* before a Nichols committee told flatly that the senior partner of the Lottery Company told him that he had bought three Senators and one Representative, the latter one of the last to leave the Packard House, 461.

New Orleans, but accepted the consulate at Liver-
pool.[1]

The dissolution of the Supreme Court of the Packard
government, which was essential,[2] as the question of
legality would come before it, was achieved by offering
one judge a collectorship, and by dangling before another a
position in a sort of international court in Egypt and so
destroying the quorum.[3]

April 16 the Conservatives so modified the adjustment
as to gain the full support of the Commission. They
passed a joint resolution to pledge coöperation, aid, and
support in executing the policy of the President; declared
their purpose to accept the war amendments in letter and
spirit; to enforce the law, rigidly and impartially, to suppress violence and crime; to promote kindly relations
between the races; to maintain public schools equally for
both races; and passed a pledge to discountenance any
persecution for past political conduct.[4] The governor
in a pledge for his people and government promised to go
in person where any disorder might menace the peace or
political rights of any citizen, adding the most emphatic
assurances that the withdrawal of the troops, instead of
causing any disorder, would prove the source of profound
gratification to his people.[5]

On the 21st the Packard body dispersed, those who
did not take their places with the Nicholls legislature
tendering their resignations. After these changes, there
were in the Senate twenty Democrats, and sixteen Re-

[1] House Repts., 45 Cong., 3 Sess., No. 140, 115.
[2] Packard threatened to appeal to it. As he had a good claim for holding
that three judges, a quorum, were acknowledged by both sides, this was a
problem. House Misc. Doc., 45 Cong., 3 Sess., No. 31, Wash., 647.
[3] His name was withdrawn from the Senate after the court had been
broken up.
[4] *Ann. Cyclop.*, 1877, 462. Virtually the terms of the Wormley Conference.   [5] *Ibid.*, 462.

publicans, four seats being vacant; and in the House, sixty-four Democrats and forty-two Republicans, eighty-six of the number having been returned by the returning-board. [1]

The Commissioners made their report on April 21 before their departure, the object fully effected. [2] Although they produced no change which the simple withdrawal of the troops would not have effected, they had given a moral weight to the unified legislature of great advantage to it. [3] On April 24, in accordance with the order of the Secretary of War, in whose opinion there did not exist "such domestic violence as is contemplated by the Constitution as the ground upon which the military power of the National Government may be invoked," [4] the troops withdrew from the city to barracks in the vicinity. And while Nicholls was receiving congratulations from all sections, Packard was yielding to necessity with a bad grace in his valedictory address. [5]

And therewith the curtain fell upon the last act in this long and weary drama. One can hardly help feeling that surely, if Louisiana had sinned, she had paid the penalty of her sins in full measure of atonement.

---

[1] *Ann. Cyclop.*, 1877, 463.
[2] For the report in full, see *ibid.*, 463–5.
[3] The writer concurs with this opinion of the *Nation* of April 26.
[4] The order was issued April 20. See *Ann. Cyclop.*, 1877, 462–3.
[5] For his address, see *ibid.*, 465.

BIBLIOGRAPHY

PUBLIC DOCUMENTS

The public documents, National and State, have been naturally the chief sources.

The Congressional *Globe* for the Forty-second Congress, the *Record* for the Forty-third and Forty-fourth Congresses.

Senate Executive Documents from the Forty-second Congress, Third Session, to the Forty-fourth Congress, Second Session.

House Executive Documents from the Forty-second Congress to the Forty-fifth Congress, First Session.

Senate Reports, from the Forty-second to the Forty-fifth Congresses.

House Reports, from the Forty-second Congress, Second Session, to the Forty-fifth Congress, First Session.

Senate Miscellaneous Documents from the Forty-third Congress to the Forty-fourth Congress, especially valuable for the testimony collected here by investigating committees.

House Miscellaneous Documents from the Forty-second to the Forty-fifth Congresses.

House and Senate Journals from the Forty-second to the Forty-fourth Congresses.

United States Statutes at Large for these sessions.

United States Supreme Court Decisions.

RICHARDSON, *Messages and Papers of the Presidents*, technically entered as House Miscellaneous Documents, Fifty-third Congress, Second Session, No. 210.

B. P. POORE. *A Descriptive Catalog of the Government Publications of the United States, 1774–1881*, Washington, 1885.

PUBLIC DOCUMENTS OF LOUISIANA

Session Laws, 1869–77.

Senate and House Journals, 1869–77. A complete set is to be found in New Orleans, at the State Library, except for the regular session of 1877, and this missing number is to be had at the city library. The set at the Congressional Library does not include the journals for the years 1869 and the regular sessions of 1872 and 1877.

House Debates, 1869, 1870, and 1871.

Senate Debates, 1870.   These few copies of debates are available only at
the Congressional Library, except the House Debates of 1871 which
are to be found at the Louisiana State Library.

Executive Documents, 1870.   At the Congressional Library.

Legislative Documents, 1869–76, except for 1873.   At the Congressional
Library.

Educational Reports, 1870–75.   Isolated copies of these reports have crept
into several of our university libraries.

Annual Reports of the Louisiana Supreme Court, volumes 21–25.

Louisiana House Report of Charges of Wickliffe against Warmoth, a
pamphlet extant in the Congressional Library.

Biennial Report of the Auditor, 1869, 1872, 1874, 1875, 1877.

Annual Report of the Secretary of State, 1877.

PRINTED COLLECTIONS OF SOURCES

T. V. Cooper and H. I. Fenton.   *American Politics*, Philadelphia, 1882.

Walter L. Fleming.   *Documentary History of Reconstruction*, Cleveland,
1906–7.   This work is valuable as it includes social and economic
aspects of Southern reconstruction collected from unofficial sources not
readily procurable elsewhere.

Edward McPherson.   *Handbook of Politics* for 1872, 1874, 1876.   Washington.   Each volume covers the two years preceding the middle of
July for the year indicated by the volume.

Tribune Almanac, New York.   Valuable for election returns and political
miscellany.

NEWSPAPER AND MAGAZINE MATERIAL OF THE UNITED STATES

Baltimore Republican, ultra-radical.

Boston *Post, Journal,* and *Advertiser*—the last-named an extremely radical
sheet.

Chicago *Times, Tribune,* and *Inter-Ocean.*   The *Tribune* wielded at this
time, probably, the greatest influence in the central West, and was not
fair to the South until toward the close of the Reconstruction period.

Cincinnati *Times.*

Cleveland *Leader.*

Harper's *Weekly*, telling and individual by reason of Nast's cartoons.

The *Independent.*   This paper reflected and itself inspired an upright and
religious element of the country.

Louisville *Commercial*, showing Southern sympathy.

Milwaukee *Sentinel.*

The Nation, 1871–77.   One of the fairest of Northern periodicals, wielding a
broad influence and offering a guide to the opinion of the more cultured
classes.

The New York *Herald, World, Times, Evening Post, Daily Bulletin,* and *Tribune.* The most important of the New York papers at this time were the *Times* and *Tribune.* Their antagonism should be remembered. The *Tribune* was, of course, Liberal Republican during the election of 1872.

North American Review, Sept.–Oct., 1877. Valuable for articles by E. W. Stoughton and J. S. Black.

Philadelphia *Ledger, Bulletin, North American,* and *Dispatch.*

Pittsburgh *Dispatch.*

St. Louis *Republican,* biased as were most of the papers.

Washington *Republican,* important, influential, but not fair.

MAGAZINES AND NEWSPAPERS OF LOUISIANA

Abeille, Bee, 1870–77, published only in French at first, but during this period portions—often whole pages—appeared in English. There were virtually two papers—a French and an English—which were not, however, exact translations of each other. Strongly conservative.

Bulletin, 1874–76, a violent, partisan organ of the Conservative party.

Crescent, January–September, 1869. A Democratic sheet—valuable, as it covers a period for which few papers are extant.

De Bow's *Review,* 1869 and 1870, New Orleans. This periodical reflected conservative feeling.

Democrat, 1874–77, the Bourbon mouthpiece, reflecting ultra-conservative views. This is the only sheet which had recourse to cartoons—usually telling.

German Gazette, representing the German element in the State.

National Republican, January–December, 1872. This paper represented the custom-house faction during the election of 1872.

New Orleans *Commercial Bulletin,* January–March, 1869, September–December, 1869, and scattered numbers to 1871. Largely devoted, as its name suggests, to mercantile matters, but valuable because it published the journals of the Assembly and thus fills gaps in the record. Its comments are colored by its Democratic sympathies but less jaundiced than the unsubsidized papers.

New Orleans *Republican,* July, 1874–June, 1877. This paper was the official organ of the Republican party until 1872 when it supported the Liberals under Warmoth's guidance. After the election it consolidated with the *National Republican.*

Picayune. While strongly conservative, this old and well-established sheet could be fairer to its opponents than the other Democratic papers. It is most valuable, as complete files are obtainable at several places in the city.

Times, 1874–1877. This paper had a checkered career: From 1863–70 it was Republican; in 1872, while supporting the Democratic party, it

34

was seized by a Republican judge and served as the organ of the negroes, but after 1875 it was again Democratic, being soon united with the *Picayune*.

The *Commercial Bulletin* for 1869, the *Republican*, the *National Republican*, and the *Times* are to be found at the Congressional Library; files of some of the papers above enumerated are accessible at the Cabildo, the New Orleans City Library, at the printing offices of the various papers, and a few at the Howard Memorial Library; but the best collection of complete files has been deposited at the City Hall.

REMINISCENCES AND OBSERVATIONS

JAMES G. BLAINE. *Twenty Years in Congress*, Norwich, 1884–6. Not unprejudiced.

GEORGE S. BOUTWELL. *Reminiscences*, New York, 1902.

J. S. BRADLEY. *Miscellaneous Writings*, Newark, 1902.

B. F. BUTLER. *Autobiography and Personal Reminiscences*, Boston, 1892.

S. S. COX. *Three Decades of Federal Legislation*, Providence, 1886.

J. A. GARFIELD. *Works*, Boston, 1893.

GEORGE F. HOAR. *Autobiography of Seventy Years*, New York, 1903.

G. W. JULIAN. *Later Speeches*, Indianapolis, 1889.

MANTON MARBLE. *A Secret Chapter of Political History*, a pamphlet issued in 1878.

HUGH McCULLOCH. *Man and Measures of Half a Century*. New York, 1888.

CHARLES NORDHOFF. *The Cotton States*, New York, 1876. A fair, impartial, account from a Northern pen. Invaluable.

JOHN SHERMAN. *Recollections*, Chicago, 1895.

S. J. TILDEN. *Writings and Speeches*, Edited by Bigelow, New York, 1882.

R. H. WILMER. *Recent Past from a Southern Standpoint*, London, 1900.

SECONDARY MATERIAL

General Works.

For a mere outline of the period the following will prove helpful:

E. B. ANDREWS. *The United States in Our Own Time*, New York, 1903.

Cambridge Modern History, United States, volume VII., New York and London, 1903.

WOODROW WILSON. *A History of the American People*, New York, 1902.

For a fuller treatment of the period, the following are valuable:

W. A. DUNNING. *Reconstruction, Political and Economic*, New York, 1907. A valuable guide to the field.

JAMES FORD RHODES. *History of the United States*. The fullest general treatment for the period of reconstruction.

JAMES SCHOULER. *The History of the Reconstruction Period*, New York, 1913.

Bibliography

D. Appleton. *Annual Cyclopedia*, for the years 1869 to 1877, New York. Besides much encyclopedic information, a great deal of source material is quoted in each volume, though in the haste of compilation, errors occurred.

Walter G. Brown. *The Lower South in American History*, New York, 1902.

Alexander McClure. *Our Presidents*, New York, 1900. Useful for the purpose indicated by the title.

C. A. O'Neil. *The American Electoral System*. New York, 1887.

E. A. Pollard. *The Lost Cause Regained*, New York, 1868.

Edward Stanwood. *History of the Presidency*, Boston, 1898. Useful for the attitude of the presidents toward Louisiana and for the elections.

J. T. White. *National Cyclopedia of American Biography*, New York, 1910.

ON PARTICULAR PHASES OF THE STATE HISTORY

W. E. B. DuBois, W. Wilson, and H. A. Herbert. Articles in *Atlantic Monthly*, 1901.

John R. Ficklen. *History of Reconstruction in Louisiana through 1868*. Baltimore, 1910. A posthumous work which carries the story only to 1869 and is, in some ways, a draft rather than a finished piece of work.

Alcée Fortier. *Louisiana, 1904*. Popular rather than scientific.

A. M. Gibson. *A Political Crime*, New York, 1885. A partisan, unreliable account of the election of 1876 in Louisiana.

Paul Leland Haworth. *The Hayes–Tilden Election of 1876*, Cleveland, 1906.

Albert Phelps. *Louisiana*, Boston, 1905. Helpful for the year, 1874.

BIOGRAPHY

Adam Badeau. *Grant in Peace*, Hartford, 1887.

C. W. Balestier. *James G. Blaine*, Des Moines, 1884.

John Bigelow. *Life of Tilden*, New York, 1885.

A. R. Conkling. *Life and Letters of Roscoe Conkling*, New York, 1884.

C. C. Eliot, *W. G. Eliot*. Boston and New York, 1904.

William Dudley Foulke. *Life of Oliver Morton*, Indianapolis, 1899.

Hamlin Garland. *Ulysses S. Grant, his Life and Character*, New York, 1896.

Parke Godwin. *Life of Bryant*, New York, 1883.

George C. Gorham. *Life of Stanton*, Boston, 1899.

Gail Hamilton. *Life of Blaine*, Norwich, 1895.

B. H. Hill. *Life of Benjamin H. Hill*, Atlanta, 1893.

GEORGE S. MERRIAM. *Life of Bowles*, New York, 1885.
HORACE WHITE. *Life of Lyman Trumbull*, Boston, 1913.

RELATING TO FINANCE

E. A. GAYARRÉ. *Political and Economic Condition of Louisiana*, 1874.
H. A. HERBERT. *Why the Solid South ?* Baltimore, 1890.
W. A. SCOTT. *Repudiation of State Debts*, New York, 1893.

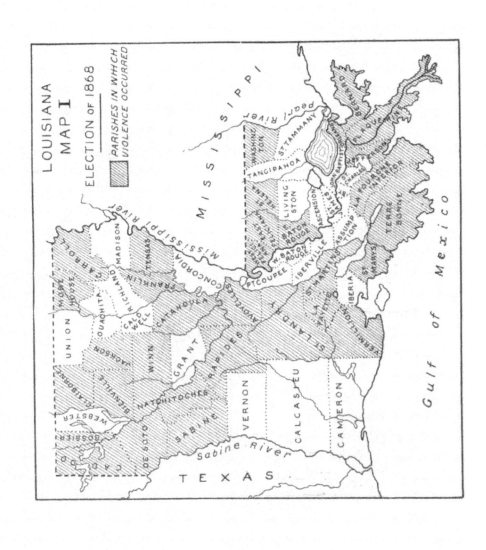

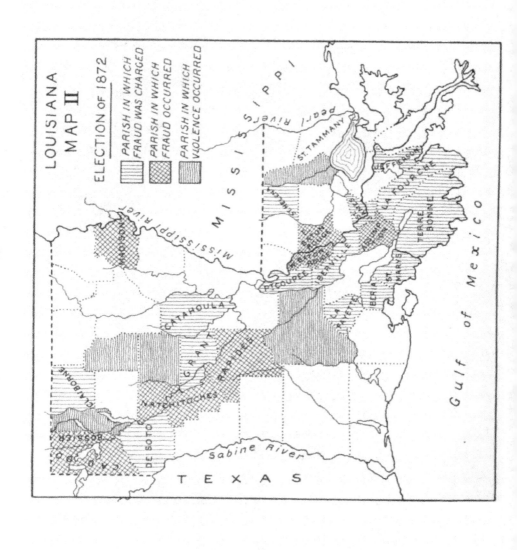

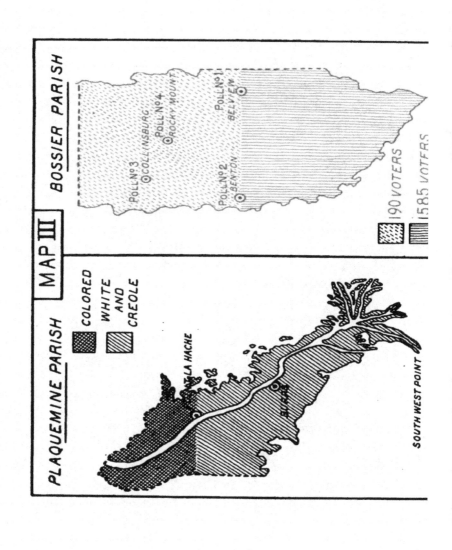

MAP III

PLAQUEMINE PARISH

COLORED

WHITE
AND
CREOLE

POINTE A LA HACHE

BURAS

SOUTH WEST POINT

BOSSIER PARISH

POLL N°3
COLLINSBURG

POLL N°4
ROCKY MOUNT

POLL N°2
BENTON

POLL N°1
BELVIEW

190 VOTERS

1585 VOTERS

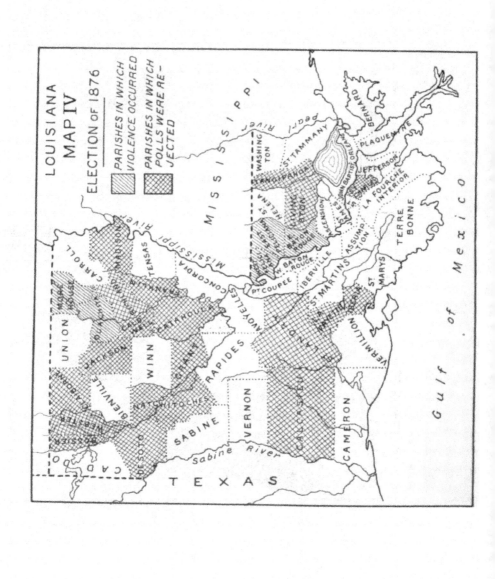

INDEX

A

Advisory Board, created, 285; breaks down, 286

Amendments, ratified, Thirteenth, 3; Fourteenth, rejected, 5; ratified, 6; Fifteenth, 42; governor's ineligibility removed, 57; Kellogg's amendments passed, 249

Anderson, J. E., flees East Feliciana, 428; alleges Republican plot, 453

Anderson, T. C., member of returning-board, 63; in 1874, 286; in 1876, 443; part in electoral ballot fraud, 464

Antoine, C. C., at convention of 1872, 146; nominated lieutenant-governor, 155, 164; in 1876, 406; bill vs. Warmoth Board, 199; opposed to compromise, 360; refuses to appoint Democrats, 426

Armstead, S., nominated Secretary of State, 161

Arroyo, Oscar, member of returning-board, 287

Augur, C. C., preserves status quo, 486

B

Banks, N. P., in Louisiana, 1862, 1; orders election, 2

Black Leagues formed, 254–256

Blanchard, B. T., election instructions of, 167 and n.

Bovee, G. E., promulgates bill without orders, 183; suspended and brings suit for office, 184; restored, 185

Brewster, O. H., speaker of Warmoth wing, 119; Carter asks reinstallment from, 128

Brown, W. G., superintendent of schools, 16; report of, 355; renominated, 406

Bryant, W. C., on banditti message, 305

Bulldozer, definition of, 413 n.

Burke, E. A., on Advisory Board, 285; agent for Nicholls, 495; interview with Grant, 497; with Matthews, 502; scheme to defeat electoral count, 503; conference with Sherman, 508; Wormley conference, 509; recalled, 518; sees Hayes, 518

Bush, Louis, speaker of Democratic wing, 476

Butler, B. F., in Louisiana, 1; supports Kellogg, 308; on election of 1876, 472 n.

C

Cameron, Simon, order to Augur, 486; partial agreement with Burke, 500; delays order for troops, 515

Campaign of 1870, 70; of 1872, 166–168; of 1874, 278–286; of 1876, 418–425

Campbell, H. J., favors Liberals, 163; forms new faction, 163; president of Warmoth Senate, 212

Carpenter, M. H., report for new election in Louisiana, 232; bill, 234; debate on, 235; speech for, 313; new election bill, 316

Carpet-bagger, attitude toward, 11–12

Carr, M., speaker of House, 24; reëlected speaker, 51; member of House, 71; made speaker and resigns, 76; effort to unseat Carter, 115

Carter, G. W., defies speaker, 24; made speaker, 76; uses patronage, 87; Warmoth on, 91; assailed Warmoth, 103; attacked by governor, 111; confidence in, 113; efforts to remove, 114–116; expelled, 119; arrest and trial,

W

Im The Story

personalised classic books

"Beautiful gift.. lovely finish.
My Niece loves it, so precious!"

Helen R Brumfieldon

★★★★★

UNIQUE GIFT

FOR KIDS, PARTNERS
AND FRIENDS

Timeless books such as:

Kids

Alice in Wonderland · The Jungle Book · The Wonderful Wizard of Oz
Peter and Wendy · Robin Hood · The Prince and The Pauper
The Railway Children · Treasure Island · A Christmas Carol

Adults

Romeo and Juliet · Dracula

Highly
Customizaate

Change
Books Title

Replace
Characters Names
with yours

Upload
Photo into
Inside page!

Add
Inscriptions

Visit
Im The Story .com
and order yours today!

CPSIA information can be obtained
at www.ICGtesting.com
Printed in the USA
BVHW082342110819
555624BV00021B/3144/P